COMPUTABILITY
OF DESIGN

PRINCIPLES OF COMPUTER-AIDED DESIGN

A Series by
Yehuda E. Kalay
School of Architecture and Environmental Design
State University of New York, Buffalo

Graphic Introduction To Programming
Computability of Design

COMPUTABILITY
OF DESIGN

Edited by

Yehuda E. Kalay

School of Architecture and Environmental Design
State University of New York
Buffalo, New York

A WILEY-INTERSCIENCE PUBLICATION

JOHN WILEY & SONS

New York / Chichester / Brisbane / Toronto / Singapore

Library of Congress Cataloging in Publication Data:

Computability of design.

   (Principles of computer-aided design)
   Papers presented at a symposium held at the State
University of New York in Buffalo, on December 6-7,
1986.
   Bibliography p.
   1. Computer-aided design—Congresses.
2. Engineering design—Data processing—Congresses.
I. Kaly, Yehuda E. II. Series: Kalay, Yehuda E.
Principles of computer-aided design.
TA174.C575 1987   620'.00425'0285   87-14745
ISBN 0-471-85387-9

Printed in the United States of America

10 9 8 7 6 5 4 3 2 1

CONTRIBUTORS

James Anderson, School of Architecture and Planning, Massachusetts Institute of Technology, Cambridge, Massachusetts

John Archea, School of Architecture & Environmental Design, State University of New York at Buffalo, Buffalo, New York

Michael F. Cohen, Department of Architecture, Program of Computer Graphics, Cornell University, Ithaca, New York

Charles M. Eastman, Formative Technologies, Pittsburgh, Pennsylvania. Current Address: Department of Architecture and Urban Design, UCLA

Stephen Ervin, School of Architecture and Planning, Massachusetts Institute of Technology, Cambridge, Massachusetts

Aaron Fleisher, School of Architecture and Planning, Massachusetts Institute of Technology, Cambridge, Massachusetts

Ulrich Flemming, Department of Architecture, Carnegie-Mellon University, Pittsburgh, Pennsylvania

James Geller, Department of Computer Science, State University of New York at Buffalo, Buffalo, New York

Mark Gross, School of Architecture and Planning, Massachusetts Institute of Technology, Cambridge, Massachusetts

Anton C. Harfmann, School of Architecture and Environmental Design, State University of New York at Buffalo, Buffalo, New York

Yehuda E. Kalay, School of Architecture & Environmental Design, State University of New York at Buffalo, Buffalo, New York

Michael K. Kim, School of architecture, University of Illinois, Urbana-Champaign, Illinois

Bruce R. Majkowski, School of Architecture & Environmental Design, State University of New York at Buffalo, Buffalo, New York

Patricia G. McIntosh, School of Architecture, Arizona State University, Tempe, Arizona

William J. Mitchell, Graduate School of Design, Harvard University, Cambridge, Massachusetts

Richard B. Norman, College of Architecture, Clemson University, Clemson, South Carolina

Gerhard Schmitt, Department of Architecture, Carnegie-Mellon University, Pittsburgh, Pennsylvania

Stuart C. Shapiro, Department of Computer Science, State University of New York at Buffalo, Buffalo, New York

Edna Shaviv, Faculty of Architecture and Town Planning, The Technion— Israel Institute of Technology, Haifa, Israel

Lucien M. Swerdloff, School of Architecture & Environmental Design, State University of New York at Buffalo, Buffalo, New York

Franz S. Veit, Cannon Design Inc., Grand Island, New York

Mathew J Wolchko, The Aybar Partnership, Garfield, New Jersey

Robert F. Woodbury, Department of Architecture, Carnegie-Mellon University, Pittsburgh, Pennsylvania

Chris I. Yessios, Department of Architecture, The Ohio State University, Columbus, Ohio

SERIES PREFACE

Computers have made their debut as design tools in many engineering disciplines, providing designers with flexible means to represent design products. In that capacity they have already demonstrated their utility in improving the productivity and the quality of the production end of the design process, much like word processors have improved the production of documents in offices.

A growing number of researchers, developers, and users of computer-aided design (CAD) systems, however, have reached the conclusion that the utility of computers in design is far from what it might become, if their use were extended over the design process as a whole, including the complete, accurate, and efficient representation of the designed artifacts and the processes that are employed in their conception and creation.

This series of five books is intended to help realize the potential of CAD, through the introduction—in an integrative form—of principles, methodologies, and practices that underlie CAD. It is intended to be used by people who wish to engage in the process of research, development, and maintenance of the new generation of CAD systems. Since the current cadre of people involved with R&D in CAD is relatively small, the series assumes that the reader has no particular knowledge of the field and thus it can be used as a text for beginners. The topics it introduces progress, nevertheless, rapidly toward the frontiers of CAD and thus make the series useful as a text for advanced courses and as reference for professionals.

The first volume, *Graphic Introduction to Programming*, introduces the basic concepts of computing that are needed to master the tool—namely, the computer. These concepts include programming, structured problem solving, and interactive computer graphics. Programming is the means through which computers are instructed how to perform the desired tasks. Structured problem solving, through algorithm design and analysis, encourages a disciplined approach to the design process as a whole and to computer-aided design software development in particular. Given the established manner of communicating design between humans, and because of the ease with which graphic and pictorial information can be disseminated compared to text and numerals, computer graphics have become the standard means of interaction with CAD systems. These three topics have been integrated and are covered through learning the programming language Pascal. This language has certain features that qualify it for this task, which include ease of comprehension, enforcing good programming practices, availability on most computers, and provision of dynamic memory management facilities.

The second volume, *Modeling Objects and Environments*, introduces the concepts of modeling real-world phenomena in the computer's memory. It covers a set of methods and techniques for representing the physical environment as symbol structures that are understood and can be manipulated by computers. The book includes the study of data structures that are particularly suitable for representing two- and three-dimensional artifacts, and operating on these structures in a way that preserves their semantic integrity. The book covers the formative and other attributes of objects, such as topology, geometry, transformations, assemblies, and general database query/update operations.

The third volume, *Modeling Design Processes*, is concerned with the representation of design as a problem-solving process. The two essential components of CAD covered include the generation and the evaluation of alternative design solutions, represented through the modeling concepts introduced in the second volume. The study of solution generation covers all design phases, including preconcept, conceptual, and detailed design. It is introduced through techniques such as knowledge representation and search strategies and relies on selected practices from artificial intelligence, database theory, linear and dynamic programming, operations research, and optimization theory. All of these topics are covered in sufficient detail for the comprehension of the central topics in the book, though of course they do not attempt to be a substitute for formal texts in their respective disciplines. The theoretical treatment of the topics covered by the book is complemented by the examples written in PROLOG, a programming language that has some powerful features useful for logic representation and manipulation. For the benefit of readers who are not familiar with PROLOG, an appendix introduces the basics of this language.

The fourth volume, *Performance Measurement Applications*, presents an assortment of task-specific applications that draw upon the model of the designed artifact and provide the designer and the knowledge-based CAD system with a variety of evaluative, simulative, and tabulative measures of the artifacts' expected performances. Written by noted experts in their respective disciplines, the applications present both state-of-the-art knowledge in specific fields relating to CAD and an integrative approach to employing computers as design consultants.

The fifth volume, *Computability of Design*, completes the series by reviewing the key topics that were presented, and by raising the fundamental issues of design computation: How can design processes be mathematically modeled? What is design knowledge, and how can it be computed? How can the design process as a whole be computed? Alternatively, how can particular design tasks be computationally assisted? This volume is based on a symposium that was held in Buffalo, New York, in December 1986, where noted experts discussed the feasibility, utility, and desirability of various approaches to the computation of design.

The series as a whole is concerned with the principles of CAD, rather than with an exhaustive survey of techniques, practices, and existing systems. Its goal is to educate students, researchers, and professionals, who will develop the CAD systems of the future and who will maintain them. It is intended to be used by designers in many engineering disciplines, rather than by computer scientists alone. It may, however, be of considerable interest to computer scientists too by exposing them to the computational concerns of design professionals.

It is recommended that the books be used in sequence, but this is not a prerequisite for their utility. Neither is adherence to the programming languages Pascal and PROLOG, which are used to exemplify the theory. It is the concepts and principles presented in the series that are of primary importance, and they transcend the technologies and techniques used for their implementation.

YEHUDA E. KALAY

Buffalo, New York
February 1987

PREFACE

The growing complexity of modern environments and the socio-economic pressures to maintain an efficient design/build cycle are forcing designers to seek new tools and methodologies that will help them cope with and manage the processes by which new artifacts and environments are conceived and created. This trend has been accelerated in the past few decades by developments in cognitive and computer sciences that provided insight to some human thought processes and produced tools to assist them. In some disciplines, such as electrical and mechanical engineering, the introduction and use of computers have significantly improved design practices and products. It is no longer conceivable, for example, to design an integrated circuit without the aid of computers. Yet, in other design disciplines (e.g. architectural design) computational design aids have attained a marginal role, at best. They have not fostered any major qualitative, or even quantitative improvements, although attempts to develop appropriate design aids have been pursued as vigorously as in other disciplines.

Why have computational design aids succeeded in improving design practices and products in some disciplines but not in others? What makes certain design methods more difficult to aid computationally than others? Is the pursuit of computational aids in such "soft" design disciplines justified? What directions of research should be followed to develop better computational design aids, or prove their development impractical? To answer these questions we must examine the nature of *soft* design processes, analyze their inherent difficulties, and the utility of the computational methods that attempt to aid them.

Design is an ill-understood process that relies on creativity and intuition, as well as the judicious application of scientific principles, technical information, and experience, for the purpose of developing an artifact or an environment that will behave in a prescribed manner.

Computable processes, on the other hand, are, by definition, well understood and subject to precise analysis. They are amenable to mathematical modeling, and can be simulated by artificial computing techniques.

Can the process of design be described precisely enough to allow its computation? Achievements in the study of human problem solving and other cognitive processes suggest that indeed it may. Yet, the very prospect of using computers to model and provide assistance in design decision-making has met with serious criticism by designers on the grounds that the inherently human process of design cannot be rendered to a computer.

This book discusses the feasibility, utility, and desirability of computing design processes or their components. It consists of contributions by leading experts in design, design methods, computer science, and computer-aided design, who convened at a symposium concerning the **Computability of Design** at the State University of New York at Buffalo, on December 6-7 1986.

The book does not attempt to answer the question of design computability, but rather to raise and explore some of the issues it involves. These issues include the modeling of design, the kinds of knowledge used by designers, and the computational methods that *have been* and *could be* applied to simulate and to assist both process and knowledge representation.

The book is organized into four parts:

1.   Design process.
2.   Design knowledge.
3.   Design computation.
4.   Design assistance.

The first part presents some general models of the design process. The chapters in this part discuss the fundamental principles of design as a cognitive process that relies on creativity and judgment, and the possibility of constructing models to study it. The second part is concerned with identification and the possible computational representation of design knowledge. The third part presents several approaches to the computer-simulation of design as a whole, its limitations, and its possible extension. The fourth part is concerned with the integration of computational design aids with traditional design practices. The chapters in this part attempt to identify the components of design that are most amenable to computation, those that are not, and how they can be integrated within a single, unified design process.

The four parts present some of the major concerns that face the computation of design. They discuss different views and approaches in each category, so both their breadth and depth are presented. The classification of chapters into specific categories is somewhat arbitrary, since no topic can be discussed in complete isolation from the others. It is done, nevertheless, to help the reader focus on the key points presented by each chapter.

Many of the discussions in the book are based on examples drawn from architectural design, one of the "softest" design disciplines to model computationally (or otherwise). Yet, the relevance of the discussions is by no means limited to architectural design. Architectural design was chosen by many of the contributors as the domain in which their theories can best be exercised, since it blends technical, social, cultural, economical, psychological, aesthetic, and other concerns in the creation of a unique spatio-temporal product. In addition to the pure intellectual challenge in computationally modeling architectural design, there is also the promise that finding computational measures that are capable of aiding the creative and judgemental components of this particular design process will prove significant. If found, they will not only increase the productivity of designers themselves, but more importantly, they may increase the quality of designed environments and their responsiveness to modern economic, environmental, and social challenges.

This book and the symposium that preceded it are the culmination of efforts by many individuals. I thank the many contributors—those whose papers were selected for inclusion in the book, and those whose papers were not. I also thank the referees for their dedicated and thoughtful review of many papers. The State University of New York at Buffalo deserves thanks for supporting the symposium through a **Conferences in the Disciplines Grant**. Many thanks to the administration of the School of Architecture and Environmental Design, for their help and encouragement. Most thanks are due to the staff and aides of the Computer Aided Design/Graphics Laboratory at the School of Architecture and Environmental Design, who assisted in organizing the symposium and compiling the book: Lois Beery, Tony Cheng, Jia-Bin Jang, Carl Nuermberger, Dhanraj Vishwanath, Wei-Jyei Wu, and Robin Wurl. Special thanks to Daniel Friedman, for his helpful editorial comments and proofreading of parts of the manuscript.

YEHUDA E. KALAY

Buffalo, New York
November 1987

CONTENTS

The Rationalizing of Design
Anton C. Harfmann   1

PART ONE   DESIGN PROCESS   9

1. Strategies for Interactive Design Systems
    Robert F. Woodbury   11

2. Puzzle-Making: What Architects Do When No
    One Is Looking
    John Archea   37

3. Designing with Constraints
    Mark Gross, Stephen Ervin
    James Anderson, Aaron Fleisher   53

PART TWO   DESIGN KNOWLEDGE   85

4. Reasoning about Form and Function
    William J. Mitchell   89

5. Development of Machine Intelligence for
    Inference of Design Intent Implicit in Design
    Specifications
    Michael K. Kim   99

6. **Models of Spatial Information in Computer-Aided Architectural Design: A Comparative Study**
Patricia G. McIntosh   117

7. **Fundamental Problems in the Development of Computer-Based Architectural Design Models**
Charles M. Eastman   133

8. **The Computability of Void Architectural Modeling**
Chris I. Yessios   141

9. **Artificial Intelligence and Automated Design**
Stuart C. Shapiro
James Geller   173

PART THREE   DESIGN COMPUTATION   **189**

10. **Generative and Evaluative CAAD Tools for Spatial Allocation Problems**
Edna Shaviv   191

11. **Expert Systems in Design Abstraction and Evaluation**
Gerhard Schmitt   213

12. **The Role of Shape Grammars in the Analysis and Creation of Designs**
Ulrich Flemming   245

13. **Design by Zoning Code: The New Jersey Office Building**
Mathew J Wolchko   273

PART FOUR   DESIGN ASSISTANCE   **293**

14. **Intuitive Design and Computation**
Richard B. Norman   295

15. **Radiosity Based Lighting Design**
Michael F. Cohen   303

16. A Partnership Approach to Computer-Aided Design
Lucien M. Swerdloff   315
Yehuda E. Kalay

17. Design Augmentation in the Architectural Practice
Franz S. Veit   337

Computability of Design
Bruce R. Majkowski   349
Yehuda E. Kalay

THE RATIONALIZING OF DESIGN

Anton C. Harfmann

School of Architecture and Environmental Design
State University of New York at Buffalo
Buffalo, New York

The study of design attempts to externalize intuitive knowledge held by designers. As more knowledge is externalized, the process becomes more complex and fragmented. Computers offer the ability to reconstruct design as a wholistic process, but what is still unclear is the degree to which computers can or should be involved. The issues raised in the paper address the core of the creative process itself and questions its computability.

☐ INTRODUCTION

Design has long been considered a uniquely human process that relies on intuition, experience, and judgment of the designer. The study of design as a process can be viewed as an effort to rationalize and externalize (or explicate) the knowledge necessary for its conduct. Externalization of design knowledge has increased the predictability and consistency of design processes, but has also tended to fragment the wholistic process of design into discrete sub-disciplines. Efforts to define how design is actually carried out can be understood as attempts to shed light on the "black box" process that transforms a problem statement into a design solution [Jones 1969] (Figure 1).

A review of the major developments in design methodology illustrates

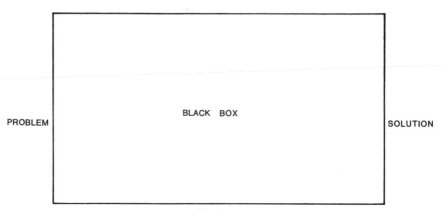

Figure 1.

how the externalization of designers' knowledge has brought about rationalization of the process.

☐ UNITY OF PROCESS AND KNOWLEDGE

Before the 15th century, design was a craft process of solving a problem through the actual creation of an artifact. The knowledge required to create the design was held solely by the craftsman or the artist. The process was controlled intuitively and followed the simple sequence of problem definition − design solution.

In complex situations, such as the creation of large buildings, this method of solving problems "in the field" led to the development of a series of sub-problems (Figure 2). These sub-problems were solved by experienced

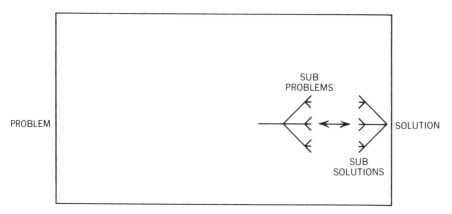

Figure 2.

craftsmen as they emerged based on knowledge accumulated through years of practice and techniques passed down through the history of their crafts (masonry, carpentry, goldsmithing, etc.). Each of these craftsmen individually held very specific knowledge about products and the processes relating to their area of expertise.

☐ ABSTRACTION AND FRAGMENTATION

Externalization and transmission of design knowledge has occurred throughout history by apprenticeship or the documentation of rules, such as the Ten Books of Architecture by Vitruvius. However, the first major step in externalizing the design process itself occurred during the Renaissance, when theoreticians sought to synthesize humanistic, philosophic ideals with practical knowledge about the building crafts. With the emergence of perspective, this era saw architects like Brunelleschi using accurate drawings and scale models to examine solutions prior to the actual construction of buildings. Renaissance architects solicited professional technical consultation from various trades to improve the quality and utility of their proposed designs [Ettlinger 1977]. The separation of the architect from the builder marked the beginning of design problem-solving as an abstract process removed from the manufacturing of the object (Figure 3). The use of scale drawings and models to represent design intentions resulted in a major change in the sequence of the design process as previously practiced; a solution could now be generated, at least conceptually, in an abstracted, accurately proportioned form, and reviewed by the related craftsmen prior to its actual construction.

With problems of increased complexity, the craft methods of solving problems proved to be too expensive and too slow [Alexander 1964]. Abstraction of the designed object, therefore, allowed a series of iterations

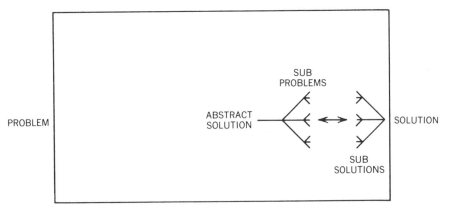

Figure 3.

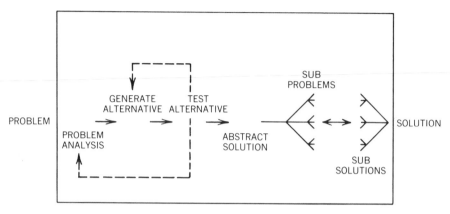

Figure 4.

to be performed for the purpose of refining the product. This iterative process suggests a further externalization of design, which includes the ability to change the solution based upon the analysis of experienced craftsmen. Iterative design, which evolved from the trial and error methods of the past, has been modeled as a generate/test cycle within the abstraction space of the proposed solution [Simon 1969] (Figure 4). Iterative methods were used, although perhaps not formally, by Sir Christopher Wren in the design of St. Paul's Cathedral, where several physical scale models were built and studied to improve and develop design ideas [Wilton-Ely 1977].

The development of means to mathematically describe the laws of nature increased the architect's ability to externalize and model design knowledge. The formulation of very specialized, sophisticated knowledge, and the development of engineering disciplines, brought further levels of separation to the design process. The expansion of design knowledge has resulted in the sub division of the process into discrete disciplines controlled by "experts." The effect this compartmentalization has had on the design process is made obvious in the numerous disciplines currently required to cooperate in the design and construction of a complex building (Figure 5).

☐ DESIGN METHODS

The next phase in the externalization process was brought about by the development of design methods that formalized and structured design knowledge itself. The design process has been categorized into basic methods for the evaluation, generation, and selection of alternative solutions.

The simplest (and hence the first) areas to be formalized are the evaluation procedures that are based on mathematical and physical principles. These include cost, structure, lighting, and energy analysis.

Methods that have been developed to generate alternative solutions range

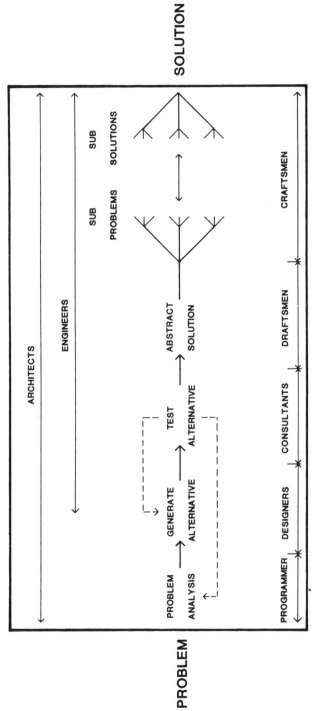

Figure 5.

from very structured and systematic procedures, such as morphological analysis, to intuitive and less structured methods such as brainstorming [Jones 1969]. Other methods attempt to employ rules or patterns that define solutions to certain specific design problems [Alexander 1977, Koning 1981].

The formalization of the process in which an alternative is selected requires a search for the solution that best satisfies the overall goals and objectives of the problem. Techniques that have been developed for this purpose involve the search through a network of possible alternative solutions for an acceptable solution [Winston 1984].

The strengths of formal design methods lie in their ability to structure and document various specific aspects of design. However, the vast amount of information that must be made explicit has hindered the designer's ability to maintain control over the process as a whole [Jones 1970].

□ COMPUTER AIDED DESIGN

Computers have been introduced to aid in the management of profuse and fragmented information externalized through the study of design. Some of the first intentions were to use the computer for the total automation of design [Cross 1977]. The first "successful" use of computers was in procedures where large amounts of numbers and equations were easily managed, such as structural and energy analysis, relieving designers from tedious tasks.

The next major advancement in CAD tools came about with the development of computer graphics [Sutherland 1963], which resulted in tools that are currently used for drafting by many designers. This use of computers, however, is very limited, and does not affect the actual process of design, except by reducing the time required to communicate the design ideas [Orr 1985]. Because this use was recognized as an underutilization of the potential of computers, three dimensional modeling systems were developed. These systems increase the efficiency of the design process by allowing the designer to review design solutions in three dimensions without the need to construct physical scale models. The computer is still viewed in this use as merely another medium for the representation and review of design solutions.

The development of CAD tools to date has utilized the existing body of externalized design knowledge for computing various aspects of the process. It is obvious that computers are not a new method for design, but rather a means to facilitate the existing established methods. It is also clear that design knowledge must be externalized before it is computed.

In reviewing the current status of the design process, we notice a much more comprehensive and complicated process than the first craft model presented. Instead of one person controlling the process and the creation of the product, the current model involves control and integration of several areas of knowledge held by different professionals. Additional complications arise in that the product itself is constructed by a different set of professionals who have had very little input during the abstract design phase. In order to cope with this separation of knowledge, several researchers have suggested an extended use of computers that would facilitate the integration of large amounts of information generated during the design process [Mitchell 1977; Eastman 1985; Kalay 1985; Coyne & Gero 1986].

To be effective, these approaches must work at several levels of abstraction simultaneously and must be as flexible as human design processes. These capacities would transform computers from their current use as design aids to "intelligent" machines capable of assisting in the creative aspects of design and would aid in the reconstruction of design as a wholistic process.

□ FUTURE DIRECTIONS

The progression of the study of design has been presented as a continuum from an intuitive, unstructured activity, to present attempts to explicitly define and compute certain aspects of design knowledge.

It seems inevitable that further externalization of the design process will occur, and that the use of computers in design will expand. Many issues concerning the incorporation of computers into design remain obscured by controversy over the "computability" of inherently human processes.

If we accept the potential computability of the design process, will the final step in the externalization be the total automation of the process? Some argue that as long as design is viewed as problem solving, all aspects could be computed. Others maintain that design (when viewed as an art) defies computability, since art by definition cannot be computed. The issues raised here address nothing less than the core of creativity. Can or should creativity be externalized? Can or should it be computed?

□ REFERENCES

Alexander C. *Notes on the Synthesis of Form*, Harvard University Press, Cambridge, MA, 1964.

Alexander C., S. Ishikawa and M. Silverstein with M. Jacobsen, I. Fiksdahl-King and S. Angel *A Pattern Language*, NY, Oxford University Press, 1977.

Coyne R.D. and J.S. Gero "Design Knowledge and Sequential Plans," *Environment and Planning B*, 12:401-442, 1985.

Cross N. *The Automated Architect*, London: Pion Limited, 1977.

Eastman C.M. "A Conceptual Approach for Structuring Interaction with Interactive CAD Systems," *Computers and Graphics*, 9(2):97-105, 1985.

Ettlinger L.D. "The Emergence of the Italian Architect," *The Architect*, Spiro Kostof, ed., Oxford University Press, New York, NY, 1977, pp 96-123.

Jones C. "The State of the Art in Design Methods," *Design Methods in Architecture*, G. Broadbent and A. Ward, ed., London: Lund Humphries, 1969.

Kalay Y.E. "Redefining the Role of Computers in Architecture: From Drafting/Modeling to Knowledge-Based Assistants," Computer-Aided Design, 17(7):319-328, September 1985.

Koning H. and J. Eizenberg "The Language of the Prairie: Frank Lloyd Wright's Prairie Houses," *Environment and Planning B*, 8:295-323, 1981.

Mitchell W.J. *Computer-Aided Architectural Design*, Van Nostrand Reinhold, 1977.

Orr J.N. "The Merits of Design Automation," *Computer Graphics World,* January 1985.

Simon H. A. "The Science of Design: Creating the Artificial," *The Sciences of the Artificial*, MIT Press, Cambridge, MA, 1969.

Sutherland I.E. "SKETCHPAD: A Man-Machine Graphical Communication System", PhD dissertation, MIT, Cambridge MA, 1963.

Wilton-Ely J. "The Rise of the Professional Architect in England during the Fifteenth Century," *The Architect*, Spiro Kostof, ed., Oxford University Press, New York, NY, 1977, pp 180-208.

Winston P.H. *Artificial Intelligence*, Addison-Wesley, Reading MA, (second edition) 1984.

PART 1

DESIGN PROCESS

An understanding of the design process is prerequisite to computationally aiding it. Attempts to explain how people design, or define what they do when they are "designing," have been the core of design methods research for many years, but a consensus is yet to be reached. Researchers agree that design is a complex activity, undertaken for the purpose of developing a strategy which, when implemented, will lead to the construction of an artifact or environment that will perform within tolerable margins of some prescribed behavior. Furthermore, many researchers agree that the processes employed by designers in their pursuit of such strategies resemble search, since no formula exists that will translate performance requirements into a self-consistent physical (or organizational) assembly of parts. Opinions differ, however, with regard to the method(s) that are used to carry out this search.

The process of search can be viewed as generating and testing alternative solutions to a design problem. The *problem solving* approach to modeling design proposes that the characteristics of the desired solution, in terms of objectives and constraints, can be formulated independently and prior to engaging in the process of seeking a solution that meets them. Accordingly, the search process is goal-directed, and can employ means-ends analysis to guide it towards the desired solution.

An alternative, *puzzle making* approach, proposes that such knowledge cannot exist prior to the search itself, since the sought solution is unique. According to this approach, the process of search resembles investigation of opportunities and limitations offered by the unique situation, without a-priori knowledge of what the solution will be like. Both interpretations perceive the solution space to be bounded by specific constraints. Initially, this space is very large, but it shrinks as design parameters are fixed and as further constraints are discovered and added to the set.

The three chapters that comprise this first part of the book present different approaches to the process of searching for a design solution. A problem solving approach that forms the basis of several different approaches (subject to different interpretations), is presented by Robert Woodbury in STRATEGIES FOR INTERACTIVE DESIGN SYSTEMS. It distinguishes between *designing*—the creation of an object that meets a set of requirements, and *defining*—the representation (graphical or otherwise) of an object, given either the (physical) object itself, or its informationally complete alternative (concept). It uses Herbert Simon's information processing model of human problem solving as the basis for developing a theory of design, and considers various computational strategies for supporting it.

An opposite approach to problem solving is presented by John Archea in PUZZLE - MAKING: WHAT ARCHITECTS DO WHEN NO ONE IS LOOKING. It models architectural design as a search for the most appropriate effects that can be attained in unique spatio-temporal contexts, through the manipulation of parts (architectural elements, attributes, and ideas), according to a set of combinatoric rules derived from precedents, symbols, and metaphors. According to this approach, design cannot be thought of as problem solving, since the problem(s) the design process attempts to "solve" cannot be formulated prior to and independently of the process of the search itself.

The third chapter, DESIGNING WITH CONSTRAINTS by Gross et al, explores yet another model of design: a model based on incrementally defining an initially ill-defined problem by adding more specific constraints that reduce the space of possible solutions. Solutions are generated by "fixing" values of design parameters, and are tested for compliance with the constraints. The selection of specific values may introduce new constraints, or affect other parameters through constraint relationships.

Although the three chapters present different approaches to modeling design, they actually complement each other: they demonstrate the breadth of the design modeling problem, and at the same time present in-depth analyses of its different facets.

1

STRATEGIES FOR INTERACTIVE DESIGN SYSTEMS

Robert F. Woodbury

Department of Architecture
Carnegie-Mellon University
Pittsburgh, Pennsylvania

An information processing model of human problem solving is used to develop strategies for the design of systems for the interactive generation of designs. Systems of this type are currently not strongly developed anywhere, nor does there exist in the literature a paradigm for their creation. Design is a task which requires different interactive support than that traditionally provided by CAD systems. In this paper, those differences are uncovered by comparison of two tasks; one, named definition in this paper, which seems to be well supported by existing systems and the other, the task of design. Use of an information processing model of human problem solving shows that differences between the tasks can be found in every potentially variant portion of the model. The information processing model is again used as a framework to propose mechanisms to support design. These mechanisms act by changing the underlying phenomena upon which the information processing model is built and thus effecting changes, either parametric or structural, in the model. The relative importance of the proposed mechanisms is discussed, leading to the conclusion that the interactive support of search is the most strategic direction for future research.

☐ THE MOTIVATION

This inquiry starts with the premise that a computer-aided media for interactive design by humans is a desirable goal to pursue. Its approach can be placed in the world of computer aids to design by referring to a classification of such aids originally by Galle [Galle 1981] and augmented by Akin, Flemming and Woodbury [Akin 1984].

1.   Automated evaluation of designs which are generated by traditional means.

2.   Interactive generation of designs using computer-assisted media.

3.   Stepwise interactive generation.*

4.   Non-exhaustive generation of feasible solutions.

5.   Exhaustive generation (i.e. complete enumeration) of feasible solutions.

6.   Generation of (sub)optimal designs.

This work belongs to the second category, of interactive generation of designs, using computer assisted media. Its approach is based upon the belief that the methods which humans use to design are intellectually challenging and exciting; in short they are fun. The joy of discovery that comes with a successful design idea and the sense of playfulness seen in the work of many good designers are among the things that should be supported and aided by a high quality interactive system. That no such systems exist today is a testament to the difficulty of the problem.

It seems obvious that computer systems, as responsive assistants to design, potentially have a tremendous advantage over purely passive media such as pencil and paper. However, current modelling systems do not seem to live up to this promise. They are instead rather good means to define something which has already been created, either on paper or in the physical world [Woodbury 1985]. In spite of much interest, beginning over twenty years ago with SketchPad [Sutherland 1963], current systems do not seem to be natural media for aiding the design and development of objects. Yet designers create and manipulate geometric representations of objects and even of things that are not physical objects (for example, a scheduling chart) continuously in the course of design. This distinction, between the capabilities of current systems for definition of form and the desired functionality of future systems to act as a medium for the design of form is the topic addressed here. This paper is meant to define a strategy for the development of interactive systems which can function as media for design. Design refers to a wide range of activities, from an individual effort at sketching plans for a piece of furniture to the workings of an interdisciplinary team creating plans for a large building complex. This paper

---

*In stepwise interactive generation, design is viewed as a sequence of transformations upon some representation. At any stage in design a set of currently feasible transformations is generated automatically. A designer guides the process of design by making a selection from that set.

addresses only a very small part of that range; design is viewed here as being done by one person, working with a medium on which representations of design are recorded.

☐ DESIGN VS DEFINE

If, as stated above, design is a different form of activity than defining something which already exists, then the two acts of definition of an object and design of an object need to be distinguished. The nature of the activity of design has been widely discussed in the literature[Simon 1973; Reitman 1964]. There is still much to be learned of the phenomenon called design, particularly in its higher level, problem restructuring, stages. The exceptions to this literature notwithstanding, for the purposes of this discussion, let design be described as:

the creation of a representation of an object which meets a set of requirements

Let definition (also referred to as *define* in this paper) be described as:

the creation of a representation of an object given either the object itself or an informationally complete alternative representation of the object*

An example of the design task is the design of a bathroom layout, given a list of client requirements and constraints, which may include cost, number of fixtures, space allocated, lighting and others (Figure 1.1) [Eastman 1970]. An example of the definition task would be the reproduction of a representation of the MBB Gehause part, a mechanical part often used in the literature as a benchmark of geometric modelling system performance (Figure 1.2).

Both of these acts, design and define, can be thought of as problems in the sense that they provide some given information and a task to perform with that information. For definition, the given information is an informationally complete representation of an object and the task is the creation of a model of that object. For design, the given information is more vague: a set of requirements on an object, and the task is the creation of a model of an object which fulfills those requirements. Further comparison of the two problems can be made by representing them in a conceptual framework for computer-augmented problem solving.

Newell and Simon [Newell 1972] propose a theory of human problem solving that provides the basis for such a framework. The theory states that human problem solving can be considered as:

---

*For example, a set of drawings or a physical model.

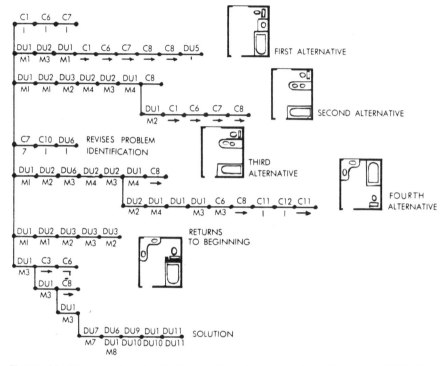

Figure 1.1. An example of a bathroom layout problem from [Eastman 1970]. Courtesy of MIT Press.

- an *information processing system* (IPS),
- using a *problem space*,
- acting by *searching*,
- influenced by a *task environment*, and
- supported by an *external memory*.

As these terms may be unfamiliar to readers of this paper, a brief discussion is included here. For a complete presentation of the theory, refer to Newell and Simon [Newell 1972], particularly chapter 14.

Human Problem Solving

The human information processing system (IPS) can be modelled as a number of memories acted upon by processors, which gain information from sensory devices and make physical actions in the real world through motor devices (see figure 1.3, after Card, Moran and Newell [Card 1983]). Each of these memories and processors have performances, the parameters of which are largely invariant across individuals. The inherent structure (or

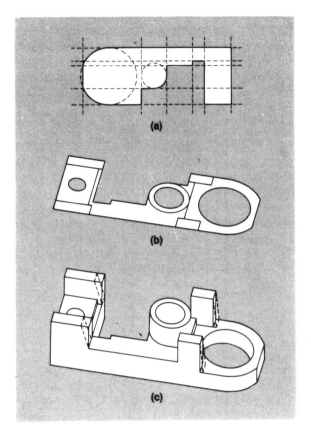

Figure 1.2. Definition sequence for the MBB Gehause part from [Hillyard 1982]. (© 1982 IEEE).

architecture) of the IPS along with these parameters dictate significant performance characteristics of the IPS as a whole which affect the capability of the IPS to engage in problem solving. For example, short term memory (STM) capacity in the human IPS is very small. This, coupled with a long write time to long term memory (LTM) ensures that only problem solving strategies which have small stocks of states are used by an unaided IPS.

Newell and Simon argue that the characteristics of the human information processing system to a large degree guarantee that the human IPS will only engage in certain classes of problem solving behavior. The behavior universally observed in typical problem solving can be characterized as "search in a problem space". Human problem solvers act by considering internal symbol structures (elements in a problem space) until a solution is found. The constituent components of a problem space are, (after Newell and Simon [Newell 1972]):

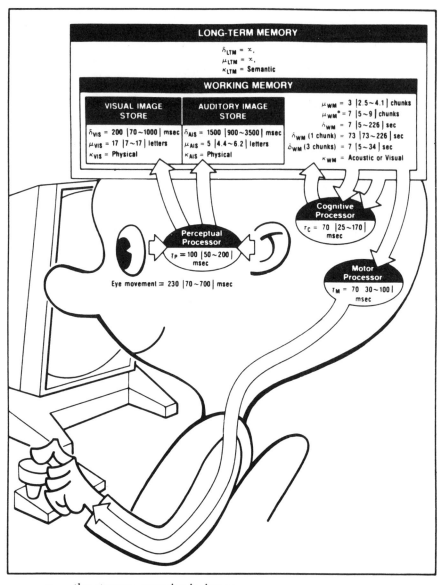

μ — the storage capacity in items
δ — the decay time of an item
$\varkappa$ — the main code type (physical, acoustic, visual, semantic)
τ — the cycle time.

Figure 1.3. The architecture of the human information processing system (IPS). [Card 1983] reprinted with permission of Lawrence Erlbaum Associates, Inc.

1. A set of symbol structures, each representing a knowledge state. These symbol structures need not exist explicitly in memory prior to generation. All that need exist is a means to generate the symbol structure through some operator.

2. A set of operators to incrementally generate new states of knowledge or to make a transition between states of knowledge.

3. An initial state of knowledge.

4. A problem, which is a description, either complete or very vague, of a final, desired state of knowledge.

5. A set of knowledge. Part of this knowledge may exist outside of the physical body of the problem solver in the form of external memory (EM). Examples of such memory are drawings, books, chessboards and computing devices.

Newell and Simon report for their subjects that the use of a problem space was invariant across subjects and tasks. They do not exclude the possibility of other environments for problem solving but also find no evidence for any such alternate environment. Simon [Simon 1973] further points out that this formalism can be used to explain complex, ill-structured domains such as design.

Problem solving occurs through a process of search in some problem space. Search involves visiting states of knowledge in the problem space in some order, according to some control structure until some goal is met. Search is thus an iterative activity, of successive application of operators to transform knowledge states. Four types of decisions must be made at every iteration in any search procedure:

1. Evaluation of existing states of knowledge against the problem requirements.

2. Selection of an existing state of knowledge on which to operate.

3. Selection of the appropriate operator to apply to the selected state of knowledge.

4. Selection of existing knowledge states to remember.

A set of policies, one for each of these types of decisions determines a search strategy. Search strategies take advantage of information in the problem space and are limited by the invariant characteristics of the human IPS. An example of search which utilizes information in the problem space is found in tic-tac-toe in which the search can take advantage of the symmetry of the game to reduce the number of existing states which are candidates for operation. An example of the characteristics of the human IPS constraining search is the use of depth first search for finding files in a hierarchical directory system [Akin 1983]. Depth first search discards all but a small number of knowledge states. It is thus a useful search strategy for the human IPS with its limited capacity for short term memory (STM).

A task environment for problem solving is the reality in which problem solving occurs. A problem is posed with reference to some state in the world, but is solved in the internal environment of a problem space. For example, a problem to solve the Rubik's cube is solved internally and symbolically and the actual environment specified by the Rubik's cube serves to provide knowledge about the world mostly in the form of constraints (and in this case also acts as an external memory device to aid* problem solving). Newell and Simon report that the constraints in the task environment are the main determinants of the problem space used by a problem solver. The task environment may also provide information which determines the type of search used in problem solving. Thus a particular task further scopes the behavior of a problem solver.

Human problem solvers are often aided by the use of an external memory to augment other memories. External memory may be immediately available to a problem solver (the area of a piece of paper in direct foveal view) or may be more remote (a book in a library). Traditionally, external memory is perceived as a passive recipient of actions made by the problem solver. It is often the medium in which a solution to a problem is described. The external memory, being outside of the human organism is the component of human problem solving most amenable to change through a computer assist.

Taken together, these five invariants, the human information processing system, the use of a problem space, the activity of search, the constraints of particular problem solving tasks and the existence of an external memory device, provide a framework for understanding a given problem solving domain.

Task Comparison

An attempt to compare both of these tasks within the framework given above immediately implies a question of fit. Are both tasks representable within the framework? Given that they are both representable, then the differences between the tasks will appear not as structural differences within the problem solving framework, but rather as differences within each element of the framework. Newell and Simon [Newell 1972] claim that their theory, while based upon observation of three types of problem solving tasks (cryptarithmetic, logic and chess) is of broad generality. They argue that the structure of the human IPS is invariant across individuals and that that structure dictates the use of a problem space in problem solving. It should be expected then, that both the design and define tasks, if attempted by a human, will be solved within a problem space. The other potentially variant characteristic of human problem solving between these two tasks is search. Newell & Simon outline a (fuzzy) distinction between "unpro-

*Or in Rubik's case, seemingly to hinder.

grammed" activities involving search and "programmed" activities involving execution of a predefined script. Both types of activity are, in a sense, problem solving, as they involve transformation of an initial set of conditions into a final set of conditions. However, we tend to observe greater use of "programmed" activities as more "mechanical", and less typical of human beings acting to solve a tough problem. Even if one of the tasks studied here was typically solved by completely "programmed" or mechanical means, then it would still be sufficiently similar to the activity of problem solving to be discussed within the Newell & Simon framework. The distinction between the two tasks would then be found in the search part of the framework, in which the activity of the highly "programmed" means could be described as non-backtracking and non-iterative compared to the methods of search used for other less "programmed" problems. The actual representations and search strategies used by problem solvers will differ between the two tasks; the degree of that difference will indicate, to a large degree, the differences between the two tasks from a problem solving point of view. Given the invariance of the human IPS and the different types of search and representation that can be discussed within the bounds of the framework, it seems reasonable to compare both tasks within the framework.

Using this framework of problem solving allows comparison of the design task with the definition task and further understanding of their differences and similarities. In both cases, the human IPS remains invariant. Nothing, anywhere, suggests that normal, healthy people have information processing architectures which differ structurally or significantly parametrically from the one outlined above. That leaves the task environment, the problem space and the search strategy as the domains in which to seek comparisons. In the absence of empirical data, I will rely on argument to make the comparisons.

The task environment for the two problems varies greatly. The nature of the ultimate product of both tasks is the same, a model of a realizable physical object. The constraints on the final object differ greatly, both in content and in fundamental structure. The constraints on the design problem are quite vague. For example, in the bathroom design problem given above [Eastman 1970], one constraint might be to provide privacy for the toilet. This is in great contrast to a possible constraint from the definition problem: the hole in the MBB Gehause part must be concentric with the outside curve. Constraints likely to be found in design problems are often geometrically non-specific, that is the constraint may not be specifiable in terms of the geometry of a part or assembly, but rather in some other set of terms, for example performance.*

Comparing problem spaces for the two problems is no mean task, as a

---

*A specific example: a building design is constrained by structural performance requirements. These demand, for their computation, knowledge of material properties and loads.

problem space is, in final analysis, inferable only from observation of actual problem solving behavior. However, certain characteristics of problem spaces for design and for definition should be inferable from the characteristics of the example problems given above, and their task environments.

Taking the five components of a problem space individually and discussing each with respect to the two task domains demonstrates the degree to which the two tasks differ.

The internal symbol structures used for design must carry very different information when compared with the definition task and are therefore likely to differ in structure as well as in content. If knowledge about a design can be described as being composed of objects and relations* then the objects of design are representations of physical objects-to-be which are constrained in location and shape by relations to other objects. Ballay [Ballay 1984] has pointed out that at any time in the design process the objects in a design can be characterized as being at a particular point along three dimensions, inclusion, coherence and precision. Inclusion is the degree to which all conditions of a design problem have been addressed in the solution. Coherence is the degree of constraint satisfaction that has occurred amongst the various parts of a design. Precision is the degree to which commitment to a particular geometric form has been made. This can be contrasted to the objects used in the definition task, which at every point in time are well-formed representations of physically realizable parts.

The relations between parts that exist during the process of design can be described along the dimensions mentioned above. As design progresses, the information in the problem space states which relate objects becomes progressively more inclusive, coherent and precise. For example, in the bathroom design problem reported by Eastman [Eastman 1970], the subject included first the main fixtures and then, only when these were committed, did he place the mirror, medicine cabinet and and towel rack. As the subject progressed, his designs became more coherent, for example, the issue of privacy became progressively more resolved. Finally, concerns of fine dimensions with respect to the human figure occur at the end of the design session, rather than at the beginning. Compared to the definition task where relations between parts are precise locational relationships, the relations of design are both less complete and more changeable in both structure and content over time.

---

*There is significant evidence for this conceptual division. Space allocation problems [Flemming 1978; Flemming 1985; Mitchell 1977] are traditionally specified in terms of units and relations. While not conclusive support for a "natural" classification into objects and relations, the mere fact that designers of space allocation problems have universally proceeded with the assumption of objects and relations is strong circumstantial evidence. The cognitive psychology literature on visual imagery uses concepts of "units and relations" [Kosslyn 1983] to build models of visual image processing. Many diagramming techniques, for example, bubble diagrams, taught in undergraduate architecture curricula have a strong "objects and relations" flavor.

Information other than that required to physically build an object is also used in representations during the process of design. A designer may make marks which do not directly signify an addition or change to an object, but rather are referents (or icons) to internal concepts relating to the object. These referents include explanatory notes, surface renderings, graphical iconic marks, grid lines and other forms of information not directly a part of a model of the object. They are traditionally two dimensional but need not be so restricted when a computer medium is used. These marks, as the first commitments toward an idea that may eventually become physically realizable, are essential to the process of design.

That the operators used on objects in the design task differ from the define task can be argued on the basis of their operands. If the operands of design, the internal symbol structures of the problem space, contain constructs which differ from those of the definition task, then the operators on those constructs will also differ. In particular, these operators will be geometrically less precise for the design task as opposed to the definition task. For example, in design objects may be placed "beside" other objects without determining a precise location for them. This is in contrast to the operations which occur in the process of definition of an object where commitment to precise location is made at every step.

Another way in which operators differ between the two tasks is in the information that is changed with each operation. If we look at operators as incremental changes to an object representation, then an operator can be viewed as substituting for some part of a representation a new part. This substitution leaves some aspects of a representation unchanged and acts to change others. In design, as opposed to definition, the information may change in fundamentally different ways during these substitutions. For example, in Eastman's bathroom problem [Eastman 1970], the subject at one point substituted two sinks in a corner vanity for a single stand-alone sink. This substitution preserved the function of the sink while changing virtually every aspect of its geometry. Compare this to making a hole in the MBB Gehause part where only local and comparatively "simple" changes to the geometry may occur.

In the third component of a problem space, the initial knowledge state, the differences between the two tasks are strongly pronounced. In design, the initial knowledge state is a statement of some conditions, which may include geometric information (a site), material information (materials of objects on the site) and a human condition (a developer owns the site). In the definition task the initial condition is complete geometric information describing an object in some other representation (i.e. possibly drawings).

The fourth component of a problem space is the problem itself. In design, it is stated in terms that may be far removed from the geometry of an object, for example, a description of some desired performance. For the definition task the problem can be much more simply stated, that the final representation be informationally equivalent to the initial one.

The last part of a problem space is the knowledge required to effectively solve the problem. In design, this knowledge set is large; for the bathroom problem knowledge of costs, building code requirements, human ergonomics, materials and building construction is needed (and all this for a very simple design problem!). In order to complete the definition task, the required knowledge is much less and is limited to knowledge of three dimensional operations on polyhedra.

Table 1.1 summarizes the differences between the problem spaces required of the two problems.

Table 1.1 Comparison of Problem Spaces for the Design and Define Tasks

PROBLEM SPACE COMPONENT	DESIGN	DEFINE
A set of symbol structures each representing a knowledge state	Information needed are incomplete models of geometric objects	Information needed are complete, well-formed polyhedral representations
	All information may not relate directly to a buildable part	All information directly relates to physical parts
A set of operators to incrementally generate new knowledge states	Operators act upon incomplete information and create new incomplete information	Operators work only on complete specification of geometry
	Operators may make large geometric changes	Operators make incremental geometric changes
	Operators apply to non-spatial representations also	Operators apply to spatial representations
An initial knowledge state	Statement of some conditions which may not be spatial	Complete spatial information in some other representation
A problem, (specification of a desired knowledge state)	Test for solution stated in ill-defined terms which may not be geometric	Test for solution very well defined
A set of knowledge	Needed knowledge is large and not given in problem statement	Needed knowledge set is strictly geometric

It seems reasonable to posit differences in the type of search used in the design task as compared to the define task. The define task should be characterized by problem solving closely akin to the "programmed activity" referred to in Newell and Simon [Newell 1972]. This type of activity can be described as the use of a highly specific algorithm in the solution of a problem, particularly an algorithm which involves little search and backtracking. An example of such problem solving is given by Hillyard [Hillyard 1982] where the intermediate states required to create the MBB Gehause part are shown in Figure 1.2. The transformation required to create each state from the previous one is clear, and in general the effects of a particular operator can be predicted in advance, making the path to a problem solution straightforward. This can be contrasted to the task of designing a bathroom as reported by Eastman [Eastman 1970] in which thirteen significant branches in a problem behavior graph occurred in the course of a twenty five minute protocol. These differences in both the amount and type of search display emphatically the differences between the two tasks.

Finally, different types of external memory would be useful to the two different tasks. Each task requires an external memory which can effectively capture the type of information used in the problem space of the task and which supports the type of search activity used. As we saw earlier, these differences are extensive. Table 2 .1 summarizes the differences between the two types of problems.

Table 1.2   Comparison of the Design and Define Tasks

THEORY COMPONENT	DESIGN	DEFINE
The human information processing system	Invariant	Invariant
Search	Search is branching and backtracking	Programmed search
Problem space see table 1	Complex, large Ill-structured	May be complex and large. Well defined
Task environment	Constraints and requirements are vague	Constraints are well-defined
External memory	Reflects differences in search, problem space and task environment	Reflects differences in search, problem space and task environment

□ STRATEGIES FOR SUPPORTING DESIGN

Consider that design can be represented using the theory of human problem solving as referred to above. That theory would represent design as a model consisting of a human information processing system searching in a problem space which is largely determined by a task environment. The behavior of the overall model is affected by its structure, its overall organization and its parameters [for example, the capacity of short term memory (STM)]. The value of that behavior, or the *performance* of the model, can be measured by:

- Its *efficiency* in both time and space. Efficiency is concerned with the resources that are used to arrive at a problem solution, not the value of the solution itself. A measure of the efficiency is the amount of time required to arrive at a solution to a given problem.

- Its *power*, or ability to find good solutions to problems. Measures of the power of a process would be taken on the usefulness of the product, the designed artifact, as a solution to the problem.

An increase in either performance characteristic of the model without a decrease in the other would be an unequivocal improvement in performance. Strategies for supporting design using interactive tools should therefore focus on improving either the efficiency or the power of the design process (or both).

These strategies may be implemented by using a computer program to change either the parameters or the structure of the model. This is exactly the purpose of a computer support to a process: that the computer should perform some task or aid in its performance to increase the usefulness of the system as a whole. An example of a change to the parameters of the model would be a computer system that could increase the speed of access of external memory. If that speed were increased to a rate comparable to the access time for STM, then the capacity of STM, a limiting parameter in the behavior of the system, would effectively be increased. An example of a change to the structure of the model would be the adoption of a stronger method than heuristic search for generating solutions. This would change the fundamental nature of the problem solving process so that it might no longer be described as search in a problem space. Various techniques of mathematical programming, for example, linear programming, fall into this category.

Taken together, strategies for increasing either the power or the efficiency of the human designer and techniques for implementing those strategies which change either the parameters or the structure of the model, suggest a classification, in the form of a two by two array, of computer assists to design. Figure 1.4 diagrams the framework for such a classification.

STRATEGY FOR:

METHOD MAKES:	increasing efficiency	increasing power
change to parameters		
change to structure		

Figure 1.4. Classification of computer assists.

In the following paragraphs are described four specific approaches to computer assists. In each case the main contribution of the approach with respect to the classification above is identified and the approach is described at length.

Search Strategies

Search is an iterative activity that requires four decisions to be made at each iteration. Informally these are:

1. Is the problem solved? If it is, stop and declare a solution, else continue.

2. Which state of knowledge will be transformed next? If no states of knowledge can be transformed, stop and declare that no solution can be found, else continue.

3. Which operator will be used on the selected state? Apply the operator.

4. Which of the existing states shall be remembered for future reference? Remember the chosen ones.

A search strategy consists of a set of policies with regard to each of these decisions. A computer can assist in search by some combination of assisting in making decisions and taking autonomous responsibility for decisions. Thus a computer assisted search strategy is one in which the policy for one or more types of decision has a computerized component. An examination of each decision type under either a computer assisted or a completely computerized decision policy yields eight simple options for computer assisted search.

1. **Computer assisted determination of a problem solution.** An approach to this option would provide the computer with a number of evaluation algorithms which could be called by the designer to examine a proposed solution to see if it meets solution criteria. Another approach would compute and describe the relevant tradeoffs of one proposed solution with respect to other already generated proposed solutions*.

2. **Computerized determination of a problem solution.** Having a computer make all tests of adequacy of a solution will work when the solution tests have some strong properties:

   > All solution criteria are well-defined and amenable to computer analysis, and

   > Either:
   > All solution criteria can be simultaneously met in a solution (strict satisficing).

   > Or:
   > All solution criteria can be combined into a single measure of value. This measure of value can be unambiguously compared against the same measure computed for other possible solutions.

3. **Computer assisted selection of a knowledge state.** Selection of a knowledge state can be predetermined by the decision policy in the search strategy, or it can determined by some knowledge of a problem†. A computer assist would be more helpful in the second case. One approach would be a program to display the search tree thus far generated so that a designer was better informed of the opportunities and alternatives available. Another approach would be to evaluate each of the states with an *evaluation function* which would produce a measure of the likelihood of each state being a solution precursor.

4. **Computerized selection of a knowledge state.** Selection of which knowledge state to operate on can be entirely automated if either:

   a. A weak method of search is used, in which case the selection is trivial, or

   b. A strong and reliable test for a solution precursor exists.

---

*This is the approach of Pareto optimality.

†This is exactly the distinction between the weak methods of search and strong knowledge based methods.

5. **Computer assisted operator selection and application**. An approach to this option would be a display of all applicable operations with some prediction of their impact on a knowledge state. The designer would select an operation and the computer would apply it to the knowledge state. A weaker form of assistance could be provided by the computer displaying the operations that have already been applied to a knowledge state. The designer would use that information to formulate and apply the operation manually.

6. **Computerized operator selection.** One approach to this option is the operator selection mechanism of means/ends analysis, in which operator selection is mapped to selection from a *table of differences*. In this table an operator is selected if it will best reduce an observed distance between a current state and a goal state. Another automated approach to operator selection is that of a knowledge driven system. Whenever the knowledge state to be operated on exhibits certain characteristics an operator may be specified. This approach lacks any formal explanation, as the characteristics which cause operator selection can be completely arbitrary. This fact has not stopped application of the idea in many knowledge based systems based upon *rules*.

7. **Computer assisted selection of knowledge states to retain.** A key idea for this option is the notion of access. As a designer develops a series of knowledge states, the computer could provide a means to characterize these states in some manner. This could be in the form of a naming convention, or could be automatic, where the state is characterized and indexed by algorithms. Version control ideas from the database field will likely be applicable here.

8. **Computerized selection of knowledge states to retain.** When weak methods of search are used, there exist simple policies for determining which states to save.

Each of these strategies for supporting search could be combined with other strategies to form more complex models of computer-assisted search. All options share the characteristic of moving some of the main cognitive activity of design, that of search, into the realm of a computing device. Thus all of the options change, to varying degrees, the structure of the model of problem solving. Some of the options, particularly those of selection of knowledge state and operators, have the effect of making feasible explorations which would be intractable by manual methods. These options act to increase the power of the designer.

Similarity Between External and Internal Representations

When designers solve problems, they use an internal formulation of the problem, known as a problem space, to carry out the information processing required to solve the problem. Almost always, designers make use of an external memory, in the form of drawings or models, to assist their memory and to help structure the process of exploration in design*. The use of this external memory implies a continual translation between it and the representations internal to a designer's mind. It can be shown [Card 1983] that the cost, in terms of time spent translating, can increase dramatically as the difference between the internal and external representations grows. The strategy then, for creating design systems, is to discover and provide external memory representations that are directly mappable into internal problem space representations.

These representations are likely to take the form of *abstractions*. An *abstraction* is a partial representation of an object, that expresses some information about the object and suppresses all other information. A well-known abstraction in architectural design is the bubble diagram, that expresses adjacencies (and possibly size) without strong specification of geometric shape and location†. Figure 1.5 shows a plan representation of a simple building and its associated bubble diagram. Abstractions such as these speak more directly to a designer than do complete descriptions, where abstract information of this type can be easily lost.

External representations of internal concepts are more than just a means to record information in a succinct and convenient manner. Once so recorded in the external world, they can be subjected to a whole range of operations and queries that are not possible within the limited scope of a designer's unaided cognition. They can be changed and manipulated according to explicit rules; their properties and implications can be formally examined. These external operations can greatly increase the utility of a representation. If a representation is both a good model of the problem space in a designer's mind and can be given formal interpretation as a mathematical object, then a great opportunity emerges. The representation can be systematically examined and used to compute its inherent implications. An example of such a symbiosis is found in the work of Flemming [Flemming 1985] who uses rectangles and a simple relation set as a representation of diverse design situations. One priority for implementation of this strategy is the discovery and formalization of a useful set of abstractions.

Designers tend to use many different, often idiosyncratic, abstractions as they design. Not all of these abstractions can be foreseen by a system designer, nor are all of these representations formalizable. As an example

---

*This external memory is necessary because of inherent limits in the human information processing system.

†Unfortunately, bubble diagrams also convey some, usually unintended, information about the placement and shape of objects. It is an all too common failing of novice designers to merely "round off" the corners of a bubble diagram and call it a "solution".

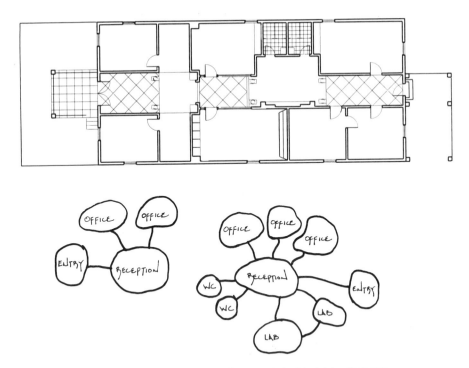

Figure 1.5. A floor plan and its associated bubble diagram.

of the richness of different abstraction types see [Laseau 1980]. An approach to the first of these problems, the lack of a complete representation set, is the combination of existing relations to build new relations. A first example is [Akiner 1985]. The second of these problems seems less tractable. The benefits of a formalizable representation are the external computations that can be performed on it. If a representation is not formalizable then the remaining benefits are simply as a repository of knowledge in external memory. This benefit could possibly be achieved by a graphic "language" convention as described by Laseau [Laseau 1980].

The strategy of making external representations that are close analogues to internal problem space representations falls into two categories in the classification of Figure 1.4. By making the external mirror the internal representations, access time to external memory is reduced, thus increasing the efficiency of the designer. By creating formal external models which can be computed, the structure of the model is changed, to a structure in which the external memory is no longer passive. This change can have an effect on the power of a designer by allowing otherwise infeasible operations to occur.

Parsimonious Input

An external medium is used in manual methods of design to augment memory. A designer interacts with that medium by creating marks on paper or by performing operations on a physical model. In some situations, very brief informal marks may be laden with meaning, in other situations, for example perspective rendering, a great deal of effort may be placed into the creation of a single representation. The early stages of design tend to make use primarily of marks of the first variety, i.e. marks that with great parsimony of effort capture their intended meaning. Just as a designer seeks to make his manual mark making parsimonious or efficient, an interactive computer system should provide very parsimonious means of creating its representations.

One of the greatest sources of parsimony of input in design could be the capture of repetitive types of representations. For example, in designing a window facade, a designer using manual media must draw each facade element (that he chooses to represent) individually. Yet these elements are highly similar and the intention of the drawing activity can be captured in a single phrase, "put windows in the facade". Another example is in the creation of tilings of the plane, a design exercise originated by William Huff [Hofstadter 1983] and recently used in a different form in a course, developed by the author, entitled *Computer Modelling in Design* at Carnegie-Mellon University. These tilings, a computer generated example of which is shown in Figure 1.6, are the product of exploration of sequential transformations on an initial tiling. At each stage in the exploration, a representation in the form of a drawing is made so that the effect of the latest transformation can be assessed. When done manually, these drawings consume a great deal of time and effort. An ability to describe the transformation directly, in terms of an operation on some part of an existing tiling, would reduce the effort required for drawing, allowing a designer's attention to be focused more upon notions of transformation.

Computer programming languages provide constructs for expressing the regularities in form and transformation described above. They are a model for formally representing sequence. Many geometric modelling systems have been based on computer programming paradigms [Fitzgerald 1981; Brown 1982] yet none, to the knowledge of the author, has brought the process part of the programming paradigm into the interactive graphical interface in a strong way. A system which supports interactive design should have explicit mechanisms for expressing and executing algorithms. These mechanisms should be presented graphically to the user.

With respect to figure 1.4 this strategy seeks to improve the efficiency of the system by changing the parameter of speed of writing on external memory.

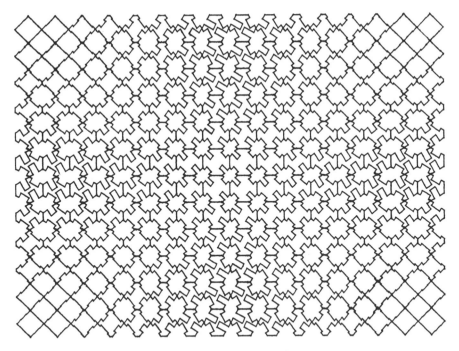

Figure 1.6. A tiling of the plane.

Design as Note Taking

The representations of design can be viewed as *notes*, which singly give some information about a design and in total specify a design to some level of completion. The term *notes* is used to emphasize that most design representations are informal, that is they may not follow consistent conventions and they may not be complete in the event that a convention is consistently used. In addition they may contain information extraneous to the specification of a design, but essential to the process of creating the design. This informality serves important purposes for designers:

- It allows the recording of ideas without a large time and effort commitment.
- Levels of informality can be used as a "code" to indicate the degree of commitment which has been brought to an idea. A drawing at small scale, done quickly, with thick charcoal is easy to change or abandon compared to a complete plan drawing, with dimensions done with ink on mylar.

- It allows for rapid change of information structuring, format and style; all important for a designer using the type of search described under the Newell and Simon model.

The computer support of note taking is problematic. In order for a computer supported note to be more useful than its manual counterpart, some of the information conveyed by the note must be extracted and explicitly represented. Yet a fundamental property of notes is their informality, their seeming non-adherence to a well formed syntax of representation. One very speculative approach to this problem is an "opportunistic" note recognizer. A system of this sort would operate by recognizing patterns in a note and making inferences from those patterns. The validity of these inferences would be manually checked. In order to work, such a system would require a strong pattern recognition facility and an ability to represent complex rules about patterns. The production system paradigm fits these requirements, but current production systems do not operate on the bitmap kind of representations that would most likely be used as the medium of note communication.

With respect to the classification in figure 1.4 this approach seeks to change the efficiency of the human information processing system (IPS) by changing the structure of the external memory that aids the designer.

☐ STRATEGY FOR DEVELOPMENT

Creating modelling systems to support the interactive generation of designs is a long range task. Priorities for inquiry in this area need to be established if such systems are to be created.

When computer tools are newly introduced to a field, increased efficiency of existing methods has traditionally been the first goal of their use [Akin 1984]. Eventually though, computation has a more profound impact on a field, for it begins to change both the structure of the methods used and the nature of the end products. A prime example is civil engineering, where computerized finite element methods introduced for the first time, a strong notion of iterative design, and the ability to "fine tune" or optimize structural performance. Similarly, in looking for strategies for developing interactive design systems, one should look first to those ideas which hold the most promise for restructuring method and changing product and secondarily to those ideas which merely seek to increase the efficiency of design.* This suggests that those strategies aimed at increasing the power of the

---

*This statement is not meant to denigrate important and essential inquiry into highly interactive operations. Rather it argues that the idea of a truly interactive design system is young and as such the limits of the idea are not fully explored. The most profound effects are liable to arise from changes to methods and products rather that efficiency of process.

STRATEGY FOR:

METHOD MAKES:	increasing efficiency	increasing power
change to parameters	internal/external parsimonious input	
change to structure	note taking	internal/external search

Figure 1.7. The strategies classified.

human IPS (the rightmost column of figure 1.4 show the most promise for developing systems for interactive design. Completing Figure 1.4 as Figure 1.7 shows that two of the strategies reported here, *search* and *internal/external* have an influence on the power of the designer. They both act by removing some of the cognitive burden from the designer and placing it in external memory.

Both of these strategies are worthy of pursuit. Search seems to be the most likely candidate for first exploration as there exists, in the field of artificial intelligence, a strong framework in which search can be studied. The use of search augmenting methods in an interactive design system relies on explicit representation of the domain being searched. This representation must have certain formal properties dependent upon the type of decision that the computer system is making or assisting. Today there appear to exist only two representation paradigms which are sufficiently formalized to fill this role; rectangular layouts [Flemming 1985] and shape grammars [Stiny 1980]. More research into formalized representations seems to be in order.

If these new formal representations are to be truly useful in design, they should map easily to internal representations that designers can maintain. Thus the strategy for making external mirror internal representations should be given a high priority. Two sources for insight into such representations seem available. One is the research into the ways in which designers work with manual methods [Akin 1979]. The other would lie in investigations into representations designers *could* use were they to have suitable supporting external representations. This second approach is more speculative, but is closer to the goal, of creating new synergies between person and computer. Making external and internal representations similar can also have the effect of transferring some of the cognitive burden away from the designer onto the machine. However, there does not exist a firm intellectual framework within which to understand how these activities would affect design, so first efforts in this area are likely to be *ad hoc*. A worthy goal would be the creation of such a thought structure that would explain in detail the role such external representations can play. These strategies, for increasing the power of the designer to create solutions, seem the most promising avenues of inquiry into the support of interactive design systems.

The other two strategies for interactive design systems fall into the categories, shown in figure 1.7, for improving the efficiency of the design process. This classification provides no means for ordering their importance, so no such ordering is reported here. Some connections to other fields should, however, be noted. The strategies, for parsimony and note-taking seem related. One goal for creating notes is to achieve a low time commitment for their construction, exactly the same goal that parsimony of input pursues. Ideas of iteration from programming languages seem appropriate here. These ideas have been formulated in a domain other than geometry. Investigation of programming ideas in a geometric domain could provide significant insight for programming language research. One approach to accomplish the note taking strategy would be a bit-map pattern recognizer. Successful development of this idea would provide insights for the field of pattern recognition in general and computer vision in particular.

In summary then, strategies for the development of systems for design are dominated by those that promise to change both the structure and the product of design. These include those strategies aimed at search and at mapping between internal and external representations. Other strategies, for increasing efficiency of design, seem to have no rank ordering of importance yet are interrelated.

The four strategies discussed here certainly do not exhaust the possibilities for approaches to supporting interactive design systems. Other ideas for building such systems can be imagined; many are latent in the extant literature and in the bewildering variety of interactive computer programs which exist today. What seems to be lacking is a conceptual structure which can give form to research efforts. A *theory* is needed; a theory which takes as its starting point the goal of creating interactive design systems, and explains in detail requirements, organizations and means of evaluation. Many of the pieces of such a theory exist today. Current understanding of designer behaviour reinforces the central notions of the Newell and Simon theory and extends those notions into more complex types of problem solving. Studies in human computer interaction provide a comprehension of the detailed, low level interaction that occurs between humans and machines. Research in automated design provides an inventory of models which suggest possible system designs. If interactive systems which truly support design are to be built, these disparate pieces must be pulled together and knit into a coherent whole.

☐ REFERENCES

Akin O. "Models of Architectural Knowledge: An Information Processing Model of Design", Phd Dissertation, Carnegie-Mellon University, 1979.

Akin O., C. Baykan and R. Rao "Searching in the UNIX Directory Space," Technical Report, Department of Architecture, Carnegie Mellon University, 1983.

Akin O. Flemming U. and Woodbury R. "Development of Computer Systems for Use in Architectural Education," Technical Report, Department of Architecture, Carnegie Mellon University, 1984.

Akiner V.T. "Topology - 1: A Reasoning System for Objects and Space Modelling Via Knowledge Engineering." In *Design Engineering Division Conference on Mechanical Vibration and Noise.* American Society of Mechanical Engineers Cincinnati Ohio, September 1985.

Ballay J.M., K. Graham J.R. Hayes and D. Fallside *Final Report Phase IV: CMU/IBM Usability Study.* Technical Report Carnegie-Mellon University, March 1984.

Brown C.M. "PADL-2: A Technical Summary." *IEEE—Computer Graphics and Applications* 2(2):69-86 March 1982.

Card S.K., T.P. Moran and A. Newell *The Psychology of Human-Computer Interaction.* Lawrence Erlbaum Associates, Hillsdale, New Jersey 1983.

Eastman C.M. On the Analysis of Intuitive Design Processes. *Emerging Methods in Environmental Design and Planning.* MIT Press, Cambridge, Mass. pp 21-37 Chapter 3 1970.

Fitzgerald W. Gracer F. and Wolfe R. "GRIN: Interactive Graphics for Modelling Solids." *IBM Journal of Research and Development* 25(4):281-294 July 1981.

Flemming U. "Wall Representations of rectangular dissections and their use in automated space allocation." *Environment and Planning B* 5:215-232, 1979

Flemming U. "On the representation and generation of loosely-packed arrangements of rectangles." *Planning and Design* December 1985.

Galle P. "An algorithm for exhaustive generation of building floor plans." *Communications of the ACM* 24:813-825 1981.

Hillyard R.C. "The Build Group of Solid Modellers." *IEEE - Computer Graphics and Applications* 2(2):43-52 March 1982.

Hofstadter D.R. "Metamagical Themas." *Scientific American* 249(1):14-20 July 1983.

Kosslyn S.M., B.J. Reiser, M.J. Farah and S.L. Fliegel "Generating Visual Images: Units and Relations." *Journal of Experimental Psychology: General* 112(2):278-303 February 1983.

Laseau P. *Graphic Thinking for Architects and Designers.* Van Nostrand Reinhold Company New York N.Y. 1980.

Mitchell W.J. *Computer-Aided Architectural Design.* Petrocelli/Charter New York N.Y. 1977.

Newell A. H.A. Simon *Human Problem Solving.* Prentice-Hall Inc. Englewood Cliffs N.J. 1972.

Reitman W.R. *Human Judgements and Optimality- Heuristic decision procedures, open constraints and the structure of ill-defined problems.* Wiley New York pp. 283-315 1964.

Simon H.A. "The structure of ill-structured problems." *Artificial Intelligence* 4:181-201 1973.

Stiny G. "Introduction to shape and shape grammers." *Environment and Planning B* 7(3):343-352 1980.

Sutherland I.E. Sketchpad: A Man-Machine Graphical Communication System. Technical Report 296 MIT Lincoln Lab 1963.

Woodbury R.F. "Computer Techniques for Designers: Strategies." In *4th Canadian Building Congress.*

2

PUZZLE-MAKING: WHAT ARCHITECTS DO WHEN NO ONE IS LOOKING

John Archea

School of Architecture and Environmental Design
State University of New York at Buffalo
Buffalo, New York

Most professionals involved in the building process work in a problem-solving mode. They state desired effects as explicit performance criteria before they initiate a decision process and then test alternative solutions against those criteria until a fit is obtained which falls within known probabilities of success. It is the thesis of this paper that architects work in a manner that is antithetical to problem-solving because they cannot explicate desired effects prior to their realization through the design process.

In an attempt to clarify architecture's uncommon mode of action, I suggest that what architects do is best described as puzzle-making. Instead of specifying what they are trying to accomplish prior to their attempts to accomplish it as problem-solvers do, architects treat design as a search for the most appropriate effects that can be attained in a unique context. They seek sets of combinatorial rules that will result in an internally consistent fit between a kit of parts and the effects that are achieved when those parts are assembled in a certain way.

Since each part or assemblage of parts must have a logical and appropriate relation to the whole effect that is achieved, the architect is primarily concerned with the completeness of the rule system that he or she superimposes on a given context. Precedents, symbols and metaphors that have attained wholeness through years or centuries of acculturization generally form the catalysts for this endeavour. By continually transforming or reinterpreting one or more of these previously completed rule systems, the architect establishes a fit between the effects that ought to be achieved and a kit of parts that is most effective for achieving those effects—thereby defining the uniqueness of the context at hand.

With regard to the making of buildings and other settings, the architect is a puzzle-maker surrounded by problem-solvers who address separate pieces of the puzzle. None of the problem-solvers has a disciplined procedure for determining how all of the separate parts ought to coalesce into an effective whole. Thus the heuristic of superimposing completed rule systems onto kits of parts and manipulating both until satisfying effects are achieved falls uniquely to the architect.

☐ INTRODUCTION

Over the past twenty years architecture has had the good fortune of attracting the attention of dedicated professionals who advocate one of several approaches to making the design process and the buildings or settings it produces more effective. Design methods, computer-aided design, system building and environment-behavior studies have at different times and different places promised to help the architect become more efficient and reliable when addressing the purposes for which buildings are built and occupied.

The promises still stand. Work continues inside and outside of academia on the computability of design decisions, participatory programming and post-occupancy evaluation. Yet despite a wealth of interactive computer-aided video imaging capabilities and volumes of corroborated research findings on how people perceive, use and feel about buildings, the main stream of American architectural education, practice and criticism seems little affected. In fact from my partially obscurred vantage point, changes in the primary architectural agenda in this country over the past decade would appear to signal a repudiation of most promises of more efficient practice and more effective architecture.

I do not know if or why this is actually the case. However, the very possibility that researchers trying to improve architectural processes and products might be pursuing agendas that are not widely shared by architectural practitioners and educators should give some pause for reflection. This paper is obviously too rough in texture to reflect clearly, but it may begin to chart some of the murky depths of architecture's pool of implicit tenets and techniques.

☐ PROBLEM SOLVING

Although most scholars trace American higher education back to the founding of Harvard College in 1636, two events occurring during the late nineteenth century had a far greater impact on the direction of higher education in this country. In 1862 the U.S. Congress passed the first Morrill Act which established land-grants to the states for the purpose of establishing colleges to train young people in the agricultural and mechanical arts. This notion of "know-how" became the founding principle of most of the great state universities at which most Americans receive their higher education. Schon [1983] points out that the founding of the privately funded Johns Hopkins University in 1876 provided the exemplary model on which most American universities were subsequently based—an assessment underscored by Piel [1986]. Johns Hopkins was founded on the notion that the application of basic scientific knowledge should be the basis for professional education—an idea that many of the first faculty members brought from Germany. I suggest that these two events were quite indicative of the ideas toward higher education prevailing in the U.S. in the late nineteenth century, that the notion of applied science or applied art remains at the core of professional education in American universities, and that the very idea that scientific knowledge and technical skills can be applied to a broad range of problems is central to all aspects of American education and the popular values that shape and sustain it.

From this point of view, the central agenda of professional education and practice is "problem-solving" [Schon 1983]. This is an enterprise in which desired effects are stated as explicit criteria and the known limitations to achieving those effects are stated as explicit constraints before a course of action (e.g., therapy, litigation, design) is initiated. The professional course of action becomes a decision process in which candidate solutions are tested against the stated criteria and constraints until a fit is attained that falls within known or acceptable probabilities of success. In order to be so clear about what they are trying to accomplish before they set out to accomplish it, problem-solvers presume that knowing can and should be separate from acting. To them, a full and independent inquiry must be completed before proper technical decisions can be made.

Most university trained professionals involved in the building process (programmers, space planners, developers, bank officials, engineers, etc.) work in a problem-solving mode and tend to view their world from this point of view. They quite logically assume that university trained architects also work as problem-solvers. I submit that this is not and never has been the case!

It is the primary thesis of this paper that architects approach design in a manner that is antithetical to problem-solving. This is because they do not and generally cannot explicate desired effects prior to realizing those effects through the full execution of the architectural design process. Architectural educators, practitioners and critics further confound this state of affairs by remaining totally inarticulate about how the design process actually contributes to the making of buildings or other settings. Instead, their literature focuses almost exclusively on the objects produced by this unspecified process—especially the internal validity of those objects as articulated value systems or exemplars of contemporary culture. Although the architect's previous works, published remarks and collegial associations are often interwoven with interpretive and evaluative statements about a given building or project, the specific sequence of decisions and tradeoffs that led to the ultimate arrangement or appearance of that object is seldom discussed.

Interestingly, most of the serious attempts to document the architectural design process have been made by non-architects or by architects with extensive training in another field [Alexander 1964; Simon 1969, 1970; Churchman 1971; Korobkin 1976; Zeisel 1981; Schon 1983; Wehrli 1986]. Not surprisingly, most of these characterize architectural design as a very complex form of problem-solving. Only Schon [1983] suggests that it might not be possible to stretch problem-solving techniques and the tenets of technical rationality on which they are based far enough to include what architects do when they say they are designing.

Before developing the major theme of this paper, I want to outline certain characteristics that the architectural design process would require to be considered a form of problem-solving. First it should be possible to state all or most of the architectural design criteria and constraints at the onset of the design process—including those pertaining to all technical, financial, legal, socio-political, organizational, experiential and perceptual aspects of a given project. Second, at the onset of the design process, a comprehensive, internally consistent and independently derived body of knowledge must exist to justify and substantiate most of the design criteria and constraints stated for all aspects of the project at hand. Finally, this comprehensive body of knowledge must be generalizable from the context in which it was developed to the specific spatio-temporal context of any given architectural project.

In sum, the potential for problem-solving exists only when there is a generalizable knowledge base which permits the specification of most (not all) of the criteria and constraints for all (not most) aspects of a given design project. While this condition may obtain in certain areas of engineering design or product design, I submit that it rarely obtains in any area of architectural design. This is because it is not possible to draw upon a generalizable knowledge base to specify many of the design criteria or constraints for most aspects of any given architectural project—especially those pertaining to socio-political, organizational, experiential or perceptual issues. The fact that architects somehow manage to produce buildings and other settings when so much of the domain within which they must operate remains indescribable at the beginning of their endeavour, suggests that architectural design involves activities other than problem-solving.

□ PUZZLE-MAKING

In an attempt to characterize the architect's uncommon mode of action I suggest that the most fundamental aspects of architectural design can best be described as a process of "puzzle-making". Instead of specifying what they are trying to accomplish independently of and prior to their attempts to accomplish it, as problem-solvers do, architects treat design as a search for the most appropriate effects that can be attained in specific spatio-temporal contexts which are in virtually all respects *unique*. A key point of demarcation between puzzle-making and problem-solving is the former's overriding emphasis on uniqueness.

Any cursory review of studio projects in schools of architecture, winners of architectural design awards or competitions, and the architectural press clearly reveals that architects are primarily concerned with unique design contexts. They prefer to design one-of-a-kind buildings on uncommon sites. When they are commissioned to design an otherwise common building on an unchallenging site, architects generally superimpose their own special agendas on the client's programmatic requirements to make each project unique.

Throughout the design process architects seek unique sets of combinatorial rules (the essence of the puzzle) that will result in an internally consistent fit between a specific kit of parts (architectural elements, attributes or ideas) and the effects that are achieved when those parts are assembled in a certain way. The key elements in the puzzle-making process are: (1) sets of combinatorial rules that delimit the domains of appropriate fit between (2) kits of tangible or intangible parts and (3) the formal, symbolic or experiential effects that emerge when the specified relationships among those parts are realized at a given point in space and time. Granted, this program is tautological. Yet it is in precisely this closed loop of redundant logic that the architect has developed a systematic program of action.

At the onset of the design process, neither the effects that the architect will attempt to attain, nor the kit of parts that will be drawn upon to attain those effects, can be specified by the architect. While both may exist in some pre-verbal or pre-visual form, neither can be fully articulated until the architectural design process is completed. In fact the whole purpose of the process is to identify appropriately matched ensembles of parts and resultant effects through successive approximations of potential means and corresponding ends.

Interestingly, neither the succession of kits of parts that are considered, nor the effects that are attained when those parts are satisfactorily juxtaposed, are explicitly related to the design program—generally stated as an interrelated series of sub-problems. Instead the architect treats the program as a catalyst for the design activity—something to be read to get some sense of direction and extent, but then to be set aside and used only as a sounding board as the design process approaches points of potential resolution. It is only through the process of designing that the architect discovers what he or she can accomplish for a given client on a specific plot of ground, and which architectural elements and attributes will be most effective in accomplishing it.

In effect the architect makes a puzzle in which each part or assemblage of parts has a uniquely satisfying position in relation to the whole ensemble. The whole ensemble in turn will reveal only a general correspondence with the requirements of the client's program, because the architectural design process is not driven by such "ends-oriented" directives. Just how a one-to-one correspondence is ultimately established between those requirements and the ensemble of elements and attributes that the architect has puzzled out, will be discussed in a later section.

□ PRECEDENTS, SYMBOLS AND METAPHORS

To this point I have done little more than bring the reader to the threshold of architecture's traditional "black-box" of intuition and creativity. However, instead of yielding to these sacred cows as the unfathomable wells from which flow the inspirations for all that is good in architecture, I should like to consider intuition and creativity as processes that are simultaneously very clever and very systematic. I begin with the notion stated above, that for the architect, each part or assemblage of parts must appear to have a logical and appropriate relation to the whole effect that is attained. This leads the architect to concentrate on the completeness and internal consistency of the combinatorial rule system that he or she superimposes on a given design context. It is clear that most architects are not clever enough to develop such rule systems anew for every project—that would approximate reinventing the calculus for every building!

So what do they do? The architects' apparent response to this dilemma is to treat precedents, symbols and metaphors which have attained their wholeness through years or centuries of acculturation, as the bases for generating rule systems for specific design projects. Jefferson's adaptation of the Maison Carree in Nimes for the Virginia State Capitol, or of Palladio's Villa Pisani in Montegnana for the first phase of his own home at Monticello, are among countless examples of the use of highly acclaimed precedents in architecture. In neither case were exact copies made. Rather, the basic rules of proportion, sequence and relief established in the precedent were taken as a starting point—a provisional rule system—in each of the latter buildings. These provisional rules were then extended, varied, reordered or juxtaposed with other rule systems (such as the Georgian facade at Monticello) until the unique demands of client, climate and circumstance were met. Exactly the same pattern was followed by countless other American architects of the 18th and 19th centuries, who modeled their works on European exemplars.

A major benefit in drawing upon a precedent in the making of architecture is that the quality of wholeness exists at the very onset of the process. The remainder of the process involves the manipulation of the initial sets of rules or the addition of new ones, until a new system emerges that is comprehensive and internally consistent enough to anticipate the range of typical and atypical circumstances characteristic of the site and the program. What drives this process is the simultaneous sorting through kits of parts (materials, senses of openness or enclosure, transparency or opacity) and the effects they produce when arranged according to the prevailing version of the architect's evolving rule system. This process comes to a logical conclusion when the effects that are attained when the kits of parts are juxtaposed according to the rule system(s) map onto the general intent of the project at hand in such a way that all unusual or special cases can be accommodated without producing undesirable effects—the point at which a puzzle has been made.

Clearly, the precedent represents the most complete, albeit the least original, starting point for the architectural design process. It clearly stood at the core of the work of the 19th century revival styles and neoclassical movements. However, symbols and metaphors also have the same potential for provisionally ordering a design project at the onset of the design process. For example, ever since Venturi et al [1972] drew attention to the normative American values embedded in the flashing lights, wipe-clean panels and parking lots of the Las Vegas strip, architects have become increasingly fascinated by the notion that many designed objects convey meanings that greatly exceed their functions. It is now widely accepted that the use of such objects or elements to launch the design process introduces a special kind of rule system in which the values associated with the kits of parts already have a built-in correspondence with the effects that the architect can expect to attain—a heuristic convenience for the designer, even if such associations are never apparent to anyone else. In effect, the analysis and manipulation of symbols allows the architect to work with rule systems that underlie and prefigure the outward appearances of architectural or non-architectural precedents.

The use of the metaphor also enables the architect to work with rules and ideas that transcend appearances. To see an architectural opportunity "as if" it had the form or function of something else has always played a central role in the design process. The building as a machine, the public square as a theater, the nursing home as an indoor village—all introduce complete packages of spatio-temporal ideas and relationships around which a coherent design activity can be pursued. The grid is perhaps the most common and powerful metaphor found in architecture, yet it is in no way intrinsic to the making of buildings. Preceeding the Greeks, carefully manipulated since the Enlightenment, raised to an art by the Modernists and systematically fractured by the Post-Modernists, grids have virtually all of the qualities of wholeness—a wholeness which they retain no mater how they are subdivided, bounded, rotated or otherwise juxtaposed.

By relying on precedents, symbols and metaphors to impart a provisional measure of completeness and internal consistency at the onset of the design process, the architect is merely acknowledging that buildings and other settings are simply too complex to be designed coherently using an incremental

approach. Instead of relying on programmatic, code and technical requirements to initiate and guide the design process, the architect superimposes an
external set of coherent rules at the onset of the process, and continues to
manipulate those rules until all of the programmatic and other requirements
have been loosely subsumed.

One of the distinguishing characteristics of puzzle-making is that it capi-
talizes on society's own peculiar mechanisms for assigning value. Not every
building that has ever been built qualifies as a potential precedent. Only
those to which critical attention, public acceptance or historical accident
bring favor tend to qualify. So it is with symbols and metaphors. Somehow the image of a nursing home as a busy intersection seems less fitting
than its image as a quiet village. The point is that the wholeness and internal consistency of the precedents or other devices introduced to guide the
design process is generally established by some segment of the society at
large, not by the architect.

In effect, by continually transforming or reinterpreting these socially val-
ued rule systems, the architect ultimately establishes a fit between specific
effects that can be achieved and a kit of parts that will be most effective for
achieving those effects, thereby defining the unique opportunity presented
by the specific spatio-temporal context at hand. For the architect there are
no problems to be solved, just a range of opportunities to be discovered
and organized within a given spatio-temporal context. The architectural
design process is not one of applying generalized knowledge to specific
cases, but rather one of basic inquiry into the essence of unique contexts.

I have taken the liberty of coining the term "puzzle-making" to characterize the architectural design process because this process, as I understand
it, does not fit neatly within any established program of inquiry such as
rationalism, empiricism, structuralism or instrumentalism [Archea 1975,
1982]. It clearly lacks the operational skepticism of empiricism and any of
its more contemporary manifestations, such as critical fallibalism [Lakatos
1970]. It also lacks the axiomatic logic of the rationalists or the contingent
logic of the instrumentalists. Perhaps the rule-seeking process of the
puzzle-makers comes closest to the taxonomic pursuits of the
structuralists—which may explain the architect's continuing fascination with
European thought from Wertheimer and Koffka through Jung, Heidegger,
Foucault and Derrida. Yet, unlike the structuralists, or even the post-
structuralists, the architect seeks no external points of verification to establish the universality or generalizability of his or her rule system(s).

The architect's mode of inquiry anticipates no observable states of
affairs! The use of precedents, symbols and metaphors is not necessarily
intended to endow buildings or other settings with specific meaning or
value, but rather to provide rule systems that are sufficiently coherent to
guide the architect's own private decision making processes. For example,
symbols are not analyzed and manipulated as criteria to be attained, but as
heuristic devices to facilitate inquiry.

Does the notion of puzzle-making simply align architecture with the arts? I think not. In fact, I suspect that architecture differs as much from the various approaches to art as it does from the applied science pursuits of the problem-solvers. Furthermore, I sense that architectural design is an enterprise that is fundamentally different than the processes followed in most other areas of design (e.g., industrial design). The key point of demarcation between puzzle-making and these other forms of inquiry or action lies in their various approaches to context.

□ UNIQUE CONTEXTS

By using the term "context" I refer to the totality of the existential here and now—arriving at, being in and passing beyond a unique point in space and time. Whether they follow an empiricist, structuralist or instrumentalist program, the sciences seek knowledge and methods that transcend the idiosyncrasies of events that occur, or observations that are made at unique points in space and time. The arts attempt to encapsulate the essence of unique contexts and put them in a form that can be made universally accessible (e.g., the framed canvas, the bound volume). Whereas the former skeptically treats events of the moment as aberrant instances of more universal principles and patterns, the latter treats them as potent microcosms or exemplars of more universal truths and values. Both treat individual contexts, situations or events as vehicles for a much more universal understanding or appreciation.

I suggest that architecture stands virtually alone in addressing singular contexts per se. It pursues the question: how will I determine what to build here and now? It is place-specific. It is time-specific. Its mode of inquiry—puzzle-making—is predicated on this condition.

What drives architecture's uncommon program of inquiry is the undeniable fact that buildings and most other architectural creations are attached to the earth at specific points in space and time. While architecture shares with the arts a fascination for discovering and expressing the essence of unique spatio-temporal contexts at the moment of encounter or intervention, it does not enjoy the artist's privilege to extract and embellish those essential values, and to package them in such a way that interpretations of the moment can subsequently be reencountered in spatio-temporally distant and dissimilar contexts [Benjamin 1969]. Instead the architect is confined to the task of limiting the domains of both inquiry and action to the circumstances of a given client, on a given site at a given point in time. Therefore the architect's professional course of action centers on a program for reconciling his or her understanding of what is already in place with his or her vision of unknown circumstances yet to come. In effect, puzzle-making is a clever commingling of "is" and "ought" that enables the architect to fashion coherent courses of action entirely *within context*.

In his development of the notion "reflection-in-action" Schon [1983] has drawn a parallel between the methods of the architect and those of the psychotherapist. Although the former deals with place-contexts and the latter deals with person-contexts, both attempt to discover the unique circumstances and opportunities presented by single cases. Both focus on the conditions prevailing in the existential here and now, including vestiges of past and anticipations of future events. Neither relies exclusively on general principles or universal patterns to diagnose problems or to solve them. Instead, both negotiate acceptable interpretations and courses of action by reflecting on the prevailing circumstances of the place or person at hand. The psychotherapist does this by interpreting his or her dialogue with the patient. The architect does this by interpreting his or her own dialogue with the client and experience with the place and the times. In both cases, the vehicle for interpretation is to overlay the dialogue with a succession of templates—precedents or prior cases, symbols or patterns of association, metaphors or analogs, or any other devices which begin to impose a measure of coherence and internal consistency on the specific case at hand.

This emphasis on unique contexts is clearly reflected in the education of the architect. In most schools there is a heavy emphasis on architectural history—a much greater emphasis on history than any other professional curriculum. There is also an uncommon emphasis on field trips, foreign study and travel—not to examine state-of-the-art building techniques, but to walk through and photograph "good" buildings and public spaces in context. Together, the history and travel constitute a total immersion in the specific circumstances and peculiarities of architectural precedents and ideas, not just for their intrinsic values, but also as potential sources of rules for subsequent design projects. This practice is heavily reinforced by the architectural journals (surrogate forms of travel), which are filled with historic and contemporary representations of built and unbuilt buildings that provide a vast pool of parts, from which every architect and architectural student is free to draw when assembling his or her own kit.

In most schools the focus of the curriculum is the design studio—a succession of increasingly complex professional projects on specific sites, which the students address through a form of role-playing [Gutman 1985]. Interestingly, the methods of design are generally not taught in direct conjunction with the activities of the design studios. In fact, most studio critics never articulate how design presumably occurs, relying instead on the widely held notion that one can only learn how to design by designing. In effect, the design studio encourages the student to develop his or her own point of view about architecture, by repeatedly mapping the lessons of history and travel onto the peculiarities of a succession of projects and sites. At no point is an explicit procedure considered which could tie these interpretations and manipulations together into an objective set of replicable protocols.

Much of the technical knowledge that most non-architects presume to be the basis for architectural education, is given relatively little emphasis compared to that given to the studio experience or to history [Gutman 1985]. Very few schools carry specific knowledge of structural or mechanical systems to the point where students are fully capable of integrating those systems with overall building design, or of prescribing their technical details. Instead, emphasis is generally placed on acquiring little more than a working acquaintance with these technical systems, with the full expectation that, in practice, such technical issues will ultimately be addressed by persons trained in other disciplines. What all of this suggests is that, at the architectural level of discourse, there are no problems to be solved, just a range of unique opportunities to be discovered and exploited. It also suggests that architecture is a verb—a way of acting within contexts for which no corroborated body of knowledge exists to provide an adequate guide for action. To treat architecture as a noun—a reference to all of the buildings that have been produced—confounds the artifact with the manner of its making. Buildings and other architectural settings are placed within unique spatio-temporal contexts which they, in turn, redefine. The process of determining what to build here and now necessarily becomes one of puzzling-out a context-specific logic that links available kits of parts to sets of desirable effects.

☐ RETREATING INTO THE PROTECTED CORE

To this point I have presented puzzle-making as the antithesis of problem-solving, without presenting any legitimate supporting evidence. In part, this is because problem-solving so predominates the world of professional activity in the United States, that little evidence surfaces to indicate the extent or character of alternative modes of professional inquiry and action. However, I sense that several historic trends give a fairly clear indication of what architectural design is, or is not concerned with.

In retrospect, it seems that whenever a body of knowledge developed to the point that the effects of a specific building attribute or system could be fully understood prior to and independently of the initiation of the design process, architects have redefined their profession to exclude responsibilities for achieving those effects. Throughout the 20th century architects have increasingly relied on other disciplines to make buildings work—beginning with the engineering disciplines and proceeding through site planners and space programmers. The problems associated with the structural, mechanical, electrical, financial and other so-called "functional" aspects of buildings have gradually been relegated to other disciplines, where they can be addressed before or after the primary architectural design activity takes place.

Ventre [1982] indicates that the architectural profession had ceded the technical aspects of buildings to civil engineers by the turn of the century. This trend was sustained in the 1950's when a committee of the AIA moved to disqualify students of "architectural engineering" as candidates for the professional examination. He also notes that a decade later, many architectural schools withdrew from colleges of engineering and affiliated with colleges of art. Saint [1983] underscores the historical tendency of the American architectural profession to disassociate itself from the technical aspects of building and to align itself with the arts.

Apparently, this pattern of shedding responsibility for certain aspects of building was balanced by attempts to strengthen control over other aspects. For example architects yielded the design of large numbers of private houses to builders and craftsmen by the middle of the 19th century. Their apparent concern was not for the technical problems associated with housing, but for the loss of control when houses they had designed for one specific site were indiscriminately reproduced and modified to fit countless sites which the architect would never see [Wright 1981].

All of this suggests that a distinction can be made between the protected core of the architectural enterprise (puzzle-making) and a protective shell which surrounds it (problem-solving). According to this assessment puzzle-making stands as the primary service offered by the architect—an essential aspect of building that is not addressed by other professions. On the other hand, problem-solving remains an unavoidable necessity when addressing the technical performance of buildings, which the architect willingly yields to other professions.

As the growth of knowledge increases the number of attributes for which the direct and indirect consequences of design decisions can be linked to those decisions themselves, an increasing proportion of the design of buildings and other settings is turned over to professionals who address problems through the application of such knowledge. This means that the protective shell surrounding the architectural enterprise continues to grow in breadth and depth as additional aspects of building design are spun off to other disciplines, such as site planning, space planning and programming.

Under these circumstances architectural practice becomes increasingly involved in a liaison activity with the professionals who populate the protective shell, and architectural practice increasingly appears to be involved with problem-solving. Nonetheless, I contend that the form of context-specific inquiry that I have labeled "puzzle-making" continues to form the essential core of the architectural enterprise, and that the problem-solving application of general principles to specific contexts is no more than a necessary, but insufficient, complement to that enterprise.

Unfortunately, well-educated non-architects often confuse architecture with the whole of building, and in doing so tend to attribute concerns for addressing technical issues to architects, which architects themselves delegate to others. This does not imply that architects have no technical concerns. It simply means that such concerns are more likely to emerge as part of a rule system fashioned to justify the effects achieved in a given context, than as fixed criteria or constraints at the onset of the architectural design process.

The technological and social positions advocated by the founders of the modern movement appeared to link architecture with problem-solving [Conrads 1975]. However, it is clear that architects never saw themselves as problem-solvers. The modern movement merely seized upon the availability of new building materials and processes to launch an inquiry into how these elements and attributes could be integrated into architecture's pool of available parts.

Consider Mies van der Rohe's design for Crown Hall in Chicago. What problems were being solved there? Certainly not the use of structural steel to frame deep bays—the clear spans produce desirable effects, but they are not innovative solutions. Certainly the use of large expanses of glass created more heating and cooling problems than it solved. Instead, Mies' design for Crown Hall seems more appropriately characterized as a search for new families of combinatorial rules that could enable new effects to evolve effortlessly out of newly available kits of parts—the discovery of new rules for displaying and joining materials.

In fact, the search for new rules for using new parts to achieve new effects seems to have constituted a generic puzzle that predominated the architectural profession's program of inquiry throughout the middle third of this century. In addition to Mies, this is clearly reflected in the work of Kahn, Rudolph, Netsch, Safdie and others. Ironically, once this program of inquiry had run its course and it became so clear what the rules for making modern buildings were that non-architects could readily comprehend them, the architect's unique mode of inquiry was no longer needed to design such buildings, the modern movement was declared bankrupt and most architects began making other kinds of puzzles.

Given the intensity of the architectural profession's preoccupation with developing new rule systems during the modern era, it is not surprising that it was during this period that most of the responsibilities for solving the technical problems associated with new building forms were spun off to engineers and other consultants. Thus, while many new technical problems were being addressed during the modern period, they generally were not being addressed by architects.

During the 20th century the architect has become the mediator between two distinct groups of problem-solvers. On the one hand are the agents of the client or society at large—mortgage bankers, developers, construction managers, building regulators and facilities programmers. On the other hand are the architect's own agents—consulting engineers, site planners and space analysts. What the architect provides is a comprehensive and internally consistent rule system for loosely accommodating the range of performance criteria and functional constraints that the agents of the client have identified for a given project. The ultimate attainment of a more precise fit between a project's programmatic and technical requirements and the form or arrangement of what eventually gets built, is generally delegated to one of the architect's own problem-solving agents. Thus the architect sustains a protective shell based on the application of publicly accessible knowledge, within which nests the protected core of an architectural enterprise based on private inquiry and discovery.

☐ CONCLUSION

Often it is suggested that the shedding of responsibility for certain aspects of buildings to other disciplines is indicative of the architect's overriding fascination with art, style, or appearance, and disinterest in more mundane technical matters. From a professional point of view this tends to cast the architect in the role of dilettante.

I suggest that this refocusing or narrowing of professional responsibility is not as indicative of architects' fascinations as it is of the domains within which their uncommon mode of inquiry is most effectively pursued. Over centuries architects have developed a mode of inquiry that works best where prevailing levels of understanding are contradictory, and where appropriate courses of action are not obvious. In effect, architects act best where the light is least, and apply their methods most effectively just in advance of the growth of "objectified" knowledge.

At one time such methods of inquiry were well suited to the full range of building technologies—even to certain basic questions of physics, mathematics and philosophy. Thus the names of Leonardo, Wren, Blondel, Jefferson, Thornton, Rutherford and even Olmstead are as intimately associated with the sciences as they are with architecture.

This association between architecture and the sciences no longer prevails. I suggest that this is because more intersubjective modes of inquiry have been pursued in the sciences, and have succeeded to the point where internally consistent bodies of knowledge have been established independently of the actions which they might or might not justify. Consequently, in most areas where architects were once active, emerging programs of inquiry have raised the possibility that problems can be specified independently of and prior to their solution, and problem-solving has become the driving force behind both action and inquiry.

Does this mean that the architect's mode of inquiry is outdated and in urgent need of augmentation through programmatic and methodological research? I think not. Rather, I sense that architecture's uncommon mode of inquiry into the unique potentials of specific building contexts will always remain operational just in advance of the inevitable growth of knowledge.

Interestingly, if the analysis presented here is accepted, the commonly understood notion of "architectural research" becomes self-contradictory. Trying to offer objectively substantiated knowledge to professionals whose stock-in-trade is shaping courses of action under precisely those conditions where such knowledge does not and cannot exist, seems like a very barren proposition indeed.

So what does all of this suggest for architecture, architectural research and the computability of design? With regard to the architectural profession, the possibility exists that it is an anachronous cottage industry that is becoming increasingly out of step with the remainder of a technological society. However, I sense that what sets architects apart from other university educated professionals is an uncommon mode of inquiry that is extremely well suited to situations in which there is no objective way of determining what ought to be accomplished until it has been accomplished through the design process. If architects would devote as much effort to making their uncommon program of inquiry explicit as they do to extolling the virtues of the idiosyncratic artifacts that it produces, they might increase both the perceived legitimacy of their professional services, and their opportunities to influence the quality of the designed environment.

As for the programmatic agenda of architectural research, I suspect that the pressing issue is to find a more appropriate constituency than the practicing architect. The various parties to building decisions who act in a problem-solving manner, and thus separate knowing from acting, would appear to be much more receptive to research findings about how buildings do or could work than most architects. Potential constituencies include most of the architect's clients, public building agencies, regulatory bodies, financial underwriters and even labor unions or consumer groups—all of whom stand to be empowered by objective knowledge about building performance.

Finally, for those interested in pursuing a methodological agenda involving the computability of architectural design, I see two fruitful avenues to follow. The first is the approach suggested for architectural research— focus exclusively on those aspects of building that lie within architecture's protective shell. This is the domain of problem-solving in which design alternatives are tested against previously stated criteria and constraints. The second may turn out to be less productive, but clearly promises to be more stimulating: to push beyond architecture's protective shell and into its protected core—its methodological commitment to acting in the face of maximum uncertainty. Here is where the methodologist may have the most to learn: the heuristic advantage of overlaying culturally valenced precedents, symbols and metaphors onto singular circumstances in order to define context-specific courses of action—the essence of puzzle-making.

☐ REFERENCES

Alexander C. *Notes on the Synthesis of Form*, Harvard University Press, Cambridge, MA. 1964.

Archea J. "Establishing an Interdisciplinary Commitment," in B. Honikman (Ed.) *Responding to Social Change*, Dowden, Hutchinson and Ross, Stroudsburg, PA. 1975.

Archea J. "Conceptual and Methodological Conflicts in Applied Interdisciplinary Research on Environment and Aging," in P. Windley, T.O. Byerts, F.G. Ernst (Eds.) *Aging and Environment: Theoretical Directions*, Springer Publishing Co., New York, 1982.

Benjamin W. *Illuminations*, Schocken, New York, 1969.

Churchman C.W. *The Design of Inquiring Systems*, Basic Books, New York, 1971.

Conrads U. *Programs and Manifestoes on 20th-Century Architecture*, M. Bullock (Trans.), The MIT Press, Cambridge, MA, 1975.

Gutman R. "Educating Architects: Pedagogy and the Pendulum," The Public Interest, 80:67-91, 1985.

Korobkin B. *Images for Design: Communication of Human Science Research to Architectural Practitioners*, Graduate School of Design, Harvard University, Cambridge, MA, 1974.

Lakatos I. "Falsification and the Methodology of Scientific Research Programmes," in I. Lakatos & A. Musgrave (Eds.) *Criticism and the Growth of Knowledge*, Cambridge University Press, Cambridge, UK, 1970.

Piel G. "Natural Philosophy in the Constitution," Science, 233:1056-1060, 1986.

Saint A. *The Image of the Architect*, Yale University Press, New Haven, CT, 1983.

Schon D. *The Reflective Practitioner: How Professionals Think in Action*, Basic Books, Inc., New York, 1983.

Simon H. *The Sciences of the Artificial*, The MIT Press, Cambridge, MA, 1969.

Simon H. "Style in Design," in J. Archea and C. Eastman (Eds.) *EDRA TWO: Proceedings of the Second Annual Environmental Design Research Association Conference*, Carnegie-Mellon University, Pittsburgh, PA, 1970.

Ventre F. "Buildings in Eclipse, Architecture in Secession," Progressive Architecture 12, 1982.

Venturi R., Scott-Brown D., and Izenour S. *Learning from Las Vegas*, The MIT Press, Cambridge, MA. 1972.

Wehrli R. *Environmental Design Research: How To Do It and How To Apply It*, John Wiley & Sons, New York, 1986.

Wright G. *Moralism and the Model Home: Domestic Architecture and Cultural Conflict in Chicago, 1873-1913*, The University of Chicago Press, Chicago, IL, 1980.

Zeisel J. *Inquiry by Design: Tools for Environment-Behavior Research*, Brooks/Cole Publishing Co., Monterey, CA. 1981.

3

DESIGNING WITH CONSTRAINTS

Mark Gross
Stephen Ervin
James Anderson
Aaron Fleisher

School of Architecture and Planning
Massachusetts Institute of Technology
Cambridge, Massachusetts

The "constraint model" of designing provides a means of demonstrating and exploring the computability of design. Designing is understood as a process of incrementally defining an initially ill-defined question, and concurrently proposing and testing possible answers. That is, not finding *the* solution to *a* problem, but finding *a* solution to *the* problem. Articulating (including inventing and modifying) the question, and exploring possible alternative answers (or designs), are two fundamental activities which can be supported by computers and the constraint model. We discuss the use of constraints to explicate design questions, circumscribe feasible regions, and specify proposed solutions, and examine the processes of search and scrutiny within a region. Naming, solving, history-keeping, block-structuring, identifying and resolving conflicts are among tasks identified that can be rendered to a computer. Questions of knowledge representation and inference making with ambiguity and imprecision are discussed. Examples of the application of the constraint model to design problems in architecture and site planning are illustrated by brief scenarios.

□ A LANGUAGE FOR DESIGNING

Two kinds of questions bar the notion that design is computable. The first is about designing, and the thing to be designed. The second, how to render some of that knowing to the machine. The second is the only new question around. How it is answered may change how design is done, but not what it is. We may understand the first better for the experience with the second. But, you start with the first. It is the beginning of wisdom. Unless begun, all else is miscellaneous ingenuity.

Design and designing are not the same. Design is domain bound; designing seems rather less so. Naval architects do not do buildings. Building architects do not do ships. Their domains overlap, but are rarely breached. However, their graphics seem similar. Do they share any other designing devices? We think so, and therefore we start with a theory of the design process. It is not a theory of the design product. It is not a theory of design. It is a theory about designing. We want it to be a good theory of designing. It is not a theory about good designing. It may make good designing more likely. We think that it describes designing across domains; that it locates the kinds and the uses of the designer's knowledge, the layers of design, and the intersection of the community of designers that would do the design.

What is a theory? A theory is to describe; to explain. It is to reduce miscellany. A good theory then goes on to reduce miscellany in places not previously considered. What needs a theory of designing to account for? Designing is invention to a set of specifications. The theory should explain the modes of reasoning, describe the location of the knowledge, and trace the reasoning deployed and the knowledge invoked as they shape the thing invented.

The set of specifications is radically ambiguous. It does not suffice, else there would be nothing to invent. Designing is engaged as much in setting questions as searching solutions. It may be single-minded. It is rarely single-tracked. The process of designing is marked by lacunae filled, ambiguities cleared, ambivalences resolved. The result of designing is the difference between the specifics charged and the details delivered. The difference cannot be unique because designing designs the questions as well as the answers.

Designing is driven by an inner logic—inner to the person and the problem—for which reason the designs can be as numerous as the designers. Varieties and variants are not all frivolous. Design is not *the* solution to *a* problem; it is *a* solution to *the* problem. Whence the art of the designer.

If this description is correct—we think that it is—then the basic operation is search, and the basic reasoning is scrutiny. It is a peculiar kind of search and scrutiny. If you are looking for something like a submarine, then a whale won't do. Shape and color are not terribly off. No matter.

A whale is not a submarine; you know that to begin with. But, just suppose you did not know that to begin with. Then your modes of searching and your methods of scrutinizing must be clever enough to discover that it is the submarine that you want as you learn that a whale won't do. Designing is looking for something whose characteristics are unfolded by the looking.

The specifications for an invention comprise sentiments that shadow purpose and performance. Sentiments are not much, but they do establish bounds within which to look. Such bounds make the search intelligent. Describing things inside the bounds requires the exercise of knowledge. Scrutinizing these things is an application of this knowledge.

The space of possible solutions bounded only by the sentiments is enormous. We said so when we described the original specifications for the invention as "radically ambiguous". An invention is a particular point in that space. You are not likely to find it searching randomly. You have not enough time to find it searching exhaustively. The space must be additionally constrained. That is the designer designing.

The theory stipulates that designing is exploring regions of feasible solutions; that feasibility is derived from the constraints chosen by the designer; that choosing constraints is how the designer uses his knowledge. The stipulation requires that every exercise of design knowledge be construable as the choice of a constraint on the space of possible inventions. We do not say, we do not intend that the designer be required to think in constraints. The purpose of the theory is to make explicit design knowing and reasoning. It is neither a study of ceremony, nor an inquiry into behavior. Ceremony and behavior are not less important. They are not our business.

We would need, therefore, to say how constraints are entered, transformed, combined, manipulated, managed. And we need to show how the accumulation of constraints becomes the invention. We develop the theory as a set of accounts that record a constraint on entry into the design; that follow its uses and transformations; that remember the succession, in time, of its states. Please notice, we have spoken as if all constraints originate from outside the machine. Within are located all the remembering, most of the manipulations, and a little of the reasoning. The theory of designing does not depend on how the processes are partitioned between designer and computer. The computer is irrelevant to the theory. However, the computability of design must hang on a theory of designing, otherwise we are miscellaneous. We shall argue in the sections that follow that this theory provides an organization for the skills that are renderable to the computer.

Designing has been described at various times, in various places, as optimizing or satisfying an objective function subject to a set of constraints. The description fails on two grounds. Objectives are almost always multiple. Two are too many. Any programming procedure would fail even were the constraints known and consistent. The constraints are not likely to be consistent because the objectives are multiple. Constraints and objectives can often be interchanged. Moreover, the constraints are not completely known. They are not just part of the problem. They are all of the problem.

An idea is a theory only if so made to permit testing. Experiment and theory are different activities but not different notions. A theory is theoretical only if it implies an experiment. Somewhere in every experiment there is a theory however crude. There is a place where this theory can be tested. We said that every exercise of the designer's understanding can be construed as a constraint. A counter-example would suffice to fail the theory—we are still looking.

□ THE CONSTRAINT MODEL

The use of constraints to manage and analyze complex problems is not new. Friedman and Leondes [1969] review the mathematical basis of the theory; Sutherland [1962], Steele and Sussman [1980] and Borning [1981], among others, describe computational implementations in various domains; and Gross [1985] has explored the application of constraint theory to design. Let us begin by introducing some terms. We describe a design as a set of "constraints" or "relations" on a set of "variables" Each variable has a "value" that the designer may set, or "fix". Some variables the designer may fix directly; others are calculated as consequences of those fixed. Every collection of constraints bounds a "region" of alternative solutions, or "variants" in an n-dimensional geometric space. The number of dimensions n is the number of degrees of freedom, or independent qualities in the design; n may be large and it changes throughout the design process as variables are introduced and/or eliminated. Each point in the region describes a complete set of variable values that meet all the (present) constraints and represents an alternative solution, or design variant. The region need not have a simple shape. It may be large in some dimensions and small in others. It may be all together in one place or in many small "islands".

The number of degrees of freedom in a design fluctuates, increasing as the designer introduces new variables, and decreasing as variable values are fixed. The region's boundaries also fluctuate as the designer adds and changes constraints. Points in the region represent "specific variants" completely specified alternatives with every variable fixed. We explore, examine, and rank variants according to various "objectives", or preferences.

Constraints are the rules, requirements, relations, conventions, and principles that define the context of designing. There are many constraints on a design and they come from different sources. Constraints are imposed by nature, culture, convention, and the marketplace. Some are imposed externally, while others are imposed by the designer. Some are site-specific, others not. Some are the result of higher-level design decisions; some are universal, a part of every design. Gravity, for example, is universal. Other constraints apply only in certain design contexts. The general position rules on windows and other facade elements that characterize facades in Boston's Back Bay are less universal constraints than gravity, but more universal than the additional constraints that operate in any particular Back Bay facade, due, for example, to the specific width of the lot.

We can describe a design problem or task as a collection of constraints and relations on attributes of the object to be designed. Then, to design is to describe constraints and to specify an object that satisfies all these constraints. For example, constraints on the design of a pencil are that it must leave an erasable mark on paper, that it be comfortable to hold. But we could design many pencils that satisfy all these constraints: hard pencils, soft pencils, red pencils, thin pencils. Design problems are atypical problems in that they have many solutions. We do not find the solution to a set of design specifications; we find one solution out of many alternatives. Although we may prefer some alternatives to others, all are solutions to the initial constraints. We can distinguish among alternatives at each step by adding constraints to the design. Adding constraints is as much a part of designing as is searching for solutions. The designing process adopts constraints, then explores for "good" alternatives in the constraint- bounded region.

Here are some examples of constraints:

1. "Bearing walls occur on 5′, 8′, or 11′ guide lines."
2. "X must be offset from Y by at least its own thickness."
3. "Kitchens must be at least 6′ × 8′ and occur only in beta zones."
4. "This window must admit at least 1 hour of direct sun."
5. "All material elements must be supported."

Constraints are always relations between variables that represent the attributes of the object being designed. In constraint 1 above, the variables represent positions of bearing walls and guide lines. In constraint 2, the variables are the positions of X and Y, and the thickness of X. In constraint 4, the amount of sun that enters the window is a variable (as, presumably, are some properties of the window itself: its position, dimension, orientation). These variables are simple; they stand for attributes of the design that can be represented by a single number. It is sometimes useful to aggregate variables to describe more complex attributes of a design. For example, a window can be a variable, its value to be chosen out of a set of possible windows. The window variable would then be an aggregate or compound variable consisting of the many simpler variables that describe attributes of windows: shape, size, material, transparency, method of opening, and manufacturer, for example. Constraint 5 expresses a universal constraint, gravity.

It is useful to distinguish between variables directly set by the designer and variables the designer controls only indirectly. In the design of our pencil, for example, we directly control the materials, length, radius, and shape of the pencil but its mass is a function of its length, radius, and materials. Architectural designers control the selection, position, and dimensions of material and space elements. Other variables in the design are determined consequentially. For example, a variable representing the privacy of a room might be related to the number of turns needed to enter the room from the nearest major access, and whether one can see in from nearby locations. Though a designer may decide to provide a certain degree of privacy, it is ultimately by adjusting the positions and dimensions of building elements that the architect affects the privacy of a place. The constraint that specifies privacy is realized by setting other variables.

Another example of an indirectly controlled variable is the amount of daylight entering a room. The designer controls daylight (indirectly), by controlling (directly) the positions, dimensions, and orientations of openings in the room's exterior surfaces. (S/he may do it in other ways as well.) The law relating amount of daylight admitted and the size, orientation, and position of each opening is a small piece of design knowledge. Good architects know this relation well.

Consider the difference between a design specification and a set of construction drawings for a building. The former consists of performance constraints—on variables that the designer can control only indirectly, such as daylight and privacy. The latter consists solely of constraints on variables the designer controls directly—the relative placement of material and space elements within certain tolerances. Design skill transforms constraints on variables such as privacy, outlook, and daylight into constraints on the positions and dimensions of material and space elements. For example, the constraint, "the room must be at least moderately light in the afternoon" is transformed to constraints on the positions, dimensions, and orientations of windows—"window sills must be at least three feet from the floor and the room must have have at least thirty square feet of window area on the west side" and ultimately to a complete specification of the window.

Most often the initial constraints describe a large region of alternatives. That is, as first stated the design problem is grossly underconstrained; a great deal of freedom remains. Novice designers typically experience a difficulty associated with this—with so much freedom it is hard to choose a course of action. Suppose in our design of a pencil we choose values for all variables except length and color. We say then that two degrees of freedom remain in the design. Within each of those two degrees, however, a large or a small range of options may remain. For example, manufacturing constraints may strictly limit the pencil to a small range of possible lengths while allowing a large range of colors. When all variables are fixed there are zero degrees of freedom. The design is complete.

But architecture is more complicated. Having designed the floorplan we may proceed to the details. The design is "complete" only relative to the constraints already adopted. New constraints may be added at any time. Instead of narrowing the range of possible alternatives, the new constraints may introduce new decisions. Consider designing a window in a wall. We may begin with constraints on the window's dimensions and position pertaining to the view, the amount of daylight, etc. At some point, not necessarily after fixing the position and dimension variables, we may begin designing the parts of the window itself. This entails new constraints and new variables. We may introduce constraints on the size of the panes and mullions, on the window's moving parts. These constraints introduce new variables to the design. These new variables are likely to be related at least loosely to some variables already known. For example, the window's overall dimension is related to the number, size, and arrangement of its panes and mullions.

At the outset there may be relatively few constraints and variables. Design proceeds from a general set of specifications to a set of specific solutions. At completion, many more constraints and variables have been introduced, and all variables have values. Thus each set of constraints and associated variable values represents only one instant (a "snapshot") of a design process.

☐ MANAGING INCONSISTENCY

Each such instant is a state of the design. In any state some variables have particular values while others are unspecified. The more values defined, the more specific the state of the design. A region of alternatives exists only if the constraints are consistent; that is, no constraints or values conflict. The region at all times consists of the set of alternatives satisfying the present collection of constraints. Often there are many alternatives and the region is very large. The designer's goal is to ultimately reduce the number of alternatives to one; the purpose of the constraint manager is to manage the many.

Each design decision would fix the value of one or more variables. A new fix can cause an inconsistency in the constraint set in two ways: alone, or in combination with variables previously fixed.

If it is inconsistent alone—that is, conflicts with some previous setting of the same variable then the resolution of the conflict is simple: the designer must make up his/her mind, or consent to carrying the inconsistency for a while.

Suppose the inconsistency is in combination—that is, arises out of several different constraints on several different variables interacting. Then the designer can:

- Withdraw the last fix; nothing is really fixed yet.
- Request a review of the previous fixes; the constraint-manager keeps a detailed history of fixes made and unmade.
- Request the services of an negotiator; many inconsistencies are likely to be minor and resolvable by rule of thumb.
- Refix some of the earlier fixes.
- Carry the inconsistency for a while; what harm can it do?
- Alter the constraint; nothing is sacred.
- Review the entire sequence of fixes; it helps sometimes to know how you got into the bind.
- Start again from scratch.
- Turn off the computer.

We intend this little example to emphasize that it is the design that is constrained, not the designer.

The constraints and the accounts are central to the theory. The constraint-manager is central to making the theory renderable to the machine. The sections that follow will examine the rendering and the characteristics of the constraint manager.

☐ PLATFORM FRAMING: BEAM AND JOIST SPANS, AND SPACING

We turn now to a small example of designing, large enough to illuminate the concept of designing as exploring constraints, small enough to be accountable in a few paragraphs: the structural problem of designing a simple platform made of beams and joists. No doubt somebody has written a computer program to produce framing plans given constraints. But that is not our aim. For us the machine is not to generate solutions to the platform design problem; rather to provide a means for designers to rapidly explore different design constraints and alternatives.

The problem of determining beam and joist dimensions, spans, and spacing in a platform is a common part of almost every building design. It comes into play in the late phases of design, not the early ones. This problem is small but it is real. Architects understand it so well they often consider it "merely engineering." The relation between floor-load, joist dimension, span, and spacing can be looked up in a handbook table, but the architect typically would know the most frequently used entries by heart. If we consider platform shapes more complex than rectangles, then the framing problem requires more attention.

A platform is constructed of a number of beams, major structural members, a certain distance apart, and joists, smaller structural pieces, resting on the beams and oriented perpendicular to them. Bearing walls may also serve as beams. Joists are either supported at their ends, or else their ends cantilever beyond the beams. In larger platforms, more than two beams will be required.

The problem is to determine for a given size platform the dimensions and positions of the beams and joists. The most important consideration is safety: the platform must support a certain load. In addition a cost is associated with each different design, a function of the number and dimensions of the beams and joists. Other factors as well may influence the framing decisions; for example, the position of the beams may be subject to other layout constraints.

Some constraints are due to the conventions of wood-frame building: framing members are available in only certain dimensions; joists are usually spaced sixteen inches on center. Beams, being larger in width and depth, have longer spans than the joists.

The simplest platform has just two beams. Suppose we start by positioning the beams. This determines the joist span. (Note that if the beams are not parallel then the joist span varies along the length of the platform.) Then we have only to determine safe joist dimensions and spacing for the expected floor load. Accept the conventional spacing of sixteen inches on center; all that remains is to select a safe joist size for a given load. The decision boils down (after adding constraints) to a question like "will 2 x 8 joists be sufficient or must I move up to 3 x 8's or 2 x 10's?".

If we also permit spacing of joists at twenty and twenty-four inch intervals then we have a few more framing options to compare. Increasing the joist spacing requires larger but fewer joists to complete the floor—a tradeoff. Should we use fewer heftier joists spaced further apart, or a greater number of lighter-weight joists spaced more closely together to build a floor with a certain expected load?

A variety of other than structural constraints may militate for one or the other way of framing the platform. Our choice may depend on the pricing schedule of lumber. One way may simply look better from underneath. Or a need to locate air ducts or other mechanical systems between joists may dictate minimum spacing.

Finally, we must make the same decisions about the beams that we have been considering with regard to the joists. Beams are just bigger joists. The same considerations discussed for deciding joist dimensioning and spacing hold also for beams. And decisions about the beams directly affect decisions about joists, for the variables "beam spacing" and "joist span" are actually the same physical quantity.

Thus we find the architect considering:

In order to cover A feet I need B beams of size C. Spacing the beams D feet apart, I will need E joists of size F, spaced G feet apart. But if I increase the distance between beams to D′ feet, (which I want to do for other reasons), I will need only B′ beams but then I must increase the joist size to F′ in order to accommodate their increased span. And if I move to smaller beams C′ then I will have to support each beam in the middle as well as at its ends.

In this mini-design there are only two main constraints: the beam relation and the joist relation. The joist relation we discussed at length above. It relates the joist span, the joist spacing, the joist dimension and the safe floor-load. The beam relation is similar; it relates beam spacing, beam size, beam span, and floor-load.

□ SOLVING IN DESIGN

Solving is an essential component of designing expertise that we can render to the machine, once we have set up our system of accounts, described the design in terms of constraints on variables. We do not claim that solving is all; as we said, designing also involves problem describing and problem inventing. But solving does play an important and central role in designing.

What is to solve? To solve is to calculate some property (variable) of a design, based on other properties (variables) of the design and the relations (constraints) of the design. When the relations between the variables are well enough specified then we can construct solving mechanisms that calculate the value of one variable given the values of others.

Designers solve all the time. Designers solve whenever a position, dimension, or other quantity is to be determined, and the decision is not arbitrary. Design decisions are seldom arbitrary. For example, in the problem of locating a window so that a certain view can be obtained from a certain place in the house, the designer solves for the position(s) of the window that satisfy the constraint. Or in determining the framing plan of a platform the designer may solve for the dimensions of the beams and joists, based on the distances they must span and the spacing between them.

Solving implies that the constraints are invertible. We can solve for the window's position given the position of the object to be viewed, or vice versa. We can fix either element first, and determine the position of the other as a consequence. (Of course this only makes sense if we control the position of the object to be viewed.)

Sometimes solving yields several solutions. Several different locations for the window may meet the view constraint. A range of joist sizes may satisfy the structural constraint. We can solve for a variable even when its value cannot be completely determined by the constraints and other fixes that are part of the design at the time. One reason to do this is to "highlight" the variable in question; to see what other variables in the design it depends on. The result of such solving may simply be a list of the constraints that reference the variable being solved for, expressed with that variable isolated. Or it may be a list of possible values for that variable. Later, in the light of further constraints and fixes, additional solving may result in a single value.

We did not say anything about the method of solving. We can find positions for the window that satisfy the view constraint by successive approximation: try placing the window, see how far off it is and in what direction, correct for the error and try again. Or we can solve by geometric construction. There need not be just one method of solving constraints.

What constraints are solvable? Lines of sight, joist dimensions and spacing are physical quantities that can be measured. These we can solve for. A line of sight is a matter of geometry; the size and spacing of joists is governed by physical laws. Though complicated, the constraints that govern these things are not complex. We understand them well enough to write equations, and our solving procedures, experts in arithmetic, algebra, and logical inference, can certainly handle them.

However, presented with the constraint "the kitchen must be nice", there is little solving we can do. "Nice" is too vague, large, and ill-defined. Perhaps we could work towards describing how to compute "nice". That is not high on our agenda, for "nice" is not particularly an architectural concept. But "nice" serves to illustrate that we can state, at least in English, constraints that we have no means to solve.

Only calculable properties can be solved for. At one extreme of the spectrum of computability is "nice"; view and structural constraints are at the other. In between these extremes lie a large number of environmental qualities such as enclosure, privacy, outlook, access, directionality, and other physical definitions. These qualities are not currently computable because they lack rigorous definition and descriptions of how to calculate these qualities from a set of plans and sections. With work we might render them computable soon. Before we can reckon with enclosure, privacy, or other environmental qualities in design, we must describe how the quality in question is related to other attributes of the design that can be specified or calculated.

Enclosure seems a likely candidate for description. For example, we might quantify the enclosure at a point as a function of the distance from that point to the nearest surrounding walls, the ratio of the height of the walls to their distance, and so forth. Calculable definition in hand, we can solve for the enclosure generated by a certain configuration of walls. And inversely, we can solve for the position, height, etc. of a wall, to achieve a desired degree of enclosure at a certain place.

No sooner than we propose one method of computing enclosure, someone will invent another that they think better describes the quality. That is all right. Different designers use the word "enclosure" differently. Our purpose is only to make descriptions of such qualities definite and comparable, using the rigorous language of constraints. Thus most designers would agree that enclosure is an important environmental quality. If pressed, at least some could describe how to calculate enclosure, at least to a first approximation, from a given floorplan. It would be interesting to compare these definitions. We would expect them to agree more than not.

Here we approach a central architectural design skill: predicting environmental qualities of a place from a description of the physical layout. The sophisticated architect understands subtle shades of environmental qualities; these qualities are determined by sensory and sensual experiences of being in a place, and part of the designer's expertise is to project into a design and imagine and describe the qualities of that place. We want to describe that projective ability in sufficient detail to compute it. Expressing environmental qualities as calculable quantities, functionally related to physical properties, is one step towards making architectural expertise explicit.

☐ WHAT SOLVING CAN WE RENDER?

We turn now to consider the various sorts of solving that we can render to the machine. We begin with algebraic and arithmetic solving because any decision concerning the dimension and position of elements in a design is likely to rest eventually on this fundamental capability.

Whenever we can express design constraints as functional relations between quantities, algebraic and arithmetic solving becomes important. We use algebraic and arithmetic solving to make inferences about and ultimately to determine quantities in a design, for example, dimensions and positions of elements. Using algebra and arithmetic we can calculate the safe dimensions of a joist based on the expected floor load, the joist span, and the joist spacing, or determine the height of a window-sill to allow a given amount of daylight to enter a room.

Algebraic and arithmetic constraints are not limited to the purely "engineering" aspects of architectural design, such as the joist-spacing and day-lighting problems mentioned above. Even design rules that describe not physical laws of nature, but architectural conventions and use-patterns can often be expressed as algebraic relations on quantities. Simple examples are proportion constraints, and minimum and maximum dimension constraints. Position rules also can often be expressed as algebraic constraints, for example: placement of elements relative to a grid, or the position rule: "place the window, its top aligned with the door's top and its right edge offset from the door by a distance equal to the width of its frame". Using analytic geometry, algebraic and arithmetic reasoning can be turned to solving geometric problems as well, bringing us closer to solving the spatial sorts of problems architects and planners work.

Algebraic and arithmetic solving can certainly be rendered to the machine. Of the many algebraic solvers that have been written, MACSYMA [Macsyma 1982] is probably the best known. MACSYMA encodes a great deal of mathematical expertise in the form of procedures that manipulate equations symbolically, simplifying and solving them by various means. We do not need MACSYMA's full capabilities for the simple algebra we expect to see in most architectural and environmental design constraints. We are writing our own more limited algebraic solving routines, beginning with those symbolic and numeric operations we need immediately.

Our algebraic solver has several components. A "solve-for" routine isolates variables in equations. Another routine solves sets of simultaneous linear equations by matrix inversion. Another eliminates variables when simultaneous constraints are not linear equations. In addition to supporting arithmetic on integer and rational numbers, we have also implemented an interval arithmetic package. An interval number has two components: an upper and lower bound; it represents a range of values. By allowing numeric variables to take on interval values, our solver can handle inequality constraints as well as equations.

Given an algebraic relation between quantities, or variables, the solver expresses each as a function of the others, isolating each variable on one side of the relation. For example, the solver will express the relation between joist dimensions, spacing, span, and safe floor load in four different ways, isolating each variable as a function of the other three. The routine that does this is called "ISOLATE-ALL-VARIABLES". Whenever any three variables have values, the fourth may be determined by substituting values for variables in the appropriate expression and then computing numerically. Then we can determine the safe floor-load for a given joist span, spacing, and size; or the proper joist size for a given floor load, joist span, and spacing; and likewise for spacing and span. The call to the solver might look like this:

```
(isolate-all-variables in joist-relation)

==> load    = F1 (size, spacing, span);
    size    = F2 (load, span, spacing);
    spacing = F3 (load, size, span);
    span    = F4 (load, size, spacing).
```

The routine ISOLATE-ALL-VARIABLES calls on SOLVE-FOR to do most of its work. The SOLVE-FOR routine requires that there be but one occurrence in the relation of the variable it is to isolate. If there is more than one occurrence, then SOLVE-FOR first invokes a "simplifier" routine to reduce the relation to single occurrence form. Working with a table of operator inverses, SOLVE-FOR locates the subexpression containing the variable to be isolated and moves that subexpression to one side of the relation. It then applies the inverse of the toplevel operation of the subexpression to both sides, "unravelling" the subexpression, repeating this procedure until the desired variable stands alone. Here is an example of SOLVE-FOR at work:

```
(solve-for x in ''2x + 3y = 16'' ) ==> x = (-3y + 16) / 2.
```

Now assume a simple syntactical parser which can accept 'english-like' input:

```
(solve-for window-width in
 "bay-spacing equals three times window-width plus twice beam-size")

==> WINDOW-WIDTH = (BAY-SPACING - (2 * BEAM-SIZE)) / 3
```

The procedure ISOLATE-ALL-VARIABLES first calls the routine FIND-VARIABLES-IN-RELATION to identify which symbols in the equation are variables and which are operator names; then it simply maps SOLVE-FOR on all those variables. For example:

```
(isolate-all-variables in "2x + 3y = 16")

==>  x = (-3y + 16) / 2 ;
     y = (-2x + 16) / 3 .
```

Why reformulate the constraint this way? First, it may prove useful simply to highlight each variable in the relation; to see it expressed as a function of the other variables may help. Second, when values are fixed for x or y these two latter equations may be used to compute the other variable. For example, if, after declaring the constraint "2x + 3y = 16", we fix the value of y to "4", then the solver uses the first equation, " x = (− 3y + 16) / 2 " to determine that "x" should be set to "2".

To carry out these computations, the solver also contains a routine called SUBSTITUTE-AND-COMPUTE-NUMERICALLY. It propagates any new variable value whether fix or consequence throughout the set of constraints. Thus, after using the fix "y = 4" to compute "x = 2", this routine may use x's new value to determine values for other dependent variables p, q, and r.

Another component of our algebraic solver deals with eliminating redundant variables. When our block-structuring routines identify constraints that share variables and hence can and should be worked together, the unit of algebraic operations is no longer the single constraint, but the group of constraints sharing variables. When the constraints are linear equations (for example: Ax + By + Cz + D = 0), and when there are as many shared variables as equations, then the solution, the set of values that satisfies the simultaneous equations, can be obtained by inverting the matrix of their coefficients. We have written code to do this.

When the equations are not linear, or when there are not enough variables to solve by matrix inversion, we can still proceed by eliminating variables. We have written the procedure ELIMINATE to do this. First we must notice that variable "x" is shared between the two constraints. The FIND-SHARED-VARIABLES-IN-CONSTRAINTS procedure (used also by the block structuring routines) does this. Then, we can call on ELIMINATE to eliminate "x" from the set of relations. It first invokes SOLVE-FOR on the first equation to find an expression for the shared variable, then it substitutes this result for x in the second equation. Successively applying this strategy to multiple simultaneous relations allows the solver to eliminate variables even when no value has been assigned.

The examples of algebraic solving all show equations or inequalities; variables represent numbers and are added, multiplied, raised to powers, and sometimes involved in trigonometric functions. Yet the solving operations we describe—isolating and eliminating variables, substituting values—may be applicable for other sorts of constraints as well. As long as all the operations have inverses SOLVE-FOR will continue to work. Might we, for example, turn some of the solving routines we wrote for manipulating algebraic constraints to work on equations in set algebra? We would certainly need to augment the existing arithmetic routines.

In addition to the algebraic solver, we have begun to code a logical solver that works on constraints stated in the form of logical implications, or IF-THEN rules. Where knowledge about designing or about the design domain can be construed as propositions and implications, a great deal of inference can be automated. For example, "If town-houses are indicated and on-street parking is unavailable then parking must be provided within the dwelling" expresses a small piece of design knowledge.

An IF-THEN rule constrains the truth values of its propositions. In the implication "if the climate is cold then thermopane windows are indicated", let variables p and q represent the propositions "the climate is cold" and "thermopane windows are indicated". Then the rule can be restated "if p then q". Logic also allows the inference "if (not q) then (not p)"; thus if we assert "thermopane windows are not indicated" then the logic solver may infer that "the climate is not cold".

When a rule like this is part of a larger set, connected to other rules, then a "logic solver" or pattern-matching inference engine can chain forward through the logical implications from a set of assertions to reach design conclusions, or backward from a design to find plausible initial settings. This sort of inference is the basis of the expert-system programs that have largely succeeded in medical decision-making, among other domains. MYCIN [Shortliffe 1976], and R1 [McDermott 1982] are well known representatives of this class of programs.

We might also want to build solvers for nonlogical reasoning. In the example above, if we assert "thermopane windows", we may not logically infer "cold climate". "P implies q" does not imply "q implies p". But what other causes might there be for thermopane windows? To find out, we would look at all the implication rules we know and select those that indicate thermopane windows. If, for example, the only way thermopane windows can be indicated is if the climate is cold, then our nonlogical solver might reasonably guess that if the designer has specified thermopane windows then the climate is cold. More likely, though, there will be several rules that result in any given condition. In that event our nonlogical solver could only list all of the possible reasons.

Finally we can provide a solver for inferring properties of things based on their membership in a class. IS-A constraints establish an object's membership in a class. For example, "a divided-highway IS A road with a median-strip between lanes". The "is a road" part of the description provides a default description for the divided highway. For example, the description of "road" may have constraints such as "hard surface", "maximum gradient", "minimum width", etc. These constraints are supplemented by the additional information "with a strip of grass between lanes" that is specific to the divided highway. And some of the default constraints inherited from "road" may be overridden in the description of "divided highway"; for example, the maximum gradient for divided highways may be lower than that for roads.

☐ TAXONOMY OF OBJECTS

Inferring properties of objects from their class suggests a data structure: a taxonomy of object types. The procedures for inferring properties of things from their declared membership in classes traverse this taxonomy, which in its simplest form is a tree, but may, when objects belong to more than one class, form a more complex directed graph.

A solver for inferring properties of objects from descriptions of their classes can be had in many object-oriented programming environments, as part of the scoping mechanisms built into the language. Built-in inheritance mechanisms are becoming almost standard features of programming languages. But were an inheritance solver not provided by our implementation language we could also have written one, using the logical solver described above, and a special set of logical implication rules for inheritance of properties.

Though many programming environments support inheritance of properties through a hierarchy of classes, few support its logical counterpart: classification of objects. To classify an object is to identify the class(es) an object belongs in (or might belong in), based on a list of its properties, and with reference to the taxonomy of objects mentioned above. For example, presented with an object X with properties "has median-strip" and "hard surface", the classifier will deduce that X may well be a member of the class "divided highways". The classifier must traverse the taxonomy tree seeking classes whose properties match those of the object to be classified. Some sticky issues arise: does a subset of the properties constitute a match? if all but one or two properties match, how should the object be classed?

□ SEARCH AND SCRUTINY IN CONSTRAINT SPACE

We said that "search" is being used particularly, perhaps peculiarly, because there is nothing there to find. There is an invention to be invented that would be located at some point in the space. It would be relatively easy to determine, in the second place, whether the invention belongs in the space. That is the responsibility of the constraint manager. The peculiarity is how to invent it, in the first place.

How much of inventing is renderable? Not all—certainly. Not none—likely. Let us suppose, for the present, that none is rendered. Then the designer designs; the constraint manager keeps accounts. The distinction is sometimes muddy. It is difficult to maintain the constraint manager in complete ignorance. Fully made, the constraint manager would also be the keeper of the designer's default knowledge, which is considerable. We have just begun to address that question. We shall return to it later. For the present, we take the constraint manager to be simplistic. He acts only on instruction. All the design knowledge is vested in the designer. Let us consider his strategems.

The first move, in any case, is the designer's. In this case, the designer comes to the constraint manager with a set of constraints and a design proposal—however conceived. It is likely, especially early on, that the proposal will be consistent with the constraints, or if not, then easily corrected. This circumstance is not accidental. The initial set of constraints will be small; accomodation is easy. Then why not try it again by iterating small additions to the constraint set, and then again. The tactic suggests a heuristic: create an ordered set of subdesigns with the property that each can be done in turn without compromising the possibility of doing the others downstream. The doings downstream will be compromised, of course. They must. They are downstream. It is the possibility of the doing that is conserved. The partition is such that the succession of subdesigns converges to the total design. We do not propose to try proving the heuristic. If we could, it would no longer be a heuristic. We shall, instead, propose an interchange between designer and constraint manager that would implement it.

We left designer and constraint manager in agreement on the opening design proposal. Consider it the first of the ordered set of subdesigns. The next one is generated in the space of the previous constraints augmented by any other objectives, issues, precedents, variables, the designer would now include. Include, means that any of the above are construed and entered as additional constraints. The constraint manager is now ready to consider a new proposition. The previous set of constraints is still enforced. Therefore, this design proposal elaborates the previous subdesign. The purpose of the heuristic—to sustain a strongly sequenced ordering—is maintained. Provided that the new constraints are consistent with the old, the logic is monotonic because every new solution is consistent with the old. If not, then you must go back, though not necessarily to the beginning.

There need not be—it is unlikely that there would be—only one elaboration per round that makes it past the constraint manager. Let us suppose that there are always several. Nor is it necessary that only one set of augmented constraints is made at each round. Then the process branches. If we understand the workings of one branch, then we shall understand them all. Let us suppose that only one set of augmentations to the constraints is made. We shall return to the matter of branching processes. They present another kind of opportunity.

Consider a stream of ordered subdesigns. A successor has been devised that passed the test of the added constraints. We can consider the stream as a sequence of "generate and test" cycles. The point is important because it provides a rationale by which to create and order the subdesigns, and because, deliberate or not, designing proceeds by trys. An effective heuristic must be informed, else it flails. Its logic does not suffice to carry it along. That is why it is a heuristic. This one is informed by the skill of the designer in sequencing the tests. Notice, that in following one stream, the search is being made in depth. That is the usual architectural mode. A stream is quite long. Following several is costful. However, staying with one stream still permits some side excursions. There may well be several subdesigns that survive a round. These variants do not quite make branches. They do widen the stream.

The heuristic would promise, but cannot assure, that each subdesign is doable. Should it turn out so, then it can take you close to the finale. If not, go back. The constraint manager keeps a good history.

We know where the heuristic is informed, what it does, that it can be realized by the constraint system. How does it do it? Each round either:

- adds new variables and constraints not connected to the old; or
- adds new variables and constraints connected to the old; or
- adds only new constraints to the old.

In the first case, the extent of the old space is unchanged. A constraint added should be construed as a relevance discovered, rather than a condition created. Then the new volume is a bounded piece of a space implicitly there and previously unbounded. The total searchable space is therefore smaller. The second case takes the first as its upper limit. The third, the second as its upper limit.

In all the cases, then, the extent of the constraint space is decreased on each round. The heuristic prunes. It provides a good tactic, if you are certain that you are headed in the right direction. It will prune the constraint space to a point. You can go no further because you have arrived.

Confidence in the direction is not a rare event; but you can't count on it. A source of variations, rather than just variants, would be a comfort. The branching process is such a source. Recall that a branch is generated when the constraint set is augmented in two different ways, which is to say, by two different tests. The order of testing can be important. You might want to keep several branches waving.

We can sort them by examining their constraint sets. Those whose constraint sets are co-consistent can be taken as variants from one stream. They do not pose a new problem. Those from inconsistent sets require choices. Either, move them in separate streams, or adjust the inconsistency thereby placing them in the same stream. All this scrutiny and manipulation is particularly suited to the skill of the constraint manager.

We have argued that the pruning heuristic provides a reasonable search strategy, and that pruning is renderable. Reasonable because at the very least, it seems convergent, and the path is retraceable. But you must say where to prune, in what sequence. We know very little that is systematic about either of these. Suppose that the space of the constraint set is comprised of disjunct subspaces. It would seem utterly reasonable, then, to prune each subspace separately, as long as pruning does not close a gap. For this purpose, we describe a diagnostic that detects separability. It is a kind of partitioning of the problem that is quite well known. We use it naively now because we are not certain how much more elaboration its present use is worth.

Suppose that there are n constraints over m variables. Please think of the constraints arrayed as an n by m matrix whose $[i,j]$ entry is zero or one. Zero, if the jth variable does not appear in the ith constraint; one otherwise. If there exists a disjunct subspace, then it should be possible, by rearranging the rows and columns of the matrix, to isolate a block in the upper left corner such that entries for all rows in the block for all columns not in the block, and for all columns in the block for all rows not in the block, are zero. The block can be located anywhere in the matrix, as could a second disjunct block. A procedure that will display and move rows or columns of a matrix is easy enough. Then the matrix can manually be rearranged to search for such a block. It can, of course, be consulted again after augmenting the constraint set to see if the subspace is still separate.

The method works. It is tedious. That is a minor matter. The major matter is that complete separability, which is to say, clean block structures, are rare events. However, the advantages of separability may justify the risks of working with approximately separate blocks. The justification is your responsibility. The approximation is, literally, an altered constraint set. Either some variables are removed from some constraints, or some constraints are entirely removed. You never have to add anything. In either case, in any case, the constraint statements can be obtained and examined. Therefore, the risks can be known, perhaps even apprized.

Searching the zero-one matrix visually for possible block structures becomes inefficient when the matrix is larger than about ten by ten. The constraint manager knows how to sort constraints by the variables they specify, and variables by the constraints in which they are included, which sortings provide hints of possible blocks more felicitously than does just looking.

You are not limited to just looking for blocks. There is nothing to prevent you from declaring them. The design of the cellar, and the design of the patio are separable problems—until the door between them has to be located. Until then, the constraint manager is managing two different problems. She does not care.

☐ PRESENTING AND REPRESENTING CONSTRAINTS

Let us accept, for the sake of argument, that the designer is expert at deciding what to try next. In any event, the designer is presently better at it than the machine. In the language of the constraint manager this means knowing which constraints to fix; where to declare separations between blocks of constraints and where to bring them together; which blocks to explore and which to leave fixed.

If the designer is concerned to establish and modify those boundaries, how can the machine support this practice? Where the intelligence which drives the search resides within the designer, how may the constraint manager engage that intelligence? Where the designer is accustomed to working in visual media, how may the machine make visible the activities of the constraint manager?

These questions are particularly relevant where a constraint model is applied to various aspects of the design process. The issues which prevail in each domain, the knowledge that relates to them—in this model a connected network of constraints—is neither universal nor unbounded. Issues are clustered. Their relevance is limited. Each issue relates to and evokes only a subset of all possible other issues.

The influence of any given constraint is limited to the networks in which it is referenced. Individual designers may explore disjoint networks, or they may shift between networks depending on circumstances. As design constraints are likely either under- or over- specified, the designer establishes separations conventionally in order to proceed. In addition, the various participants in the design endeavor do not always share views of the problem. This leads to additional separations because of particular constraints which are incommensurable. An important aspect of designing with constraints, then, is managing multiple disjoint networks. This takes the form of exploring the means to effect and the consequences of constraint proliferation among bounded networks.

This view implies three activities that the constraint manager must support. The first is to manage the scope of each constraint by identifying the domains within which the constraint is effective, yet to allow this to evolve when the constraint is introduced into some new domain or removed from an existing one. The second is to control proliferation of constraints among domains. The last is to indicate which domain is active at any stage of a design process.

This does not lead to a demand for a language of "meta-constraints", which would automate shifts of focus and of knowledge among domains; we do not know enough about the design process to describe those meta-constraints. What is more, the things we do know imply that the practice of design frequently establishes the appropriateness of constraints according to the circumstances and idiosyncrasies of practice rather than according to any logic. In the beginning, it is more valuable to set the constraint manager in a system which helps designers observe this practice. We reserve the problem of automating management of a field of constraint networks until we have more experience with using these tools.

Designers who work on paper perform these three activities in their own ways. They depict active constraint networks, shift their attention between them, record modifications to a set of constraints, and note the links among them by making and arranging physical records. These records appear as drawings, specifications, and correspondence which represent the contents of and the relationships among the various networks. Designers often trace a drawing, or make sketches of an aspect of a more extensive design in order to select and identify a limited set of constraints. They denote, by physical proximity or graphical keys, the significance of the relationship between the various views. Designers also depend on naming, numbering, and filing systems (for example the cross-reference systems for specifications or working drawings) to denote the relations between networks of constraints.

A discussion of how to render this activity to the machine should begin with the large amount of work that has already been done on the issue of presentation. The constraint model offers a means to extend these methods to the tasks outlined above.

The issue of representation and presentation has always been significant to the inventors of automated design tools. Conventional "computer aided design" tools use a central 3-d geometric model, often with associated non-geometric attributes, and predetermined methods (projections, windows, etc.) to view this model in several different ways. Relations among domains are managed through methods which allow and control access to the central model or database.

Such systems provide two means to represent the facts of a design:

- *Assertion constraints* on entities and properties: this wall is here, is this size, and is made of this material.

- *Transformational constraints* on views: a line segment appears solid when seen in elevation, but should show as dashed when hidden in a section view; this wall, at a given location in 3d space, should be seen at this location in 2d space.

Two additional features may extend the expressive power in such modeling systems:

- *Transformational constraints* on properties (procedural generation): a material could depend on the size of an element; an area could be derived from the dimensions of an element; the dimensions of an element may derive from those of its setting;

- *Relational constraints* on properties: corners close; lines are orthogonal; an element's area is affected by its context and by neighboring elements, while it is also affected by its own constituent elements.

Assertion constraints are simple. They fix the values of properties. The transformational constraints are a special case of relational constraints. The former provide a one-way path, while the latter provide for inference in both directions. To specify a binary relational constraint is to either specify a transformational constraint which is invertible, or to specify two transformational constraints—one to map in one direction, and one to map in the other.

Users of automated tools that are based on detailed three-dimensional geometric models often find that relational constraints are too expensive, while transformational and assertion constraints are usually not sufficient. Aside from the desire on the part of practitioners from the various design disciplines to emphasize their own domains by reassimilating and re-representing all data, it is not practical - and sometimes not possible - to project the central model for each individual design discipline.

Thus designers of computer aided design systems are faced with issues as:

- When a design is projected into 2d, to produce contract documents, where do annotations appear, and how do any modifications percolate back to the global model?

- If one agent modifies some aspect of the design, how are modifications assimilated into all other representations. Must each be reconstructed from the global model?

One key to resolving these problems is the realization that it should not be the appearance of design proposals that is exchanged, but the constraints. Where the design is represented by constraints, rather than geometric details, the problem is to specify the scope of particular constraints, rather than to specify transforms of geometric data.

As the designer proceeds, these decisions as to the constitution of domains, as to the relations among domains, and as to the order of presentation of domains need to be recorded. They begin to represent, independent of the particular designed object, the design method itself.

This introduces two aspects into the designer's language.

- There must be terms to describe the content, and visible relationship of presentations of design proposals. These proposals may be maintained by one constraint manager—as with successive versions—or they may evolve within unrelated and incompatible constraint managers—as with practitioners in distinct fields.

- There must be terms to describe the parallel substantive relations among the distinct models. These terms specify the scope of constraints, the rules which govern their proliferation from one domain to another, and the rules which determine how propagated constraints are assimilated. Some of these rules will be verbal— following the precedents of programming language design—some will be expressed visually—mimicking the actions of the architect at the drawing board.

□ A GRAPHICAL INTERFACE FOR SEARCHING

Consider how designers might work, with computers containing a sophisticated graphical system and constraint manager on their desks. All objects described by a single constraint network are identified with one presentation. Each presentation might, for example, comprise a number of viewing surfaces. Each surface is analogous to the different 2d projection ports that one can establish in some automated drafting systems. They are all located in one bounded region of the screen, to denote their relationship.

The position of presentations on the screen could denote the constraints placed on relations of constraints among the presentations. Placing one presentation over another would cause any constraints which may be propagated from the superior presentation to be resolved within the inferior presentation. Additional explicit, drawn connections would bind presentations according to explicit rules which specify which constraints of each presentation are to be known externally, under what conditions they are promulgated, and how they are assimilated.

Where, for example, the designer has a primary presentation which depicts the geometry of a design, and an alternative presentation which depicts a structural or energy analysis, the geometric presentation might have a number of perspective views, as might the analytical presentation. The contents of a view could be changed as a consequence of changes made within a related presentation. The particular change would be governed by the constraints which link them, and their proximity. Thus, if the analytical presentation is moved on screen to be near to the geometric, then it might assimilate any changes made in the latter. The reverse happens if the geometric presentation were moved.

The designer would pursue a sequence of projection and evaluation steps. As this is going on, there would be a "presentation constraint manager" which observes the designer's activities, and records the contents of presentation and the relations created among them. The same set of presentations and relationships could then be available on another occasion for another design.

□ NAMING CONSTRAINTS

We must consider now some issues raised by specifications for scope, promulgation, and assimilation of constraints among presentations. As the presentations multiply, the exploration becomes a breadth-first search, and the issue becomes how to share the knowledge among presentations.

A network of constraints originates either as a set of constraints expressed by the designer, or as a copy of an existing network. When a designer is working in a number of domains, it is likely she will initiate new search paths by adopting constraints from an existing domain and then transform them. Although it is also possible for domains to appear without reference to each other, that is less likely.

The names of constraints, rather than the names of members, are communicated between domains. As the designer works, the constraints in the respective domains are modified. New relations and fixes appear. Constraints are eliminated. At some point names will no longer be shared. This suggests that it is necessary to employ relative naming: constraints are applied to named elements of objects which are identified by type and original value, rather than by name. Where the assimilation mechanism depends on names to match constraints, provisions are made for translation. Constraints are named and typed, according to the things which they constrain.

Proliferation of constraints can be controlled at a number of levels. Where constraints are typed, according to object type or according to whether the constraint is assertion, transformational, or relational, proliferation could be controlled by type. As with internal propagation, external proliferation could occur immediately when the internal constraints are modified, or it could occur upon demand. This would make distinctions possible between presentations which are mutually dependent, simply dependent, and independent. Once a constraint is rephrased in a domain, it is handled as any other internally generated constraint. The assimilation operation could generate a new version of the constraint set, or it could supplant the old value, with or without internal propagation.

☐ USING CONSTRAINTS

As another example of some of the ideas about constraints we have presented so far, we consider now an example of using constraint in the domain of site planning and design, since we have some experience with it, and are developing tools for teaching site planning incorporating the ideas of the constraint manager.

A typical site planning problem might go like this:

> Given a site of n acres, with bounds and natural features as shown, prepare a plan for x residential dwelling units, of types a, b and c, and y square feet of commercial space. Include provisions for automobile and pedestrian access, consider the needs of handicapped and elderly citizens, provide play areas for children of all ages. Preserve existing natural systems as much as possible, provide for adequate drainage, erosion control, and economical maintenance over time, and allow for change in patterns of use and growth over the next twenty years.

The types of information required for site planning and design include hydrologic and topographic maps, traffic flow and marketing studies, knowledge of horticulture and construction technology. The designing process demands constraints related to human behavior and perception, civil engineering criteria, and notions of sensuous form and choreographed movement.

We consider three different kinds of site planning knowledge, and therefore of constraints and constraint management: definitional, functional, and preferential. The distinction among these is somewhat artificial, and is not necessarily preserved by the constraint manager system, but does serve to illuminate what designers know, and how they use it. (The order given is approximately in the order of firmness, or in reverse order of frequency of modification, re-examination and relaxation, but this correlation is not essential or even recognized by the constraint manager.)

Definitional constraints provide the base level on which others are built. They include both composite and geometric definitions and provide the components for higher level constraints. For example: "A road consists of one start-point, zero or more horizontal-curves, and one end-point"; "an end-point is either an intersection, a cul-de-sac or a hammer-head", "a cul-de-sac is a closed-loop with a minimum radius of 80 feet", etc.

Definitional constraints are formed largely of IS-A and HAS-PARTS relationships, with reference to a lower-level dictionary of geometric and algebraic terms and relations. These may seem basic, but they are not trivial: naming and identifying elements is the first step to taming magic, and realizing explicit design. In defining basic components, the designer articulates values and establishes a personal palette of elements. From a pedagogic point of view, the definitional process reveals a design student's familiarity with the particular design domain.

By way of the set membership primitive relationships (IS-A, HAS-PARTS, etc.), definitions serve to structure the hierarchy of elements and families, which shapes the way the design problem will be explored, and how the design solution will evolve.

Many design elements and families may have standard definitions, and handbooks and regulations provide us with these. Conventional definitions may be simply loaded as defaults as required, but the opportunity to define an idiosyncratic or personal set of elements has potential for liberating designers from unstated assumptions and providing a laboratory for exploratory and innovative conceptions (e.g: "a road is a string of nodes and links"; "a node is either a long-view, a close-view, or a dead-spot"; "a link is either a straight-run or a gentle-arc"; "a gentle-arc is a part of a circle with a minimum radius of 100 feet", etc.). Simply adopting a set of personal aliases (different names) for otherwise conventional terms may be beneficial to the designer in communicating with him/herself and making an internal mental model of the design. Some of the distinction between inside (the computer) and outside (the designer) will no doubt be reflected in changing names for things, with the designer often one step ahead of the constraint manager (for example, call that last accumulation of benches, bricks, trees and lamps "the plaza"; call those four plazas "the arena" and so on...).

Functional constraints describe relationships between elements (variables) and reflect, for example, natural law, engineering or construction practice, or designers' invention (e.g. "a drainage-course must be located at the base of each slope over 10 feet in length", "circular-curves must be separated by a straight-tangent of more than 100 feet, or not at all", "each park-bench must be within 20 feet of a shade-tree", etc.)

These kinds of constraints are made up of geometric, topological and adjacency relationships like CONNECTED-TO, NORTH-OF, INSIDE often with reference to the names and set-memberships defined in the definitions. Once again, functional constraints for a particular domain will over time and use be built up into a dictionary of common defaults, and they may also be ad-hoc user-defined with reference to a common dictionary (for example, "All park benches must be PROTECTED"; "an element is PROTECTED if it is either within 20 feet of a shade-tree, or at the base of a wall, or on the south side of an evergreen", and so on.)

Functional constraints serve to limit the size of search space and to select sub-areas of interest within the universe of possible worlds opened up by definitions. In rendering functional constraints, the designer is certainly revealing her knowledge of standard practice, but also beginning to make assertions about personal preference leading toward a unique design. We distinguish functional from preferential constraints (although the distinction is fuzzy at best) in that they refer to some more or less objective (commonly agreed upon) performance criteria, and not personal preference. Naturally preference is exercised in choosing which functional contraints to recognize—that is designing.

Preferential constraints are the most capricious and arbitrary, and may be the least amenable to discovery and articulation—at least until we have a cohort of designers who have learned to use the constraint manager. Some such constraints may be based on simple mathematical or topological relations (e.g. "all groups should number 3 or 5 or more—never 2 or 4.", "the ratio of length to width for play-rooms should be 0.8", "never have two activity-centers in a row", etc.) Preferential contraints are the most likely to have complex clauses and exceptions—they may also require a complex chain of connected procedures or calculations (e.g. "if a node has a long-view then the planting should be sparse unless the slope is steep or the road is curvy in which case the planting should be dense...") These constraints can be built out of all of the kinds of relationships found in the other two types of constraints. We believe one of the greatest challenges to constructive use of the constraint manager by designers will be in their ability to first articulate for themselves—and then later for the constraint manager—what are their constraints.

We should note that the order of constraints indicated above—from definition through functional to preferential—is not central or even relevant to constraint-based exploration. Indeed, sometimes personal preferences will serve at the beginning to limit explorations of technically feasible solutions. We do imagine, however, that certainly in the beginning, and for some time as we learn to work with the contraint manager, constraints for such qualities as 'image', 'feel', and 'sense of place' will be the hardest to describe in renderable—computable—terms.

To this point, the intelligence and knowledge that drive the search processes are outside the computer. The constraint manager keeps the game honest. To get beyond this point, we think that we shall have to have some years of experience with designers using the constraint manager to express and explore their knowledge.

☐ REPRESENTING DESIGN KNOWLEDGE WITH CONSTRAINTS

The discussions of beams and joists, and houses and roads described the content, representation, and uses of the designer's knowledge in particular settings. In setting out the particulars of the interactions between designer and constraint manager, we proposed the kinds of competences that can be rendered the machine to realize such interaction. We proposed to locate these competences in the constraint-manager. These competences—solving, relating, inferring, matching, sorting, accounting, recording, are not exotic—thank goodness. A constraint-manager need not be a dull grind. Teaching one to be somewhat intelligent and rather knowledgely is not a simple job. It is doable.

We propose, in keeping with our notion that design knowledge is representable as constraints, to shape the repository that comprises the constraint-manager's knowledge to the same form as the constraints entered by the designer. It will use the same syntax, access the same procedures, be accessible to the same procedures. In particular, it will be under the protocol, control and scrutiny of the constraint manager.

Knowledge is not permanent, although some things, like trigonometry, can last a long time. Repositories should be mutable. In particular, one might be shaped to the requirements of precedent, fashion, use, occasion, the designer's idiosyncracies.

☐ LIMITS TO REPRESENTING DESIGN KNOWLEDGE WITH CONSTRAINTS

The discussions of beams and joists, and houses and roads also uncovered some non-renderable knowledge. Consider the roads, for example. We took them to be primitives of the design, generating their own constraints. Designating primitives is a dangerous practice. A road can, equally well, be considered a fix entertained to satisfy the prior constraint that the people who live in the houses on the site be able to get in and out and around. We do not know how to render the argument which would infer a road, given that constraint. Likewise, we know how to manipulate beams and joists. We would not know how to invent them.

We said that successive design proposals in the search process were generated by the designer. We do not know how to instruct the constraint-manager in that competence.

Our recourse in all these instances is simple. What we cannot render to the machine, remains for the designer. We are certain, we think, that ultimately there will remain at least one non-renderable. We think—we are not certain—that we do not stand close enough to the ultimate for discomfort, and that there are many more renderables remaining to be rendered.

All instances of non-renderables seem vaguely to require creative acts. The presumption is circular because creativity is defined to be non-inferential. An inference missing is not necessarily an inference lacking. Whether a design was inferred or created cannot be argued a priori. Whether inferences can be constructed that would account for the design can be argued—a posteriori. The argument is worth considering. It is likely that more inferences are missing than lacking. They just might not have been articulated.

Nevertheless, we shall hold the presumption that creativity is non-renderable. It seems the safer choice. Then we must consider competences that might support creativity. Should they be quiet? Or obtrusive? That would be a rather different state of affairs. It edges toward a reversal of roles. The constraint manager may now become the nag. Some software systems provide a choice. At first, we shall try to remain quiet. It's safer.

Our proposition is relatively modest. It originates in the observation, hardly new, that the throes of creativity surface in the making of marks, usually on paper. They can be as simple as the mathematician's ideograms, or as elaborate as an artist's studies. They are tentative (Mozart was a deviant in this respect.) They are visual. They assert the eloquent connection between looking and inferring. A picture is an argument. How the argument is argued is obscure. The stream from eye to brain has been mapped only as far as the visual cortex. Programs that do visual pattern matching end with the pattern. We begin with the pattern.

An architect usually makes two kinds of pictures. One kind diagrams relations; the other shows forms of shape and volume. The first kind is topological. Some are better than others, but being non-literal, the making is not fussy. (Line weight and choice of media are not so important in diagrams and "back-of-the-envelope" scribbles.) In the part on searching, we described such a diagram, and showed the argument that it illustrates. That was the zero-one matrix. The second kind, unfortunately, requires a rather more elaborate apparatus, more attention to medium and detail. Fortunately, the apparatus exists. It need not be invented. CAD systems would have the capabilities in the details (line weight, color, scale, etc.) They are less felicitous in the organization and manipulation of knowledge.

What are these felicities? The constraint manager must be able to read the drawing, which means:

- distinguishing icons from literals,
- understanding labels and quantities,
- assigning data to labels.

So far, nothing new.

- associating labels with constraints,
- associating quantities with fixes, and
- altering the drawing to make it consistent with the constraints.

These are new. In this application, the drawing replaces verbalized constraints and fixes. The designer is bilingual (verbal and graphical); the constraint manager should match that skill.

There is something else. The last competence: altering the drawing to make it consistent with the constraints, is not very hard if the constraint manager has the drawing in the first place. Suppose it hasn't. Then it is very much harder, because a drawing made by the designer is very likely to be furbished with constraints unstated, and therefore, unknown to the constraint manager. Does it fill in, and risk becoming a nag, or does it draw walls without windows, houses without roofs, toilets without plumbing? It is clear that the constraint manager will have a style, perhaps several styles. We are most interested in what our colleagues think these styles should be.

One may object—several have—that when the rendering is done there will be a lot left over because the machine is highly verbal and design is highly intuitive. We wonder about the intuitive because we observe that architectural intuitions are rare among dentists. Most intuitions are learned. We think that things thought to be non-verbal and non-quantitative are confused with the ambiguous and imprecise. Ambiguity and imprecision are not defects in any sense that is pathological. The constraint-manager can handle imprecision. It is treated as interval data. We would like to make the constraint manager competent to detect ambiguity. That's harder. Loading that difficulty on the syntax of the language is the wrong solution. Leaving it to the semantics of the constraints and the competence of the solver seems better. That is hard. Clearly, more work needs to be done....

□ CONCLUSION

We have argued a theory of designing and derived from it a description of the uses and organization of computing in design. The computer is not a consequence of the theory. It is an application of the theory. Therefore it is also a vehicle by which to prove and improve the theory. We think that we have a nice experiment underway. It is of the kind of making knowledge knowable. This enterprise has a long history—ours is only a more fashionable setting. We expect that the theory of designing with constraints will prove to be more robust than any manifestation of that theory in computer software, but software is our next step.

□ REFERENCES

Macsyma "MACSYMA Reference Manual," The Macsyma Group, Laboratory of Computer Science, M.I.T. Cambridge, MA 1982.

Shortliffe E.H. *Computer-based Medical Consultations: MYCIN*, American Elsevier, 1976.

McDermott J. "R1: A Rule-based Configurator of Computer Systems," *Artificial Intelligence*, 19(9):39-88, 1982.

Friedman, G.J. & Leondes, C. "Constraint Theory, Parts I, II, III." IEEE Transactions on Systems Science & Cybernetics, Vol SSC-5, #1, #2, #3 1969.

Sutherland, I. "Sketchpad—A Man-Machine Graphical Communication System." Technical Report #296, Lincoln Laboratory, Massachusetts Institute of Technology, Cambridge, MA 1963.

Steele, G., and Sussman, G.J. "CONSTRAINTS—A Language for Expressing Almost-Hierarchical Descriptions." *Artificial Intelligence*, 14: 1–39, 1980.

Borning, A. "Thinglab—An Object-Oriented System for Building Simulations Using Constraints." Proc. Fifth International Joint Conference on Artificial Intelligence, pp 497–498, 1979.

Gross, M. "Design as Exploring Constraints." Doctoral Dissertation, Massachusetts Institute of Technology, Cambridge, MA 1985.

PART 2

DESIGN KNOWLEDGE

The importance of knowledge for carrying out both complex and common tasks has been established and demonstrated by developments in artificial intelligence. In particular, researchers like Simon and Newell demonstrated the importance of using knowledge in solving "wicked" problems, for which no strong solution procedures exist. Design is one of the most difficult problems people solve, and accordingly it requires the application of considerable knowledge.

To be able to computationally aid design, at least some of this knowledge must be formalized and made accessible to the computer. Without it, the computer can only be used as an extravagant pencil. This part of the book deals with three related questions underlying the computability of design knowledge:

1. What is the nature of design knowledge?
2. How can it be computationally represented?
3. How can it be computationally used?

The nature of design knowledge is explored in Chapters 4 and 5. In REASONING ABOUT FORM AND FUNCTION William Mitchell explores the issue of (computationally) fitting form to function. He points out the relationship between design knowledge and the semantics of languages, both used to communicate and to support the formation of ideas. He discusses the limitations of generative expert systems that can explore only formative combinatorial properties of standard elements, and proposes that in order to be able to engage the more difficult issue of design synthesis, the knowledge bases of such systems will have to include a variety of empirically derived and validated knowledge of rich and sophisticated architectural forms.

In Chapter 5, DEVELOPMENT OF MACHINE INTELLIGENCE FOR THE INFERENCE OF DESIGN INTENT IMPLICIT IN DESIGN SPECI-

FICATIONS, Michael Kim challenges the possibility of relating form and function as advocated by Mitchell. In his exploration of the nature and source of design knowledge, Kim demonstrates the paradox in attempting to define the qualities of a designed artifact (its function) prior to its construction, and the use of those specifications to construct it (to give it form). He points out the pitfalls in attempting to use the rich and semantically laden language of architecture to define new structures (e.g. the word "door," which is associated with a whole gestalt of form, materials, etc.), and advocates a teleological search for the client's true intent implicit in the design specifications.

The computational representation and use of design knowledge is discussed in Chapters 6 through 9. First, a comparative analysis of four methods of computationally representing and utilizing design knowledge and information are presented by Patricia McIntosh in MODELS OF SPATIAL INFORMATION IN COMPUTER-AIDED ARCHITECTURAL DESIGN: A COMPARATIVE STUDY. She explores the nature of spatial information as it is represented and used for decision making in architectural design, according to paradigms developed by Mitchell, Eastman, Kalay, and Coyne-Gero. Two of the major aspects of computational design knowledge are stressed: the representation of spatial relationships, and the generation of form.

Some of the major problems in attempting to computationally represent design information are discussed by Charles Eastman in FUNDAMENTAL PROBLEMS IN THE DEVELOPMENT OF COMPUTER-AIDED ARCHITECTURAL DESIGN MODELS. Eastman points out how solids modeling failed to revolutionize architectural design, although it promised to do so by providing a unified database for all the building information. He proposes that the reason for this failure is due to the inherent properties of drawings, which are not simple sectional projections of a 3D model. Rather, they are context-dependent abstractions of the designed artifact, and thus require knowledge for their appropriate presentation. Furthermore, drawings allow "fuzziness" in defining the artifact, and hence the sharing of design responsibilities between the architects and builders, something that solid modeling does not permit.

An alternative approach to modeling architectural spaces is presented by Chris Yessios in THE COMPUTABILITY OF VOID ARCHITECTURAL MODELING. Yessios presents the theory and implementation of void modeling, an approach that accommodates the representation and manipulation of a class of objects that are containers of other objects, such as space enclosures. His approach extends solid modeling by adding a level of semantics that makes it possible to computationally distinguish solids from voids, and thereby resolve some of the limitations of solids modeling that were discussed by Eastman.

Finally, a more general approach to solving the problem of design knowledge computational representation is presented by Stuart Shapiro and

James Geller in ARTIFICIAL INTELLIGENCE AND AUTOMATED DESIGN. They discusses how powerful AI techniques can be applied towards the development of intelligent design/maintenance assistant systems, where the the ontology and epistemology of some design tasks can be represented through semantic networks. This method of knowledge representation also enables reasoning about objects and forms, their position (absolute, relative, and "fuzzy"), their attributes, and the mechanisms of attribute inheritance along class, part-whole, and relevance hierarchies.

4

REASONING ABOUT FORM AND FUNCTION

William J. Mitchell

Graduate School of Design
Harvard University
Cambridge, Massachusetts

One of the hopes raised by the development of expert system technology is that this technology will make it practical to build CAD systems that reason usefully about relations between form and function. Given a specification of functions to be performed, for example, a system might suggest appropriate spatial arrangements and material choices. Conversely, given a site or a room or an architectural element, in some particular context, a system might suggest the highest and best use. If we take such possibilities seriously, we must confront the question of the logical character of the relations between form and function. Under what circumstances, and in what sense, might we say that "form follows function?" In this paper I will sketch some answers.

☐ THE UTILITY OF GEOMETRIC AND MATERIAL PROPERTIES

To claim that "form follows function" in some given physical system is to claim, at the very least, that the system's significant geometric and material properties can be shown to have some utility; they are not merely irrelevant accidents. A stronger claim that might be made is that they have greater utility than other obvious possibilities. A classic analysis of form, in these terms, is the ancient physician Galen's treatise, *On the Usefulness of the*

Parts of the Body (translated by May, 1968).* In this treatise Galen attempts to establish the functions of various human organs, to show that their significant geometric and material properties are appropriate to these functions, and to demonstrate that other obvious alternatives would be inferior.

Let us consider, for example, his analysis of the hand. First the issue is formulated:

> Come now, let us investigate this very important part of man's body, examining it to determine not simply whether it is useful or whether it is suitable for an intelligent animal, but whether it is in every respect so constituted that it would not have been better had it been made differently.

Then the utility of the cleft shape of the hand is considered:

> One and indeed the chief characteristic of a prehensile instrument constructed in the best manner is the ability to grasp readily anything of whatever size or shape that man would naturally want to move. For this purpose, then, which was better—for the hand to be cleft into many divisions or to remain wholly undivided? Or does this need any discussion other than the statement that if the hand remained undivided, it would lay hold only on the things in contact with it that were of the same size as it happened to be itself, whereas, being subdivided into many members, it could easily grasp masses much larger than itself, and fasten accurately upon the smallest objects? For larger masses, the hand is extended, grasping them with the fingers spread apart, but the hand as a whole does not try to grasp the smallest objects, for they would escape if it did; the tips of two fingers are enough to use for them. Thus, the hand is most excellently constituted for a firm grasp of things both larger and smaller than itself. Furthermore, if it was to be able to lay hold on objects of many different shapes, it was best for it to be divided into many differing members, as it now is, and for this purpose the hand is obviously adapted best of all prehensile instruments. Indeed, it can curve itself around a spherical body, laying hold of and encircling it from all sides; it surrounds firmly objects with straight or concave sides; and if this be true, then it will also clasp objects of all shapes, for they are all made up of three kinds of lines, convex, concave and straight.

Next it is suggested that two hands are better than one for grasping large and heavy objects:

> Since, however, there are many bodies whose mass is too great for one hand alone to grasp, Nature made each the ally of the other so that both together, grasping such a body on opposite sides, are in no way inferior to one very

---

*For an excellent history of attempts by biologists to analyze relations between form and function, see Russell (1916).

large hand. For this reason, then, they face toward one another, since each was made for the sake of the other, and they have been formed equal to one another in every respect, a provision suitable for instruments which are to share the same action.

Finally, the usefulness of variation in the sizes of fingers, and of the opposition of the thumb to the fingers is analyzed:

Now when you have considered the largest objects that man can handle with both hands, such as a log or rock, then give heed, pray, to the smallest, such as a millet seed, a very slender thorn, or a hair, and then, when you have considered besides how very many bodies there are that range in size from the largest to the smallest, think of all this and you will find that man handles them all as well as if his hands had been made for the sake of each one of them alone. He takes hold of very small objects with the tips of two fingers, the thumb and forefinger, and slightly larger objects with the same two fingers, but not with just the tips; those still larger he grasps with three fingers, the thumb, forefinger, and middle finger, and if there are any larger yet, with four, and next, with five. After that the whole hand is used, and for still larger objects the other hand is brought up. The hand could act in none of these ways if it were not divided into fingers differently formed; for it was not enough in it itself for the hand merely to be divided. What if there had been no finger opposing the four, as there is now, but all five of them had been produced side by side in one straight line? Is it not clear that mere number would be useless, since an object to be held firmly must be either encircled from all sides or at least laid hold of from two opposite points? The ability to hold an object firmly would be destroyed if all the fingers had been produced side by side in one straight line, but as it is, with one finger set opposite the rest, this ability is nicely preserved; for this one finger has such a position and motion that by turning very slightly it acts with each of the four set opposite to it.

The final conclusion seems inescapable:

Hence it was better for the hands to act as they do now, and Nature therefore gave them a structure suited to such actions.

□ CONDITIONS OF FUNCTIONAL ADEQUACY

Such analyses can be carried out not only of natural systems, but also of designed artifacts. In the *Physics* (Book II, Chapter IX), for example, Aristotle asked: "Why is a saw like this?" He then answered:

In order that it might have the essential character of a saw and serve for sawing. This purpose, however, could not be served if it were not made of iron. So if it is to be a saw, and to do its work, it must necessarily be made of iron.

The positivist architectural theorists and historians of the nineteenth century were fond of analyzing architectural form in similar fashion. Consider, for example, a classical temple roof. In a famous analysis, Auguste Choisy (1899) suggested that such a roof could fail to provide shelter in two ways: if the pitch were too flat, then the water would not drain away; but if the pitch were too steep, then the tiles would slide off. Therefore, he suggested the physical property of pitch "is ruled by this double condition."

The important point to note here is how these authors establish a relation between form and function by making use of the idea of a condition of functional adequacy. They assert that there are certain necessary conditions (adequate hardness, appropriate shape) of functional adequacy. These can be satisfied by possession of certain geometric and material properties (having a blade made of iron, or a roof pitch of a certain angle). Hence, it is claimed, the presence of these geometric and material properties is explained. This is a stronger claim than merely that these properties are useful. But is it logically justified?

In order to examine the logic of the situation it will be useful to set up a general scheme for this sort of argument. This may be done as follows:*

1.   At a certain time t, a system s functions adequately in a context of kind c.

2.   System s functions adequately in a context of kind c only if a certain necessary condition n is satisfied.

3.   Whenever system s has property p, as an effect, condition n is satisfied.

4.   Hence, at time t, system s has property p.

So, for example, we might paraphrase Aristotle's argument thus:

1.   A saw s adequately cuts wood.

2.   A saw adequately cuts only if the blade is sufficiently hard.

3.   Whenever the material of the blade is iron then, as an effect, the condition of sufficient hardness is satisfied.

4.   Hence the blade of saw s is made of iron.

In similar style, Choisy's argument may be paraphrased:

1.   A temple roof s adequately provides shelter in a natural setting.

2.   A temple roof adequately provides shelter in a natural setting only if:

---

*This analysis closely follows Hempel (1965).

The water drains away.

The tiles don't slide off.

3. Whenever the roof pitch is as shown then, as an effect, these conditions are satisfied.

4. Hence the pitch of roof s is as shown.

Is such an argument formally valid? Intuitively, most people would guess that it is not. Such suspicion is well-founded. Although we may readily grant that all the premises (1, 2, and 3) are true, and that so is the conclusion (4), the rules of logical inference do not license us to draw the conclusion from the premises. Technically speaking, the fallacy is one of affirming the consequent in regard of premise 3. To make this evident, we need only consider the following obviously fallacious argument of similar form:

1. The Parthenon is a monument of European architecture.

2. A building is a monument of European architecture only if it is in Europe.

3. Whenever the Parthenon is in Paris then, as an effect, the condition of being in Europe is satisfied.

4. Hence the Parthenon is in Paris.

☐ UNIQUE SATISFACTION OF THE CONDITIONS

A slight alteration, however, to premise 3, as follows, would suffice to convert this into a formally valid argument:

3. *Only* when the Parthenon is in Paris is the condition of being in Europe satisfied.

In other words, we assert that the necessary condition stated in 2 is uniquely satisfied by being in Paris. But, of course, we pay a price for achieving formal validity in this way. Now premise 3 is empirically false; we know that being in many different cities (including Athens) would satisfy the condition.

Similarly, we can rewrite our premise 3 about the saw as follows:

3. Only when the material of the blade is iron is the condition of sufficient hardness satisfied.

But we know that iron does not uniquely satisfy the condition; the blade might equally well be made of steel, or bronze, or some other hard metal.

Along the same lines, Choisy's argument about the temple roof might be "saved" by rewriting the third premise as:

3. Only the pitch in question satisfies the conditions.

But this seems implausible.

☐ THE ROLE OF FUNCTIONAL EQUIVALENCE CLASSES

A way around these sorts of difficulties can be found, though, if we make use of the concept of functional equivalence. We let P be the class of all those properties which are empirically sufficient to satisfy condition n under the specified circumstances. In other words, a property p will be included in P if and only if its realization in system s, in a context of kind c, would be empirically sufficient to ensure the satisfaction of condition n. (We must say "empirically sufficient" to indicate the satisfaction of n by p must be a matter of empirical fact, not just of pure logic. Thus we exclude trivial items, such as n itself, from P. We must also provide, for technical reasons, that P has at least one member). The class P, then, is a functional equivalence class.

Now we can set out a valid argument, relating form to function, as follows:

1. At a certain time t, a system s functions adequately in a context of kind c.
2. System s functions adequately in a context of kind c only if a certain necessary condition n is satisfied.
3. P is the class of all properties that empirically satisfy condition n under the specified circumstances.
4. Some one of the individual items p, which is included in the class P, is present in system s at time t.

Thus, we might, for example, empirically define the class P as consisting of the values iron, steel, bronze, and so on for the variable *material*, and validly conclude that some one of these is present when a saw cuts wood. Or we might, by experiment, find a range P of temple roof pitches from which water drains and for which tiles do not slide off, and validly conclude that some one of these is present when a temple provides shelter in a natural setting.

The problem now is, however, that this kind of argument relating form to function tends to be weak and unilluminating. First, the class P extends indefinitely, and potentially is very large. Secondly, the argument gives no ground for expecting the occurrence of any particular item p from P, rather than one of its (potentially many) functional equivalents.

□ SET-PREDICATE FORMULATION

The root of all these difficulties is that our universe of discourse is not well-defined. (The technical concept of a universe of discourse was introduced into formal logic by Augustus de Morgan in the nineteenth century. For our purpose here, we can define such a universe as the set of all objects that enter into, or are regarded as admissible, in a particular discussion or problem formulation).

Now universes of discourse usually may, quite reasonably, be specified in a variety of different ways, so as to have different memberships. Let us consider again, for example, Aristotle's argument about the saw. We might find it reasonable to say, here, that the relevant universe of discourse is the set of metals available for use by craftsmen in Ancient Greece, and we might specify the universe by giving a list of these metals. Alternatively, we might choose to say that the relevant universe is the set of all hard metals and alloys that we know about today, and so give a very much longer list.

Within a given universe of discourse, a subset P can be specified by stating the conditions of membership. For example, we might define P as the set of all metals which meet some objective test of hardness. Technically speaking, we use a predicate applied to a universe U to specify a subset P of functional equivalents.

Now let us reconsider Choisy's argument about temple roof pitches. The universe of discourse might reasonably be defined as the range of pitches from 0 degrees to, say, 89 degrees. Let us assume that variation takes place in small discrete increments of, say, one degree. Thus we have a universe U of 90 possibilities. The predicate "sufficiently steep to give adequate drainage" now specifies some subset A. Similarly, the predicate "sufficiently shallow that the tiles don't slide off," now specifies some subset B. The set P of functionally adequate pitches, then, is the intersection of A and B. In other words, the members of P satisfy both predicates.

When particular predicates are applied to a particular universe U in order to specify a subset P, three possible situations may result:

1. P is empty; nothing in the universe is functionally adequate.
2. P contains exactly one member; form follows function, in this respect, in a strong sense.
3. P contains more than one member—perhaps many; there are functional equivalents in the universe, so form follows function only in a weak sense.

We may conclude, then, that the question of whether form follows function is not one to be argued as a matter of universal principle. We cannot expect an answer of yes or no. It is, instead, a matter of empirical fact relative to some particular formulation of the issue. When we establish large universes of discourse, when we give very broad functional descriptions, and when we can only adduce weak conditions of functional adequacy, then we are likely to find that there are many functional equivalents. But when universes of discourse are more restricted, when we specify function more narrowly, and when we can adduce strong conditions of functional adequacy, then we may well find that function much more closely determines form.

□ LANGUAGES OF ARCHITECTURAL FORM

Clearly then, any satisfactory account of relations between form and function must be based upon:

1. Specification of the system in question's functions—that is, the behaviors that make it of value to us.
2. Specification of the relevant universe U of geometric and material possibilities—the possible alternative forms of the system.
3. Specification of the relevant conditions of functional adequacy—the predicates which apply to U to establish a subset P of functionally adequate possibilities.

The system's functions might simply be stated verbally, or the relevant behaviors might be described in terms of values on some measurement scale, with numerical constraints establishing acceptable ranges. Similarly, the conditions of functional adequacy might be stated in the form of simple empirical rules, as in our saw and classical temple example, or they might take the form of mathematical laws relating relevant behavior to the values of geometric and material variables, together with constraints on the values of these variables.

Typically, positivist and functionalist architectural theorists have focused upon understanding system behaviours (structural, thermal, and so on), and conditions of functional adequacy, but have neglected systematic consideration of universes of form possibilities. Thus, in the end, their theories of design synthesis have remained incomplete and unsatisfactory. Such theories may provide an adequate foundation for design by parametric variation of standard elements, or by combinatorial assembly of a kit of parts, but hardly begin to address the centrally important issue of formal innovation in design.

This difficulty with functionalist design theory was pointed out nearly thirty years ago, in a famous essay by Sir John Summerson (1957), entitled, "The Case for a Theory of Modern Architecture" Summerson wrote:

The conceptions which arise from a preoccupation with the programme have got, at some point, to crystallize into a final form and by the time the architect reaches that point he has to bring to his conception a weight of judgment, a sense of authority and conviction which clinches the whole design, causes the impending relationships to close into a visually comprehensible whole. He may have extracted from the programme a set of interdependent relationships adding up to a unity of the biological kind, but he still has to face up to the ordering of a vast number of variables, and how he does this is a question. There is no common theoretical agreement as to what happens or should happen at that point. There is a hiatus. One may even be justified in speaking of a missing architectural language.

□ CONCLUSIONS

It seems to me that Summerson is right. If expert systems that reason about form and function are to move beyond the relatively trivial realms of parametric design and combinatorial assembly of standard pieces to engage the really difficult issues of design synthesis, their knowledge bases will have to contain not only rules relating behaviours to geometric and material variables, but also adequate knowledge of the vocabulary and syntax of rich and sophisticated language of architectural form.

□ REFERENCES

Aristotle, *The Physics*, Loeb Classical Library, Harvard University Press, Cambridge, MA, 1957.

Choisy, A. *Histoire de l' Architecture*, Editions Vincent Freal et Cie, Paris, 1964 (Reprint).

Galen, *On the Usefulness of the Parts of the Body*, (trans. M.T. May), Cornell University Press, Ithaca, 1968.

Hempel C. "The Logic of Functional Analysis," in *Aspects of Scientific Explanation,* The Free Press, New York, 1965.

Russell, E.S. *Form and Function*, John Murray, London, 1916.

Summerson J. "The Case for a Theory of Modern Architecture," *Royal Institute of British Architects Journal*, vol 64, 1957.

5

DEVELOPMENT OF MACHINE INTELLIGENCE FOR INFERENCE OF DESIGN INTENT IMPLICIT IN DESIGN SPECIFICATIONS

Michael K. Kim

School of Architecture
University of Illinois at Urbana-Champaign
Champaign, Illinois

This paper illustrates the poverty of the current practice of designing buildings based on the design specifications, and introduces an alternative approach particularly appropriate in the coming age of machine intelligence. It is argued that the attempt to design design specifications as reliable design guides can only lead to a paradox, and therefore, the resulting specifications are necessarily inappropriate as such guides. Rather, the design specifications and the design itself should be developed simultaneously, in light of each other, toward the fulfillment of the design intent. To that end, this paper presents the logic of uncovering the design intent and the teleological structure implicit in the client's expressed desire. Machine intelligence which can effectively uncover the teleological structure and design intent is also presented. Further, the potential of the same machine intelligence as an "idea generator," the next phase of development of the "designing machine," is demonstrated.

□ INTRODUCTION

Behind every design, there is the intent to create some particular thing or particular situation of some specific value. Through the building design, we try to create the specific physical setting which, by virtue of the specific physical characteristics which we purposely create, would enhance our well-being in some particular way which we regard as desirable. The current practice of design begins with Design Specifications* which describe the design objectives, the design criteria, and other pertinent **deontic descriptions** [Rittel 1974]† about the building, i.e., the description about the way the building ought to be.

The practice of prescribing the design before actually designing the building sounds entirely logical; after all, it seems absurd to say that one could design without knowing what it is that is to be designed. Yet, any experienced architect knows that there is no set of design specifications which he/she can follow without modification in order to arrive at a reasonable design. As the design progresses, the architect usually realizes that the design specifications, no matter how good it appeared at the outset, no longer function as appropriate guides for the design. The specifications may very well need to be modified, supplemented, and revised as the design progresses if the architect is to get the kind of design which was originally intended.

The architect knows that what the client wants is a building which can really fulfill the client's purposes, even if the building does not exactly meet the particular design specifications. It is, the architect knows, not the design specifications, but the client's design intent implicit behind the specifications, that really matters. After all, the set of design specifications is, like the design itself, no more than someone's belief about what the design ought to be if it is to accomplish what the design is intended to accomplish. If the belief behind the specifications is to be tenable, it must be based on a reliable understanding of the relevant facts. If it is not, then one could err in specifying the design just as easily as in actually designing.‡ If this is the case, then why should the design possibilities be unduly

---

*Design specifications, in this paper, is used as a generic term denoting a class of descriptions of what the building ought to be like. In practice, depending on the situation, various terms are used to denote specific ideas about the building, such as design objectives, design criteria, etc. The building program is also a description of this type. In this context, perhaps it is proper to call such a description a design prescription.

†Human beings almost instinctively improve their setting. For this, we individually have a sense of how things ought to be. This kind of knowledge is called Deontic Knowledge (After [Rittel 1974]). Deontic description is an externalization of one's deontic knowledge.

‡In fact, specifying is designing, and designing is specifying. Designing tends to imply a process of defining, or specifying if you will, the assemblage of physical elements in a particular configuration. Specifying tends to imply a process of defining desirable attributes of an object to be designed. Both are attempts to prescribe the nature and the properties, physical or qualitative, of the same object that we try to produce.

limited by the design specifications? Instead of blindly following the design specifications as if it were the Bible for the design, a good designer should be critical about the propriety of the design specifications itself as the prescription of what a successful design ought to be like. The designer must, therefore, be ready to revise, modify, and supplement the specifications whenever necessary in much the same way as we change our design in light of what we learn about the particular design as the design progresses.

However, before actually exploring the design possibilities, no one can really know what is wrong with the design specifications, and therefore can not know how to write the specifications "right" the first time; the problems can only be discovered as the design progresses. Why is this? This paper discusses the necessary impropriety of the design specifications, the paradoxical nature of "designing" design specifications, and the appropriate mode of design practice under such a paradoxical situation. This paper will also develop the logic of uncovering the "real" design intent implicit behind explicit design specifications, and introduce the principle of developing machine intelligence which can effectively assist architects in designing their buildings to meet the design intent, thus producing the buildings that accomplish what they are intended to accomplish.

□ THE NECESSARY IMPROPRIETY OF DESIGN SPECIFICATIONS

Specifying a building design is the process of stipulating the properties or the characteristics of the building which are believed to be desirable or required for the building if the building is to accomplish the original intent of the client.* Every design creates some thing or some situation of some specific value, and every set of design specifications is a description of a means of creating such. Therefore, behind every set of building design specifications there is an implicit assumption that the building to be created following the specifications would manifest the specifically desired quality by virtue of having the prescribed properties and characteristics.

Furthermore, what is also implicit in the set of design specifications, if it is meant to be strictly followed, is the belief that a building thus created would be better, or at least not worse, than those which do not meet the specifications. Put in another way, the implicit belief is equivalent to the following:

> Let B be the set of all buildings which meet the design specifications S, and let B' be the set of all buildings which do not. Then
>
> $b > b'$, for all $b \in B$ & for all $b' \in B'$.

---

*The term "client" is used as a generic term referring not to the person who pays for an architect's services, but to the people affected by the design, and therefore to those people who the architects are supposed to serve.

How valid is this implicit belief? Value judgement is object specific and context dependent [Musso and Rittel 1969].† Without knowing exactly what it is that is evaluated under what situation, no one can make a sensible evaluation. Furthermore, what matters most in evaluating anything is the evaluation of the evaluation criteria themselves, or, in the context of our discussion, the evaluation of the design criteria or the propriety of the design specifications. Of course, such an evaluation is also context dependent, and therefore cannot be properly made without knowing exactly what the evaluative context is. The problem is particularly acute in design. Since to design is to come up with something new, until the design is completed, no one can really know what the specific new building will be like, how the physical context will be affected, and, most importantly, how our evaluative system itself will be changed because of the experience of the very design.‡ How, then, can anyone say that a better design can be produced by simply following the design specifications?

Perhaps, the most which a design specification can imply is:

> Let B be the set of all buildings which meet the design specifications S, and let B' be the set of all buildings which do not. Then

$$b > b', \text{ for some } b \in B \ \& \ \text{for some } b' \in B'.$$

How informative is such a specification? Does it tell us anything new? We all know that some things are better than some other things. What we do not know is what the "right" kind is, and what the "wrong" kind is. Design specifications neither specify which of those buildings that *do* meet the specifications are good ones, nor, more importantly, do they specify which of those that *do not* meet the prescription are still good ones. What is prescribed by the design specifications, therefore, does not mean very much at all. The conditions which make supposedly good buildings (those meeting the specifications) bad, and supposedly bad ones good, are external to the design specifications. Without further supplementary conditions, the design specifications do not tell us anything really conclusive, and therefore, fails to be functional as a definitive guide for designing.

To be functional, design specifications ought to be further supplemented by the pertinent external conditions in one way or another. Clearly, there can be only three logically exhaustive ways of internalizing the necessary external conditions:

---

†Evaluation varies depending on several general parameters: what is being evaluated, when, with regard to what purpose, and under what circumstances. See [Musso and Rittel 1969] for the detailed argument.

‡For example, a similar situation is the familiar experience of shopping for a particular item because we regard its specific features as desirable, but actually buying a similar item possessing features we may have previously considered undesirable.

1. Internalize all the necessary conditions at the outset, before beginning the design.
2. Internalize the necessary conditions as the design progresses.
3. Internalize the necessary conditions after completing the design.

The third case is clearly absurd, and need not be discussed. The second case is what is happening in practice. Whether or not the second case has to be, necessarily, the case is obviously dependent upon whether or not the first case can be possible. The next section explores this issue.

□ THE PARADOX OF DESIGNING DESIGN SPECIFICATIONS

If we are going to internalize at the outset all the necessary external conditions—the conditions which would make those designs with the "desirable" characteristics undesirable, and those which lack the "desirable" characteristics still desirable—then we must at least know what the external conditions are, or equivalently, what the additional deontic statements necessary for the reliable evaluation of all possible design alternatives are. In other words, for each of the possible deontic statements,* one has to assess (1) the relevancy of the particular deontic statement as a criterion for assessing yet unknown design alternatives, as well as (2) the validity of the particular deontic statement [Kim 1980].†

In order to make these assessments, one has to know the design implications as well as the context for the evaluation. The dilemma is that the particularities of the very design which has yet to be developed, supposedly in accordance with the design specifications consisting of the very deontic statements which are being evaluated, constitute both the design implications and the evaluative context of the deontic statements. Therefore, in order to derive the "perfect," or "complete," specifications for a design, one has to know all the design implications of the specifications, i.e., all the particularities about all the possible design solutions. Likewise, to derive those design solutions, one has to have the very design specifications which has yet to be derived. This is paradoxical [Kim 1984]. The "complete" design specifications is either *impossible* because we do not know enough about their design implications; or *unnecessary* because we already know all about what the design solution is like.

Therefore, design specifications can never be written completely prior to the design. The only remaining possibility for developing design

---

*We already know this is an impossible task. We can never know all the possible statements.
†In addition, we have to assess the acceptability of the side or after effects resulting from attempts to accomplish the goal. See [Kim 1980].

specifications is, then, supplementing and modifying the design specifications, explicitly or implicitly, as the design progresses. And this is exactly what occurs in the practice of design. Such a mode of practice is neither an accident nor a sign of the weakness of specifiers or designers, and follows necessarily from the nature of the design process. Though frustrating, there is essentially no escape from such a mode of practice. We could, however, improve the process. The rest of this paper will explore such a possibility.

☐ SIMULTANEOUS DEVELOPMENT OF THE DESIGN AND THE DESIGN SPECIFICATIONS IN LIGHT OF THE DESIGN INTENT

It is obviously true, in a way, that the design specifications can only be supplemented as the design develops: both the design specifications and the design itself are descriptions of the same thing, and therefore, both are known simultaneously as we find out more and more about the design as we work on it. What the design is, or can be, is also what the design ought to be, because nothing which cannot be can be the way it ought to be. Designing is a process of explorative learning. It begins with knowing nothing about the design solution and ends with knowing "everything" about the solution. Between these two points, there is a successive exploration of what the design possibilities are, what their limitations could be, and what their implications and effects might be, and so on. Through this exploration is the growth of the knowledge which is uniquely relevant to that particular design, and can not be acquired otherwise. At every point in the design process, the designer assesses the potentiality of the design idea, explores and hypothesizes its appropriate developmental directions, further develops and refines the idea enough to see what it might entail, and in light of such insights, assesses whether or not the hypothesized design direction is in fact the right direction.

Such a judgement can not be made entirely within the knowledge derived from the design and the design specifications alone. Design is a goal-oriented activity, and behind every design, there is a specific set of goals which is intended to be achieved through the design. Therefore, the frame of reference for the judgement of the rightness or the wrongness of the direction of the design development is whether or not the goal, or the design intent, can be successfully fulfilled through the particular design idea when fully developed and implemented. More often than not, such intent is not explicit, and needs to be uncovered.

Even when the intent is explicit, whether or not the intent itself is appropriate is still questionable. Intent itself is goal oriented, and behind every intent, there is the higher order intent for which the intent of the lower order is nothing but a means. Perhaps the particular intent might be an appropriate one, or perhaps not. The issues concerning the evaluation of the propriety of design intent have been discussed extensively elsewhere [Kim 1980], and shall not be repeated here, except to say that fulfilling the design intent of a lower order may not necessarily be a desirable solution because the intent of the lower order itself may not be a desirable means of fulfilling the intent of the higher order, even if the higher order intent is, in fact, an appropriate one. An appropriate design approach, then, is one that uncovers the structure of the intent, or the **teleological structure**, as it will be called in this paper, implicit behind the design specifications, and works toward fulfilling the design intent of the "highest order."*

□ INFERENCE OF THE TELEOLOGICAL STRUCTURE AND THE DESIGN INTENT IMPLICIT IN THE DESIGN SPECIFICATIONS

When someone specifies what the design ought to be, the implicit belief in the specifier's mind is:

1. If S_i can be done, then the state S_{i+1} will follow.
2. S_{i+1} ought to be the case.
3. Therefore, S_i is the desirable prescription of the design.

On the other hand, underlying the belief that S_{i+1} is desirable, is the similar belief that:

1. If S_{i+1} can be done, then the state S_{i+2} will follow.
2. S_{i+2} ought to be the case.
3. Therefore, S_{i+1} ought to be the case.

This argument, called the **Teleological Explanation** [Kim 1986] is a way of corroborating the plausibility of one deontic statement by means of another in light of the means-end relationship between the two, and can be expressed in its normal form as follows:

$$[S_i] \leftarrow [S_{i+1}] \wedge (S_{i+1} \leftarrow S_i)$$

where:

*Whether there could be "The Goal of the Highest Order," and what it could be, if it exists, is beyond the scope of this paper. The "highest order" in this paper, is meant to be understood as that point in the teleological structure that a person believes, unquestionably and on its own merit, as desirable.

$[S_i]$: Deontic statement about the state S_i, i.e. S_i ought to be the case.

$[S_{i+1}]$: Deontic statement about S_{i+1}

$(S_{i+1} \leftarrow S_i)$: Factual statement about the cause-effect, or means-end, relationship between S_{i+1} and S_i; i.e. if S_i, then S_{i+1}

In this paper, [ ] denotes a deontic statement, and ( ) denotes a factual statement.

This is read as "S_i ought to be the case because S_{i+1} ought to be the case, and if S_i can be done, then S_{i+1} will follow." In general, the plausibility of a deontic statement $[S_i]$ in light of some "undisputable" deontic statement $[S_{i+n}]$ can be established through a series of teleological explanations as follows:

$$[S_i] \leftarrow [S_{i+1}] \wedge (S_{i+1} \leftarrow S_i)$$
$$[S_{i+1}] \leftarrow [S_{i+2}] \wedge (S_{i+2} \leftarrow S_{i+1})$$
$$[S_{i+2}] \leftarrow [S_{i+3}] \wedge (S_{i+3} \leftarrow S_{i+2})$$

$$\cdots\cdots\cdots$$

$$[S_{i+n-1}] \leftarrow [S_{i+n}] \wedge (S_{i+n} \leftarrow S_{i+n-1})$$

Suppose one prescribes S_i because he/she believes that doing S_i is an efficient way of accomplishing S_{i+n}. Then we can say that S_{i+n} is the implicit design intent behind the explicit design prescription S_i. In this case, the teleological structure behind the design prescription S_i, or the structure of the believed means-end relationships leading from S_i to the accomplishment of S_{i+n}, is:

$$S_i \rightarrow S_{i+1} \rightarrow \cdots \rightarrow S_{i+n}$$

Now, provided that we know the teleological structure implicit behind the design prescription, we can uncover the implicit design intent of the "highest order" behind the design specifications by tracing up the teleological structure. In that case, the structure of the intent can be made readily "visible." When it is "visible," the likelihood of arriving at successful designs can be significantly increased. Therefore, the design would meet the design intent more closely, rather than simply meeting the design specifications which themselves could be an undesirable solution for fulfilling the design intent.

Undoubtedly, the teleological structure is not necessarily linear, or tree-like, but more likely an inter-twined lattice. The implicit design intent, therefore, can be accomplished by more than one means, and each of these means, in turn, could be accomplished by many further means. Similarly, doing one thing is likely to lead to more than one effect, some of which might be desirable, and some of which may not be. As an example, the teleological structure for a hypothetical case may be like the following:

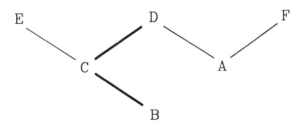

In this example, D and F are both the effects of A (or A is a means to both D and F), B is a means to C, and C is a means to E and D. Suppose F is an undesirable state, and C and E are not undesirable. Further, suppose that D is the design intent behind the explicit design prescription A. In this case, it is clear that C and A are both the means to D. The execution of A, however, will bring the undesirable side effect F, while the execution of C will not. Hence, C is more likely to lead to A more acceptable design than the prescribed means, A. However, one might choose to do B instead of C as a way of fulfilling the design intent D, if such a choice has other benefits, such as being easier to implement, since B is also a means to C. The example illustrates that, if the design intent implicit in the explicit design specifications can be uncovered, then it is more likely to elicit the design prescriptions and design solutions which are more acceptable or more desirable than what is specifically prescribed by the design specifications.

Elsewhere [Kim 1980], it was illustrated that there exists the duality relation between causal relations and teleological relations. To be specific, when [a] and [b] are two deontic statements, and (a) and (b) are two factual statements, such that between (a) and (b) there exists a causal relation, then there also exists a teleological relation between [a] and [b].

For instance, let

a: eating
b: being hungry

Then, from the causal relationship between the state of eating and that of not being hungry, we know that the following holds:

(a) → (¬b).

Now suppose that we have a need not to be hungry, or in other words, ought not to be hungry. Then, provided that eating is the necessary and sufficient condition for not being hungry, we know that we ought to eat. That is to say, the following proposition also holds:

$$[\neg b] \rightarrow [a]$$

Or, we might say that we ought to eat because we ought not to be hungry:

$$[a] \leftarrow [\neg b].$$

Behind this enthymeme, there is the implicit belief about the causal relations between (a) and ($\neg$b):

$$(\neg b) \leftarrow (a)$$

Thus, the complete belief is:

$$[a] \leftarrow [\neg b] \wedge ((\neg b) \leftarrow (a)).$$

This is the teleological explanation of why one ought to eat, and it illustrates the point that from the causal structure of various events, we could:

1. systematically construct the corresponding teleological structure as a duality of the former,
2. derive teleological explanations about our deontic beliefs, and
3. uncover the implicit design intent behind the explicit design specifications by tracing up the teleological structure.

For instance, suppose that one of the design requirements (a specification of how the building ought to be) is being quiet:

[quiet]

Then, suppose that the effect class [Kim 1980] of being quiet, that is, the exhaustive set of the effects; or to be precise, the "believed effect" class (E) of being quiet, is

$$\begin{aligned}
E(quiet) = \ &((\text{less distraction} \cup E(\text{less distraction})); \\
&(\text{serenity} \cup E(\text{serenity})); \\
&(\text{less exciting} \cup E(\text{less exciting}))),
\end{aligned}$$

then the implicit design intent, or the goal (G) behind requiring quiet must consist of one or more of the elements of the effect class. That is,

G(quiet) ⊂ ((less distraction ∪ E(less distraction));
(serenity ∪ E(serenity));
(less exciting ∪ E(less exciting)))

The set can be expanded by replacing its elements with, for example,

E(less distraction) = ((high productivity ∪ E(high productivity));
(being peaceful ∪ E(being peaceful)))

G(quiet) ⊂ ((less distraction;
(high productivity ∪ E(high productivity));
(being peaceful ∪ E(being peaceful));
(serenity ∪ E(serenity));
(less exciting ∪ E(less exciting)))),

In this example, one may find, for instance, that the design intent behind requiring (quiet) is (high productivity). If that is the case, then coming up with the building which is more conducive to high productivity rather than merely being quiet but otherwise not conducive to productivity, is the way the design ought to be. In fact, the resulting building may not be quiet at all.

This kind of design approach, that is, designing for the implicit design intent of the highest order, rather than the explicit design specifications, by tracing up the teleological structure, is a particularly desirable approach. By uncovering the teleological structure of the prescriber, we may even find the errors in the belief about the teleological relations between the events, and therefore find out that the particular design prescription is incorrect. Upon the correct understanding of the teleological relationships, the prescriber him/herself could denounce the particular prescription.

□ DEVELOPMENT OF MACHINE INTELLIGENCE FOR TELEOLOGICAL INFERENCE

The above discussion illustrates a method for uncovering the implicit design intent by tracing up the "believed teleological structure" that is behind the explicit design prescription, which in turn can be discovered or constructed from the cause-effect relationships that hold, or are believed to be held, among various events associated with the design situation. Such a teleological structure can also make the range of design solution possibilities, as well as their implications, readily visible. This can aid the designer or the design prescriber in arriving at more desirable design solutions.

The process discussed above can be greatly enhanced if appropriate machine intelligence can be made available. With the aid of such machine intelligence, we can, as we do with our own brain, almost instantaneously and effortlessly trace up and down a teleological structure to uncover the design intent, assess its propriety, explore the range of possible solution strategies, and deduce their implications. The development of such machine intelligence is within our reach, and particularly promising, with the advancement of super-computing technology.

Efforts at developing such machine intelligence have been made recently under the sponsorship of the US Army Construction Engineering Research Laboratory under the project title *Development of the Goal-Defining Artificial Intelligence System.* The project is one component of a much larger project, *The Design of a Designing Machine*, which includes several other components besides the **Design-Prescriber**, such as the **Design-Information-Inquirer, Design-Idea Generator, Design-Describer**, and the **Design-Prognoser**.

The Designing Machine is essentially a knowledge-based system. The core of the system consists of numerous "knowledge nodules." Various kinds of "associative links" interconnect these knowledge nodules in such a way that the activation of any one nodule and the "firing" of any particular kind of "link" of specific interest automatically activates a host of other nodules. The activated nodules are associated with the initial nodule in the particular way that is represented by the specific type of link.

For instance, an extensive list of reasons why "Privacy" might be wanted can be easily constructed by activating the knowledge nodule "Privacy," and firing the "is-a-means-to" link. The result is the activation of all those nodules which *"Privacy" "is-a-means-to"* (First Order Goal),* all those which *"Privacy" "is-a-means-to" "is-a-means-to"* (Second Order Goal), all those which *"Privacy" "is-a-means-to" "is-a-means-to" "is-a-means-to"* (Third Order Goal), and so on. Also, various strategies of designing for privacy can be found by activating the same nodule "Privacy," but firing, instead, the link of type "means-are." The result is the activation of all those which *"are-means-to" "Privacy"* (First Order Means), all those which *"are-means-to" "means-to" "Privacy"* (Second Order Means), all those which *"are-means-to" "means-to" "means-to" "Privacy"* (Third Order Means), and so on.

Although the only kind of knowledge link needed for the development of Design-Prescriber or Goal-Definer, a component of Designing Machine, is "is-a-means-to" type, the knowledge base itself is being developed with

---

*If circumstance A directly leads to the desired circumstance B, then we say that A is a first-order means to B (A can "produce" B), and B is a first-order goal of A (B can "be produced" by A). However, if A leads to B, and B leads to C (C being the desired circumstance), then A is a second-order means to C, and C is the second-order goal of A.

"eight pronged connections" between the knowledge nodules so that it can support the entire Designing Machine. They are:

"is-a-means-to"
"means-are"
"is-a-part-of"
"is-the-whole-consisting-of-(...)-organized-according-to"
"is-a-crude-version-of"
"is-a-refined-version-of"
"is-the-class-containing"
"is-a-member/subclass-of"

From the operational point of view, the machine is designed to make both the necessary inquiries and the inferences. The purpose of inquiry is two-fold:

1. to learn about the particular user's specific knowledge, right or wrong, pertaining to the design, and his/her value system, so that the machine can properly "advise" the user, and

2. to further enrich the knowledge base.

As for making inferences, the Design-Prescriber is designed to fire the "is-a-means-to" links automatically up to that level of the teleological hierarchy which the user regards as being unchallengably desirable objectives. The machine constructs the resultant truncated teleological structure as an "hypothesis" of the client's or prescriber's likely teleological structure. The user is consulted to confirm or correct this hypothesis. At the same time, the machine asks the user about how strongly he/she feels about various desired ends, thus "mapping" the landscape of the user's value system. This map of the client's value system will play an important role when the machine operates in the "designing mode."

The Designing Machine, when fully developed, is expected to have the capacity to dynamically shift its "attention" from one mode to another such as from prescribing to "idea-generating," and vice versa, depending on the way the design progresses. In the current machine implementation, with several of its components still in their conceptual stages, the machine is (temporarily) set up to shift into the idea-generating mode when, by refusing further challenge of her/his design objectives, the user truncates the tracing of the teleological structure.

The logic of "idea generation" in this system is what may be called "reflexive design," where the kernel of the design idea is "generated" by "associative recall." For the machine to operate on this basis, an efficient machine understandable representation of architectural knowledge is necessary. While neither the full scale study of the architectural knowledge representation nor the development of the design-idea-generator are within the scope of the project described in this paper, some exploratory work has been necessary to assess the viability and developmental direction for designing the designing machine as a whole. The principle of **Reflexive Design** and a **Configurational Descriptive System** enabling symbolic operation and computation have been explored to some extent, and shown to be viable. The following example shows the operational characteristics of the Design-Prescriber. The elementary operational concept of the idea-generation process is illustrated at the end of the example.

□ CONCLUSION AND THE DIRECTIONS FOR FURTHER RESEARCH

Through the project presented in this paper, the viability of the Design Prescriber, or Goal Definer, has been presented as an effective machine intelligence system which can successfully aid the designer uncovering the client's design intent and his/her value structure so that better design solutions can be obtained. The system, however, is still in its experimental stage. To be fully operational, it needs to incorporate a much richer knowledge base. Undoubtedly, "nurturing" the machine with new knowledge will be an ongoing process.

At the same time, other components of the Designing Machine, particularly the Idea-Generator and the Idea-Prognoser, need to be further developed. As this paper discusses, the operational principles of these components have already been conceptualized. However, these systems should be further developed and "materialized," so that proper prognoses and appropriate developmental adjustments can be made in designing the Designing Machine.

Further research must include the work on the development of an innovative machine understandable, and computable, design descriptive language. The language should be appropriate for the description of the design idea while it is still in its embryonic stage. The development of such a language is essential for properly harnessing machine intelligence for design. Efforts are continuing, and the outlook is promising.*

---

*For example, a workshop for the design of a Machine Understandable Design Language was held in April, 1986, at the University of Illinois at Urbana-Champaign. Also, "Innovative Design Descriptions" was chosen as the theme for 1986 Symposium of CIB W78, Working Commission on Integrated Computer-Aided Design. The symposium was held in September, 1986, in Washington, DC. Presently, a computable symbolic design descriptive system is being developed by the author. The outlook is promising, and a primitive version has been utilized in the "Example Run" presented in this paper.

An Example Run

—————————Run—————————   —————————Comments—————————

PLEASE ENTER YOUR DESIGN OBJECTIVE(S).
\>\>\>((QUIET)(PRESTIGE)(PRIVACY))

The client describes what the design ought to be like.

IS THE DESIRABILITY OF (QUIET)
CONTESTABLE? (Y/N \<CR\>)
\>\>\>Y

WHY DO YOU BELIEVE THAT (QUIET)
IS ABSOLUTELY DESIRABLE?
THAT IS, DO YOU HAVE ANY REASONS IN MIND? (Y/N \<CR\>)
\>\>\>N

OKAY, THEN I WILL HELP YOU.

THE FOLLOWING IS A LIST OF POTENTIAL REASONS
IN ADDITION TO THE REASONS YOU HAVE GIVEN
FOR YOUR DESIRING (QUIET):

    1). LOW DISTRACTION.
    2). LACK OF EXCITEMENT.

Machine traces the possible reasons behind the explicit objectives.

TELL ME HOW STRONGLY YOU FEEL THAT THE CASE
SHOULD OR SHOULDN'T BE. INDICATE YOUR ASSESSMENT
BY SELECTING YOUR RATINGS FROM THE MENU BELOW.

Machine requests ratings to aid in mapping the users value structure.

LIST OF EFFECT, IMPLICATIONS							
1). LOW DISTRACTION............	ABS UNDES	HLY UNDES	UNDES	DSN'T MTR	DES	HLY DES	ABS DES
2). LACK OF EXCITEMENT............	ABS UNDES	HLY UNDES	UNDES	DSN'T MTR	DES	HLY DES	ABS DES

DO YOU STILL THINK (QUIET) OUGHT TO
BE THE CASE EVEN IF ALL THE REASONS FOR DESIRING
(QUIET) AS YOU PRESENTED ARE FULFILLED? (Y/N \<CR\>)
\>\>\>N

Machine wants to find out if the explicit objective is desired on its own right, or only as a means of accomplishing something else.

IS THE DESIRABILITY OF (LOW DISTRACTION)
CONTESTABLE? (Y/N \<CR\>)
\>\>\>Y

The implicit objectives are now considered as the desired objectives, and the reasons for such desire are similarly traced.

WHY DO YOU BELIEVE THAT (LOW DISTRACTION)
IS ABSOLUTELY DESIRABLE?
THAT IS, DO YOU HAVE ANY REASONS IN MIND? (Y/N \<CR\>)
\>\>\>N

OKAY, THEN I WILL HELP YOU.

```
THE FOLLOWING IS A LIST OF POTENTIAL REASONS
IN ADDITION TO THE REASONS YOU HAVE GIVEN
FOR YOUR DESIRING (LOW DISTRACTION):

   1). HIGH PRODUCTIVITY.

TELL ME HOW STRONGLY YOU FEEL THAT THE CASE
SHOULD OR SHOULDN'T BE. INDICATE YOUR ASSESSMENT
BY SELECTING YOUR RATINGS FROM THE MENU BELOW.
```

LIST OF EFFECTS IMPLICATIONS	RATING SELECTION						
1). HIGH PRODUCTIVITY.....................	ABS UNDES	HLY UNDES	UNDES	DSN'T MTR	DES	HLY DES	ABS DES

```
IS THE DESIRABILITY OF (PRESTIGE)
CONTESTABLE? (Y/N <CR>)
>>>Y
```

After one original objective has been traced to the user's satisfaction, the next original objective is traced.

```
WHY DO YOU BELIEVE THAT (PRESTIGE)
IS ABSOLUTELY DESIRABLE?
THAT IS, DO YOU HAVE ANY REASONS IN MIND? (Y/N <CR>)
>>>N


OKAY, THEN I WILL HELP YOU.

THE FOLLOWING IS A LIST OF POTENTIAL REASONS
IN ADDITION TO THE REASONS YOU HAVE GIVEN
FOR YOUR DESIRING (PRESTIGE):

   1). HIGH STATUS.
   2). HIGH VISIBILITY.

TELL ME HOW STRONGLY YOU FEEL THAT THE CASE
SHOULD OR SHOULDN'T BE. INDICATE YOUR ASSESSMENT
BY SELECTING YOUR RATINGS FROM THE MENU BELOW.
```

LIST OF EFFECTS IMPLICATIONS	RATING SELECTION						
1). HIGH STATUS....................	ABS UNDES	HLY UNDES	UNDES	DSN'T MTR	DES	HLY DES	ABS DES
2). HIGH VISIBILITY....................	ABS UNDES	HLY UNDES	UNDES	DSN'T MTR	DES	HLY DES	ABS DES

```
ACCORDING TO WHAT YOU HAVE BEEN TELLING ME, IT SEEMS
TO ME THAT YOUR 'REAL' DESIGN OBJECTIVES IMPLICIT
BEHIND THE EXPLICIT INITIAL OBJECTIVES ARE:

   1). HIGH PRODUCTIVITY.    ABSOLUTELY DESIRABLE
   2). HIGH SECURITY.        ABSOLUTELY DESIRABLE
   3). HIGH STATUS.          HIGHLY DESIRABLE
   4). LOW ACCESSIBILITY.    UNDESIRABLE
   5). LACK OF EXCITEMENT.   UNDESIRABLE
   6). HIGH VISIBILITY.      UNDESIRABLE
```

After the teleological structure behind all the originally stated objectives have been traced to the user's satisfaction, the machine presents its hypothesis of the user's implicit design intent.

DO YOU HAVE ANY MORE DESIGN OBJECTIVES TO ADD? (Y/N <CR>)
>>>N

The machine requests the user's confirmation, or correction if necessary, of the machine's hypothesis about the user's design intent.

WOULD YOU LIKE TO MODIFY THE LIST OF
IMPLICIT OBJECTIVES? (Y/N <CR>)
>>>N

DO YOU HAVE ANY DESIGN STRATEGIES IN MIND
THAT WOULD FULFILL THE ABOVE OBJECTIVES? (Y/N <CR>)
>>>N

The machine enters the "idea-generating" mode. In future implementations, "idea-generating" and "value mapping" will become more intertwined.

OK. I WILL TRY TO HELP YOU FIND SOME.

HERE IS A LISTING OF POSSIBLE MEANS:

   1). OFFICE TYPE 4.

THIS IS THE TREE OF EFFECTS/IMPLICATIONS/PROPERTIES
OF (OFFICE TYPE 4)

   1). HIGH SECURITY.
   2). HIGH PRODUCTIVITY.
   3). HIGH STATUS.
   4). LOW COST.

The machine presents its "idea" about how the user's design intent could be fulfilled, based on what it knows about "what can do what," "what is like what," etc.

In addition, the machine presents what it "knows" about the particular solution so that the user may make a more informed design decision.

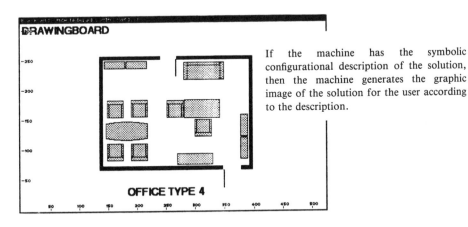

If the machine has the symbolic configurational description of the solution, then the machine generates the graphic image of the solution for the user according to the description.

```
WHAT DO YOU THINK?

PLEASE DECIDE ON ONE OF THE FOLLOWING
WITH RESPECT TO (OFFICE TYPE 4).

    A). I WOULD LIKE TO FURTHER DEVELOP THIS IDEA.

    B). IT IS INTERESTING, BUT LET'S SEE WHAT THE
        NEXT STRATEGY, IF AVAILBLE, IS LIKE.

    C). THIS STRATEGY IS NOT WORTH PURSUING ANY FURTHER.
>>>A
```

The user is asked to assess the whole situation, make appropriate decisions, and direct the machine.

☐ REFERENCES

Kim M.K. "The Structure of Inquiry and Explanations in Design," a paper presented at the Workshop on Machine Understandable Design Language, University of Illinois, Champaign, IL. April 1986, Being edited for publication.

Kim M.K. *Appropriate Directions for the Application of Artificial Intelligence to Building Design and Evaluation,* A Report for the U.S. Army Construction Engineering Research Laboratory, Champaign, IL, 1984b.

Kim M.K. Unpublished lecture (on tape, being transcribed) for the Course, Architecture 15-8b, "Logics of Design/Planning," Harvard University, Graduate School of Design, Cambridge, MA, Spring 1984a.

Kim M.K. *Counter-Modeling as a Strategy for Decision Making: Epistemological Problems in Design,* Dissertation, Berkeley, CA: University of California, Berkeley, 1980.

Musso A. and H. Rittel "Uber das Messen der Gute von Gebauden," in Jurgen Joedicke (ed.), *Bewertungsprobleme in der Bauplanung,* vol. 1 of *Arbeitsberichte zur Planungsmethodik,* Stuttgart: K. Kramer, 1969.

Rittel H.W.J. Unpublished lecture for the course, Architecture 130, "Introduction to Design Methods," University of California, Berkeley, CA: Fall, 1974.

6

MODELS OF SPATIAL INFORMATION IN COMPUTER-AIDED ARCHITECTURAL DESIGN: A COMPARATIVE STUDY

Patricia G. McIntosh

School of Architecture
Arizona State University
Tempe, Arizona

This paper explores the nature of spatial information as it is represented and used for decision making in architectural design. The point of departure for this discussion is a well known model of design problem solving. The vehicle for this investigation is the comparison of four paradigms for computer-aided design systems. The conceptual models for computer-aided architectural design and the spatial models incorporated in these models are discussed. Two major aspects of spatial modeling are investigated: the representation of spatial relationships and the generation of form. Finally, directions for future research in this area are outlined.

☐ INTRODUCTION

Facile spatial manipulation of a design with the aid of a computer is a long-standing goal of comprehensive computer-aided design systems [Sutherland 1963; Mitchell 1977]. Because of the nature of architectural design, and for reasons of economy and consistency, a computer-aided design system should support the transformation of the evolving design through the stages of the design process, from schematic design to final production drawings. In addition to representing the shapes that compose a design, the system should also represent the interelationships between, and the constraints on, the spaces that give meaning to spatial configurations. The system should also allow for the manipulation of this information at semantic levels appropriate for architectural design.

As spatial modeling tools, two-dimensional drawings and automated systems that focus on renderings of the building, whose databases are static collections of lines, fall short of this goal. The attachment of labels and nongeometric attributes, such as bill-of-materials information, to these line assemblies is but an evolutionary progenitor to the spatial semantics that are actually required to model the designer's intentions about space or to simulate spaces as they exist in reality.

The possible nature of the ideal design tool ranges from a passive modeling tool to an intelligent design partner [Kalay 1985]. Such models would undoubtedly be very complex, perhaps beyond the limits of present day theory and technology. However, the combination of advances made in geometric modeling in the past two decades and developments in the fields of artificial intelligence and cognitive science auger a bright future for understanding and modeling decision-making in architectural design.

This paper explores the nature of spatial information as it is represented and used for decision making in architectural design. The point of departure for this discussion is a well known model of design problem solving. The vehicle for this investigation is the comparison of four paradigms for computer-aided design systems. The conceptual models for computer-aided architectural design and the spatial models incorporated in these models are discussed. Two major aspects of spatial modeling are investigated: the representation of spatial relationships and the generation of form. Finally, directions for future research in this area are outlined.

□ EFFICACY OF DRAWINGS AS DESIGN TOOLS

One motivation for the study of spatial models of buildings is the inadequacy for computation of traditional means of communicating spatial information in designs. Two-dimensional drawings are limited; they do not explicitly or completely model even the three-dimensional geometry. Present day so-called CAD systems are limited in the breadth and depth of the design process to which they can be applied. Automated systems designed to produce working drawings are not design tools. Automated manipulation of two-dimensional renderings has limitations similar to the manual production of drawings: the semantically rich part of the model remains in the designer's mind.

Architectural drawings are spatially fragmented (the plan view is detached from the front and side views). Fragmentation is problematic when updating drawings, for spatial information changed in one view must be changed in the other views as well, and there is no way to guarantee that the separate views will be consistent. As drawings change, the implications of the change to other parts of the design are not automatically propagated. As iconic models drawings lack the structure to be manipulated in a semantically sophisticated fashion.

Drawings also are inadequate representations of constraints on spaces and of relationships between spaces. As much spatial information is implicit, an expert individual must mentally assemble the three-dimensional model. Drawings show just the geometrical configurations; the meaning of the juxtaposition is not contained in the drawing itself and must be inferred (cursory labels such as room names are considered sufficient annotation to imply relationships).

On the other hand, the advantages of drawings are their conciseness, portability, and simple production requirements. The creation of drawings seems to help designers understand space and spatial relationships. The hand sketch is semantically charged: although its geometry is inexact, it is precisely this rough-edged character that assists the designer in externalizing preconceptions of spatial organization.

Thus, it is not the implicit nature of much of the information about the design as it is represented in a drawing that is problematic. It is because of the way this information is represented, that much of the information about the design is not automatically or computationally accessible for the kinds of design tasks for which it is required.

☐ THE NATURE OF SPATIAL INFORMATION

In architectural design spatial information is ubiquitous; it is the milieu of the designer and it is something to be manipulated in the designers' mind and on paper as naturally as language itself. However, when one seeks to externalize the design for computational purposes, either the cognitive structures that the designer uses to create these models must be discovered and mimiced, or systems that contain models that designers would find natural and convenient to use must be developed [Coyne 1985].

Spatial information consists of the shapes that are used to delineate space, the spaces between the shapes, the relationships of the shapes and the spaces to each other, and the meaning or purpose attached to the spaces and their relationships. This meaning is what is often referred to as the semantics of architectural space. The semantics of space are derived from many sources and are manifest at many levels of abstraction. In the overall design of a building, the architect may intend to express some broad cultural sentiment. Typically, within this statement there will be several primary functions that require spatial expression. Other spaces may then be required to link and support the primary spaces. In addition, the technological subsystems, from enclosure to plumbing, will require spatial consideration to permit them to function as a whole.

The nature of mans' relationship to physical objects in the world and his perception of those objects has been a preoccupation of philosophy for all of history. Daley [1984] conjectures that the fundamental processes by which designers design is innate and beyond the capability of linguistic discourse to describe. In his essay, "The Structure of Ill-Structured Problems," Simon speculates that one of the mechanisms by which architects solve complex design problems has to do with the structure of the a priori knowledge that they have about designs that work [Simon 1984]. More recently, the emerging field of cognitive science has begun to examine, not the biological apparatus, but the cognitive structures that must necessarily be present in the human mind for people to solve problems in the fashion that they do [Pylyshyn 1985; Akin 1982; Sowa 1984].

□ A MODEL OF DESIGN PROBLEM SOLVING

Architectural design has been characterized as a "wicked" problem [Rittel 1984] because the initial design problem is usually incompletely specified and often enfolds only as the design proceeds. Even when a solution is reached, it is frequently difficult to test whether the solution is an appropriate one.

Simon [1984] has defined a general problem solver, which requires the following information in order to work on a problem:

1. a description of the solution state, or a test to determine if that state has been reached;
2. a set of terms for describing and characterizing the initial state, goal state and intermediate states;
3. a set of operators to change one state into another, together with conditions for the applicability of these operators;
4. a set of differences, and tests to detect the presence of these differences between pairs of states;
5. a table of connections associating with each difference one or more operators that is relevant to reducing or removing that difference.

Simon characterizes the architectural design problem as a combination of a general problem solver, working on a well-structured subproblem, and a retrieval system that continually modifies the problem space by evoking new constraints and sub-goals. The problem solving system operates in a serial fashion, using only small amounts of information at any one time. He asserts that the comprehensive structure of the problem is not known at the outset of problem solving: it evolves over time.

☐ PARADIGMS FOR COMPUTER-AIDED ARCHITECTURAL DESIGN

Since spatial modeling is but one aspect of design, a discussion of models of the overall design problem process is appropriate. The purpose of this overview is to give a context to spatial modeling as it is carried out within the whole in the design process, and to identify how it is influenced by the overall process of design.

Mitchell Model

Mitchell [1977] advances a paradigm for computer-aided architectural design as a design problem characterized by:

- a data structure, which consists of variables describing the relevant properties of potential solutions.
- a set of operators, which may be applied to variables to change the state of the data structure. These operators, together with the rules of their application, define a state-action graph, and implicitly establish a set U of potential solutions;
- a set of constraints and/or objectives that defines a goal set G of acceptable solutions;
- a solution generation procedure that produces a set S of potential solutions for consideration. S may or may not intersect G.

This comprehensive CAAD system would be used for the storage and retrieval of design data, automatic generation of solutions to well-defined problems, and evaluation of solutions.

Eastman Model

Eastman proposes "abstractions" as a conceptual approach to design with a CAD system. A design abstraction is defined to consist of [Eastman 1985]:

- Design data
- a set of operations or other tools to manipulate the data;
- a set of relations that is always maintained in the data;
- a set of tests and performance conditions that can be evaluated from the data.

Mappings would exist between abstractions as different abstractions might have different data types.

Eastman characterizes an abstraction as a design sub-language. The entities in an abstraction consist of building components such as walls, doors and windows. The entities for a particular abstraction are identifiable by the condition that they are individually created or manipulated or that they have relationships with other entities in the abstraction. The relations between the entities are managed by the abstraction. The operations in an abstraction include mappings from previous abstractions, definition of design alternatives, and editing functions to transform one design alternative into another. The sequence of abstractions forms a procedural net.

Kalay Model

Kalay [1985] has developed a conceptual framework for a knowledge-based computer-aided design system. It consists of two major components: a planning component and a design state representation component.

The planning component is responsible for directing the design process from beginning to end. It consists of a sequence of goals, a set of evaluation procedures, and a controller that employs heuristics to determine the next goal to be achieved.

The second major component is the design state representation component, which keeps track of the design as it emerges and maintains its integrity. The design state representation consists of a database that stores the objects being designed and the links between them, and a consistency maintenance subsystem that maintains database integrity by propagating changes brought about by transitions in design states.

Coyne-Gero Model

Coyne [1986] and Gero propose a three-layer linguistic model of the design process for layout planning in buildings consisting of a language of form, a language of actions, and a language of plans.

The first layer, the language of form, is generally what has become known as a shape grammar. This grammar does not operate on building components, but uses dimensionless spaces as vocabulary elements. The second layer is a language of actions, that provides control for the language of form. The relationships among actions, both serial and parallel are represented as a procedural net. The third layer is a language of plans which is described as dealing with meta-planning knowledge. This level provides a way of ordering the actions in the second level. Its grammar consists of scheduling rules. The structure of these plans is a hierarchical graph.

Comparison of Overall Models

Mitchell's formulation, the earliest of the four, contains the basic components of a CAAD problem solving system. It contains, for example, the concept of a solution generation procedure, whose counterpart in later models is the hierarchically structured planning component. In the Eastman model this top level planning component is absent: each abstraction is independent from all others, except for mappings to other abstractions. The knowledge about other abstractions is contained within an abstraction itself. The Kalay and Coyne-Gero models both contain top-level planning components that determine the order in which design goals will be solved. Both of these planning models create a hierarchy of goals and subgoals. In the Kalay model the design phases constitute a sequence of goals, with each goal being made up of a hierarchy of subgoals. The planning language in the Coyne-Gero model serves a similar purpose. Coyne and Gero [Coyne 1986] state :

> The levels within this graph make explicit the semantic relationships between the tasks. They can be considered as similar to macro operators in a structured computer program or, in this context, it is perhaps more meaningful to talk about a schedule of tasks.

☐ MODELS OF SPATIAL INFORMATION

The previous discussion created a framework within which to view spatial modeling. The decisions that affect the definition of space occur at a level below the uppermost planning level, though the upper level certainly affects spatial decisions. Thus, having set the stage with the overall design process, the spatial aspects of each model will now be addressed.

Mitchell Model

Mitchell [1977] outlines a symbolic description of space that consists of elements, attributes associated with elements, relations between elements, and the organization of subsets of elements into hierarchies:

> The elements employed as the basis for a description might, for example, be abstract geometric entities such as square or cubic modules, functional elements such as rooms, or physical components such as columns, beams, and slabs. For different purposes, it is appropriate to utilize descriptions based upon different types of entities. Thus a circulation analysis might employ a description of a building as a set of rooms, while a structural analysis would employ a description in terms of physical components.

He gives a partial list of attributes of an element as geometric; such as dimensions or location; physical, such as weight or thermal conductivity; and economic, such as cost or availability. He notes in passing the dilemma of explicitly storing versus computing some attributes.

Relations between elements mentioned are adjacency requirements, connections between rooms, and structural connections. With respect to relationships, he again notes the dilemma of explicit versus implicit representation.

A possible organization of elements is described as subsets of hierarchies [Mitchell 1977]:

> For example, we might say that a building consists of (owns) a set of major departments, each department owns a set of suites, each suite owns a set of rooms, each room owns a set of surfaces, each surface owns a set of components, and so on. Different design algorithms may utilize descriptions at different levels in such a hierarchy. For instance, a site plan layout algorithm might appropriately treat a building as a set of major wings to be located while a detailed cost analysis algorithm would treat it as a set of components. For this reason, comprehensive building descriptions which are intended to be operated upon by a variety of different algorithms are typically structured in hierarchical fashion.

He also notes the use of instances of elements to eliminate repetition in the stored building description.

Eastman Model

Eastman does not set out a formal spatial model, but gives examples of some early development work on a schematic design system [Eastman 1985]. He gives examples of three abstractions that were developed in this work, that at the time they were developed, were meant to be used serially with no provision for backtracking to deal with inconsistencies.

The first abstraction consisted of single-line floor plans, the elements of which were walls, doors, and windows. The spaces formed by the walls were given labels. A hierarchy of windows and doors embedded in walls was maintained. The wall connectivity that formed spaces was also maintained. The second abstraction incorporated the elements and relationships of the first and added sections for walls, doors, and windows, and floor/ceiling sections and floor-to-ceiling heights. The third abstraction transformed the two-dimensional floor plans along with floor-to-ceiling heights into a three-dimensional model.

Eastman notes some shortcomings of the system, most of which relate to inflexibility of the decision making process and the way that relationships were maintained. He points out, for example, that facades were determined by floor plans and could not be evaluated directly, and that constraints of earlier abstractions could not be modified by a later one. Useful insights into the design decision making process were gained [Eastman 1985]:

> Some decision sequences were unrealistic. For example, wall sections were defined prior to assignment. In reality, wall sections are typically defined as a secondary product of the desired finishes desired for different spaces. It is the two spaces on each side of a wall that determine wall construction, especially finishes, not the other way around.

Kalay Model

Kalay discusses the symbolic description of the building as a design state representation. In this model the design state component of a system consists of a database in which is stored the objects and the links between them, and a consistency maintenance sub-system that insures by propagating changes that the integrity of the database is maintained [Kalay 1985]:

> The database comprises the symbolic representation of objects and assemblies, and the relationships between them. It stores not only the objects and the links that represent design states, but also most of the knowledge that pertains to them. Every object includes both descriptive and functional knowledge: the descriptive knowledge is comprised of the form and the other properties of the object, such as geometrical information, location, material, cost, etc. The functional knowledge describes how the object should be manipulated and used, and what the relationships are between the various parameters. Together, these two kinds of knowledge constitute an 'abstract data type', a term coined by program language developers to describe a consistent unit of information. Links between individual objects transform them into a network of interrelated parts of one whole.

Kalay describes three kinds of links between objects: part-whole, master-instance and group. The part-whole relationship links objects into a hierarchy similar to the one described by Mitchell. This relationship provides a way of propagating locational change information.

The master-instance relationship puts every object into a class of objects. The class has a set of characteristics that apply to both data and operations. An instance has a set of parameters such as size, location, and orientation. The master-instance relation eliminates redundancy and thus enhances the integrity of the database. It also is a means of propagating change: if the master object changes, so do all the instances. Selective inheritance of master properties by the instance is also mentioned.

Group relationships are described as the most general kind of relationship. These relationships bind together sets of objects that share some common property. This is a way of linking objects for change propagation in both directions. The example given is the relationship that expresses a perpendicularity constraint between two walls: if either of the walls is moved, the other must be moved accordingly. This relationship is contrasted with part-whole and master-instance in that it must be explicitly defined, whereas the former types of relationships are implicit. A conditional component of this relationship is also described where the relationship is either exercised or relaxed depending on the nature of the change.

Coyne-Gero Model

In the linguistic paradigm of design proposed by Coyne and Gero, the languages of form and action most directly generate the spatial representation. The language of form generates some of the geometric and topological information for shapes and spaces of a layout, while the language of actions creates configurations of spaces and this contributes the architectural semantics to the layout. An interesting aspect of the language of form is the use of dimensionless spaces rather than a vocabulary of building elements [Coyne 1986]:

> There may be any number of ways of formulating object level grammars, but a useful type of rule is that which takes dimensionless spaces as vocabulary elements and operates on these. This is an attempt to capture something of the "fluidity" of spatial representation during the design phase.

The language of actions that operates on the dimensionless spaces adds context to the shapes. An example is given where the shapes are assigned variable names and a predicate 'put' indicates where the shapes should be placed in relation to each other. For example

```
put bathroom east_of bedroom
put dining_room east_of kitchen and north_of living_room
```

The effect of the language of actions is described as follows [Coyne 1986]:

> Rules that transform states can also be regarded as actions. These actions constitute a language of actions. In this language the way in which the action operates (as rules) can be ignored. So we only consider their names. The relationship between these actions, however, is important. The "artifact" (final state) of the language consists of a sequence of actions that provides the control for the language of form. There are two useful relationships to consider: serial and parallel relationships. In serial relationships actions are configured in the order in which they are to be executed. In parallel relationships actions are arranged in groups as conjunctions and disjunctions. It is therefore possible to represent actions with varying degrees of commitment to order. These relationships can be represented in a procedural network.

☐ COMPARISON OF SPATIAL MODELS

Mitchell Model

The Mitchell model offers some basic insights into the representation of spatial information. It is the earliest of the four models; as such, it lacks the benefit of recent research in artificial intelligence. However, based as it is on a model of problem solving that has endured [Simon 1969], it has all of the essential ingredients of later models.

Eastman Model

The Eastman model uses the notion of abstract data type to represent, not single objects in a design, but the entire design state. The motivation for the abstraction definition appears to be the packaging of convenient sets of objects, object relationships, and evaluations for a particular stage within a design process, for implementation purposes. This has intuitive appeal as a way of representing designs at different stages of development, and different degrees of form definition.

One of the components of an abstraction is the set of operations required to create and change the design state. It appears that this component contains the actual operation, rather than just descriptive functional knowledge about how the operations affect the design. From a conceptual point of view, the lack of separation between the design state representation and the means of its creation is questionable.

Kalay Model

The design state representation of Kalay gives a conceptual framework with which to understand the organization of space in a design of a building. Of the four models, this one gives the clearest and most complete account of a design state. The design state is represented as objects and the links between objects. An object includes descriptive knowledge and functional knowledge, which together are characterized as an abstract data type. The definition and classification of object links as part-whole, master-instance, and group provide an encompassing set of relationships with which to structure objects into a whole building. It is conceptually appealing that, by their nature, the part-whole and master-instance relationships provide for model consistency. The group relationship, even in the simplest of examples, poses as yet unanswered design state transition problems. Finally, the separation of the design state from the process of design gives much needed clarity of representation.

Coyne-Gero Model

The Coyne-Gero model is a very interesting experiment in the explicit representation of semantic knowledge. In fact, only some of the semantics are made explicit. In the examples given, only one kind of object link is used, the group link as defined by Kalay. The 'put' operator establishes relationships of next-to, north-of, south-of, east-of, and west-of. When an object is located (put) with any of these relationships, other objects with other links are potentially affected. The obvious question then is: what is the structure of these interrelationships, or alternatively, how are the ripple effect dependencies found?

This is not necessarily an implementation problem: it may be more readily dealt with as a representation problem. In terms of representation one can either represent all object links explicitly or perhaps employ an inference mechanism to deduce the existence of relationships. The implication here is that by making some relationships at a certain level explicit, other relationships that were not explicitly represented can then be inferred.

The interface of the language of form to the semantics of the language of actions speaks to the difficult problem of specifying appropriate geometries with which to represent design concepts as they emerge. The rewriting rules of language may be a way of specifying transitions from more abstract representations of design concepts to more concrete ones.

This model does not separate a design state from the transformations required to generate a design. However, it should be possible to create a separate symbolic representation from the the language, although this is not discussed by Coyne and Gero. By the same token, the state transitions in the Kalay model could be stored, to give essentially the same kind of information as is given in the Coyne-Gero language model.

☐ SPATIAL SEMANTICS AND THE REPRESENTATION OF FORM

One of the most significant problems to be faced in the development of computer-aided design systems is the present inability to incorporate rich geometric models into rich design decision making models. Eastman [1985] points out this difficulty with respect to solid modeling techniques. The difficulty is the degree of specificity of geometric information required to define such models. Solid models are too well defined for the early stages of design, where line drawings or graphs more appropriately describe the initial definition of space.

One approach to the incremental definition of space is the Euler operations [Baumgart 1974]. These operations were developed in the context of machine vision. Their virtue is that they build mathematically correct three-dimensional polyhedral descriptions out of simple elements: vertices, edges, and faces.

Another approach to the provision of a rich set of geometric operations to be used at various stages of design is described by this author [McIntosh 1982]. This approach extends the boolean operations to operate on graphs, polygons, and polyhedra. Regularized operations between the different object types are defined.

Yet another approach to the requirement for different types of geometric information at the different stages of design can be found in mechanical engineering [Henderson 1984]. This scheme shows how contextual features relevant to mechanical part design, such as fillets and pockets, can be extracted from existing mathematical polyhedral models.

Of the four models, Eastman and Coyne-Gero deal explicitly with the problem of fitting the representation and generation of form into an overall model of the design process. The Eastman model addresses the very difficult problem of definition of geometry from abstract to more concrete representations of form. Although the Eastman experience points out some of the geometric transition problems, no formal model of these transitions is forthcoming. Although Eastman's abstractions are intended to deal with this problem, their description does not include a full account of how this would be accomplished.

The resolution of this problem is significant because it lies at the heart of the geometric modeling problem in computer-aided architectural design. If total regeneration of geometry at each phase of design is to be avoided, this type of design state transition must somehow be resolved.

Eastman also points out the problem of coordinating relationships established in one abstraction with those established in succeeding ones. He suggests that some mechanism for backtracking must be established to deal with situations of this type. It is in this regard, the lack of an explicit and separate planning component to coordinate design state transitions, that the abstraction model is most problematic.

The Kalay model, with its planning component and consistency maintenance subsystem, at least offers a formal mechanism for dealing with transition problems. This model, by its explicit representation of a design state, which is separated from the procedural aspects of its generation, gives an indication of how the transition problem might be approached.

In the Coyne-Gero model, the language of form addresses the difficulty of choosing appropriate geometric entities for particular stages of design. What is noteworthy in this model is the integration of a shape grammar into the larger model of the design process. However, the issue of transition from more to less abstract geometric models is not discussed. Though the layered linguistic formalism ties the design process into a neat package, further experiments with this model are necessary in order to understand its implications in a broader context than the plan layout example presented.

☐ DIRECTIONS FOR FUTURE RESEARCH

In order to build better computer-aided design systems, a sound theoretical basis must be established. One aspect of this is the human cognitive structures and mechanisms for solving design problems and for understanding space. Related to this and contingent upon it is the continuing development of paradigms for computer-aided design systems.

In spatial modeling several more specific problems have emerged. The first is the structuring of design state representations to contain appropriate semantic levels of information for computation. A closely related problem is that of representing the geometry of space at appropriate levels of abstraction. A clearer understanding of the structure of goal and constraint satisfaction is also required. The final problem is that of finding transitions between different spatial representations.

☐ CONCLUSIONS

The immediate objective of this study was to gain an understanding of the state of the art in the development of paradigms for computer-aided design in general and spatial modeling in particular. Since the introduction of the Mitchell model a decade ago, the theory of computer-aided design systems has developed very slowly. It was not until the mid-eighties, when the results of research in artificial intelligence were applied to the computer-aided design problem, that this theory took a quantum leap forward. Until this time there were few appropriate techniques with which to model the architectural design problem in a comprehensive way. Parts of this process, such as, geometric modeling, computer graphic renderings, and energy and structural analyses, are relatively well-understood. Findings from AI research begin to provide the necessary tools with which to tackle the "wicked" part of the architectural design problem.

☐ ACKNOWLEDGMENT

This work was supported in part by a National Science Foundation Grant #MSM-8504886.

☐ REFERENCES

Akin O. *Models of Architectural Knowledge: An Information, Processing View of Architectural Design,* Ph.D. dissertation, Carnegie-Mellon University, 1979.

Baumgart B. *Geometric Modeling for Computer Vision,* Ph.D. dissertation, Stanford University, 1974.

Coyne R.D. and J.S. Gero "Design Knowledge and Sequential Plans," *Environment and Planning B,* 12:401-418, 1985.

Coyne R.D. and J.S. Gero "Semantics and the Organization of Knowledge in Design," *Design Computing,* 1(1):68-89, 1986.

Dalay J. "Design Creativity and the Understanding of Objects," *Developments in Design Methodology,* ed. N. Cross, John Wiley, pp. 291-302.

Eastman C.M. "A Conceptual Approach for Structuring Interaction with Interactive CAD Systems," *Computers and Graphics,* 9(2):97-105, 1985.

Henderson M.R. *Extraction of Feature Information from Three-Dimensional CAD DATA,* Ph.D. dissertation, Purdue University, 1984.

Hillier B., J. Musgrove and P. O'Sullivan "Knowledge and Design," *Developments in Design Methodology,* ed. N. Cross, John Wiley, pp. 245-264, 1984.

Kalay Y.E. "Redefining the role of computers in architecture: from drafting/modelling tools to knowledge-based design assistants," *CAD J.,* 17(7):319-328, September 1985.

McIntosh P.G. *The Geometric Set Operations in Computer-Aided Building Design,* Arch.D. dissertation, College of Architecture and Urban Planning, University of Michigan, 1982.

Mitchell W.J. *Computer-Aided Architectural Design,* Van Nostrand Reinhold, 1977.

Pylyshyn Z.W. *Computation and Cognition,* MIT Press, 1984.

Rittel H.W. and M.M. Webber "Planning Problems are Wicked Problems," *Developments in Design Methodology,* ed. N. Cross, John Wiley, pp. 135-166, 1984.

Simon H.A. *The Sciences of the Artificial,* MIT Press, 1969.

Simon H.A. "The Structure of Ill-structured Problems," *Developments in Design Methodology,* ed. N. Cross, John Wiley, pp. 145-166, 1984.

Sowa J.F. *Conceptual Structures,* Addison-Wesley, 1984.

Sutherland I.E. "Sketchpad: A Man-Machine Graphical Communication System," *Proc. SJCC,* 23:329-346, 1963.

7

FUNDAMENTAL PROBLEMS IN THE DEVELOPMENT OF COMPUTER-BASED ARCHITECTURAL DESIGN MODELS

Charles M. Eastman

Formative Technologies
Pittsburgh, Pennsylvania

Solid modeling promised to revolutionize architectural design by providing a single unified database for a complete building description, which could be used for automatic generation of drawings and as a basis for various analyses. The promised revolution has, however, not been realized, for reasons inherent to architectural drawings and practice, rather than to the inadequacy of solid modeling itself.

Drawings are context-dependent abstractions of the designed artifact. Therefore they cannot be generated simply by sectional projections from a solid model. Attempts to automatically extract drawing information from solid models have been made, but they suffer from various limitations.

Drawings allow "fuzziness" in defining the artifact, which solid modeling does not. This fuzziness facilitates joint decision making among architects, engineers, and builders, each of whom can elaborate parts of the design that were left undefined by the other.

A more realistic role for solid modeling in architectural design is their use as one of several means of representation, along with 2D drawings and physical scale models.

□ INTRODUCTION

In the early 1970's, research in architectural computer-aided design became directed towards a revolutionary set of objectives:

- To allow users to design directly in three dimensions, using solids modeling. The solids model would allow complete development, from schematic design through construction drawings.
- To produce plans, sections and elevations automatically, as sectional orthographic projections from the 3-D model.
- To associate material and other properties with each shape, so as to allow integration of energy, lighting, structural and other forms of analyses in the computer-aided designing process.

The goal was to create a new design medium that would greatly enhance the capabilities of designers. The rationale for such a development seemed obvious*:

- The only way to guarantee that all the drawings of a project would be geometrically consistent was to base them on a single 3-D model. All projections made from the model would represent a single 3-D layout.
- Architects are creating 3-D objects. Solids modeling provides the capability to directly view in perspective the results of candidate designs; thus it should be a more appropriate design medium than any limited to the 2-D of paper and pencil.
- Working in 3-D should prove more effective than using multiple 2-D presentations, by allowing the integration of lighting, energy and a number of other analyses in the decision-making process. Design thus would be enriched by more powerful analytical tools.
- A full 3-D model would allow designers to expand their role in the building process. They could check interferences, provide better information for cost estimation, and otherwise gain better control over projects.

Many researchers developed tools that contributed to the realization of this goal.† The goal seemed accomplishable, and the revolution imminent.

---

*An early presentation of this concept was given by the author in: "The use of computers instead of drawings in building design," *Journal of the American Institute of Architects*, pp. 46-50, March 1975.
†Other early expositions on computerized building models were: D.P. Greenberg, "Computer graphics in architecture," *Scientific American*, pp. 98-105, May 1974, and William Mitchell's book *Computer-Aided Architectural Design*, Petrocelli Charter Press, 1977.

Over ten years have now elapsed since this goal was identified and, while solids modeling has become readily available on low-cost computing equipment, and the ability now exists to gain quicker perspective views of candidate designs, this approach to architectural design has not be fulfilled.

In this paper, I present my view of why this goal will not be achieved in the near term. In doing so, I will relate a set of new research issues that must either be resolved or re-defined if the computer is to significantly advance as a design tool.

□ THE DIFFERENCE BETWEEN GEOMETRIC PROJECTIONS AND CONSTRUCTION DRAWINGS

It may have been thought that the main reason architects did not directly design in 3-D is the lack of adequately flexible representations for 3-D design. Clay, chipboard and other physical materials are too rigid and incorporate structural and other constraints that do not allow the flexibility needed for design. It should be noted however, that some architects, for example Antonio Gaudi, relied on 3-D models for much of their design work. And models are used heavily today for detail studies and massing studies. As has been learned with solids modeling, the representational medium was not the issue.

It was originally expected that the generation of construction drawings could be automated. That is, the description of a building in the form of a computerized 3-D model was to be the authoritative representation of the design. It would incorporate an unambiguous shape definition of all elements, their light reflectances and their engineering properties. From this model could be extracted an infinite number of reports. Plans and elevations could be thought of as examples of geometric reports in plan, section, elevation or other formats (similar, in a sense, to graphs generated from business data). Many other reports and analyses could be generated from a fully defined geometric model, including complete material lists, isometric and exploded views, examination of different construction sequences, evaluation of spatial conflicts among erection equipment and robots, and so on.

The electronic building model was expected to become the contract document that is transmitted to the contractor and owner. Contractors could then generate drawings and reports as required: perspectives, exploded isometrics, sections, plans, as needed by different members of the building team. Owners could use the model for a wide variety of evaluations, including review of layouts with their staff, planning work flow, and so on.

It was recognized that institutional obstacles were involved with accomplishing this goal. Drawings are recognized as legal documents, while computer models are not. Liability insurance of architects covers certain information which is usually represented in drawings; it certainly does not cover all of the information represented in a computer model. But it was assumed that these social issues would be resolved if the benefits to society were evident.

But there are many other issues that have kept models from being practically used as a base for the generation of drawings: issues of how design decisions are made, and how information is presented.

Design decisions rely upon a pre-defined and fixed set of presentation formats, where each entity is defined graphically multiple times, once for each format. Model driven, automatic drawing generation thus consists of extracting the right presentation format for each entity; which is either stored explicitly in the model or must be computed from it and from a set of presentation rules. Hidden line removal can be provided when desired, and notes and dimensions may be added to the projection in which they are to be presented.

Examples of systems that incorporate automatic drawing generation based on explicitly stored presentation formats are the Computervision CADDS-4X, and the McAuto BDS systems. The strengths of these systems are their good treatment of textual notes and dimensions; and rapid display of formatted drawing information. Their shortcomings are their poor support for defining new construction components (whose presentation must be explicitly defined for each format); preventing user-modification of presentation formats; difficulty in generating not-to-scale drawings (such as are required for structural and piping drawings); and lack of support for complex presentation formats (such as floor plans where changes in ceiling height are shown as dotted lines).

Another approach to automatic generation of drawing is procedural, rather than data driven. This approach uses procedures that, when executed, compute the desired presentation convention from data they extract from the model about each entity, and from rules stored outside the specific model (such as orthographic, centerline presentation of walls, or their replacement with symbols). Line weights can be computed from a set of assignment rules; then projected, possibly with hidden lines removed, on the selected projection plan.

An example of systems that use procedural drawing generation is the Calma DDM system. Its strengths are consistency with the concept of a database schema with multiple views; allowing easy user-definition of new construction components; and allowing user definition of new presentation formats. Its weaknesses are the high cost of computing a new set of drawing presentations. Layout of textual and dimensional information is also a problem, as the drawings are revised; and layout of not-to-scale drawings and their management in multiple revisions is difficult.

Neither of these approaches works well, because the complexity of presentation drawing conventionally used in the construction industry exceeds their capabilities. This may eventually change, not only because of enhancements to the CAD systems, but also because of redefinition of presentation standards. The ANSI, DIN and other standards that define presentation formats for drawings pay little attention as of yet to the move toward computerization. With over 50% of design fees typically going to the production of drawings, and with the increasing use of CAD in their production, it is evident that standards that cover the electronically produced drawings must be developed.

Even with a relaxation of external standards, the following issues remain an obstacle regarding the formatting of information on drawings:

- The version-to-version maintenance of presentation format information, entered either by the user or automatically, such as: not-to-scale drawings; note and dimension layout; line weigh selection.
- Complex projections that include information both in front of and behind the cutting plane.

The technology of drawing extraction from a 3-D model requires significantly more research. But even if these issues of projection could be resolved, the issues in the next section would keep the goal of 3-D modeling from being fulfilled.

□ DESIGN ABSTRACTIONS

Over the history of design, paper both forced and allowed designers to abstract issues associated with their design. Architecture is complex; it involves circulation and material flows, massing, structural, air conditioning as well as visual and many other concerns. Various 2-D representations have evolved that allow these issues to be considered alone or with a few other issues, without requiring full definition of the 3-D geometry of the components involved. That is, designers could abstract the full design to focus on particular issues. Particular design variables could be examined in isolation, without the complexity of a fully completed design; decisions could be factored and sequenced by selecting the issues to be addressed and their corresponding 2-D representations to allow their evaluation. Thus circulation diagrams, single line floor plans, vertical sections with airflows, structural grids, and site plans are all abstractions that ignore some design variables by not representing them, and allow detailed examination of the relationships among other variables.

The complex form of problem solving called design, as practiced today, does not rely on one representation; rather it uses many. Each representation provides a means to investigate a portion of the design and to make decisions about it. The use of multiple representations is an integral and necessary part of complex design problem solving. Multiple representations break down the issues and allow them to be dealt with piecemeal; otherwise they would be overwhelming in their complexity. Thus solids modeling could never be the one and only representation of design; it could only be one of several.

Today most computer tools allow only one or a limited number of abstractions of the total design. Manipulation of the underlying model is cumbersome and not conducive to creative design. The organization of multiple abstract representations is an important research issue, not only for architecture, but for all design fields.

□ DESIGN AS JOINT DECISION MAKING AMONG MANY PARTICIPANTS

In architectural school it is not commonly discussed that, for large projects, the architectural drawings will not be those used in actual construction. It is also not acknowledged that architectural drawings do not resolve all layout decisions and that, after selection of the contracting organization, the contractor makes shop drawings from which the building is actually constructed.

The need for two sets of drawings points out certain inefficiencies in the current organizational practices in the construction industry. It also emphasizes the fact that architectural drawings are an incomplete specification of the building project. In the United States, architectural drawings hardly ever specify the dimensions and routing of pipes, ductwork and wiring. Certain joint conditions, for example around the edge of hung ceilings or floor tiles, are often left to the craftsman to work out. The architect can specify how he wants it done or he can leave the decision to the craftsman. Historically, the relation between architect and craftsman has been quite involved, and they have worked closely together. A 3-D model, on the other hand, would define all these details exactly and would not easily support the current give-and-take between the architect and the craftsmen, regarding design responsibilities.

Typically, 20 to 30 design professionals contribute to the final definition of a building's design and layout decisions. They include the multiple engineering consultants, the contractor, construction management groups, various tradesmen, as well as the architectural and interior designers.

Because of these realities, it has not become the practice to use 3-D solids modeling as the base representation for the derivation of construction drawings. While 3-D modeling can be very useful during schematic design, it is too elaborate for the level of detailing practiced by architects. 3-D modeling should be viewed as an optional representation to use in working out special detailing issues, just as 3-D physical models are used for that purpose today. But as a result, design development cannot assume that a 3-D model will be available for the generation of presentation documents.

Recognizing these realities leads to the secondary recognition that 3-D design tools must allow for mixing their use with a variety of 2-D abstractions. That is, it is desirable to move from 2-D abstractions to 3-D models and back again, with most of the detailed design development done in one or the other dimensionality.

☐ SOME FUNCTIONAL REQUIREMENTS FOR A DESIGN ORIENTED CAD SYSTEM

If solids modeling will not serve as the core representational scheme within architectural CAD, then another approach involving multiple representations is required. Since each representation is only partial; that is, a particular abstraction, consistency will have to be maintained in some explicit manner between the representations, possibly by using expert system and rule checking.

How to organize and use multiple representations becomes a research issue in design problem solving*. An early questions is—what are the best representations to use to support resolution of particular issues, such as circulation, massing and site planning, external visual character? Then it is appropriate to determine how these representations can be integrated so as to allow iteration between them. Is the best approach to use a single complex database model with multiple views of it, or should there be several small modeling schemes with well defined mapping functions between them? Various concepts, such as abstract data types and data object inheritance are useful here.

The selected approach should allow both iteration of decisions and different development sequences. Adding or replacing one abstraction that is useful in the design of one technology with another for the design of another technology, is highly desirable, for example, for regular HVAC versus solar based design. Thus abstractions are likely to be organized both by the set of building functions being satisfied (e.g. structural, environmental), and by the technologies used to satisfy them (e.g. solar vs. regular HVAC, catenary vs. rigid beam structures). Any rigid set of abstractions will probably fail in the long run. Thus a generalized scheme for integrating varied representations as the design process progresses seems a desirable goal. Being able to make decisions on estimated data, then later to evaluate the estimates and iterate them, is another important capability.

Only by seriously addressing these issues will researchers be able to develop more powerful computer-based design tools for designers.

---

*The author has developed these issues somewhat in "Abstractions: a conceptual approach for structuring interaction with integrated CAD systems," *Computers and Graphics*, 9(2):97-105, 1985.

□ CONCLUSION

It is obvious at this point that solids modeling has not fulfilled its initial promise. The most common assumption is that adaptable and user friendly solids modelers are lacking and this is why they have not been successful. I suggest that there are other reasons. In other design fields, where one organization produces and uses the same drawings for both design and construction, the value of solids modeling will be greater. This is the case in the mechanical and process plant design areas.

It has often been said that the benefits of computerization seldom result directly in improved productivity of the automated task. Rather it is the re-examination of procedures and their rationalization in light of articulated objectives that leads to improved performance and productivity. Computer models of buildings, as the output representation of design, identify many of the inefficiencies now existing within the fragmented practices of the building industry.

8

THE COMPUTABILITY OF VOID ARCHITECTURAL MODELING

Chris I. Yessios

Department of Architecture
The Ohio State University
Columbus, Ohio

Solid modeling has proven inefficient as a computational aid to architectural design. A theory and computational method called void modeling has been developed to accommodate a class of objects which are containers for other objects. Examples include space enclosures, which are the primitive elements in architectural compositions. The basic computational techniques of void modeling are presented. They show void modeling to be highly efficient in addressing the syntactic and semantic requirements of architectural design.

☐ INTRODUCTION

In order to deal with design computability, it would normally be desirable to first identify what design, and in particular, architectural design is. However, design means different things to different people. I shall therefore bypass the issue. Any definition of design can only be expected to be self-defeating, as it would by necessity negate those unpredictable aspects of design which constitute its essence.

Even though we cannot (or simply should not) attempt to define design, we may address the issue of whether or not design is computable. I propose that we follow Artificial Intelligence's paradigm and define computable design to be all those processes that produce results which would be considered "design" if they were executed by humans. I further propose that we may still establish some basic distinctions and criteria that would allow us to develop and evaluate computable design-oriented strategies and processes.

The first basic distinction is that design consists of *conceptualization* and *execution*. While conceptualization is apparently the most essential part of design, execution is also critical since a design concept can only be of value when it can be executed and materialized in some physical and/or aphysical form.

Conceptualization incorporates an extensive range of activities which are expected to be different from one designer to another. We generally agree that design conceptualization comprises *analysis* and then *synthesis,* or *problem recognition* and *definition* followed by *problem solving,* where there is usually no clear distinction between the two stages as the process cycles back and forth. Because of this, some view design as an ill-defined problem solving process, while others refuse to see it as problem-solving. This discussion underlines why it would be inappropriate to attempt to define design completely, since any definition would be overly restrictive. Whatever the case of design conceptualization, I claim that design execution comprises much better understood processes and can thus be defined and computed. This paper deals with procedures that use computational methods to *execute* design.

The term *computable,* as used in this presentation, means that an algorithmic process can be defined and implemented on a computer to produce results which satisfy the requirements posed by the problem area in question. We shall define *architectural modeling* to be the methods, processes, and operations which lend themselves to the generation of informationally complete architectural models. The requirement that the architectural models be informationally complete implies that they incorporate all the attributes inherent in architectural models, which (a) allow us to extract whatever information is relevant and applicable, (b) allow them to behave as architectural models when they are operated upon, and (c) allow the operands and the resulting artifact to preserve their attributes and character as architectural entities throughout the execution of an operation.

The latter requirement guarantees the computability of architectural modeling. That is, it is not enough to say that a process produces results. These results should be such that they preserve their ability to represent a certain type of entity, the same kind of entity upon which the computable process was applied in the first place.

From the practical point of view, architectural modeling generates physical models of buildings and their environments, which are complemented by a variety of aphysical attributes. The construction of physical scale models has been a method practiced by architects for centuries. When implemented on the computer, internal representations are used that can produce images of 3-D building models. It is also desirable that the internal representations lend themselves to the production of modeling abstractions appropriate for a variety of analyses, engineering calculations, and construction specifications.

Over the past fifteen years, *solid geometric modeling* has been viewed as the appropriate method for accommodating the requirements of architectural modeling. More recently, solid modeling has gained in popularity as we have developed a better understanding of its procedures [Mortenson 1985]. It is considered the cure which would transform what are currently drafting oriented CAD systems into design machines. The majority of the current commercial solids modeling systems have been imported from Europe, where their development was triggered by the pioneering work of I. Braid [Braid 1973]. In this country, architectural researchers were among the first to contribute to the development of solid modeling [Eastman 1976; Borkin 1978]. Ironically, as we fell in love with solid modeling and its set theoretic operations of union, intersection, and difference, we somehow failed to recognize its inefficiencies for architectural modeling.

Consistent with the trends, we at OSU's Computer Aided Architectural and Environmental Design Laboratory (CAAED Lab) devoted much research effort towards the use of solid modeling in architectural design [Yessios 1978]. By the early eighties, we had to conclude that solid modeling is simply not capable of expressing and accommodating architecture [Yessios 1986]. Since then, we have concentrated on the development of another type of geometric modeling which we have called *void modeling*. Void modeling is a general method which has applications beyond architectural design. It is applicable to all fields that deal with and require the modeling of containers of fluids or gasses. It is proving highly efficient in accommodating architectural modeling, where the main primitives are containers of spaces or space enclosures.

The most significant aspects of void modeling are that it suffices in the representation of the most critical attributes of architectural elements and is also highly computable. That is, procedures can be defined and implemented that are capable of processing and operating upon voids in ways that the voids used to represent space enclosures retain their original character. Void modeling also lends itself to the integration of 2-D and 3-D representations. Above all, void modeling offers the means to deal with architectural design during its soft and dynamically tentative states, while a design solution is still unknown and under exploration.

Architectural modeling in itself, whether based on solid or void modeling techniques, is not a producer of design concepts nor solutions. It is a computational tool through which designs can be executed. It is not a means that leads to automated design but to computer assisted design, where the human designer retains the control of conceptualization, design decision making, and value judgements. To enhance these creative processes, modeling is required to respond in a direct and consistent manner. Above all, it is required that modeling relieve the user from tedious tasks of design execution by undertaking such tasks and carrying them to completion in ways which reflect the properties of the object being modeled. It is in this sense that void modeling has proven superior in accommodating architectural design. How this is done is the theme of this presentation, which is by necessity condensed. A more complete elaboration on architectural void modeling can be found in Yessios [1986].

□ VOID MODELING

Void modeling is based on the recognition that certain classes of physical objects are containers of fluids, gasses, or even solids, and that their structural system and semantics can be dealt with in a direct fashion, rather then by simulating their behavior through solid modeling.

The *void,* which is the main primitive of void modeling, consists of a *contained* part and a *container.* The container is a "skin" of an initial zero width. It can be assigned a variety of attributes, including width. Different portions of the skin may be assigned different attribute values, any of which can be freely changed during the process of modeling.

The most significant feature of a void is that its contained part and its container can behave independently when they are operated upon. The practical implication of this feature is that each of a void's parts preserve its distinct character and attributes when operations are applied. Figures 8.1 and 8.2 illustrate this feature.

Assume that we need to derive the union of two pipes, shown in section in Figure 8.1. Were they represented as solids, then the result would have been as in 8.1(a). Obviously, this result is not satisfactory since the flow of the fluid or the gas which the pipes may contain is interrupted. One can, of

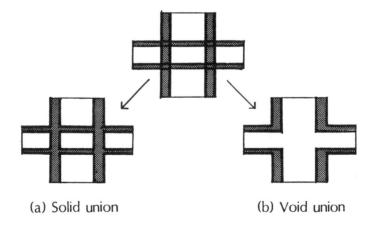

(a) Solid union   (b) Void union

Figure 8.1. Solid versus Void union.

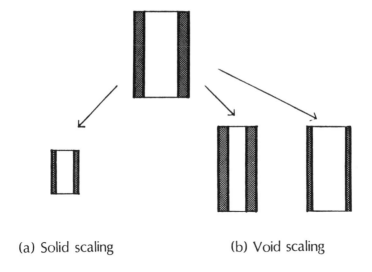

(a) Solid scaling   (b) Void scaling

Figure 8.2. Solid versus Void scaling.

course, "clean" the resulting union to achieve the desired result, but it is certainly preferable to derive the appropriate result directly. This can be achieved by applying a void modeling union, assuming the operands are represented as voids. The latter result is shown in Figure 8.1(b).

Another operation, scaling, is illustrated in Figure 8.2. Were the pipe represented as a solid, then the scaling operation could only affect the whole object in a uniform manner. Were it represented as a void, then its contained and container parts could be scaled independently of each other.

Void modeling is applicable to all those fields which require the modeling of objects which fall under the class of voids. This presentation deals with the use of void modeling for architectural design. Readers with interests in fields other than architecture should have no major difficulty in recognizing the analogies which would make the computational techniques presented here applicable in their respective areas of interest.

Void modeling can be made to include solid modeling as one of its subareas. Consequently, void modeling can be viewed as a universal method of physical geometric modeling. We shall later see how this generalization can be applied to architectural modeling.

□ THE GENERATION OF A VOID ARCHITECTURAL MODEL

The simple example shown in Figure 8.3 will be used to illustrate and discuss the workings of void architectural modeling. In the following discussion and throughout this paper, the terms "vector line" and "curve" are

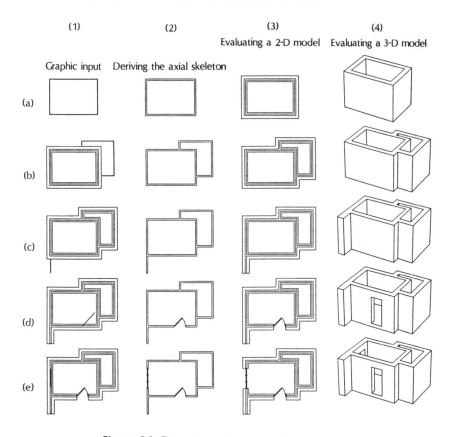

Figure 8.3. The void model generation process.

used with the same meaning. Also, whenever a value is assigned to an attribute, it should be understood that it may be explicitly entered by a user or it may be defaulted by a system.

Assume that a closed vector line, representing walls of a building, is drawn, as shown in Figure 8.3(a1). Generate a copy of the vector line in opposite direction, as in Figure 8.3(a2). This pair of reversely coincident vector lines are called *axial skeletons*. Assuming that a width value has also been assigned to each of the segments of the axial skeleton, then a 2-D rendering, as shown in Figure 8.3(a3), can be derived. We shall call the latter an *evaluated 2-D model* of a building floor plan. Next, assuming that a pair of height values have also been assigned to each of the points of the axial skeleton, a 3-D building model, as shown in Figure 8.3(a4), can be derived. We shall call the latter an *evaluated 3-D model*.

In step (b), a new wall line is drawn as shown in Figure 8.3(b1). Both of its end points lie on previously drawn walls. A reversely coincident copy of the drawn line is generated and the axial skeletons are updated as shown in

Figure 8.3(b2). Assuming that the required width and height values for the new segments have been assigned, a 2-D and 3-D model can again be evaluated, as shown in Figures 8.3(b3) and 8.3(b4), respectively.

In step (c), a wall line, only one end point of which lies on an existing wall, is drawn. After going through the same procedures, evaluated 2-D and 3-D models are derived.

In step (d), a door opening is introduced. The graphic input consists of two points which represent the position of the door's centroid and its swing. These points are associated with attributes which describe the door to be generated, including its width, which is used in step d2 to update the axial skeleton structure. On the basis of the newly adjusted axial skeleton a 2-D and 3-D model is evaluated, as before. Step (e) is quite similar, except that now a window opening has been generated.

One can proceed and execute a variety of graphically entered editing operations, such as add/delete walls, add/delete windows, doors, or plain openings of a variety of types, cut walls, move/eliminate plan portions, etc. All these are *editing operations* which affect the topology of the axial skeletons. Other classes of operations affect the geometry of the axial skeletons. They are the *attribute assignment* (and reassignment) operations and the *symmetry operations* of translation, rotation, scaling, and reflection. Finally, the topology and geometry of a void are affected by *compositional operations* such as simple arrangements and the set theoretic operations of union, intersection, and difference. The computability of the void modeling versions of a few of these operations will be discussed later.

The simple example in Figure 8.3 has shown how void architectural models are computable from single line sketches, which have also been assigned some attributes. In summary, the process is as follows:

1. The single line sketch becomes the basis for the derivation of the axial skeletons. The axial skeletons are the only constants of the void representation. They are complemented by a variety of attributes, which are variables. That is, their values can be changed at any time during the model generating process.

2. On the basis of the axial skeletons and their attributes, an evaluated 2-D model can be generated. This is done by applying a parallel line (or plane) procedure to derive the "wall" lines. An evaluated 2-D model can be readily plotted as a floor plan representation.

3. On the basis of an evaluated 2-D model and the associated height attributes, an evaluated 3-D model can be generated. This is done by appropriately tracing the floor plan (2-D model) to generate the faces of a 3-D model, assuming boundary representation for the 3-D model.

It should be noted that the axial skeletons and their attributes already constitute a complete representation of a void model. Much of the information in this representation is implicit from the point of view of being able to actually render either a 2-D or a 3-D graphic representation of the object being modeled. Because of this, we may call it an unevaluated model. From the unevaluated model, an evaluated 2-D model can be computed. The inverse is also computable; that is, 2-D models can be derived from 3-D models and unevaluated models can be derived from 2-D and 3-D evaluated models. The following sections elaborate more on some of these distinctions and the applicable computational procedures.

□ THE AXIAL SKELETON REPRESENTATION

The axial skeletons are the containing "skins" of voids. They always come in pairs: one axial skeleton line for each side of the skin. By definition, an axial skeleton curve is *positive* when it has a clockwise direction; otherwise it is *negative*. All exterior curves are positive. Negative curves delineate the perimeters of interior spaces. Thus, the contained part is always on the left side of an axial skeleton, when traced in a forward direction. In void modeling, there is always an exterior curve which contains the (infinite) universal space and at least one interior curve which contains a finite space inside the void.

We may initially assume that corresponding segments of axial skeletons are coincident. This is consistent with the initial definition that the containing skin is of zero width. It is also consistent with the way we derive axial skeletons in the example of Figure 8.3; that is, by generating reversely coincident copies of the vector lines drawn. When the condition that corresponding segments of the axial skeleton be coincident is satisfied, we call the void *regular* (Figure 8.4(a)). When some of the corresponding segments of the axial skeleton of a void are not coincident, the void is *irregular* (Figure 8.4(b)). The regular/irregular distinction is of procedural significance. In regular voids, the links of corresponding axial skeleton points are readily available. In irregular voids, they are not. Most of the discussion in this presentation will be restricted to regular voids. Yet, in many of the illustrations (such as in Figure 8.3), coincident axial skeletons are shown at a distance from each other. This is simply done to facilitate viewing them.

An internal void data structure can be implemented as shown in Figure 8.5. Each point of a void occupies a 9-cell word or row. Two sets of links in cells 3 and 4 and 5 and 6 are available. Cells 3 and 5 are links to the previous point and cells 4 and 6 are links to the next point, thus allowing direct backward and forward tracing. The pair of links in cells 3 and 4 represent a *space* or *room* tracing. The pair of links in cells 5 and 6 represent a *skin* or *wall* tracing. It is also possible to combine the two sets of links and jump from one to the other at pre-specified types of points, to apply a variety of mixed tracings. Two such tracings are illustrated in Figure 8.6.

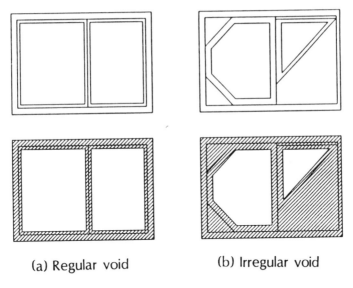

(a) Regular void   (b) Irregular void

Figure 8.4. Types of voids.

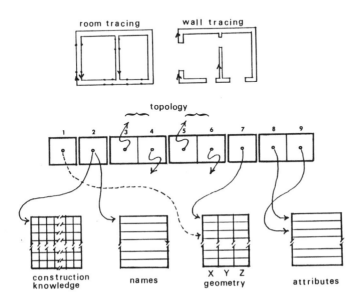

Figure 8.5. The void data structure.

The two sets of links in cells 3 & 4 and 5 & 6 constitute the backbone of the void data structure. Each curve in the data structure has a clearly identifiable header and is always closed. We shall see later how a tree structure can be derived and used to access all the curves of a void through their headers in a hierarchical order.

Cell 7 points to the geometry (x, y and z coordinates) of the points on the axial skeletons. Cell 1 will eventually (after a 2-D model is evaluated) point to the geometry of the points on the wall lines. There is always one and only one such point corresponding to a point on the axial skeleton.

Cell 2 contains the indices of the rooms (interior and exterior) to which the respective point belongs. These indices are both numeric identifiers of individual spaces and pointers to alphanumeric names that can be used to identify spaces. Cell 2 also contains pointers to a construction knowledge base, which consists of information about architectural elements such as doors and windows. Finally, cells 8 and 9 contain (begin and end) pointers to lists of attributes such as wall widths and heights, material, color, etc.

□ COMPUTING AND TRACING AN EVALUATED 2-D MODEL.

From an implementation point of view, computing an evaluated 2-D model means filling cell 1 (pointers to the geometry of wall points) of the void data structure. The procedure involves the generation of parallel lines to the left of each segment of the axial skeletons, at distances equal to the width values assigned to the respective axial segments. The intersection points of pairs of consecutive parallel lines are the points of the wall lines. The parallel line procedures need to be generalized to be able to handle degenerate segments (line segments whose endpoints are the same point). Degenerate segments occur at wall edges and the sides of door and window openings.

An evaluated 2-D model, from the point of view of architectural design, is the equivalent of a structured floor plan. By "structure" we mean that it is a linked system of points and lines that can be traced in a variety of ways and for a variety of purposes. It is not simply a collection of lines, as would be the case with a drafting oriented system.

The *space* or *room* tracing (illustrated in Figure 8.5) is capable of tracing the closed curves that delineate the internal or external spaces. The *skin* or *wall* tracing (also illustrated in Figure 8.5) is capable of depicting the walls which make up a floor plan. A variety of *mixed* tracings are also possible. Two examples are shown in Figures 8.6(a) and 8.6(b). The first is used to derive the interior bottom faces (floors) of building models. The second is used to derive the horizontal faces of window and door openings. Referring to the void data structure discussed in the previous section, the room

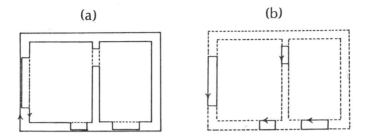

Figure 8.6. Mixed tracings.

tracing utilizes the links in cells 3 and 4; the wall tracing utilizes the links in cells 5 and 6. The mixed tracings combine the two sets of links by jumping back and forth at pre-specified points. The tracings illustrated in Figure 8.6 switch links at door and/or window opening points.

All types of tracings can be applied to either the axial skeleton lines or to the wall lines. Tracings are useful for *drafting* purposes, including *automatic dimensioning,* for *capturing data* and *extracting knowledge,* for executing *spatial analyses*, and for *computing 3-D models.*

A floor plan can be drafted by applying a wall tracing (Figure 8.7). Note that the closure of the vector lines given by a wall tracing makes the generation of hatch lines an almost trivial task. Diagrammatic representations of floor plans can also be easily generated and drafted through a room tracing. Depending on the scale of a drawing and the detail required, drafting-oriented tracings may be applied to either the wall or the axial skeleton lines.

The void data structures lend themselves to tracings that allow us to capture and extract information about the models they represent. By applying room tracings, the dimensions, the areas, and/or the volumes of "rooms"

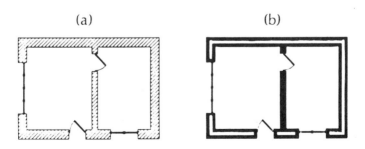

Figure 8.7. Drafting.

can easily be computed. By applying wall tracings, lengths of walls can be depicted and become the basis for computing bills of materials. Similarly, door and window schedules can be computed by applying either a room or a wall tracing. The void data structure also lends itself to the computation of the spatial relationships of a model, as we shall see in the next section. Such spatial analyses offer the means to acquire knowledge about architectural functions, if a relatively large number of plans depicting known solutions to similar architectural problems are processed.

□ THE HIERARCHICAL STRUCTURE OF VOIDS

The simple examples which have been used so far may mislead the reader to believe that a single interior curve suffices to delineate an interior space. The plan in Figure 8.8(a) shows that this is not necessarily the case. It is therefore necessary to compute the spatial relations of a void model in order to correctly identify the spaces of which it consists and the curves that delineate each space. In the general case, the spaces contained by a void are hierarchically structured; a tree structure will be used for the representation of the spatial relationships of a void.

Having identified the curves in the plan with numeric indices, each curve can be represented by a node in the tree structure. Each node is marked with a " + " sign if it represents a positive curve or with a "-" sign if it represents a negative curve. Each node in the tree branches to nodes representing the spaces that are contained by it at the next level. The resulting tree is shown in Figure 8.8(a). A node marked with a 0 has been used as a root. It represents the universal space within which the void model exists.

It should be noted that the tree in Figure 8.8(a) was derived on the basis of room tracings. Had we applied wall tracings, a different tree structure would have been derived. Such a tree structure is shown in Figure 8.8(b). Unless otherwise explicitly stated, room tracings are applied whenever spatial tree structures are derived.

Having derived the hierarchical tree structure of the void (floor plan) in Figure 8.8(a), we can now make some observations that will next guide our tracings:

- A positive curve is not always an exterior curve.
- Curves of the same sign (positive or negative) are at every other level and two consecutive levels cannot be of the same sign (both positive or both negative).
- The delineation of an interior space may require more than one curve.

Descendants of node A are all lower level nodes which can be reached

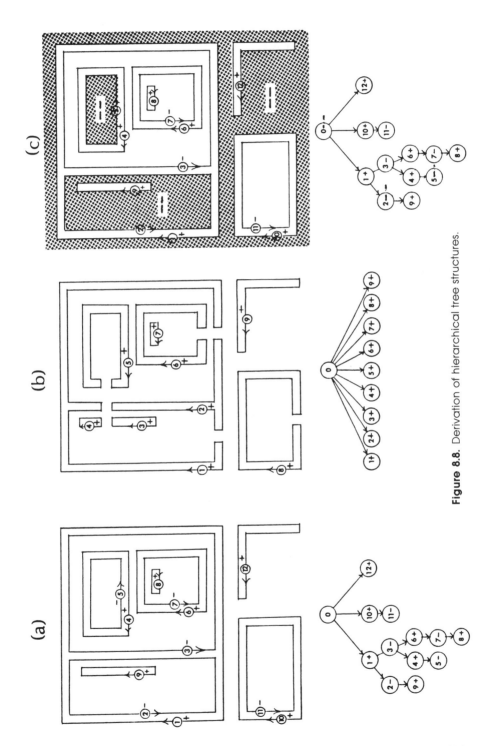

Figure 8.8. Derivation of hierarchical tree structures.

153

when tracing the branches of node A, all the way to the terminal nodes (leaves). Immediate descendants to node A are only the next level nodes to which node A branches. Different portions of a void model can now be traced by the following rules:

- All exterior curves are given by the first level positive nodes.
- The interior spaces are given by the negative curves and their immediate descendants (which are always positive), if any.

We shall see, next, that while the above rules suffice for a certain class of void models, they cannot sufficiently accommodate the general case. Having a method to deal with the hierarchical structure of spaces and with spaces that are within other spaces, we also have the opportunity to deal with exterior spaces that are inside buildings (or voids in general).

Assume that interior spaces "2" and "5" of the plan in Figure 8.8(a) are designated to be "open" spaces. That is, they are exterior spaces inside the exterior perimeter of a building. Figure 8.8(c) shows the same plan with the open spaces shaded and marked with a double minus sign ($--$). Note that for the sake of consistency, we have now applied the same markings to the universal exterior space. The double minus signs are also carried to the tree representation, which otherwise remains the same. We can now use more accurate wording to express the general rules by which different parts of a void may be traced.

- All exterior curves are given by the positive nodes which are immediate descendants of double negative nodes. They are complemented by the double negative nodes which are their direct (but not necessarily immediate) descendants, if any.
- The interior spaces are given by the single negative curves, which are complemented with the next level positive curves to which they branch (immediate descendants), if any.

□ COMPUTING AN EVALUATED 3-D VOID MODEL

The evaluated 2-D model is a complete representation of a 3-D model. To be able to render a 3-D model, however, further evaluation is required. Two different types of 3-D models can be derived: a solid or a void 3-D model. While a solid model is simpler to derive and suffices for the production of renderings, it does not preserve the attributes of the original void model. Furthermore, it cannot behave as a void when operated upon. Consequently, when it is desirable to further operate upon a model directly through its evaluated 3-D form, a void model is required. For the computation of both the solid and the void model, the required information is extracted from the 2-D model in almost identical manners. What is different is the 3-D data structure into which the 2-D data structure is transformed. I shall first outline the solid model computing procedures and then further elaborate the generation of the 3-D void model.

For solid models, I shall assume a boundary representation, where the following conventions apply: Each boundary face is delineated by a closed curve, the positive direction of which is clockwise when viewed from outside the solid. A face can be delineated by more than one curve, only one of which can be positive. Thus any additional curves, which can only be negative, represent holes on the face. The collection of bounding faces should be closed. That is, they should completely cover the surface of the solid.

The model of a building consists of horizontal and vertical faces. By convention, the horizontal faces are parallel to the X-Y plane; the Z direction is used for the height and is considered to be the vertical direction. The faces of the top and bottom ends of a building, as well as the top and bottom ends of door and window openings, are also horizontal. They correspond closely to the evaluated 2-D model or the floor plan of a building. We shall initially assume single story buildings, where their bottoms and/or tops may be closed or open. The 3-D model computing procedures can easily be expanded to derive multi-story models, as we shall see later. To generate a building model, the horizontal faces are derived first by executing an appropriate tracing of the 2-D floor plan model and by assigning appropriate Z (height) values. The Z values are extracted from the attribute lists to which the 2-D model points. The vertical faces are computed next from the horizontal faces. These procedures are as follows:

- Referring to the tree representation in Figure 8.8(c), the top faces of an *open top* building model are given by the positive curves, complemented by the single negative curves, which are their immediate descendants, if any. All curves are derived by applying a forward room tracing (Figure 8.9(a)). Assuming a flat top end, all top faces of an open top building are assigned the same Z value.

- For *closed top* building models, two sets of top faces are required: the exterior and the interior. Both the exterior and the interior faces are derived as outlined for exterior and interior curves in the previous section. Different Z values are assigned to both the exterior and interior faces. The process is illustrated in Figure 8.9(b).

- To derive the bottom faces of an *open bottom* building, the windows (if any) are deleted from the 2-D model, and a tree structure is derived by applying a wall tracing. The bottom faces are again given by the positive curves, complemented by the negative curves to which they branch, if any. Backward tracings are applied and all faces (if more than one) are assigned the same Z value. The process is illustrated in Figure 8.9(c). It was based on the tree structure shown in Figure 8.8(b).

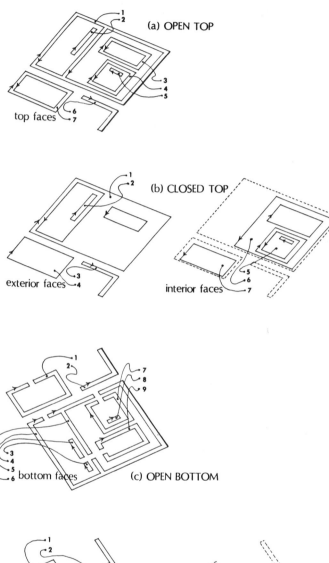

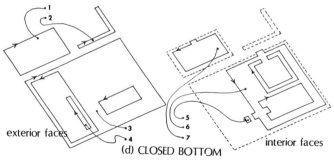

Figure 8.9. Derivation of horizontal faces.

- Two sets of bottom faces, exterior and interior, need to be generated for *closed bottom* building models. After deleting the windows, a tree structure is constructed by applying the mixed tracings illustrated in Figure 8.6(a). Then the exterior bottom faces are given by positive curves complemented with the double negative curves that are their descendants, if any. The interior faces are given by the single negative curves that are their immediate descendents, if any. Backward tracings are applied and each set of faces (exterior and interior) is assigned different Z values.

The horizontal faces of door and window openings are derived as follows:

- The upper horizontal ends of doors and windows for open and closed top building models are derived by applying the mixed tracing shown in Figure 8.6(b) in a forward direction and by assigning the corresponding Z values, which may be different for each door and/or window.

- The lower horizontal ends of windows only, for open and closed bottom building models, are derived as for the upper ends, except that the mixed tracing of Figure 8.6(b) is applied backwards. Note that lower horizontal faces for doors need not be derived, as they have been incorporated in the faces generated for the bottom end of the building model.

Having derived the complete set of horizontal faces, they now provide the basis for generating the vertical or wall faces. Observe that each boundary segment of a horizontal face corresponds to a reversely coincident horizontal segment of some vertical face. Also, all boundary segments that are coplanar with the same vertical face belong to that face or to more than one face that are coplanar. Therefore, the process of constructing vertical wall faces consists of depicting all the sets of coplanar boundary segments in the horizontal faces and appropriately connecting them through the introduction of vertical segments.

To execute the above procedure, we establish an orthogonal system of coordinates W,Z, where W is the horizontal and Z is the vertical axis (Figure 8.10). Assuming we are constructing the far right exterior face of the floor plan in Figure 8.8(c) and that the model to be generated has both its top and bottom open, apply the following procedure:

- From the horizontal faces generated for an open top and bottom building model, pick the segments that are coplanar to the far right vertical face. These segments are shown with heavier lines in Figure 8.9. Reverse their direction and plot them in the W, Z system of coordinates, by positioning them parallel to the W axis and at the appropriate Z position (Figure 8.10(a)).

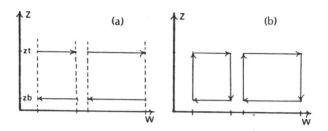

Figure 8.10. Generation of vertical wall faces.

- Connect matching end points by introducing vertical segments (Figure 8.10(b)). Each directed vector line segment has an initial and a terminal end point. Two such vector segments match if the terminal point of the first and the initial point of the second lie on the same vertical line.

This process generates, for each set of vertically coplanar boundary segments, one or more closed curves, which bound the vertical wall faces. To generate all the vertical faces of a building model, all sets of vertically coplanar segments are picked from the horizontal faces.

The discussion so far has concentrated on the evaluation of 3-D solid models. The derivation of 3-D void models is not too different. The same procedures apply; except that rather than tracing wall lines, axial skeleton lines are traced leading to the generation of 3-D axial skeleton faces. These again come in pairs of reversely coincident axial planes, each bounding one side of the void's skin, and are of an initial width 0. They also carry a variety of attributes, including wall width values, from which wall faces can be computed through the application of parallel plane procedures. In addition, the axial skeleton faces are linked and thus constitute a structured system of 3-D faces that can be traced in a variety of ways and purposes. As in 2-D, the 3-D void data structure is receptive to a variety of operations under which it preserves its attributes and its void character.

☐ MODELING LEVELS OF ABSTRACTION

Any entity that we model can be viewed at different levels of abstraction or detail. Actually, in any model, it is desirable to be able to incorporate only as much detail as is required by the targeted application or analysis. In a similar fashion, architectural models need to be constructed at different levels of abstraction. The most commonly required levels are the following:

1. The *volume level,* where buildings and other elements are represented as solid volumes and with very little detail.

2. The *building level,* where each building is modeled with its walls and spaces and all the other details which completely describe its form and function.

3. The *construction level,* where each building element, such as a wall, is shown with its structural details.

The architectural designer requires the capability to work at any of the above levels of abstraction, depending upon the current stage of the design process and his/her personal preferences. As design work proceeds at one level of abstraction, models at the other levels should be automatically generated and be readily available.

What is really required and proposed here is a single internal data structure from which models at different levels of abstraction may be extracted. Thus, this requirement is no different from the rather widely recognized requirement for 2-D/3-D integration. 2-D representations should be considered yet another level of modeling abstraction.

I have already shown how void modeling can accommodate drafting as a direct byproduct of its modeling procedures. We have also seen how models at the building level can be extracted from the void data structure. We shall next see how models at the volume level can be extracted from the same data structure. There are at least two computational methods, each addressing distinct semantic requirements, which may be applied for the generation of volume level models. We shall discuss them both.

The structured drawing in Figure 8.11 contains the floor plan we used earlier to generate models at the building level (Figure 8.8). It is the shaded portion of the drawing, where the isolated walls have been deleted, since they are of no relevance to volume level modeling.

Each area in the drawing of Figure 8.11 is also marked with a number enclosed in a diamond shape. These numbers represent the height (Z values of top ends) for the respective areas. We shall use this drawing to derive a solid object. We shall assume that its base (bottom end) is at height 0.

As before, we construct a tree structure (Figure 8.11), to depict its spatial relations. The tree structure is derived from room tracings applied to the axial skeleton lines. For the generation of volume level models, all tracings will be applied to axial skeleton (rather than wall) lines. Note that in addition to the outer universal space (node 0), there is one node marked with a double negative sign $(--)$. This corresponds to interior curve 12, which has been assigned a height of 0 (or the same height with the base). By convention, this is interpreted to mean that the respective area is open (a hole).

As before, the faces that bound the surface of the solid object are assumed to be either horizontal or vertical. We shall first trace the 2-D plan to derive the horizontal faces. We shall then derive the vertical faces from the horizontal.

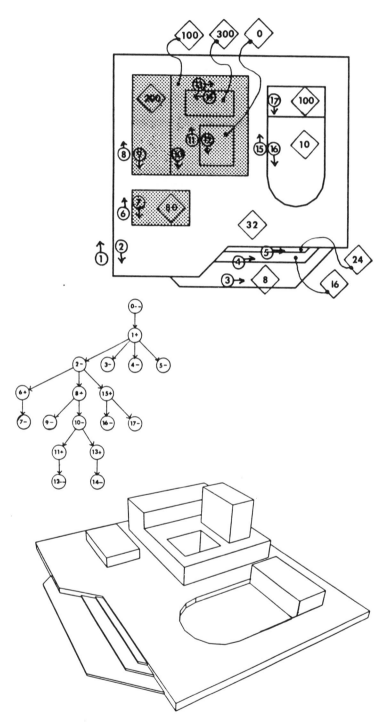

Figure 8.11. Derivation of volume level model.

- The horizontal *bottom* faces are given by the exterior curves (positive curves which are immediate descendants of double negative curves). They are complemented by the double negative curves, which are their direct descendants, if any. They are traced backwards and assigned Z = 0 for their heights.

- The horizontal *top* faces are given by the single negative curves, complemented by the positive curves which are their immediate descendants, if any. They are traced backwards and assigned the Z values corresponding to those marked on the 2-D drawing.

It should be noted that the above procedures are almost identical to those used for the generation of the bottom faces for a closed bottom building model. The only difference is that we now do not have to deal with door openings and we trace axial skeletons rather than wall lines. Similarly, the vertical or side faces can be generated as before, except that we have to make an extension to our previous procedures to accommodate the case where two bounding segments of the generated side face may intersect each other.

The case arises in situations such as the one isolated in Figure 8.12. The generation of the side face for the segments coinciding at the highlighted position in Figure 8.12(b) gives us the boundary vector line shown in 8.12(c). Notice that two segments intersect at point p. When such cases arise, the intersection is resolved and the closed boundary line is decomposed into two closed curves. Note that they are in opposite directions, which is appropriate since they are delineating faces bounding reverse sides of the solid.

Another computational method for deriving a solid model (volume level) from a 2-D structure is illustrated in Figure 8.13. We retain the 2-D structure exactly as it was in Figure 8.8, but apply the following procedures:

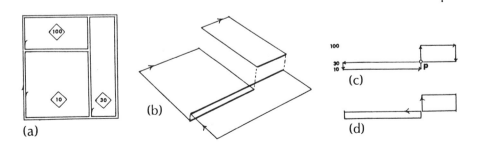

Figure 8.12. Resolution of intersecting boundary segments.

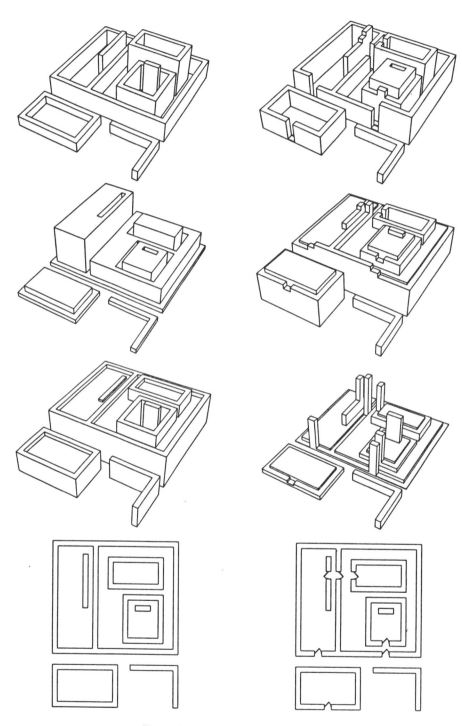

Figure 8.13. Volume level models.

- Transform all wall lines into pairs of reversely coincident axial skeletons. The new axial skeleton structure may be evaluated to generate new wall lines, but it is not necessary as we shall only need to trace the axial skeletons.

- Assign height values to the spaces in the drawing and apply the 3-D model computing procedures as above. Figure 8.13 illustrates a variety of models at the volume level, that were derived on the basis of the transformed 2-D drawing and variable sets of height values.

The procedures discussed so far in this section have shown that at least two levels of abstraction can readily be computed from the same 2-D void representation. The derivation of models at a construction level is illustrated in Figure 8.14. To compute such models, in addition to the 2-D void

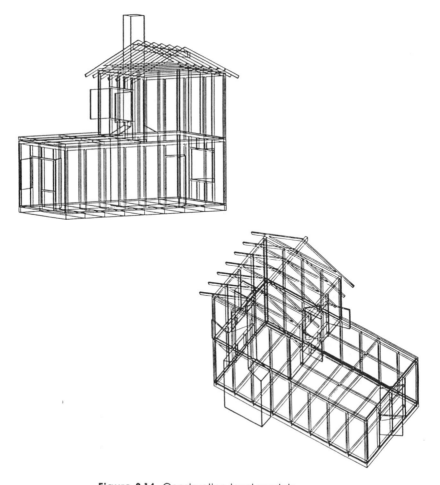

Figure 8.14. Construction level models.

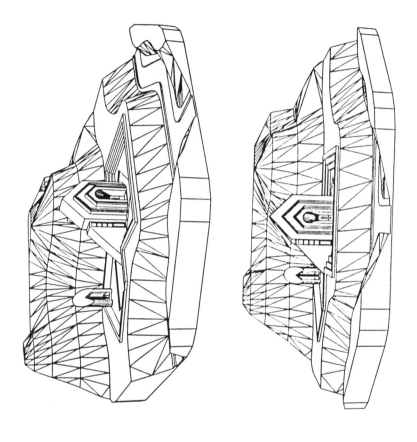

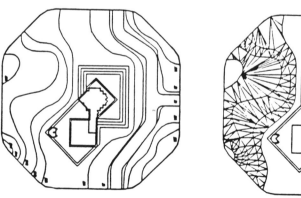

Figure 8.15. Landform models.

representation of a building, we need a definition of the structural system to be employed. The latter can best be represented through generative grammars. Space does not permit me to elaborate fully, but the interested reader is referred to [Kubicek 1985] for a discussion of the methods which may be employed.

The 3-D model computing procedures we have discussed have also demonstrated that void modeling representations allow us to generate solids in addition to voids. Because of this capability, it can be claimed that void includes solid modeling and can thus be viewed as a general method of geometric modeling.

The examples I have shown may, of course, lead to the erroneous impression that only solids that are bounded by horizontal and vertical faces exclusively can be generated. This is not so. The void modeling methods can accommodate any form. While space does not permit me to elaborate further here, the generative power of void modeling is clearly shown by the land form models in Figure 8.15. For a discussion of these procedures, the reader is referred to [Burmesch 1985].

□ OPERATIONS ON VOID MODELS

Earlier, editing procedures were used to interactively sketch a floor plan, which then led to the derivation of evaluated 2-D and 3-D models. After a void model has been generated, or even while it is being generated, we need to be able to manipulate its form by applying either symmetry transformations (translation, rotation, scaling, or reflection) or compositional operations. In this section, I shall discuss the most significant of these operations; namely scaling, arrangement, and set theoretic operations. We shall see how the behavior of a void under these operations is different from the behavior of a solid.

The results derived when applying solid scaling versus void scaling have already been illustrated in Figure 8.2. The advantage of the void scaling is that it allows the containing and the contained parts to be scaled independently of each other in a semantically consistent manner.

To *scale* the space enclosed by a void, the axial skeleton is scaled and the evaluated 2-D and 3-D models are recalculated, using the same width and height attributes for walls, doors, and windows. Note that the result of such an operation is a scaled up or down space, but all the other elements (such as wall and door/window widths, building heights, etc.) retain their original sizes. Such a result is consistent with architectural modeling semantics.

To *scale* the width of walls, door/window openings, heights, etc., the respective attribute values are scaled up or down and the model is reevaluated. This independence of the elements of a void model under the scale

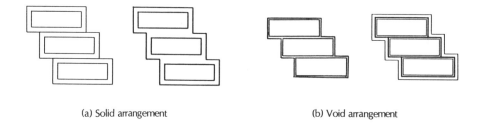

(a) Solid arrangement   (b) Void arrangement

Figure 8.16. Arrangements.

operation also offers us the opportunity to deal with incremental scaling. For example, prefabricated windows come in sizes which differ by integer increments of 2" 4" or 6" Consequently, a 77% scaling of a window opening makes no sense, in the general case. The same is true for other attributes, such as wall widths, since they also depend upon their structural details and can only be scaled incrementally. Incremental scaling may be accommodated by attaching to respective attributes knowledge about the acceptable increments and their upper and lower limits. This knowledge may be permanent or it may be entered at model generation time.

The *arrangement* operation is defined to be the generation of *n* copies of an object that are positioned in a way such that each copy begins where the previous ends. The positions of the copies in an arrangement can be generated by explicit symmetry transformations, most commonly translations, or an automatic procedure may be available which generates appropriate positions, given *n* copies of an object. The arrangement operation can also be extended to apply to cases where the elements to be arranged are not all copies of the same object. The solid modeling version of an arrangement is shown in Figure 8.16(a), while the void modeling version is shown in Figure 8.16(b). The advantages of the void version are obvious.

To derive a void modeling arrangement, the interior axial skeleton curves are arranged, as appropriate, and the exterior axial skeleton curves are unioned to derive a single exterior curve. Then, evaluated 2-D and 3-D models can be computed as before.

The semantic difference between solid and void modeling techniques are most distinctly underlined by the set theoretic operations of *union, intersection*, and *difference*. Given the two space enclosures A and B shown in Figure 8.17, the results of the solid modeling version of the union, intersection, and difference are shown on the left; the results of the void modeling version are shown on the right. Again, the superior ability of void modeling to accommodate architectural design semantics are apparent.

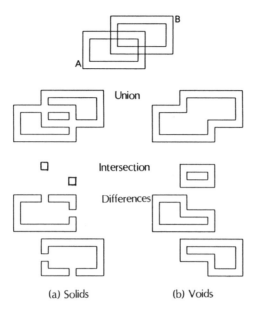

Figure 8.17. Set theoretic operations.

The void set theoretic operations are executed upon the axial skeletons as follows (Figure 8.18):

- For the union (A ∪ B), derive the union of the interior axial skeletons of A and B and the union of the exterior axial skeletons separately, and combine the results. The process is illustrated in Figure 8.18(a). The intersection (A ∩ B) is computed in the same manner, except that the intersections of the interior and exterior axial skeletons, taken separately, are derived. The process is illustrated in Figure 8.18(b).

- For the difference A-B, compute the difference of the exterior axial skeleton(s) of A minus the interior axial skeleton(s) of B, and the difference of the interior axial skeletons of A minus the exterior axial skeletons of B, and combine the results. The difference B-A is the reverse of A-B. The derivation of both is illustrated in Figure 8.18(c) and 8.18(d).

The void version of the set theoretic operations can be applied to either the 2-D data structure and have the corresponding 3-D model evaluated, or they can be applied to the 3-D data structure directly. Figure 8.19 shows results derived when 3-D void models are given as operands to the set theoretic operations.

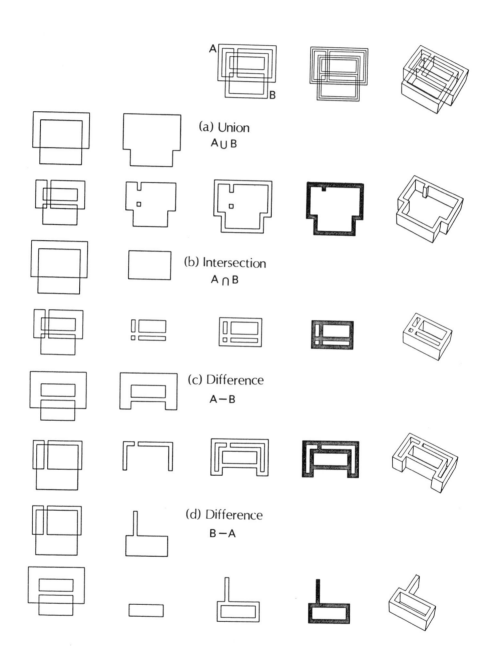

(a) Union
A∪B

(b) Intersection
A∩B

(c) Difference
A−B

(d) Difference
B−A

Figure 8.18. Set theoretic operations of voids.

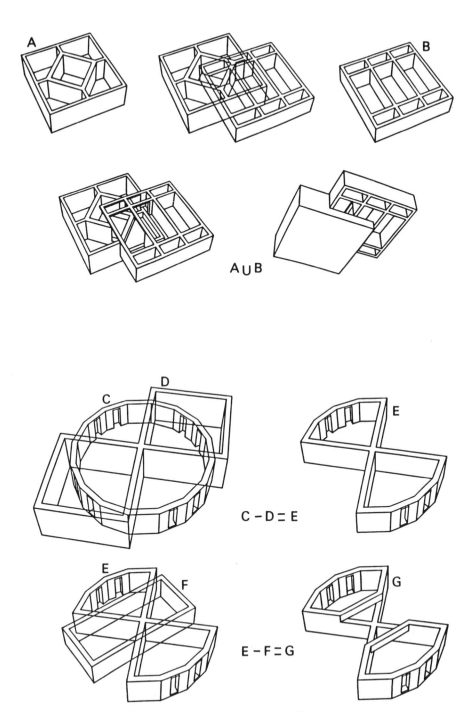

Figure 8.19. 3D void union and difference.

□ MULTI-STORY BUILDING MODELS

The operations we discussed in the previous section can be used to generate multi-story building models. A number of similar or dissimilar copies of previously generated single story building models can be arranged vertically or a number of single story models can be unioned. While these are certainly appropriate methods to generate multi-story buildings, in practice

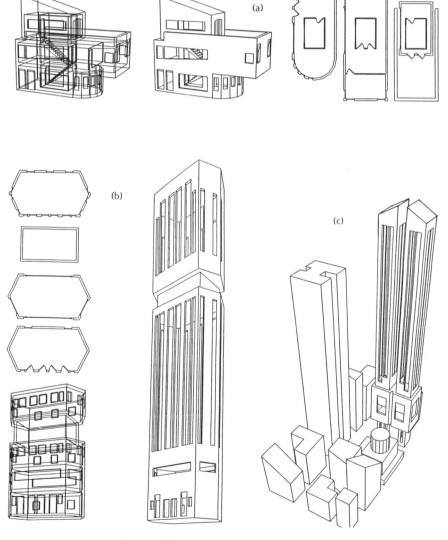

Figure 8.20. Derivation of multi-story building models.

multi-story buildings are generated on the basis of floor plans. The same floor plan may be applied to all the stories or a variety of plans may be mixed as a building rises vertically. It also turns out that it is computationally more efficient and direct to generate a building model (void or solid) from a set of floor plans, rather than generating it piecemeal and then composing the parts together.

The computational procedures that generate multi-story buildings from plans (evaluated 2-D models) are a generalized version of the procedures already discussed earlier. All the horizontal faces are generated as before by applying the appropriate tracing to respective floor plans. However, as the horizontal faces are being generated, conjoint and coplanar faces are unioned, where the union operation is in 2-D and generalized to be able to handle the union of positive with negative curves, which is frequently required. We shall also now take the term "horizontal" to mean a face at any slope which is not vertical or virtually vertical; in other words, any face which is not a wall face. The generation of the vertical (wall) faces is as before.

The generation of multi-story buildings is illustrated in Figure 8.20. In 8.20(a), a three-story building model is constructed on the basis of the three floor plan variations. The procedures do not require that the floors have flat ends, but from a practical point of view it usually does not make sense not to have flat ends. The case is different with the top ends of top stories, when it is frequently desirable that different parts of a plan end at different heights.

Figure 8.20(b), illustrates the derivation of a high-rise building on the basis of four floor plans. It also illustrates the "stretching" effect which results from a scaling applied to the height attributes. Finally, Figure 8.20(c) illustrates how volume level and building level models can be mixed or how one level of modeling abstraction can be applied to one portion of a plan and another level to another portion. Needless to say, the computational efficiency of this capability leads to a prudent use of memory.

A detailed discussion of the multi-story building model generating procedures can be found in [Chen, 1986].

□ CONCLUSION

A substantially developed, but still under investigation, theory of void modeling and its computational methods as they apply to architectural modeling, have been presented. The development of void modeling was undertaken in order to address the deficiencies of solid modeling, when applied to architectural design. The majority of the procedures discussed have been tested by implementing them in the Architectural Modeling, Design and Drafting System of The Ohio State University (Archimodos), the development of which has been supported in part through a contract with the IBM

Corporation. The initial release of Archimodos has been complemented with modules developed as Master Thesis projects (see references).

Void modeling and its implementation in Archimodos does not attempt to automate design conceptualization, but rather design execution. We have taken the position that design conceptualization and problem solving should remain the realm of the human user/designer. However, the designer should be relieved from a variety of tedious tasks of execution and have his/her design model automatically constructed for him/her correctly and speedily. This way, a modeling system can enhance design without dictating it. We are attempting to do so by incorporating constructive knowledge about how buildings are and how they behave within the modeling representation and structure itself, rather than in the form of an externally attached knowledge base. This is the essence of void modeling as it applies to architectural design: allowing buildings to be constructed as buildings and to behave as buildings when they are operated upon. Given that buildings are configurations of spaces, void modeling, to the extent it has been developed, has proven highly computable and efficient.

☐ REFERENCES

Borkin H.S., J.F. McIntosh and J.A. Turner "The Development of Three-Dimensional Spatial Modeling Techniques for the Construction Planning of Nuclear Power Plants" *Proceedings of Siggraph 78*, ACM, August 1978.

Braid I.C. *Designing with Volumes*, Cantab Press, Cambridge, England, 1973.

Burmesch F.H. "The Site Model Generator" Master Thesis, Department of Architecture, The Ohio State University, Columbus, OH, December 1985.

Chen H.L. "The Multi-Story Building Model Generator" Master Thesis, Department of Architecture, The Ohio State University, Columbus, OH, December 1986.

Eastman C.M. "General Purpose Building Description System," in *Computer-Aided Design*, January 1976.

Kubicek F.L. "OPUS 2x4: A Wood Framing Construction Computer System" Master Thesis, Department of Architecture, The Ohio State University, Columbus, OH, December 1985.

Mortenson M.E. *Geometric Modeling*, John Wiley & Sons, 1985.

Yessios C.I. "A Notation and System for 3-D Constructions," *Proceedings of 15th Design Automation Conference*, ACM, Las Vegas, NA, June 1978.

Yessios C.I. "What has yet to be CAD" in *Proceedings of ACADIA 86*, The Association of Computer Aided Design in Architecture, Houston, Texas, October 1986.

Yessios C.I. *Architectural Modeling*, Arch 844.04 Lecture Notes, Department of Architecture, The Ohio State University, Columbus, OH 1986.

9

ARTIFICIAL INTELLIGENCE AND AUTOMATED DESIGN

Stuart C. Shapiro
James Geller

Department of Computer Science
State University of New York at Buffalo
Buffalo, New York

Artificial Intelligence (AI) offers to the design task the use of powerful systems that can be knowledgeable assistants to the human designer. Knowledge Representation techniques can be used to specify the ontology and epistemology of the particular design task so an Intelligent Interface, in general, and an Intelligent Drafting assistant, in particular, can discuss the task with the designer using the same concepts that he uses. Investigating Knowledge Representation formalisms for such aids in the context of developing a Versatile Maintenance Expert System (VMES) has uncovered a number of interesting concepts that seem useful for a wider class of design domains. These concepts are presented after a general discussion of the role of AI in design, and an introduction to a particular AI Knowledge Representation system. The role of design aids and Intelligent Interfaces in VMES is presented as an example of the use of such systems.*

*This work was supported in part by the Air Force Systems Command, Rome Air Development Center, Griffiss Air Force Base, New York 13441-5700, and the Air Force Office of Scientific Research, Bolling AFB DC 20332 under Contract No. F30602-85-C-0008, which supports the Northeast Artificial Intelligence Consortium (NAIC).

☐ ARTIFICIAL INTELLIGENCE AND DESIGN

The task of design presents intelligent humans with a large number of complicated problems. Artificial intelligence (AI) is the research area which attempts to discover how to program computers to solve the sort of problems intelligent humans tackle. One use of AI in design might be to have an AI system that would do the design itself, perhaps viewing design as a search through a design-problem space. In this paper, however, we will discuss two aspects of the application of AI as design aids for human designers — the application of Knowledge Representation to drafting systems, and the use of Intelligent Interfaces. After some introductory remarks, we will give a brief introduction to the AI system we are using, present some results of our investigations into the applications of AI to design, and, finally, show how this fits into a Maintenance Expert System we are developing.

The Role of Knowledge Representation

Modern computerized drafting systems supply their users with a wealth of powerful modeling tools. A typical drafting system deals with objects, their visual and non-visual attributes, and their mappings into graphical representations. However, such a system is only a powerful set of pens, it is not an assistant that "knows" what the designer is talking about. To be intelligent, an assistant must be knowledgeable. Knowledgeable computer systems are known as "Knowledge-Based Systems" (KBSs), and are a very active area of AI research and development.

We can identify three roles that people play in the design and use of KBSs. First, there are people who design and implement KBSs without regard to any particular application domain. We can refer to such people as the KBS Designers, and to the results of their efforts, using terminology from the field of Expert Systems (ESs), as "KBS shells." Second, there are those who particularize KBS shells to given application domains. They are called "Knowledge Engineers" (KEs) in the ES world, and we can refer to the results of their efforts as KBSs *simpliciter*. Finally, there are the "end-users" who use KBSs as tools to get particular jobs done.

The job of a KE is usually perceived to be interviewing a person already knowledgeable (at an expert level) in the application domain, and recording that person's knowledge in a form that the KBS shell can use. However, if the KBS shell is flexible enough, there is an additional task for the KE: to design the "form" in which the knowledge is to be recorded. This task is the Knowledge Representation (KR) task, and we will refer to the KE performing this task as the "Knowledge Representation Engineer" (KRE). (The KRE's task has jocularly been called "notational engineering.") The KRE's first task is an analysis of the knowledge primitives in the domain. He must define the domain's ontology (the kinds of objects and attributes contained in the domain), and its epistemology (the sorts of things one may know about the domain, and the ways of knowing them). A flexible KBS shell will permit the KRE to do this declaratively, *i.e.* without re-programming the shell.

The KRE can supply a vocabulary of conceptual objects, relations, and attributes without a limit on the level of object abstraction. For example, one can take the system's representation of an object, and its representation of the depiction of the object on the screen, and create an explicit non-procedural mapping between them. This mapping itself can be reified, which makes it in turn amenable to serving as an object in a propositional context. This example only involves two levels of abstraction and is frequently useful. For instance, it may be used to assert the validity of a mapping that might be limited to particular circumstances.

The declarative representation of these objects has the additional benefit of placing them in the domain of possible end-user queries. Whatever is a concept for both system and user can be discussed by them. The user can tell the system about them, and can ask the system what it currently knows about them. The system can have rules that specify how to reason about them, how to derive new attributes from old ones, and even under what circumstances to infer the existence of objects it hasn't been explicitly informed about.

A Knowledge-Based drafting system can be an intelligent assistant to a designer, rather than just a powerful drawing tool.

Intelligent Interfaces

Recently, there has been increased interest in the contributions AI can make to the design of interfaces. There was both a workshop and a panel on Intelligent Interfaces at the 1986 AAAI sponsored National Conference on Artificial Intelligence, and DARPA has recently funded a program on Multi-media Interfaces.

Our own view, [Shapiro 1986a] is that an intelligent interface needs the following capabilities: it should know about the topic under discussion, not merely be an isolated, modular, general purpose interface; it should know about communication issues, including what is on the screen, and the relationship between what is being communicated and the way it is being communicated; it should have a user model, so it has an idea of what the user knows, doesn't know, and what the user is trying to accomplish. The KBS-based drafter we are developing can be seen as an appropriate intelligent interface to a more extensive design system.

General Introduction to SNePS

The SNePS Semantic Network Processing System [Shapiro 1979; Shapiro 1986b] is the KBS shell we use, and we will use the SNePS formalism in the remainder of this paper. For the reader not familiar with SNePS, we will first give a short introduction to the basic properties that distinguish it from other semantic network systems.

SNePS, unlike semantic network systems of the KL-ONE, KRYPTON family, [Brachman 1985; Brachman 1983] but like Anderson and Bower's HAM, [Anderson 1973] is a propositional semantic network system. *i.e.*, the main ingredient of SNePS networks are assertions, constructed from case grammar-like frames [Fillmore 1968]. This does not imply that SNePS cannot support KL-ONE type class hierarchies and inheritance [Tranchell 1982], but that this feature is less prominent in SNePS. SNePS is a fully intensional knowledge representation system [Shapiro 1986b] — it can represent imaginary, non-existing, and even impossible objects, as well as abstract objects, and multiple guises of a single object as if they were separate objects.

SNePS handles full predicate logic with universal, existential, and numeric quantification. A number of non-standard connectives that improve expressibility are available, including both a default operator and a true negation. SNePS supports forward, backward, and bidirectional inference, in contrast to many other systems which permit reasoning in only one direction. For instance, the OPS5 expert system shell does only forward inference, whereas PROLOG does only backward inference. In SNePS, the same rule syntax can be used for either type of reasoning; there are no specific forward or backward rules. SNePS permits the use of recursive rules, either directly recursive or indirectly recursive [McKay 1981]. A relevance logic based [Anderson 1975; Shapiro 1976] extension to SNePS permits its use as a truth maintenance system [Martins 1983].

Another advantage of SNePS is the total order independence of rules and clauses in the rules, in effect eliminating the painful mixed procedural-declarative semantics of PROLOG. This higher degree of flexibility permits very natural representations, especially for natural language rule expressions. However, the required computation times are usually longer than for PROLOG programs.

Although the major purpose of SNePS is not to be a functional model of the brain, as opposed to, for instance, Anderson's ACT system [Anderson 1983], SNePS has been designed with a high degree of cognitive validity in mind. This is expressed by a differentiation between conceptual and non-conceptual relations, by the impossibility of PROLOGish retract-like forced forgetting (except for debugging purposes), and by the accessibility of all information about a concept from the concept itself.

A number of different SNePS interfaces have been designed, containing several natural language parser/generators for subsets of English, a frame-like editor, a logic programming language, and several graphics interfaces. In our description of knowledge structures we will liberally use the "Lispish" notation of the SNePS User Language (SNePSUL), or our standard graphical representation of SNePS networks.

Knowledge Representation in SNePS

In this section, we will discuss an example SNePS network to introduce the syntax and semantics of some of the representational structures we use in our work on VMES, the Versatile Maintenance Expert System [Shapiro 1986c]. Figure 9.1 shows an Adder-Multiplier, a simple experimental device that has been used in the field of hardware maintenance research by a number of people. This object consists of three multipliers and two adders. Figure 9.2 shows part of the semantic network that describes this device. Rectangles in Figure 9.2 represent concepts of real or imaginary objects. Circles represent propositions about these objects. The network can be read as follows: D1 is an object of type M3A2; D1A1 is of type Adder and is a part of D1; D1M1 is of type Multiplier and is a part of D1; D1A1F1 is a Full Adder and is part of D1A1; etc.

The SNePSUL commands that create the network of Figure 9.2 are:

```
(define part-of object type)

(build object  D1A1
       type    Adder
       part-of D1)

(build object  D1M1
       part-of D1
       type    Multiplier)

(build object  D1
       type    M3A2)
       part-of D1A1
       type    Full Adder)

(build object D1A1F1
       part-of D1A1
       type    Full Adder)

(build object  D1A1F2
       part-of D1A1
       type    Full Adder)
```

The first define command defines the arcs to be used in the system. Arcs can be followed, for retrieval purposes, in either the forward or backward direction, guaranteeing the universal accessibility of every node from every other node that is related to it.

The set of build commands creates the actual network. Note that every build command will result in the creation of one "m..." node. These

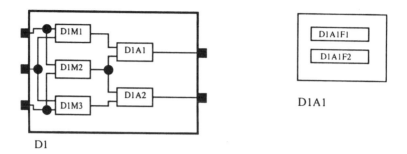

Figure 9.1. The Adder Multiplier and one of its parts.

nodes, as described earlier, correspond to propositions in the system and cannot be created directly by the user. In other words, it is not possible for the user to create an arc connecting two nodes named by him, guarding users against creating non-conceptual propositions, objects the SNePS theory of mind does not permit.

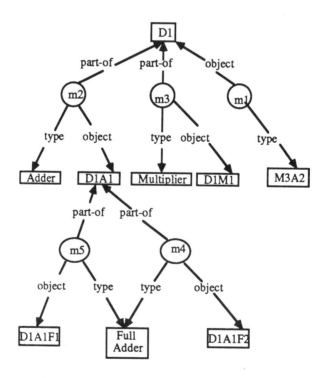

Figure 9.2. A piece of semantic net.

☐ AN ANALYSIS OF IMPORTANT ELEMENTS OF DESIGN KNOWLEDGE

Having introduced the SNePS KBS shell, we will now discuss the ontology and representational constructs that we, in our role as KREs, have found to be necessary for creating descriptions of graphical depictions of simple circuit boards.

Objects and Forms

The first fundamental unit we need to deal with is the displayable *object*. In order to create a picture of an object it is necessary to specify a *form* for it. Every form has a dual role. On the one hand, it can be used to create a picture of that form. On the other hand, it is a conceptual unit in the knowledge representation system and can be manipulated as such. Picture creation is done by a Lisp graphics function whose name is identical to the form concept in the network, and whose arguments are the coordinate positions of the place the form is to be drawn. So, if the form of a particular gate is specified by the function `gate-form`, the gate would be drawn at position (100, 300) by evaluating the Lisp form:

```
(gate-form 100 300)
```

The degree of specificity of a form varies. While the form of an integrated circuit or a transistor is totally fixed, the form of a wire is dependent on the position of the ports it connects. If a user wishes to display an abstract object then he has to supply a symbolic form for it.

Positions

The next essential ingredient for a drafting system is the concept of *positions*. There are several possible ways of specifying positions. In a traditional CAD system, positions are only expressed in an absolute or relative manner based on coordinate values. This is an ability that a KBS should also have. However, knowledge-based design systems should also be able to deal with relational specifications, such as the specification that a certain element should be near or to the left of another element. This, of course, introduces a certain fuzzyness in the representation. However, in many cases this is exactly what a designer would like. It permits him to think in concepts that are natural to him, and it avoids unnecessary specificity. In other words, a knowledge-based drafting system permits one to specify spatial relations with a reasonable degree of imprecision.

The following SNePSUL commands show first our representation for relative coordinate positions, and then for fuzzy positions:

```
(build object   gate-1
       relpos   (build x 100 y 200)
       rel-to   gate-5
       modality function)

(build object   gate-2
       relpos   left
       rel-to   gate-1
       modality function)
```

The first SNePSUL command will create a piece of SNePS network representing the proposition that gate-1 is 100 units to the right and 200 units above gate-5. The second one asserts that gate-1 is to the left of gate-2. The `modality` slot is used to differentiate between different arrangements of an object in a functional representation (wire plan) and a physical representation (picture of the board).

Attributes

Attributes can either be of objects or of pictures of objects. An example of an attribute of a picture is *blinking*. A blinking picture can help a user focus his attention on a currently interesting object, without expressing anything about the object itself.

An example object attribute we have been using is the faultiness of a gate. The proposition that gate-1 is faulty would be represented by the network built by the command:

```
(build object   gate-1
       attr     (build atrb-cls state
                      atrb     faulty
                      modality function))
```

In order that the system know how to display a faulty gate, we tell it that the state attribute maps to the `state-to-color` function:

```
(build attr     state
       mod-func state-to-color)
```

Each attribute function, such as `state-to-color`, is actually a functional that takes a form function and an attribute value as arguments, and returns a modified form function. So, again, if gate-1 had the form represented by the function *gate-form*, and given that gate-1 is in the state of being faulty, and that the attribute function for state is *state-to-color*, gate-1 would be displayed as faulty at coordinate position (100, 300) by evaluating the Lisp form:

```
(funcall (state-to-color #'gate-form 'faulty)
         100 300)
```

Notice that representing different attribute dimensions (state, color, size, etc.) by different attribute functionals explicates the way that different attribute dimensions are, in fact, different.

In this technique, the information of how to display a faulty gate is procedurally encoded in the state-to-color functional. An alternative is to store the information declaratively in the network, such as by a proposition built by the command:

```
(build attr     state
       atrb     faulty
       mod-val  red)
```

This proposition says that the attribute of being in a faulty state is to be shown by making the display red. The fact that red is a value of the color attribute is stored by a separate proposition.

Class Hierarchy

An important feature of most knowledge representation systems is their ability to handle *classes* of objects (and also hierarchies with many levels of classes). This permits a user to associate an attribute with an entire class instead of a single object. For example, one could express the fact that all integrated circuits expect ground potential on their pin 0 by associating this fact with the class of all integrated circuits.

Classes have two important features that are valuable for design systems (and KR systems in general). The first is that by asserting that an object belongs to a certain class, a lot of new knowledge is immediately available about it. This is called inheritance along a class hierarchy. The other valuable feature is that this type of representation seems to correspond to the way people organize their knowledge. Therefore the naturalness of the use of classes also improves the general communication between user and system.

Part Hierarchy

Another feature that is common in AI systems is the use of *part hierarchies*. Much of the knowledge about physical objects can be organized as facts that express a part-whole relation between different objects. This applies also and especially to design systems.

Our own research has shown that the concept of inheritability which was mentioned for class hierarchies is also applicable to part hierarchies, but with a difference that we have not seen discussed in the previous literature. For instance, the attribute of a special transistor of being "twice as large as an average transistor" is inheritable by its parts. On the other hand, if a circuit board is known to be faulty, nobody would want this attribute to be inherited by all its parts. That would defeat the very purpose of a diagnosis system.

In class hierarchies, the only attributes that are not inheritable, are those that apply only to classes. For example, the cardinality of a class is not applicable to, let alone inherited by, its individual members. In the part hierarchy, however, there are non-inheritable attributes, such as faultiness, that are applicable to sub-parts, just not to be inherited by all of them.

The representation that we are using for inheritable attributes is the same as the representation for non-inheritable attributes, and is, in fact, identical to the example of faultiness given in an earlier section. However it is possible to assert in the network about a certain attribute that it is inheritable, simply by pointing to it with an `inheritable` arc. For example:

```
(build inheritable size)
```

The display program which interprets the network automatically queries for inheritability if it has to expand an object with attributes into parts. The results of this query determine whether or not the parts of the object are displayed as having the attribute.

Inheritability, as an attribute of other attributes, is a meta-attribute. The fact that we are representing it explicitly and declaratively gives the user the power to experiment with different attributes, and to postpone the decision about which of them is inheritable.

Our findings about inheritance can be extended to other hierarchies, which we refer to as *relevance hierarchies*. Relevance hierarchies are an abstraction of a number of different hierarchies used in the literature, including topic hierarchies [Haan 1986] and hierarchies of spatial universes (containment hierarchies) [Fahlmann 1979].

☐ THE VMES SYSTEM

The research described in this paper is a part of the VMES (Versatile Maintenance Expert System) project, which deals with hardware maintenance for mixed analog and digital circuit boards. By using the features of a knowledge based architecture, a high degree of versatility has been achieved [Shapiro 1986c].

The specific significance of our work is that frequently electronic devices have fairly short life cycles. A new board is designed and quickly comes

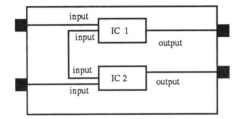

Figure 9.3. An invalid connection.

into use in the field. There is little time to design elaborate test procedures or equipment, or to educate a large number of technicians and users. Usually, the only real expert on the device is its designer, and he is already involved with another project when the first problems in the field come up. Our research is directed toward the design of a KBS-based drafter that the designer will use to help design a new device. This design stage will be the "Knowledge Acquisition" stage of the VMES, which will then be able to advise maintenance technicians on the maintenance and repair of the device that it helped design.

The maintenance system can also be used as a part of the design system, since it can be used to detect impossible designs which do not conform to certain integrity constraints. An example of such an impossible design in the circuit board domain would be if a new device that is described to the system has two chips with their input ports connected to each other, but neither connected to an outport of any other chip (Figure 9.3). Another example would be if two points are electrically connected to each other by two separate wires (Figure 9.4).

VMES implements a large number of the concepts which have been described in the previous sections, i.e. part and class hierarchies, inheritance, attributes, etc. It expects to talk to two different types of end-users. On the one hand are maintenance technicians with a limited amount of education and training. On the other hand are the designers that enter a description of a new device into the system. These two types of end-users

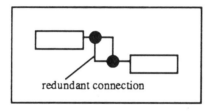

Figure 9.4. A redundant connection.

have different user interfaces, but both interfaces are required to be natural and user-friendly.

The need to create descriptions of circuit boards quickly and without "programming" requires a system that has fairly general knowledge about circuit boards, and that can be adapted to a new device in a short time and with a natural dialogue. To achieve this the system has to *understand* much about the objects of the domain, like wires, inverters or integrated circuits. The use of a Knowledge Representation language is a precondition for achieving such understanding. Use of a component library also permits a rapid change from one device to another. If a new device does not contain any new components, then it is only necessary to describe the new wiring.

Our approach to the design of Intelligent Interfaces may be explained by a description of three interfaces that are part of VMES. The main user interface is a Knowledge-Based graphics component. This program, named display, takes a piece of semantic network as argument and uses it to generate a pictorial representation of the stored knowledge. display works as a generator, quite comparable with a natural language generator. Only redundant permanent auxiliary storage is used by display. In other words, the semantic network plus the Lisp functions describing primitive forms are the only knowledge sources for the computation and creation of device depictions.

We are working on displaying devices under the assumption that no coordinate positions are given. We refer to this activity as intelligent machine drafting (IMD). We are attempting to provide a procedural model of some of the knowledge that a draftsman has about space and arrangement of electronic components. display tries to arrange components of the system in what it "thinks" is a graphically appealing way, using several variations of an equal-spacing algorithm. Unlike VLSI routing or layout programs, which usually try to find some space-optimal solution, display assumes that there is ample space to solve the placing problem.

The second interface is a natural language understander (NLU), implemented by using an augmented transition network (ATN) [Woods 1970; Shapiro 1982] semantic grammar. A user can create classes of objects, assign (predefined) forms to them, name members of these classes, assign them attributes, and then display them, all with commands from a (fairly limited) subset of natural language. The NLU uses the same KR constructs as are used by display. This enables it to demonstrate its understanding of declarative sentences by drawing the object(s) mentioned using appropriate graphic indicators of the asserted attributes.

The third interface is the readform facility, which allows a user to create Lisp form functions simply by drawing objects. readform permits a user to create pictures of objects from simple primitives like lines, circles, boxes etc. He can also design a form off to the side, on a kind of scratch pad, and then add this form repeatedly to the object being designed. readform will assume that the form created on the side is the form of a class of objects, and that the repeatedly added instances are members of that class. These members will also be assumed to be parts of a main object, consisting of the primitives placed before and after using the scratch pad. readform verifies some of its assumptions by querying the user, e.g. asking for a name of the suspected class. If the user supplies the requested names then readform will create a network structure that asserts the class and part relations and will even store the positions of the parts relative to their super object.

☐ CONCLUSIONS

AI offers to the design task the use of powerful Knowledge-Based System shells. Knowledge Representation Engineers particularize these KBS shells to the particular design domain by specifying the ontology and epistemology of the domain. This permits the end-users to discuss the design task with the KBS as if it were a knowledgeable assistant.

We discussed two aspects of KBSs useful for design. Intelligent Interfaces know the task being performed, know about the objects, relations, and attributes being discussed, and know how to express these concepts to the user. Intelligent Machine Drafters (IMDs) are knowledgeable assistants to the designer, besides being powerful drafting tools.

We have been developing a Versatile Maintenance Expert System (VMES) that would be able to help a maintenance technician repair a device that had been designed so recently that there would not have been time to give the technician training on how to repair it. The VMES would acquire its own knowledge of the device by serving as an IMD to the original designer.

In our roles as KREs for VMES, we have identified the following concepts as useful for an IMD and for an Intelligent Interface to a design system: objects; forms of objects; absolute, relative and "fuzzy" positions; attributes of objects and of pictures of objects; attribute functionals; object attribute to picture attribute mappings; class, part, and relevance hierarchies; and meta-attributes, such as inheritability.

☐ ACKNOWLEDGMENTS

We would like to thank the other members of the VMES team, Mingruey R. Taie, Sargur N. Srihari, and Scott S. Campbell for valuable discussions; Dale Richards from RADC for administrative support; Bill Eggers, Michael Rosenzweig, Jim Carney, and Carl Mercer for working on several generations of "Readform"; and finally Lynda Spahr, our secretary, for being a pearl in general.

☐ REFERENCES

AAAI *Proceedings of the Fifth National Conference on Artificial Intelligence*, Morgan Kaufmann Publishers, Los Altos, CA, 1986.

Abbott C. "Introduction to the Special Issue on Computer Music," *ACM*, Computing Surveys, 17(2):147-289, June 1985.

Anderson A. and N. Belnap *Entailment: The Logic of Relevance and Necessity*, Princeton University Press, vol.1, 1975.

Anderson J.R. "A Spreading Activation Theory of Memory," *Journal of Verbal Learning and Verbal Behavior*, 22:261-295, 1983.

Anderson J.R. and G.H. Bower *Human Associative Memory*, V. H. Winston and Sons, Washington, D.C., 1973.

Ballard D.H. and C.M. Brown *Computer Vision*, Prentice Hall, 1982.

Brachman R.J., R.E. Fikes and H.J. Levesque "KRYPTON: A Functional Approach to Knowledge Representation," IEEE Computer, 16(10):67-73, 1983.

Brachman R.J. and H.J. Levesque *Readings in Knowledge Representation*, Morgan Kaufmann Publishers, Los Altos, CA, 1985.

Boden M.A. *Artificial Intelligence: How Machines Think*, Simon & Schuster, NY, 1985.

Brachman R.J. and J. Schmolze "An Overview of the KL-ONE Knowledge Representation System," *Cognitive Science*, 9(2):171-216, 1985.

Charniak E. and D. McDermott *Introduction to Artificial Intelligence*, Addison Wesley, Reading, MA, 1985.

Fahlmann S.E. *NETL: A System for Representing and Using Real-World Knowledge*, MIT Press, Cambridge, MA, 1979.

Fillmore C.J. "The Case for Case," *Universals in Linguistic Theory*, ed. E. Bach and R. T. Harms, Holt, Rinehart, and Winston, NY, pp. 1-88, 1968.

Gardner H. *The Mind's New Science: A History of the Cognitive Revolution*, Basic Books, NY, 1985.

Haan J. de and L.K. Schubert "Inference in a Topically Organized Semantic Net," *Proceedings of the Fifth National Conference on Artificial Intelligence*, Morgan Kaufmann, Los Altos, CA, pp. 334-338, 1986.

Hayes-Roth F., D.A. Waterman and D.B. Lenat *Building Expert Systems*, Addison-Wesley, Reading, MA, 1983.

Hofstadter D.R. and D.C. Dennett *The Mind's I*, Bantam Books, NY, 1981.

Hunt M. *The Universe Within*, Simon & Schuster, NY, 1982.

IJCAI *Proceedings of the Ninth International Joint Conference on Artificial Intelligence*, Morgan Kaufmann Publishers, Los Altos, CA, 1985.

McCalla G. and N. Cercone "Approaches to Knowledge Representation," *Computer*, pp. 12-18, Oct. 1983.

McKay D.P. and S.C. Shapiro "Using Active Connection Graphs for Reasoning with Recursive Rules," *Proceedings of the Seventh International Joint Conference on Artificial Intelligence*, Morgan Kaufmann, Los Altos, CA, pp. 368-374, 1981.

Martins J.P. *Reasoning in Multiple Belief Systems*, 203, SUNY at Buffalo, Dept. of Comp. Sci., 1983.

Nilson N.J. *Principles of Artificial Intelligence*, Tioga, Palo Alto, CA, 1980.

Peat F.D. *Artificial Intelligence: How Machines Think*, Simon & Schuster, New York, 1985.

Shapiro S.C. and M. Wand *The Relevance of Relevance*, 46, Indiana University, 1976.

Shapiro S.C. "The SNePS Semantic Network Processing System," *Associative Networks: The Representation and use of Knowledge by Computers*, ed. by Nicholas V. Findler, Academic Press, NY, pp. 179-203, 1979.

Shapiro S.C. "Generalized augmented transition network grammars for generation from semantic networks" *The American Journal of Computational Linguistics*, 8(1):12-25, 1982.

Shapiro S.C. and J. Geller "Knowledge Based Interfaces," *AAAI-86 Workshop on Intelligence in Interfaces*, ed. Bob Neches and Tom Kaczmarek pp. 31-36, August, 1986a.

Shapiro S.C., S.N. Srihari, M.R. Taie and J. Geller "VMES: A Network Based Versatile Maintenance Expert System," *Applications of AI to Engineering Problems*, 1986c.

Shapiro S.C. and W.J. Rapaport "SNePS Considered as a Fully Intentional Propositional Semantic Network," *Proceedings of the Fifth National Conference on Artificial Intelligence*, Morgan Kaufmann, Los Altos, CA, pp. 278-283, 1986b.

Tranchell L.M. *A SNePS Implementation of KL-ONE*, TR-198, Dept. of Comp. Sci., SUNY at Buffalo, 1982.

Winston P.A. *Artificial Intelligence*, Addison-Wesley, Reading, MA, 1984.

Woods W.A. "Transition Network Grammars for Natural Language Analysis," *Communications of the ACM*, 10:591-606, 1970.

PART 3

DESIGN COMPUTATION

Of all the attempts to apply computers in design, the most comprehensive and intellectually challenging are attempts to automate the design process as a whole. "Design machines" preceded computational design aids, which gradually gave way to computer-aided drafting when the magnitude of the problem was realized.

Recent advances in artificial intelligence, coupled with over two decades of research in computational and other design methods, raise the possibility of design automation once again. This has already been achieved in some engineering disciplines, such as the design of integrated circuits. Its feasibility in other disciplines has also been demonstrated.

The four chapters in this part of the book discuss possibilities and experiences in automating architectural and other "wicked" design processes, using some of the techniques developed in artificial intelligence and CAD research.

Edna Shaviv presents the three major components of design automation: Analysis, synthesis, and evaluation of design alternatives. In ON GENERATIVE AND EVALUATIVE TOOLS FOR SPATIAL ALLOCATION PROBLEMS, she re-introduces the classical problem of architectural space allocation. Two computational approaches to solving layout design problems in floorplans are presented. The first approach is generative, based on three spatial allocation algorithms. The second is evaluative, based on three qualitative measures. She discusses the feasibility and utility of each approach, as well as their respective disadvantages, and proposes their integration as a solution.

In Chapter 11, EXPERT SYSTEMS IN DESIGN ABSTRACTION AND EVALUATION, Gerhard Schmitt discusses the principles of rule-based expert systems, one of the most promising developments in the automation of design (and other cognitive processes). He provides an overview of rule-based generative systems, and shows through examples how they can be applied in solution synthesis and evaluation.

The principles related to the derivation and use of shape grammars, another significant development in design automation, are introduced by Ulrich Flemming in THE ROLE OF SHAPE GRAMMARS IN THE ANALYSIS AND CREATION OF DESIGNS. Flemming demonstrates how shape grammars can be generated from a particular corpus of architecture, then used as a means to analyze and to synthesize buildings of the same kind.

In DESIGN BY ZONING CODE: THE NEW JERSEY OFFICE BUILDING, Mathew Wolchko extends the notion of shape grammars by including procedural computations in addition to grammar rules, where rules alone are insufficient. He demonstrates the use of this extended generative method by its application to non-homogeneous though related building forms.

10

GENERATIVE AND EVALUATIVE CAAD TOOLS FOR SPATIAL ALLOCATION PROBLEMS

Edna Shaviv

Faculty of Architecture and Town Planning
The Technion—Israel Institute of Technology
Haifa, Israel

Computer-aided design tools for generating architectural layouts and for evaluating design alternatives are compared. Both types of tools rely on a careful analysis of the relationships between occupants' activities, the physical dimensions required for the activities, and other architectural constraints. The ability to derive new, original, and efficient architectural solutions by using computational generative tools, and the ability to improve given alternative solutions by using computational evaluative tools, are discussed. It is argued that the techniques of design generation and evaluation should be integrated to form a unified computational design model.

☐ INTRODUCTION

The complexity of architectural design layout problems, known as *spatial allocation problems*, has given rise to several computational approaches intended to assist their generation and evaluation. Generative approaches use computers to produce building layouts, while evaluative approaches use computers to appraise design solutions that were generated computationally or manually.

Spatial allocation algorithms were first developed more than twenty five years ago [Koopmans 1957]. Between 1957 and 1970, over thirty different programs were developed for automatic generation of architectural floorplans, using optimal or quasi-optimal layout methods*. Most of the programs were developed for non-interactive batch processing and ran on mainframe computers.

The advent of interactive user interfaces in the 1980's caused a gradual decline in the development of computer programs for generating layout solutions. The trend today is to develop integrated systems in which the solution is developed manually by the architect, and is then introduced to the computer for appraisal [Maver 1977]. Although such human-machine interactive systems show much promise, most commercial integrated CAD systems support no appraisal techniques, and their comprehensive geometric databases are used only for creating working drawings and perspective images.

Rather than dismiss design generative systems as inferior to current CAD systems or design evaluation tools, this paper examines some of the limitations of automated solution generating systems, points out some of their advantages, and proposes that they should be combined with design evaluation systems to yield better results.

The paper presents few models that were developed in the Technion [Shaviv & Gali 1974; Kalay & Shaviv 1979] for the purpose of solving design layout problems by means of generative and evaluative methods. These models stress in particular the importance of relationships between activities for which the building is designed, the physical dimensions that these activities require, and many other architectural constraints. The advantages and disadvantages of the generative and the evaluative approaches are discussed along with the models, and a case is made for their integration.

□ AUTOMATIC GENERATION OF OPTIMAL OR QUASI-OPTIMAL BUILDING LAYOUTS

Early research in automatic floorplan generation was motivated by the search for an *optimal* or *quasi-optimal* building layout, subject to architectural constraints. Some approaches that were developed for this purpose attempted to create a layout that minimized a certain objective function, such as the volume of circulation between the constituent activities [Armour & Buffa 1963; Whitehead & Eldar 1964; Lee & Moore 1967; Agraa &

---

*These approaches are summarized in CAP—Computer Architecture Programs Vol. 2 [Stewart, Teicholtz & Lee 1970].

Whitehead 1968; Shaviv & Gali 1974]. However, most algorithms for obtaining quasi-optimal building layouts required too much computer time, or trivialized complex architectural problems. Later efforts were focused, therefore, on the search for *feasible* solutions that responded to a given set of constraints without any objective function [Johnson et al 1970; Negroponte 1970; Eastman 1971]. Since not all design criteria could be computationally represented (such as aesthetics and constructability), the generated solutions were often not satisfying. Moreover, the constraint satisfaction approach could be transformed into an optimization approach by selecting one of the feasibility constraints as an objective function. This approach was subsequently replaced by algorithms that automatically generated *all* feasible solutions, allowing the architect to choose the preferred solution by applying additional, non-computable criteria to the selection process [Grason 1968; Mitchell et al 1976; Flemming 1978; Galle 1981]. However, due to algorithmic size complexities, many of the approaches that were developed for this purpose were limited to architectural problems composed of fewer than 16 entities, for which manual floorplan layout generation is not difficult [Earl 1977]. Most practical architectural problems for which the generation of floorplan layouts is difficult contain more than 40 entities, and lie, therefore, beyond the capabilities of the exhaustive enumeration approach.

It appears, therefore, that the optimization approach would be most suitable for solving the design layout problem, if a simple algorithm could be found that would yield a solution within a reasonable time, and which could be applied to complicated architectural problems. Such models were developed by Shaviv & Gali [1974], and will be presented here briefly. They are based on random and heuristic techniques rather than on a path-oriented method, allowing for the generation of different quasi-optimal design alternatives. The architect can then choose the preferred solution by adding criteria that were not embedded in the model.

The originality of design solutions that are generated by means of automatic generators of the kind discussed here could be addressed in two ways: for "small" problems exhaustive enumeration could be employed, so that all possible solutions would be investigated*. For problems that are too large to be investigated exhaustively, some heuristic techniques that can randomly sample the entire space of solutions can be used. By comparison, non-exhaustive systematic search techniques that follow a predetermined path in the space of alternative solutions may not reveal innovative solutions that lie too far down the search path (a problem that is known as the "horizon effect"). The space allocation models of Shaviv & Gali that are described in the following are based on such a random interchange technique.

*Consider, for example the model for designing sun-shades, [Shaviv, 1975] or the CAD tool for the design of solar communities, [Shaviv, 1985].

Formulation of the Models

The Shaviv and Gali models for generating a quasi-optimal solution by randomly searching the space of feasible solutions can accommodate up to 100 activities of different floor areas, each comprised of up to 196 modular grid units. They are based on minimizing the following objective function:

$$\text{Minimize } G = \Sigma_i \Sigma_j W_{ij} D_{ij}$$

where W_{ij} is a weight factor representing merits of adjacency between activities i and j, and D_{ij} is a measure of the Euclidean, the rectilinear, or the minimal distance between these activities.

The adjacency merits scale is comprised of subjectively defined *indifferent, possible, preferable, very preferable, necessary,* and *disturbing* adjacencies. A geometrically increasing scale was chosen, after different alternative scales were examined by evaluating their impact on the resulting solutions (the *disturbing* relationships are negative). The model allows, alternatively, to define the adjacency merit weights in an objective manner, by weighting the value of circulation (number and frequency of trips, and the loads carried), the mutual disturbance between activities, and other subjective criteria (see [Shaviv & Gali 1974]).

The models enables the allocation of activities in several arbitrarily prescribed floors, and the allocation of up to three staircases or elevators (the stairs need not be continuous from one level to the next). The distance between any two activities is calculated through the staircases that yield minimum distances. The location of the staircases and their nature (continuous or not) can be determined by the designer or by the models. In the latter case, the models search for the optimal location based on circulation considerations, consistent with other architectural constraints. The effect of climbing stairs to a given height, as compared with walking a given distance, is an input parameter that may vary from one problem to another (since the situations in a school and in a hospital, for example, are obviously dissimilar.

Various types of architectural constraints have been included in the models, such as forcing the allocation of given activities to a specific floor, or requiring natural illumination for certain activities. If an activity requires natural illumination, the models will place it adjacent to an external wall or an internal court which is added for that purpose dynamically.

Mutual disturbances between activities are treated as constraints that categorically demand separation between two activities. Alternatively, they can be weighted and included in the evaluation of the objective function. Although in most cases mutually disturbing activities will not be placed adjacent to each other, a few exceptions may occur. When a categoric demand for separating two activities is implied, yet their placement in proximity to each other improves the overall value of the objective function, specific technical solutions may be employed, such as separation by acoustic walls. The architect will have to compare and evaluate the extra cost of employing such technical solutions with the added value of the objective function gained by placing the mutually disturbing activities in close proximity.

The Principles Underlying the Models

The search for a quasi-optimal layout commences with a randomly generated initial layout, whose objective function evaluation is compared with another layout in which the location of 2N activities have been interchanged (N > = 1). If the new layout improves the objective function, it replaces the initial layout and becomes the current "best solution.". The search continues until the objective function can no longer be improved, that is, until a minimum has been reached. The activities to be interchanged are selected at random, yet consistency with the various constraints is enforced. Simultaneously interchanging more than two activities (N > 1) was found to be useful in reducing the likelihood of generating local minimums, but requires considerably more computing resources (Figure 10.1). Yet, the difference between a local minimum obtained by interchanging a single pair of activities (N = 1) and the almost absolute minimum obtained by interchanging multiple activities (N > 1) was found to be usually small.

It is interesting to rank the final solution in terms of the best and worst theoretical allocation of activities in a given grid. Figure 10.2 shows the decrease of the objective function (compared to the value of the initial layout). The convergence on a minimum-valued function is initially fast; consequently, there is no real need to start out with a "good" initial guess, since the number of interchanges saved that way is very small. After a relatively small number of interchanges, a plateau is reached and the solution is not improved. Instead, equally good different alternatives are produced, that can be stored by the program (the current implementation stores up to ten alternative solutions). Thus, by starting out with different initial layouts, many alternatives can be generated.

Figure 10.2 also demonstrates that random interchanges are particularly useful at the early convergence stages, since the convergence at that stage is fast; and randomness, unlike systematic interchange techniques, (see [Armour & Buffa 1963]) facilitates variety. On the other hand, once a plateau has been reached, it may be desirable to resort to a systematic interchange technique [Shaviv 1985].

MATRIX OF WEIGHTED ADJACENCY MERITS

	1	2	3	4	5	6	7	8	9	10	11	12	
1	0	9	2	2	1	8	7	3	6	4	1	1	-reactor
2	9	0	1	5	3	4	3	1	2	5	1	1	-control
3	2	1	0	8	9	1	1	2	3	1	9	7	-mechanical workshop
4	2	5	8	0	7	1	1	2	3	1	7	9	-electrical workshop
5	1	3	9	7	0	2	1	1	3	1	8	8	-cold machines room
6	8	4	1	1	2	0	7	1	3	2	3	3	-hot machines room
7	7	3	1	1	1	7	0	2	9	8	1	1	-purification
8	3	1	2	2	1	1	2	0	8	6	2	2	-administration
9	6	2	3	3	3	3	9	8	0	4	3	3	-utilities
10	4	5	1	1	1	2	8	6	4	0	1	1	-radiation haz control
11	1	1	9	7	8	3	1	2	3	1	0	8	-mechanical store
12	1	1	7	9	8	3	1	2	3	1	8	0	-electronic store

INITIAL LAYOUT 1

1	2	3	4
5	6	7	8
9	10	11	12

G = 578

INITIAL LAYOUT 2

1	4	7	10
2	5	8	11
3	6	9	12

G = 572

OPTIMAL LAYOUTS

SINGLE INTERCHANGES FOR LAYOUT 1

10	9	8	3	N = 1
7	1	4	11
6	2	12	5	G = 453

SINGLE INTERCHANGES FOR LAYOUT 2

2	4	5	3	N = 1
1	6	12	11
10	7	9	8	G = 451

MULTIPLE INTERCHANGES FOR LAYOUT 1

5	6	1	2	N = 6
3	4	7	10
11	12	9	8	G = 447

6	1	2	5	N = 2
7	9	4	3
10	8	12	11	G = 449

Figure 10.1. Matrix of weighted adjacency merits, two initial random layouts and optimal layouts obtained by the Point Model for a nuclear reactor.

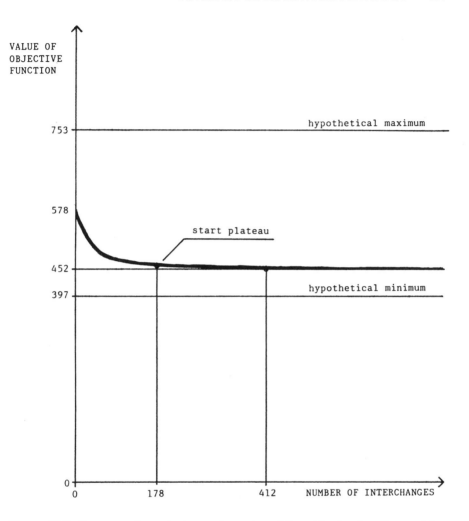

Figure 10.2. Correspondence between the value of the objective function and the number of interchanges.

The Structure of the Models

The models operate in two levels of abstraction: (a) a dimensionless level, where activities are represented as nodes in a graph (the PM model); and (b) a level where the activities are represented by proportionally dimensioned rectangles (the AM model) or by an appropriate number of modular grid units (the PAM model). The difference between the latter two models is their ability (or inability) to handle predetermined building contours: the PAM model can incorporate predetermined outer contours, as well as pre-assigned locations of select activities. The AM model, on the other hand, cannot guarantee that the outer contour of all floors is identical. Unlike the PAM, however, it allows predetermination of the contour of individual activities. The decision of which one of the two methods to use depends on the particular problem at hand.

The point model (PM) allocates activities in the building to the different floors, considering the shortest routes offered by the different staircases. It treats the problem with a high level of abstraction: all activities are represented by squares of an equal size placed on an orthogonal grid, thus allowing for mutual interchange of all activities. This makes the solution insensitive to the initial guess and guarantees its convergence towards the absolute minimum.

The purpose of the PM is to create a good layout for the AM and PAM models, where the actual areas of each activity are considered.

The point-area model (PAM) incorporates the actual area required by each activity into the layout generated by the PM by allocating to each activity the proper number of atomic units it is comprised of (Figure 10.3).

This method of allocating basic units systematically, after an initial layout has been reached (through the PM random techniques), is preferable to other methods that consider each basic unit an activity whose affinity to other basic units of the same activity is very high. Although the high weight of affinity between these units would cause the PM algorithm to keep all basic units of the same activity together, it also reduces the sensitivity of the model to affinities between different activities. The PAM model

(a) MATRIX OF WEIGHTED ADJACENCY MERITS

	1	2	3	4	5	6	7	8	9	10	11	12	
1	0	9	2	2	1	8	7	3	6	4	1	1	-reactor
2	9	0	1	5	3	4	3	1	2	5	1	1	-control
3	2	1	0	8	9	1	1	2	3	1	9	7	-mechanical workshop
4	2	5	8	0	7	1	1	2	3	1	7	9	-electrical workshop
5	1	3	9	7	0	2	1	1	3	1	8	8	-cold machines room
6	8	4	1	1	2	0	7	1	3	2	3	3	-hot machines room
7	7	3	1	1	1	7	0	2	9	8	1	1	-purification
8	3	1	2	2	1	1	2	0	8	6	2	2	-administration
9	6	2	3	3	3	3	9	8	0	4	3	3	-utilities
10	4	5	1	1	1	2	8	6	4	0	1	1	-radiation haz control
11	1	1	9	7	8	3	1	2	3	1	0	8	-mechanical store
12	1	1	7	9	8	3	1	2	3	1	8	0	-electronic store

Figure 10.3. Input and output for the nuclear reactor problem with actual areas incorporated in the PAM: (a) matrix of weighted adjacency merits; (b) random initial layout; (c) optimal layout; (d) freehand interpretation of the computer output obtained in (c).

(b) RANDOM INITIAL LAYOUT

13	8	1	10	1
1	5	1	3	12
11	2	6	1	9
6	1	4	13	1

G = 6649

(c) OPTIMAL LAYOUT

INDEX, ITERAT, K, HAT, NTOTS, NDUP   1105   2   4545   0   2

5	12	11	8	13
5	4	3	9	8
2	1	1	1	10
6	1	1	1	7
6	1	1	1	13

G = 4545

END ITERAT ITERMAX ARE = 8973000

(d) FREEHAND INTERPRETATION

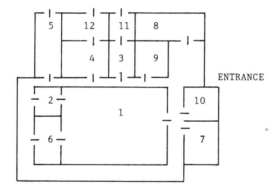

Figure 10.3. (Continued)

retains its sensitivity to affinities between all units, as well as the unity of each activity [Shaviv 1985].

The area model (AM) is an alternative approach to the PAM method. Instead of using modular grid units, each activity is assumed to reside in a rectangle (the ratio of the length to the width of which may vary during the convergence to the optimum layout within prescribed limits). The optimum

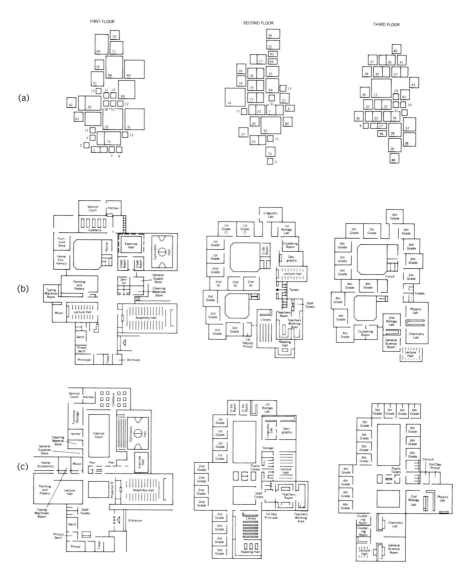

Figure 10.4. (a) Optimal layout for a junior high and a high school in three floors. (b) and (c) are different freehand interpretations of the optimal output.

rectangle that contains each activity is determined by searching a list of possible values that are consistent with furniture, structural materials, or housing regulations.

The AM starts out with a blown-up result of the PM layout. The center of every activity is placed on a very large grid and is represented by its (predetermined) rectangular area, without overlaps. The blown-up layout is sized to leave spaces between all activities, so that internal courts can be added, should they be desired for daylighting.

The AM operates by contraction of spaces and interchange of activities. The contraction "squeezes" the empty spaces between activities, while the interchanges attempt additional permutations between activities, similar to the PM. The interchanges are accompanied by attempted rotations of 90 degrees, or by attempted changes in the proportions of the rectangles within the prescribed bounds. An interchange is rejected if the objective function is not improved, or if the two activities cannot be fit within their proper rectangular areas. Obviously, an interchange must be consistent with the various constraints.

The handling of daylighting and required orientation is dynamic. For example, if an activity requires northern orientation but is not adjacent to a northern external wall, an internal court is added dynamically to the north of it. When this activity is moved from inside the building to a location adjacent to a northern wall, the internal court is deleted. Since the addition of an internal court increases the circulation cost, the model attempts to relocate such activities to the perimeter of the building and eliminate internal courts if possible.

The most important advantage of the AM is the fast generation of solutions in the case of large variations in the areas between activities. We have made successful runs with 84 activities composed of up to 196 modular basic units, with areas varying by a factor of 50. The CPU time required to generate the three-floor scheme depicted in Figure 10.4 was 193.26 sec. on an IBM 370/168.

Critique of the Generative CAD Approach

The PM algorithm, combined with the AM algorithm, resembles the way architects frequently generate floorplans. They start by attempting to understand the relations between the activities, using techniques such as non-dimensional bubble diagrams. Next, they add areas and reallocate activities. The models described here can perform both these steps faster, and can generate several different alternative layouts by using random interchanges. Consequently, the solutions obtained are, in principle, equal to or better than ones obtained manually, and original concepts for design solution can be revealed.

Yet the results produced by the computer do not qualify as final layouts:

They are only good conceptual, schematic solutions. The architect can proceed from them to design the building manually, then use evaluation techniques, such as the ones discussed later, to refine the conceptual solution.

□ EVALUATION OF BUILDING LAYOUTS

Evaluation and appraisal approaches were first developed in the early 1970's, predicated on the conviction that human creativity makes the use of computers for design generation unnecessary. Computers, therefore, should be used to aid designers by evaluating design proposals in a comprehensive yet uncumbersome manner [Maver 1970].

During 1978-79, an evaluative approach to the problem of designing standard dwelling units for the Ministry of Housing in Israel was developed in the Technion [Kalay & Shaviv 1979]. It was motivated by our belief that a large variety of design parameters could be evaluated computationally more accurately than they could be evaluated manually or through a generative approach. We also believed that qualitative, as well as quantitative appraisal could be performed by computational methods, including evaluations of the character of the connection between activities, the compliance of the layout with respective privacies required by various activities, and the life cycle flexibility of the dwelling unit as a whole.

The Evaluation of Activities Layout in a Dwelling Unit

The particular properties of dwelling units, especially their small dimensions, promote a different set of design values from those commonly found in complex buildings with a large number of occupants and activities. For example, the Euclidean distances between various activities are of secondary concern to the mutual spatial relationships between them. Moreover, Euclidean distances in a dwelling unit are poorly defined. It is practically impossible, therefore, to express in some continuous and monotonic way the improvement in the layout due to changes in the distances between the activities. Consequently, both the weights W_{ij} and the distances D_{ij} in the objective function G that were discussed earlier must be defined qualitatively rather than quantitatively.

Relationships between activities in a dwelling are determined by the following primary factors: the respective degrees of privacy of each activity; the affinity between the activities; and the mutual disturbances between them. The Mutual Spatial Relationships (MSR) between the activities can be defined by a dimensionless, discrete space of access configurations, rather than by relative proximities.

By limiting the model to one floor (which is the most common

8 RELATIONS TYPES TO ANY TWO ACTIVITIES IS DETERMINED BY THEIR PRIVACY - RELATIVE AFFINITY AND RELATIVE DISTURBANCE. THE DEGREE IS INDICATED BY ONE OF THE FOLLOWING LETTERS:

    A - BEST RELATION
    B - GOOD RELATION
    C - POSSIBLE RELATION
    D - BAD RELATION

    P - PRIVATE ACTIVITY (INVOLVES
        ONE PERSON ONLY)
    F - SEMI-PRIVATE ACTIVITY (INVOLVES
        FAMILY MEMBERS ONLY)
    G - GUEST ACTIVITY (GUESTS
        AND STRANGERS)

    N - NO AFFINITY OR NO DISTURBANCE
    M - MODERATE AFFINITY OR MODERATE
        DISTURBANCE
    S - STRONG AFFINITY OR STRONG
        DISTURBANCE

THE 8 RELATION TYPES ARE DESCRIBED IN THE COMPREHENSIVE RELATEIONS MATRIX WHICH FOLLOWS.

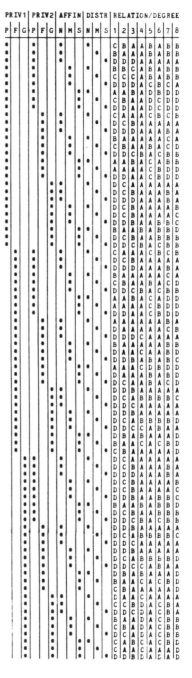

Figure 10.5. The 4D-8D vectors correspondence between a given access configuration and elements in the MSR space. The weighted adjeacency merits are marked by the letters A–D. Reprinted with permisssion from [Kalay and Shaviv 1979], Pergamon Books Ltd.

configuration of dwelling units in Israel) we have defined eight types of access configurations in the MSR space, as follows:

1. Both activities are in the same space.
2. The two activities are in adjacent spaces, with a partial partition between them.
3. The activities are in adjacent spaces that are connected by a door.
4. The activities are in spaces connected by a private corridor.
5. The activities are in spaces connected by a non-private (semi-public) corridor.
6. The activities are in spaces connected by a third space containing semi-public activities.
7. The activities are in spaces connected by a space containing private activities.
8. The activities are located in remote spaces.

These configurative access definitions replace the proximity factors in the evaluative objective function. The definition of the weighted adjacency merits (W_{ij}) is somewhat more difficult, due to the lack of metrics in the MSR space, which prevents the development of a simple scale where the elements of the MSR space are arranged according to some monotonic quality function.

Instead, we enumerated (in the form of a four-dimensional vector) the different factors that affect the relationships between any two activities: the privacy required by each of the two activities, the affinity between them, and the mutual disturbance between them. Each such 4D vector was then associated with a unique eight-dimensional vector that determines the quality of each of the MSR's access configurations with regard to the privacy conditions described by the 4D vector, on a scale of four degrees of merit (Figure 10.5): (A) Best, (B) Good, (C) Possible, and (D) Bad. Given two activities, the corresponding 4D vector that describes their properties can be ascertained, and the quality of their spatial access configuration (as found in the floorplan) can be determined from the associated 8D vector.

To evaluate a floorplan, the user need only provide the layout itself, with the exact locations of doors and activities. The transformation of a given physical layout into the symbolism of the MSR space is performed by the program: the program determines the MSR relative access configuration of each pair of activities, using the existence of walls, openings, or intermediate spaces as decision criteria. In this last case, the character of the activity in the intermediate space is determined by the program as well. Given several openings in each space, and hence several routes for connecting the activities, the program chooses the best spatial access configuration as defined in the 4D-8D correspondence table, assuming the dweller will use the best route if given a choice.

Given the transformed floorplan, the program computes and summarizes the number of connections of each merit, and the overall value of the given floorplan relative to an ideal configuration where all accesses are of the best kind (Figure 10.6). The worst access configurations are spelled out explicitly.

In comparing two layouts we face the problem that not all activities have the same importance; consequently, a poor connection between two activities of one kind does not equal a poor connection between activities of another kind. Therefore, we have defined a scale for the relative importance of activities, which is based on two categories: (1) essential activities, and (2) non-essential activities. Each category is subdivided into dominant and subordinate activities. An activity is essential if it must exist in the dwelling unit (e.g. a kitchen). A dominant activity is one that dictates the character of the space in which it is located (e.g. food preparation is the dominant activity in a dine-in kitchen). Using this scale of importance, an index of performance of the given design alternative can be calculated (see [Kalay & Shaviv 1979]), and different design alternatives can be evaluated and compared according to this index.

The Evaluation of the Dimensions of the Rooms in a Dwelling Unit

The area required by each room in the dwelling is a function of the number of the activities it contains, their character, and the space required to perform each activity. These factors also depend on the size of the family that occupies the dwelling, and their standard of living. One room may contain different activities: furniture can be moved around, and each possible arrangement considered as a different layout alternative. This fact is important for the evaluation of the flexibility of the dwelling, in terms of accommodating families of different sizes, as will be discussed later. The dimensions of each room are considered invariant, because standard buildings in Israel are built from heavy materials, therefore partitions in dwellings cannot be easily moved.

For each activity we define the *core* area, which is the physical area occupied by furniture, and a *field area*, which is the area that is used to access the core. The core must not overlap any other core or field. Similarly, no overlap is permitted in the fields of dominant activities. However, there can be an overlap of 40% or 80% in the fields of essential or subservient activities, respectively.

Given these rules, we can calculate the required room area (X) according to the activities it contains. We found that the real room area (Y) was typically much larger than the calculated area X, especially in small rooms. The reason for these differences is assumed to be psychological, and is due to the inconveniences and discomfort in small crowded rooms. In comparing the actual area of rooms in eighteen different floorplans with the calcu-

```
            1   2   5   6   7   8  10  11  12  16  17  22  23  25  26  28  29  31  32  33

1-ENTR-     5   8   8   5   5   5   5   8   8   8   8   8   8   8   8   8   8   8   8   8
            A       A   A   B   B   B   A   A   A   A   C   D   A   A   A   A   A   A   A
2-GEST-     5       8   8   5   5   1   1   3   8   8   8   8   8   8   8   8   8   8   8
            A           A   A   A   B   D   D   B   A   A   A   A   A   A   A   A   A   A
5-UTIL-     8   8           1   3   3   8   8   8   8   8   8   8   8   8   8   8   8   8
            A   A           A   A   A   A   A   A   A   A   A   A   A   A   A   A   A   A
6-WASH-     8   8   1           3   3   8   8   8   8   8   8   8   8   8   8   8   8   8
            A   A   A           A   A   A   A   A   A   A   A   A   A   A   A   A   A   A
7-COOK-     5   5   3   3           1   5   5   8   8   8   8   8   8   8   8   8   8   8
            B   A   A   A           A   A   A   A   A   A   A   A   A   A   A   A   A   A
8-BREK-     5   5   3   3   1           5   5   8   8   8   8   8   8   8   8   8   8   8
            B   B   A   A   A           A   A   A   A   A   A   A   A   A   A   A   A   A
10-PLAY-    5   1   8   8   5   5           3   8   8   8   8   8   8   8   8   8   8   8
            B   D   B   B   A   A           A   A   A   A   A   A   A   A   D   D   A   B
11-STU -    5   1   8   8   5   5   1           3   8   8   8   8   8   8   8   8   8   8
            B   D   B   B   A   A   D           B   A   A   A   A   A   A   B   A   A   B
12-OUTD-    8   3   8   8   8   8   3   3           8   8   8   8   8   8   8   8   8   8
            A   B   D   D   A   A   B   B           D   A   A   A   A   A   A   A   A   B
16-SDAD-    8   8   8   8   8   8   8   8   8           1   1   1   1   1   4   4   4   4
            A   A   A   A   A   A   B   A   D           B   C   D   C   A   A   A   A   A
17-SDAD-    6   8   8   8   8   8   8   8   8   1           1   1   1   1   4   4   4   4
            A   A   A   A   A   A   B   A   B   B           C   C   A   A   A   A   A   A
22-SLAD-    8   8   8   8   8   8   8   8   8   1   1           1   1   1   4   4   4   4
            A   A   A   A   A   A   B   A   C   B   D           C   A   C   A   A   A   A
23-SLAD-    8   8   8   8   8   8   8   8   8   1   1   1           1   1   4   4   4   4
            A   A   A   A   A   A   A   A   A   D   C   C           C   A   A   A   A   A
25-WRCH-    8   6   8   8   8   8   8   8   8   1   1   1   1           1   4   4   4   4
            A   A   A   A   A   A   A   A   A   A   A   A   C           A   A   A   A   A
26-WRCH-    8   8   8   8   8   8   8   8   8   1   1   1   1   1           4   4   4   4
            A   A   A   A   A   A   A   A   A   A   A   A   A   A           A   A   A   A
28-WRCH-    8   8   8   8   8   8   8   8   8   4   4   4   4   4   4           4   4   4
            A   A   A   A   A   A   A   A   A   A   A   A   A   A   A           A   A   A
29-TLCH-    8   8   8   8   8   8   D   8   8   4   4   4   4   4   4   4           1   4
            A   A   A   B   A   A   A   A   A   A   A   A   A   A   A   A           B   A
31-MKUP-    8   8   8   8   8   8   D   8   8   4   4   4   4   4   4   4   1           4
            A   A   A   A   A   A   A   A   A   A   A   A   A   A   A   A   A           A
32-SLPR-    8   8   8   8   8   8   8   8   8   4   4   4   4   4   4   4   4   4
            A   A   A   A   A   A   A   B   A   A   A   A   A   A   A   B   A   A
33-WRPH-    8   8   8   8   8   8   8   8   8   4   4   4   4   4   4   4   4   4   1
            A   A   A   A   A   A   B   B   A   A   A   A   A   A   A   A   A   A
```

STATISTICS:

NUMBER OF FIRST GRADE CONNECTIONS = 312 - 82.11%
NUMBER OF SECOND GRADE CONNECTIONS = 32 - 8.42%
NUMBER OF THIRD GRADE CONNECTIONS = 10 - 2.63%
NUMBER OF FOURTH GRADE CONNECTIONS = 26 - 6.84%

INDEX OF ALTERNATIVE = 4708 - 82.42%

BAD CONNECTIONS:

BETWEEN ACTIVITIES: ENTR AND SLAD
                      ENTR AND SLAD
                      GEST AND PLAY
                      GEST AND STUD
                      UTIL AND OUTD
                      WASH AND OUTD
                      COOK AND OUTD
                      PLAY AND STUD
                      PLAY AND MECH
                      PLAY AND TECH
                      OUTD AND SDAD
                      SDAD AND SLAD

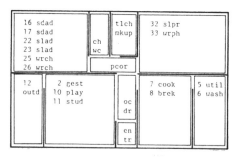

Figure 10.6. Comparison between the required and realized access configurations in the MSR space. The corresponding elements of the MSR are marked by numbers and the quality of the realized mutual relationships are marked by letters. Reprinted with permission from [Kalay and Shaviv 1979], Pergamon Books Ltd.

206

(a)

SUMMARY OF KITCHEN

A = 1.08163
B = 0.11834
R = 0.86767

SUMMARY OF LIVING AREA

A = 0.87214
B = 0.37259
R = 0.75731

SUMMARY OF DINING AREA

A = 0.81871
B = 2.49031
R = 0.91767

SUMMARY OF FAMILY LEISURE

A = 0.96474
B = 1.32855
R = 0.90175

SUMMARY OF ONE CHILD SLEEPING SPACE

A = 0.83422
B = 2.39705
R = 0.89872

SUMMARY OF TWO CHILDREN SLEEPING SPACE

A = 1.05097
B = 0.66674
R = 0.82847

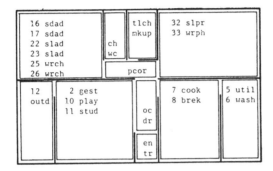

(b)   SUMMARY OF DIMENSIONS - ALTERNATIVE NO. 3

R. NO.	RO.SIZE (RAREA)	RO.SIZE (SAREA)	S.DIFF. (HS)	% DIFF. (% RS)	WIDTH (CRW)	R.WIDTH (CWDTH)	W.DIFF. (DCR)
17-BALC	5.26	4.00	1.25	31.25	1.50	1.60	-0.10
	5.26	6.00	-0.75	-12.50	1.50	1.60	-0.10
	5.26	8.00	-2.75	-34.38	1.50	1.60	-0.10
2-LIVG	14.00	13.85	0.15	1.12	1.50	3.20	0.30
1-ENTR	1.50	1.50	0.0	0.0	1.00	1.10	-0.10
5-KITC	0.75	7.31	1.44	19.75	2.50	1.40	1.10
	8.75	7.74	1.01	13.06	2.50	1.40	1.10
	8.75	8.39	0.36	4.32	2.50	1.40	1.10
6-UTIL	5.25	3.30	1.96	59.25	1.50	1.00	0.50
8-CHDR	12.00	14.45	-2.45	-16.96	3.00	2.80	0.20
20-PCDR	2.50	1.00	1.50	150.00	1.00	0.90	0.10
10-CHWC	2.00	1.10	0.90	81.82	1.00	0.80	0.20
9-CHB1	3.00	2.52	0.48	18.81	1.50	1.50	0.0
12-PMSL	12.00	8.81	8.19	36.15	3.00	2.70	0.30
21-OCDR	2.00	1.00	1.00	100.00	1.00	0.90	0.10

UNACCEPTABLE FUNC. SPACES:

STANDARD-3
   1 - BALC (17)   DEVIATION FROM MINIMUM -34.38%
   2 - CHD2 (8)   DEVIATION FROM MINIMUM -16.96%

SCORES:

STANDARD-3   12% - 39.98%

Figure 10.7. (a) Area correlation parameters. (b) Evaluation of the dimensions of rooms in a dwelling unit.

lated area for the activities in those rooms, we found a linear correlation between the real area Y and the calculated area X, of the form $Y = AX + B$, as shown in Figure 10.7a. Note that the parameter B is relatively large in rooms that contain much traffic, such as living rooms; while it is relatively small in rooms that house many activities but relatively little traffic, such as kitchens.

To evaluate the area of each room, we list the required areas and the minimum width for each activity, according to the number of people in the family and according to three standards of living, stored in memory. The given area and width of each room of the layout is computed and compared with the required area and minimal width, defined by the activities contained in the room. The differences between the required and designed areas are summarized (Figure 10.7b). If the analysis shows that the area of the room is smaller than required, and if the room contains non-essential and subservient activities, these activities are removed from the room and the area is re-evaluated for the remaining activities. This procedure follows the assumption that the residents of this dwelling will adapt it to their most effective use. The implication is that the architect's effort to enrich the design by adding more activities may yield a non-realizable solution. This dynamic adaptation of the layout to realizable conditions demonstrates the inclusion of some generative techniques in an otherwise evaluative model; such as relocating the removed activities to other rooms where there is enough space to accommodate them, or adding the minimum required missing area to the room in order to contain the removed activities. These changes may later be incorporated manually in the floorplan.

The Evaluation of the Flexibility of a Dwelling Unit

The model evaluates the degree of adaptability of the dwelling to different families and to different possible continuous changes in the family structure during its life cycle. This evaluation is based on the assumption that each stage in the family's life cycle has certain physical implications in terms of the number of activities and the spatial standards required by them. The model determines the degree of adaptability of a given dwelling unit to each of these requirements.

The determination of the requirements may change with the target population. In this model we consider families of one to five members. (More than 90% of the families in Israel have fewer than six members.) No distinction was made between sexes. These conditions yield 17 different family profiles (Figure 10.8a). The physical requirements of each profile, in terms of the required activities and the areas required by them are classified.

Next, the combinatorial tree of the different possible life cycles that can be supported by the given layout is computed. A life cycle is defined as a

MATRIX OF FAMILY PROFILES

A FAMILY PROFILE IS REPRESENTED BY A VERTICAL SECTION IN THE MATRIX.
AN ASTERISK INDICATES THE MEMBER OF THE FAMILY.

```
            1  2  3  4  5  6  7  8  9  10 11  12 13  14  15  16  17

1 - PARN -  *  *  *  *  *  *  *  *  *  *   *  *  *   *   *   *   *
2 - PARN -     *  *  *  *  *  *  *  *  *   *  *  *   *   *   *   *
3 - BABY -        *        *  *            *  *  *
4 - CHLD -           *        *     *  *   *  *       *   *
5 - CHLD -                       *                        *
6 - CHLD -                                                *
7 - ADLT -           *     *        *  *      *  *    *   *   *
8 - ADLT -                             *        *            *   *
9 - ADLT -                                                       *
```

b. **FLEXIBILITY MATRIX OF ALTERNATIVE NO. 3:**

PROF.NO	VALID	OVLR PR	RUM OVP	DIMLNS	CONNECT
1	1	1	6	81.22	95.84
2	1	2	6	81.22	95.84
3				0.0	0.0
4	1	5	6	84.31	87.69
5				0.0	0.0
6				0.0	0.0
7				0.0	0.0
8	1	2	6	73.73	88.24
9				0.0	0.0
10				0.0	0.0
11				0.0	0.0
12				0.0	0.0
13				0.0	0.0
14				0.0	0.0
15				0.0	0.0
16				0.0	0.0
17				0.0	0.0

```
 _____
|                           |        | tlch | 32 slpr   |
| 16 sdad                   |        | mkup | 33 wrph   |
| 17 sdad                   | ch     |      |           |
| 22 slad                   | wc     |------|           |
| 23 slad                   |        |      |           |
| 25 wrch                   |        | pcor |           |
| 26 wrch                   |        |      |           |
|-------|-------------------|--------|------|------|----|
| 12    |  2 gest           |        | 7 cook| 5 util |
| outd  | 10 play           |  oc    | 8 brek| 6 wash |
|       | 11 stud           |  dr    |       |        |
|       |                   |--------|       |        |
|       |                   |  en    |       |        |
|       |                   |  tr    |       |        |
```

c.

NUMBER OF SATISFIED FAMILY PROFILES - 7
PROFILE - 1
PROFILE - 2
PROFILE - 3
PROFILE - 4
PROFILE - 5
PROFILE - 6
PROFILE - 8

NUMBER OF STATISFIED LIFE-CYCLES - 2

Figure 10.8. (a) Matrix of family profiles. (b) Flexibility matrix of a given design alternative. The table lists the family profiles that the given alternative fits and the total agreement between the dimensions and connections requirements. (c) Summary of all family profiles supported by the design alternative and the total number of life cycles.

sequence of family profiles. For example, a possible sequence would be comprised of a couple, a couple with a baby, a couple with one child, and finally a couple with one adult child. After the child leaves home, we again have a family of two and then one member. To support this life cycle, a dwelling must satisfy the demands of family profiles 2,3,4,7,1 (see Figure 10.8a). The combinatorial tree of families of one to five members contains 620 different life cycles. The physical requirements of the 17 different family profiles and the combinatorial tree of the family life cycles are stored in the model's database.

The flexibility of a given layout is determined by computing the different alternatives for allocating activities in the rooms, and by computing the number of family profiles these alternative allocations support (see Figure 10.8c). The flexibility index of the dwelling is determined by the number of different life cycles these family profiles comprise.

Critique of the Evaluative Approach to CAD

The evaluative approach presented here supports a detailed and sensitive evaluation of the connection between the activities, the dimensions of each room, and the flexibility of the dwelling unit, both qualitatively and quantitatively. The model is shown to be capable of deriving these qualitative and quantitative merits from a geometrical representation of the layout, augmented with a list of activities contained in each room. Furthermore, it is able to find the best connecting path from room to room, and determine what activities should be removed from a room for lack of space. It can evaluate the required dimensions of these rooms, the profiles of families that the dwelling unit can support, and the number of life cycles these family profiles comprise.

Much like other evaluative design tools, this program can help the designer make decisions about needed improvements. Nevertheless, all design solutions are generated manually, and have to be presented to the computer by the designer.

□ CONCLUSIONS

The approaches presented in this paper were devised to deal with the complexity of design layout problems, using generative or evaluative techniques. The generative approach enabled us to reach new and original solutions that might not be considered otherwise. On the other hand, the evaluative approach allows better understanding of the details and consequences of alternative solutions. However, the design of the layout must be carried out manually.

A generative program can produce an unlimited number of design solutions in one execution, while the evaluative programs can analyze only one design solution at a time. Moreover, the evaluative programs require more detailed description of the building and its environment than does a generative program. Hence, evaluative tools are not frequently used in the initial design stages, where most of the important design decisions are made, but rather in the later stages, after most of these decisions have already been made. On the other hand, generative design tools are typically developed explicitly for use in the initial design stages, to assist the generation of appropriate, original solutions.

We maintain that these two techniques should not be separated. They should be considered components of one, continuous design process. It seems that the order of using these two techniques should be as follows:

1. Alternative design solutions should be generated automatically, according to design requirements formulated as constraints and as an objective function.

2. The generated alternatives should be evaluated and appraised by means of automatic evaluation programs. This stage would include a very detailed and sensitive evaluation of each requirement and would allow the refinement of the proposed design.

3. The deficiencies of the proposed solutions, identified by the evaluation step, should be rectified through the automatic or manual generation of new and better design alternatives. This process of generation/evaluation should be iterated until a design solution that meets all the requirements is found.

The combined use of computational generation and evaluation techniques will help designers find better solutions to the architectural layout problem than could be derived manually.

☐ REFERENCES

Agraa O. M. and B. Whitehead "Nuisance Restriction in the Planning of Single Story Layout," *Building Science 2*, 291, 1968.

Armour G. C. and E.S. Buffa "A Heuristic Algorithm and Simulation Approach to Relative Location of Facilities," *Management Science* 9(2):294-309, Jan. 1963.

Eastman C. M. "Heuristic Algorithms for Automated Space Planning," 2nd Int. Joint Conf. on Artificial Intelligence, British Computer Society, pp. 27-39, 1971.

Earl C. F. "A Note on the Generation of Rectangular Dissections", *Environment and Planning B*, 4(2):241-246, Dec. 1977.

Flemming U. "Wall Representation of Rectangular Dissections and their use in Automated Space Allocation," *Environment and Planning B*, 5(2):215-232, Dec. 1978.

Galle P. "An Algorithm for Exhaustive Generation of Building Floor Plans", *Communications of the ACM*, 24(12):813-825, Dec. 1981.

Grason J. "A Dual Linear Graph Representation for Space-Filling Location Problems of the Floor Plan Type," *Emerging Methods in Environmental Design and Planning*, G.T. Moore (Ed.) Proc. of the Design Methods Group, 1st Int. Conf., Cambridge, MA. 170-178, 1968.

Johnson T. E., G. Weinzapfel, J. Perkins "Image: An Interactive Graphics-Based Computer System for Multi-Constrained Spatial Synthesis", Department of Architecture, M.I.T., Sept. 1970.

Kalay Y. & E. Shaviv "A Method for Evaluating Activities Layout in Dwelling Units," *Building and Environment*, 14(4):227-234 Dec. 1979.

Koopmans T.C. et al. "Assignment Problems and the Location of Economic Activities," *Econometrica*, 25(1):53-76, Jan. 1957.

Lee R. B. & J. M. Moore "CORELAP - Computerized Relationship Layout Planning," *Journal of Industrialized Engineering*, 18(3), March 1967.

Maver T.W. "A Theory of Architectural Design in Which The Role of the Computer is Identified," *Building Science*, 4:199-207, Mar. 1970.

Maver T. W. "Building Appraisal" *Computer Applications in Architecture*, J.S. Gero (Ed), Applied Science Publishers Ltd. London, 63-94, 1977.

Mitchell W. J., J. P. Steadman & R.S. Liggett "Synthesis and Optimization of Small Rectangular Floor Plans," *Environment and Planning B*, 3(1):37-70, June 1976.

Negroponte N. *The Architecture Machine*, MIT Press, Cambridge, MA. 1970.

Shaviv E. & D. Gali "A Model for Space Allocation in Complex Buildings", *Build International*, Applied Science Publisher Ltd, England, 7(6):493-518, 1974.

Shaviv E. "A Method for the Design of fixed external Sun Shades," *Build International*, Applied Science Publisher Ltd, England, 8(2):121-150 1975.

Shaviv E. "A Model for the Site Layout of Solar Communities," *Sunworld*, 9(4):113-115&128, 1985.

Shaviv E. "Layout Design Problems and Their Systematic Approach," CAAD Futures, Proc. of the Int. Conf. on CAAD, Technical University of Delft, Sept 1985.

Stewart, Teicholtz & Leehitecture Programs", *Center for Environmental Research*, Boston, 2, 1970.

Whitehead B. & M. Z. Eldar "An Approach to the Optimal Layout of Single-Story Buildings," *The Architects' Journal*, 17:1373-1380, June 1964.

11

EXPERT SYSTEMS IN DESIGN ABSTRACTION AND EVALUATION

Gerhard Schmitt

Department of Architecture
Carnegie Mellon University
Pittsburgh, Pennsylvania

Design abstraction and design evaluation are fundamental processes to represent and predict the performance of an architectural product. In a rational decision making design context, algorithmic and knowledge-based computer programs can support these processes. Expert systems are an evolving class of architectural tools which promise significant advantages over traditional and first generation computer aided abstraction and evaluation approaches.

Part one compares the traditional models underlying design abstraction and design evaluation. The general characteristics of these models are described followed by a discussion of knowledge based and expert systems and their potential to improve traditional methods.

Part two deals with design abstraction. We assume that a number of valid paradigms for design abstraction have been developed and are applicable. In absence of a general computer based representational language for architecture, languages such as LISP, PROLOG, OPS5, and OPS83, are used to simulate and understand the process of design abstraction.

Part three addresses design evaluation. It is built on the same computational paradigm as design abstraction. Expert front ends can improve the accuracy of simplified evaluation programs and they allow even the novice user to perform accurate evaluations. As compared to traditional computational methods, reliable results can be achieved with drastically reduced time commitment and computing power, which is particularly important in the conceptual design stages.

□ ARCHITECTURAL ABSTRACTION AND EVALUATION

The process of design, since its formal inception, has maintained a singular goal: the production of good buildings. The process itself, the teaching of design, the evaluation methods and criteria, are subject to change and depend on the state-of-the-art in research and technology. Abstraction supports both the generative and the analytical phases of design. Recent developments in the fields of Artificial Intelligence and Psychology provide the theoretical basis to build fundamentally new tools to support the architectural design process, in particular for design abstraction and evaluation. Before the presentation of these tools, it is necessary to describe the underlying traditional models for design abstraction and evaluation and their roles in the design process.

Traditional Models of Abstraction

The concept of abstraction in architectural design is historically linked to the level of complexity of the product. Abstraction developed along the paradigm change from *making* buildings to *planning* buildings. First applications of abstraction involved the representation of existing structures and can be characterized as an attempt to recreate reality. Any representation of the built reality involves abstraction, as the only perfect representation of reality is the artifact itself.

Abstraction relies on the existence of a *model* that both the creator of the abstraction and the individual interpreting the abstraction agree on. The use of an identical or at least similar model is critical in the successful translation from reality to abstraction and then back to reality. Architects have developed powerful models of abstraction, most notedly in the area of graphics.

A more difficult application of abstraction is the prediction or simulation of reality. The representation of reality uses an existing building and, through abstraction, reduces it to a drawing; in the reverse sense, a non-existent but planned building envisioned by a designer is taken from an abstracted drawing to reality. The same means of abstraction are applied to represent an existing floor plan or to represent the floor plan of a building under design. It is this bi-directional character of abstraction that makes it particularly suited for the application of computational models.

Graphic Language: An Abstraction

Analogies between the linguistic paradigm and the architectural design process are an emerging field of architectural research [Coyne 1986; Goel 1986]. Laseau proposes a graphic language that has grammatical rules comparable to those of verbal language [Laseau 1980]. The nouns, verbs, and modifiers in verbal language represent identities, relationships between nouns, and qualifications and quantifications of identities, respectively. Graphic language, inherently explicit, needs a grammar, a vocabulary, elements and operations that establish identities, relationships, and modifiers. Graphic language represents vocabulary as symbols composed of point and line primitives, those being its elements. It represents relations with proximity and the thickness of connecting lines. It represents modifiers by varying symbol size and line weight. Coyne's and Goel's work focuses on the formalization of relations between the linguistic paradigm and the design process, thus establishing a more general and fundamental approach which is particularly interesting for computer based applications.

Graphic language is, other than verbal language, both sequential and simultaneous. Though the proposed graphic language paradigm can benefit from parallel structures in verbal language, it must not obscure the fact that it does not sufficiently represent all complexities of the design process. "The successive stages of the process are usually registered by some kind of graphic model. In the final stages of the design process, designers use highly formalized graphic languages such as those provided by descriptive geometry. But this type of representation is hardly suitable for the first stages, when designers use quick sketches and diagrams . . . It has been accepted for years that because of the high level of abstraction of the ideas which are handled at the beginning of the design process, they must be expressed necessarily by means of rather ambiguous, loose graphic language. Such a language would register the information exactly at the level of abstraction it has, and it would facilitate communication and cooperation among designers" [Bonta 1972]. Until recently, computer aided abstraction meant the quicker execution of the final design stages by taking advantage of the rules of descriptive geometry and the new machines' computational power. The more enigmatic earlier design stages were not supported.

Generative and Analytical Aspects of Abstraction

Practical design problems seldom have one best solution. Every entry into a design competition represents the best solution for the participant, but not necessarily for the jury. The competition participant works from a set of criteria and experiences acquired beforehand. The jury applies predefined criteria to the solutions, and combines them with the stimulation evolving from the review of the entries. In both cases, abstraction is used for architectural problem solving. The competition participant employs abstraction to simplify and reduce the design problem to its essential elements. Subsequently, abstraction becomes a means of *generating* solutions. The jurors, on the other hand, apply abstraction via a stepwise process of compliance checking and extraction of important characteristics to finally facilitate the comparison of products. In this case, abstraction supports *analysis* and judgement.

Different levels and traditional methods of abstraction are available to the designer. Abstraction through graphic language was described above. The building program itself, expressed as functions and associated areas, attributes and requirements, is an abstract, yet not sufficient description of the design. The room names, their adjacency and proximity requirements represented in a matrix, are another form of abstraction. The popular bubble diagrams, and the less often produced space schedule diagrams are means of abstraction. Kinesthetic maps, representing the kinesthetic or dynamic experiences of a person moving through space, represent abstract models to support a well defined aspect of the design problem.

Abstraction is employed to represent and test different aspects of the entire design problem. It is the designer's responsibility to set priorities, weigh the importance of each aspect, and come to a final decision. The product is a set of syntactic drawings. The meaning, or semantics, is supplied by the viewer who uses in an ideal situation the same underlying model as the designer.

Traditional Models of Evaluation

Abstraction and evaluation are closely related. Evaluation of architectural design is based on abstraction. As absolute architectural evaluation is not possible and a contradiction in itself, it needs abstraction to evaluate aspects of a building or a design (see Figure 11.2). The example of the design competition offers valuable insights in the evaluation process as well. Whereas the designer is forced to concentrate on the generative capabilities of abstraction in order to deliver a product in a given time frame, the analytical or *evaluative* aspects of abstraction are used to check every design solution against the defined goals. The jurors are faced with a set of solutions and must select one as the best. They apply abstraction mainly as an analysis tool, less for generative purposes. It is interesting to note that often entries which violate some of the requirements are placed among the best. In these cases, the designer has purposely or by accident changed the priorities or weighting of the criteria and the jury has accepted this or discovered a benefit in doing so. A reason might be that different meanings or semantics can be assigned to the same drawing or syntactic representation—a formidable challenge for any computer implementation attempt.

Evaluation of Existing Buildings and Building Design

The quality of design is often directly proportional to the quality of the criteria applied for the evaluation. Constraints such as density or minimum distances between buildings are an example for regulative and quantitative criteria which are frequently supplemented by qualitative criteria such as contextual concerns. Quantitative performance can be measured; consequently, quantitative criteria are relatively easy to establish and verify. Examples are energy consumption, yearly maintenance costs, or temperature conditions. In fact, cost or energy budgets, minimum U-values for building materials, and similar thresholds are now established and accepted design and evaluation criteria. Qualitative criteria such as thermal or visual comfort and user satisfaction are more difficult to establish and measure. Although extremely important—94% of the average life-cycle cost of office buildings is related to personal cost—user satisfaction is seldom a hard criterion. If, for example, a new building develops severe air quality problems resulting in a 25% employee absentee rate, then this will be much more damaging from a cost standpoint than the introduction of a quality assurance process during design and construction [Hartkopf 1981]. This example shows that the present process of evaluation of existing or planned buildings is at least incomplete, if not misleading, due to the fact that some of the fundamental evaluation criteria are not quantifiable.

First Generation Computational Tools supporting Abstraction and Evaluation

Abstraction has two major advantages: it simplifies the exposure of the underlying structure of an entire system by showing only the significant parts, and it frees the designer from extraneous drawing while manipulating symbols representing entities. The first characteristic requires the designer to understand the system and to assign meaning to the abstraction. Until recently, computational methods offered no help in this process. Computers are helpful, however, in freeing the designer from repeatedly drawing complex entities. In general, the first generation computational tools, based on algorithmic programs, were able to facilitate the syntactic, but not the semantic tasks of the designer. Possible shortcomings are associated with this approach: by facilitating the syntactic part of representation, designers may actually forget the useful aspects of abstraction and reduction, i.e., the semantic aspects. The growing libraries of standard elements available with commercial drafting packages are an indication. Standard elements do not only include primitives such as chairs and tables, but standard templates are available for entire rooms and buildings. Although working with large assemblies, or chunks, is effective for the experienced designer, it may be overwhelming and incomprehensible for the novice. The mere assembly of lines to form a syntactic vocabulary will not improve design if the designer does not understand the meaning and place of the graphic vocabulary.

Figure 11.1 demonstrates a first generation computer aided abstraction applied to a chair by Charles Rennie Mackintosh. The sequence 11.1a-11.1b-11.1c-11.1d shows abstraction applied analytically to represent the artifact: 11.1a is a photograph of the original chair, 11.1b a manually produced abstraction of the chair showing the front and side elevation. 11.1c is the result of scanning the manual drawings into the computer, and 11.1d is a view of the resulting computer model. The sequence 11.1d-11.1a would show the generative character of abstraction: 11.1d would be the result of a design process that starts with the intention to design a chair and the creation of an abstract computer model. The computer model can be used to generate all orthographic views and dimensioned working drawings which are necessary to build the chair. Not surprisingly, the generative use of abstraction turns out to be easier than the analytic approach.

Similar observations are in place for the first generation evaluation packages. Concentrating on the readily computable aspects of a building or a design, simulation meant the often meaningless computation of performance aspects that had little or no impact on the real behavior or quality of the building. Examples are early energy analysis packages and cost analysis packages. Due to the inability of the programs to handle non-quantifiable but common-sense problems, their usefulness was limited. The same applies for first generation spatial layout programs. In general, the first computational tools for abstraction and evaluation were well suited for the solution of well defined questions, but not for real architectural problems which are ill-defined and under-constrained. In fact, these early evaluation and abstraction programs, not developed by architects, and lacking user-friendly interfaces, still have a questionable reputation in parts of the architectural community [Schmitt 1985a].

Figure 11.2 gives an example for a first generation computer aided design evaluation. The diagrams on the top show the abstract representation of two different buildings in terms of thermal zones. The zoning diagrams were developed manually in order to represent the building as a model that the analysis program, in this case DOE-2.1.B, could understand. The graph shows an hourly simulation of the electricity consumption from January (left) through December (right). An experienced energy analyst will conclude from this graph and from studying floor plans and climate that the building is internal load dominated and has a high air conditioning load because of its configuration and equipment. Traditional computer analysis cannot provide this explanation.

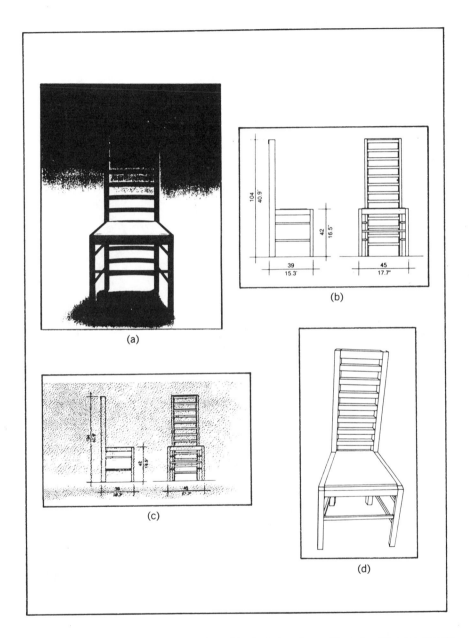

Figure 11.1. First generation computer aided abstraction. Chair by Charles Rennie Mackintosh.

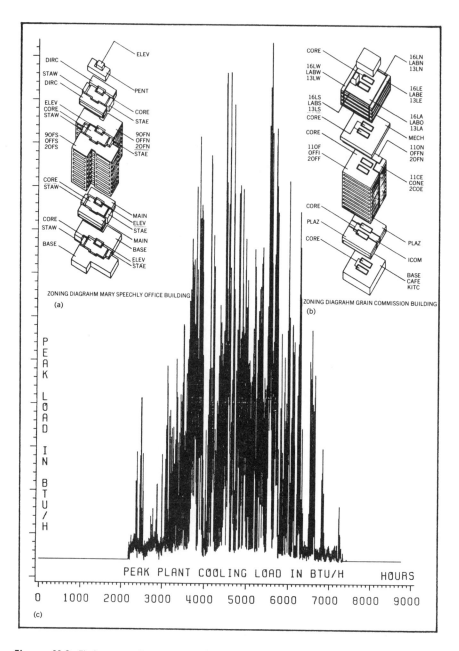

Figure 11.2. First generation computer aided design evaluation: Energy simulation with DOE-2.1.B.

Architectural Expert Systems

Architectural Expert Systems (AES) are expected to solve many of the problems of the first generation tools for abstraction and evaluation, i.e., supply computer aided abstraction and evaluation tools with reasoning capabilities. Although the concept of expert systems has matured and produced impressive results in areas such as medicine and geology, its applications in architecture so far are limited. One reason is the graphic character of traditional architectural representation and the fact that this abstraction hides most of the meaning of the drawing—not to the designer, but to the computer. The languages and shells to build expert systems that exist today were not developed for architectural applications. Rather, architectural researchers have selected existing systems for their implementations.

Architectural expert systems are rule-based and/or frame-based systems that provide the means for codifying the problem-solving know-how of human experts. Expert systems are appropriate if the problem-solving technique can be described as a set of situation-action rules. Rule-based expert systems share a number of key properties. "They incorporate practical human knowledge in conditional if-then rules. Their skill increases at a rate proportional to the enlargement of their knowledge bases. They can solve a wide range of possibly complex problems by selecting relevant rules and then combining the results in appropriate ways. They adaptively determine the best sequence of rules to execute, and they explain their conclusions by retracing their actual lines of reasoning and translating the logic of each rule employed into natural language" [Hayes-Roth, 1985].

Although this description seems rather optimistic, rule-based systems have a definite place in the architectural design process. Unlike algorithmic programs, they have the potential to solve ill-structured design problems. They are able to acquire the necessary knowledge through a series of iterations in which the human expert observes the performance of the system, criticizes it, inspects the knowledge base used, and suggests expansions or modifications. Expertise in a task domain, such as architecture, requires substantial knowledge in that domain. The effective representation of architectural domain knowledge is therefore a condition for the success of an AES. The representation and reasoning facilities in an AES must integrate various kinds of knowledge into a coherent knowledge base that can effectively support the system's activities [Fikes 1985] (see also Figure 11.5c). Experience has shown that none of the major languages used in Artificial Intelligence such as OPS or LISP is able to satisfy this request. Consequently "semantic networks" and "object-oriented" representation languages based on frames were developed [Hendrix 1979]. Frames provide structured representations of objects or classes of objects. They are equipped to capture the way architects typically think about and organize their knowledge. They provide a structural representation of relations and the equivalent of different levels of abstraction. To utilize the advantages of rule-based and frame based systems, schemes have been developed including both frames and rules [Aikins 1984].

The first architectural implementations of rule based and frame based systems are characterized by the limitations of the languages used. Successful implementations were developed for spatial layout [Flemming 1986a], participatory design [Kalay 1985], composition [Gero 1985], and geometric reasoning using knowledge based systems [Woodbury 1986]. Attempts of formalizing architectural abstraction and evaluation will be described in the following sections.

☐ EXPERT SYSTEMS IN DESIGN ABSTRACTION

Developing expert systems for architectural design means to explore the traditional concept of abstraction on an advanced level. Expert systems are in the first place a vehicle to externalize and formalize hidden and implicit knowledge used in design. If experiences in geometric modeling, drafting, and database management are an indication, computer supported abstraction will fundamentally change the process of design for the individual. This section provides an introduction to the relation between the human and the computational aspects of abstraction. A description of computer assisted abstraction applied to architectural design generation and representation precedes an overview of search methods that use abstraction to generate solutions. Two implementations of the discussed methods conclude the section. For the following discussion we will concentrate on the generative aspects of abstraction.

Abstraction and Architectural Design Representation with Computers

Abstraction is a crucial process in the generation, evaluation, and representation of design. Both the generation and evaluation of design depend on a valid internal representation in the designer's memory or in a computer. The creation and manipulation of this representation require abstraction. One purpose of architectural abstraction, then, is to translate between the internal representation and the envisioned artifact. This translation can range from simply mapping properties of the artifact to the internal representation to a high level interpretation of both artifact and internal representation. Traditional computer programs are well suited for the mapping process, whereas knowledge based systems are better suited for the interpretive end of abstraction. An important by-product of the development of architectural expert systems is the externalization of the abstraction process because the representation must be explicit and unambiguous for the computer.

In order for an architectural expert system to use architectural domain-specific knowledge, it needs a knowledge representation language. This language must be able to communicate the expert's knowledge to the system. It must have the ability to explain the system's knowledge to the expert, and the system must be able to use the information it has been given. Different kinds of domain knowledge must be incorporated, such as objects and relationships, vocabulary definitions, constraints, heuristics, processes, uncertain facts and disjunctive facts [Fikes 1985] (see also Figure 11.5c). The representation of this knowledge as rules and frames has been described above. For the typical designer, however, they are applicable for a very limited set of problems only.

One of the main problems in implementing an architecturally oriented representation language is the productivity aspect of architectural programming. Since the invention of compilers in the 1950s, only incremental productivity improvements have been achieved. Two earlier approaches in the automation of software development known as "program analysis" and "program synthesis" [Frenkel 1985] have striking parallels in the architectural design process and are therefore appealing for architectural programmers. The goal is to elevate the communication between machine and human to a similar level in specific domains. Only if the communication between human and computer is freed from low level obstacles and limitations, it will be possible to develop effective representations of architectural abstraction.

A considerable amount of groundwork has been undertaken to understand and describe human abstraction [Simon 1969] and abstraction applied to the architectural design process [Akin 1986]. Akin's findings on the representations of design in human memory have the advantage of being computer compatible. Of particular interest for computer assisted abstraction is the description of the two basic modes of representation available to the designer: the verbal-conceptual and the visual mode. An example for the verbal-conceptual mode would be the word "window" which could represent an infinite number of different windows. An example for the visual mode would be a specific view of a specific window with which we can associate only one verbal-conceptual schema, i.e., "window". Several representational paradigms consistent with the distinction between the visual and the verbal-conceptual schemata exist. Two of them, productions and chunks, are of relevance to this discussion:

Productions, also known as if-then rules, are simple control structures with a Left-Hand-Side (LHS) and a Right-Hand-Side (RHS). The LHS contains a condition, the RHS the associated action. Productions can be combined into a production system to simulate more complex design patterns. Production systems are quite robust and generic and are developed in growing numbers for microcomputer applications (see example 2).

Chunks are defined as an organizer of hierarchical, multi-associative links in memory [Chase 1973]. In problems dealing with spatial arrangements, chunks have proven to be the most robust information structure. The human memory organizes tokens into clusters or chunks that have one or more common relationships binding them together. By nesting chunks within chunks, multi-leveled hierarchies can be achieved. Commercial database management programs make use of this organizational principle, and some advanced microcomputer drafting programs provide almost parallel structures to chunks that allow the buildup of multiple hierarchies (see example one and Figure 11.3).

Productions and chunks are frameworks that support the cognitive process of interpretation or inference. They are therefore well suited to be modeled with production systems or combinations of production systems and CAD systems. Productions and chunks, implemented in computer programs, are thus an important externalization of design representation and abstraction in human memory.

Architectural Reasoning and Search with Computers

Inductive reasoning has been identified as one of the major forces in the human design process [Akin 1986]. Architectural concept transformations and manipulations can be explained as induction processes, and there seems to be a direct relation between the richness of associations between concepts and the experience of the designer. Architectural inductive reasoning with computers goes back to drawing-understanding systems [Herot 1974] and sketch interpreting systems [Taggart 1971]. In the absence of a fundamental theory on architectural knowledge representation, the computer implementation of architectural and geometric reasoning systems is in its infancy [Woodbury 1986]. A second important aspect of the architectural design process is goal directed search [Kalay 1985]. An array of computer based search methods have been developed to support and simulate human search processes (see examples one and two). Abstraction is applied constantly in the search process. Given the desire to arrive at a satisfactory solution, this process involves discovery and invention. According to David Pye, invention

> can only be done deliberately, if the inventor can discern similarities between the particular result which he is envisaging and some other actual result which he has seen and stored in his memory. . . An inventor's power to invent depends on his ability to see analogies between results and, secondarily, on his ability to see them between devices [Pye 1964].

This statement supports our assumption that design discovery is based on discernment and selection and not on random generation of alternatives. Similar findings in psychology [Simon 1969] can be applied to architecture. Architectural search is taking place on a general, global level and on specific, local levels. Typical search methods employed on a global level are depth-first search and breadth-first search.

Depth-first search uses the analogy of an inverted tree with branches that connect nodes. The method is also not well suited to guarantee design optimization because each decision is influenced by the constraints of the previous decisions. In spite of the shortcomings of this method, experts are using it extensively [Newell 1965; Hunt 1975]. This applies particularly for experienced architects working in well understood problem fields.

Applying the analogy of the inverted tree to breadth-first search, the designer would allocate attention horizontally rather than vertically. Typical applications are the selection of a solution from a few architectural prototypes that adhere to the most critical constraints of the design problem. Solutions are likely to be found in a shorter time. In the architectural design process, the breadth-first search is followed by a depth-first search after a feasible solution has been identified.

On a local level, specific goals of the designer can be achieved with an array of possible search strategies, of which the Generate-And-Test method, Hill-Climbing method, and Heuristic Search or Means-End-Analysis (M-E-A) are particularly suited for computer implementation:

Generate-And-Test (G-A-T) is considered a weak method because it merely requires a procedure to generate possible candidates for a solution and a procedure to test whether the candidates are indeed solutions. The difficulty in finding a solution is proportional to the size of the set and therefore not feasible for large design problems. In spite of its limitations, the G-A-T method is very popular in architectural computing due to its ease of implementation.

The Hill-Climbing (H-C) method is closely related to the G-A-T method. Only those newly generated solutions are accepted that are better than the best solution developed to this point. If a better solution is found, it replaces the previous best one. The method has a slight drawback in that it does not encourage the consideration of a worse solution than the best current solution (local peak), which might finally lead to a better overall (global) solution.

Heuristic Search or Means-End-Analysis (M-E-A) is used in many management science and theorem proving programs where a search within an exponentially expanding space of possibilities is necessary. The search must be controlled and focused by the application of heuristics. Akin proposes 15 heuristic rules—among them divide-and-conquer, constraint hierarchy, and first idea—to be used in discovering a good architectural solution [Akin 1986].

Expert systems in other domains such as Civil Engineering use the same control strategies to direct search [Maher 1985]. These search strategies make use of various levels of abstraction. By employing the search strategies for the exhaustive or non-exhaustive generation of designs, the operations on the abstracted objects—objects could be the artifact itself or other abstractions—are moved from the designer to the computer. The computer then performs some of the "mechanical" activities such as inferencing and branching—much in the way the computers started to perform mechanical drafting tasks. Whereas the quality of computer generated drawings is dependent on the degree to which the laws of descriptive geometry have been discovered and implemented, the quality of computer aided abstraction and inference making depend on the degree to which the human design process is understood and formalized.

Example 1: Generating Elevations Using Hornbostel's Architectural Language

Example one demonstrates the architectural knowledge-based application of computer structures similar to chunks in human memory. The computer assumes three crucial tasks to generate building elevations using architectural language: storing and maintaining a graphical database of architectural *symbols* in various levels of abstraction, maintaining a set of *relations* between those symbols, and a *grammar*. The symbol library is maintained by a general purpose drafting program. The knowledge necessary to express the relations between symbols and the grammar are expressed as rules. The program is implemented in AutoLISP and takes advantage of the block structure built into the general drafting program. These blocks are drawing elements (points and lines) or vocabulary (assemblies of points and lines, such as doors and windows) that can be supplied with attributes. Blocks can be nested several levels deep, that is, one block can be constructed of other blocks which again consists of blocks on a lower level. The user can redefine blocks and thus refine levels of abstraction. In Figure 11.3, for example, we replace the verbal-conceptual symbol "window" (11.3a), first with simplified visual window symbols (not shown) and then with the orthogonal representation of different window types (11.3c). Figure 11.3d shows the completed elevation. The exercise is particularly effective in the teaching of architectural styles.

The program uses production rules and the LISP evaluator as inference engine. The user input is facilitated by the possibility of programming custom menus that allow symbol selection and input. This can happen verbally and visually via an expanded set of LISP functions such as "getpoint", "getdistance", and "getangle". The program is ideally suited for quick proportional studies of Hornbostel's architectural language and to represent the complex real artifacts such as windows and details, with abstracted symbols. Its significance lies in the use of a complete "infrastructure" provided by a professional drafting program, thus allowing the programmer and the user to communicate with the computer on a high level of abstraction.

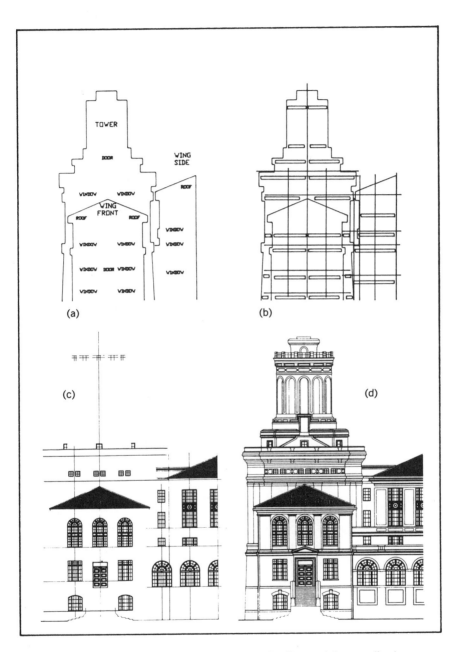

Figure 11.3. Expert systems in abstraction—the Beaux-Arts consultant.

Example 2: A Medieval Architecture Consultant

The Medieval Architecture Consultant incorporates some of the search methods and the representational paradigms of visual and verbal-conceptual schemata described above. It supports the process of abstraction with verbal and graphical means. The program focuses on medieval religious French architecture for two reasons: the encountered building types can easily be classified and abstracted, and the interdependency of qualitative-political and quantitative-technological factors is evident and can be formalized. The Medieval Architecture Consultant combines several programs: a graphics program provides the expert system with a graphical output and with a graphical knowledge acquisition module, and drafting and database management programs provide the system with functional utilities. The system deals with the relationship between the construction of religious buildings in medieval France and historical conditions. It features the generation and graphic display of various possible religious building types, their graphic insertion into a map of France, and the inference of a historical statement from the distribution, type, and number of the buildings in a certain area of France.

The system is implemented at a high level of control abstraction and can therefore easily be changed to represent other aspects of design, history, or evaluation. As an example, for building diagnostic applications, the program would present a set of possible building failures, ask for their location in the building plan, and suggest strategies for correction. Another possible application is interactive participatory design where the user designs within given constraints and receives feedback whenever constraints are violated. A more elaborate graphic knowledge acquisition module features general facilities for site and architectural symbols definition, insertion of symbols into the site, and incorporation of the resulting knowledge into the expert system environment in form of production rules.

Knowledge Representation and Control Strategy

The expert system is implemented in a microcomputer version of OPS5. All historical and factual knowledge is represented in the form of rules. The graphics program, DRAW, and the knowledge acquisition module are implemented in C and are based on the Graphical Kernel System (GKS). The program is thus a hybrid implementation with the expert system controlling procedural support programs. The control strategy is forward chaining. The user interface is menu driven in the OPS5 environment, and icon driven in the graphic parts. The graphic output for the expert system is performed by calling DRAW, after creating a data file containing the drawing in DRAW format. The original version of the program was completely implemented in OPS5. The execution speed was greatly improved by using C procedures for the entire process of graphics data generation.

Sample Session

The user begins by defining the kinds of religious buildings that will later be used for the history session. A number of choices are presented in the form of short menus (see Figure 11.4b for a sample OPS5 rule). Selections include the time period, building type, building location, the kind of religious order, and the financial situation of the builders [Brooke 1974]. If these parameters prove to be insufficient to characterize a building adequately, more specific rules can be easily added. If enough evidence is assembled for one particular building type, the program will pass control to the graphics program DRAW. In this way, the user "learns" from the program by trying out several input combinations and immediately seeing the architectural result, displayed by DRAW (see Figure 11.4a).

Subsequently, the user has the choice of inserting the different possible configurations into the map of France, which is divided into five regions for this purpose. The user picks an icon and inserts it into the appropriate region (see Figure 11.4c). The necessary knowledge can be taken from an appropriate source, such as an architectural history book. By inserting the object into the appropriate region, the user "teaches" the program. The program will accept the input in graphic form and convert this information into OPS5 rules. Once control is passed back to the expert system, the result of the graphic interaction will be analyzed and the most likely political situation, based on the input, will be described. If this political analysis conflicts with the user's knowledge, two reasons can be isolated. The first problem may be an error in the graphical input. This can be corrected immediately. The second reason may involve the rules in production memory that assess the political situation based on the building distribution in the region which are incomplete or do not apply to this region. In this case, the production memory knowledge must be changed or enhanced.

Conclusion

The systems presented in the two examples support various levels of computer assisted abstraction. This happens through operating in the visual mode by calling built-in graphics functions or external C procedures, or through operating in the verbal-conceptual mode by using the interfaces constructed within LISP or OPS5. The main objective of the examples was to facilitate the attachment of semantic information to a purely syntactic representation. The meaning of graphic symbols can be assigned graphically or verbally. One of the most interesting experiences with the systems was the users' change of attitude towards developing rules and abstractions: after an initial learning period, the users clearly concentrated on the more friendly visual construction of rules. Abstraction seems to be greatly facilitated if the objects can be represented graphically in different representations.

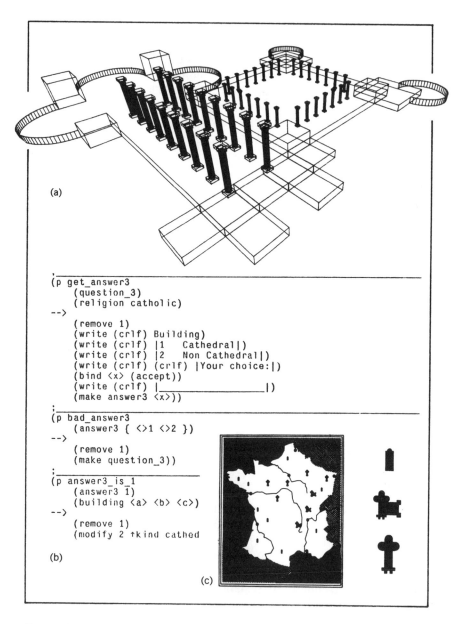

(a)

```
;
(p get_answer3
    (question_3)
    (religion catholic)
-->
    (remove 1)
    (write (crlf) Building)
    (write (crlf) |1    Cathedral|)
    (write (crlf) |2    Non Cathedral|)
    (write (crlf) (crlf) |Your choice:|)
    (bind <x> (accept))
    (write (crlf) |_____|)
    (make answer3 <x>))
;
(p bad_answer3
    (answer3 { <>1 <>2 })
-->
    (remove 1)
    (make question_3))
;
(p answer3_is_1
    (answer3 1)
    (building <a> <b> <c>)
-->
    (remove 1)
    (modify 2 ↑kind cathed
```

(b)

(c)

Figure 11.4. Expert systems in abstraction—the medieval architecture consultant.

230

☐ EXPERT SYSTEMS IN DESIGN EVALUATION

Expert systems in architectural design evaluation have three major applications: to facilitate rule-of-thumb estimations, to provide intelligent front ends to algorithmic programs, and to improve the accuracy of large simulation programs. Expert systems in design evaluation often fulfill diagnostic and analytical purposes. This section introduces design evaluation expert systems as computer programs that allow forms of domain-specific reasoning. The description of a design exercise follows which incorporates the use of various evaluation expert systems that support the final judgement of the design product.

Design Evaluation Expert Systems

Evaluation describes judgement applied to the results of analysis. Consistent with this definition, design evaluation expert systems should consist of two components: an analysis and a judgement component. The analysis component computes a particular quantifiable aspect of design, the judgement part will compare the results with the computer's internal knowledge. Computer aided analysis of design began with the understanding and formalization of the performance of artifacts. The complexity and reliability of the resulting programs is proportional to the capabilities of the employed computer software and hardware. Missing decision capability of the programs was compensated by the experience and knowledge of the programmers. The validity of analysis was controlled and checked directly by the programmer. As long as languages allowed only the manipulation of quantitative data, evaluation was reserved to the human programmer (see Figure 11.5b). The step from batch programs towards interactive programs was an important improvement in user friendliness. The production of meaningful evaluation results was facilitated by the addition of graphic pre-processors and post-processors, while at the same time the necessary human knowledge base to perform performance analysis was reduced (see Figure 11.5a).

The most significant improvement in design evaluation systems was the development of languages that permit the integration of qualitative decisions into the analysis process. This allows a larger class of users to achieve relatively exact analysis results without having to acquire extraneous background knowledge—provided that the knowledge is found within the program. Rule based and expert systems fulfill exactly this task. This observation holds true for all architectural evaluation areas, as Figures 11.5b and d show. The graphs demonstrate that the factual knowledge about the object to be evaluated remains constant. Figure 11.5b shows the shift in knowledge placement and representation from human memory to computer memory over time for constant accuracy of prediction. The human knowledge necessary to achieve meaningful analysis results is decreasing over time,

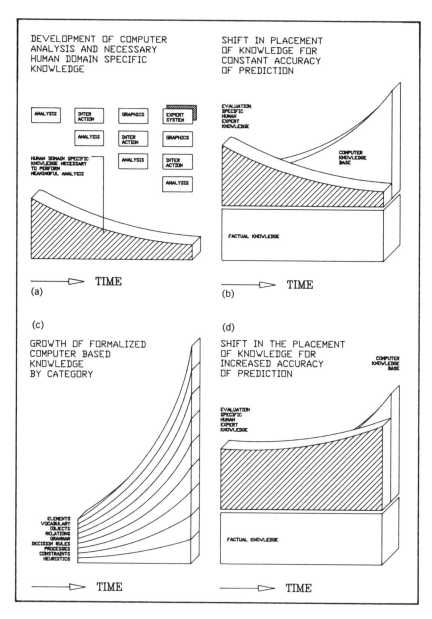

Figure 11.5. Expert systems in design evaluation: development of computer tools over time.

whereas the computer knowledge base is growing exponentially. Figure 11.5d indicates the shift in knowledge placement and representation over time for increased accuracy of prediction. Figure 11.5c schematically shows the increase of formalized and computer compatible knowledge over time by category.

Knowledge-based programs will not replace, but supplement human judgement and validated analysis programs. Most of the algorithms in analysis programs are verified and implemented efficiently. Rule-based programs should be reserved for solving ill-defined parts of the analysis for clarity and efficiency reasons. As our experience with rule-based systems shows, most of the analysis problems can be solved in the algorithmic approach. Even complex rule-based programs can be converted to algorithmic programs once the problem structure has been externalized. Figure 11.6 is a schematic representation of possible expert system applications in the early design phases. These applications range from rule-of-thumb estimation programs in the conceptual design phase to more sophisticated systems consisting of expert front ends and algorithmic programs in design development.

Developing expert systems for successful evaluation of design is by far more complex than building generative expert systems. Although both kinds of expert systems are based on related abstract models, the knowledge base for achieving a meaningful result from an evaluation must be orders of magnitude larger than the knowledge base needed to generate solutions adhering to given constraints. The reason is that evaluation expert systems are built to produce an assessment of the real world artifact—which can be verified directly to determine the usefulness of an evaluation—whereas the generative expert system may begin from a limited set of assumptions and knowledge completely under the control of the designer. Exact criteria exist for the quality assessment of evaluation programs, while the criteria for generative systems are only under development. A review of the literature reveals that designs generated by rule-based systems are generously complemented with human interpretation of the potential of such systems [Flemming 1986a; Gero 1985; Stiny 1986], whereas the quality of evaluation programs is measured against their verifiability and accuracy. An evaluation program is considered worthless if it does not assess or predict reality closely.

Sample Application: Expert Systems in Conceptual Design Evaluation

Within the framework of rational decision-making, the evaluation of a design consists of two steps: its performance analysis according to individual criteria, and an overall judgment that indicates whether the design is satisfactory or, when alternatives are under discussion, which of the competing candidates should be selected; in the latter case, this selection nor-

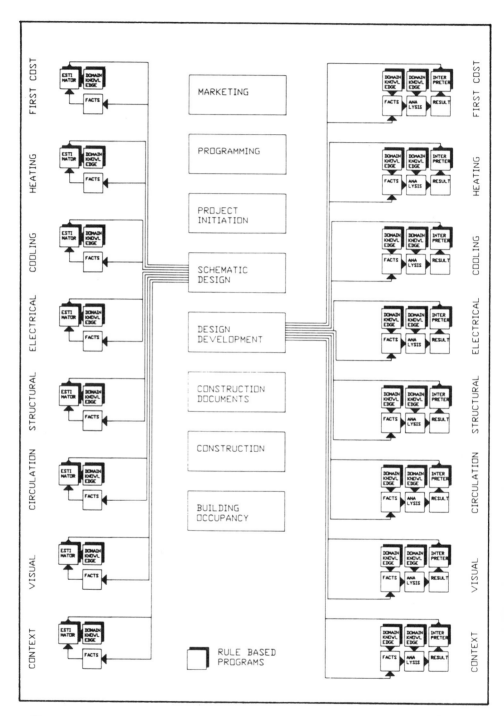

Figure 11.6. Typical applications of rule-based systems in the schematic and early design stage.

mally implies an evaluation of trade-offs because no alternative can be expected to be best with respect to every criterion. Expert systems are well suited for the comparative evaluation of early design concepts. Performance criteria include energy consumption, first and life cycle cost, circulation efficiency, and structural feasibility. To evaluate these criteria in a consistent and systematic way, traditional algorithmic computer programs are used. The evaluation of criteria that are not measurable is supported by rule-based systems and by visualizing the concepts using 3-D modeling and graphics packages.

Some traditional mainframe computer programs offer the possibility to simulate and compare more than one aspect of performance. The DOE-2.1.C program, for example, will compute how a change in the geometry of a window influences daylighting in the adjacent room; temperature changes in that room; its heating, cooling, and electricity consumption; the energy consumption of the entire building; the life cycle cost of the building; and the load change on the associated power, heating, or cooling plant. This is possible only because the causal relations and interdependencies between the simulated performance aspects are known and have been incorporated in the program. Most microcomputer programs, however, deal with the simulation of much simpler causal relations between design changes and simulated building performance. The use of various algorithmic and knowledge-based programs to achieve a complete evaluation implies that the results of individual programs must be collated and set in relation to each other. Evaluation expert systems can support this process. The following evaluation criteria are selected for the example (see Figures 11.7a and b):

First Cost. The necessary parameters for first cost evaluation of a particular design concept are extracted directly through the extract capability of the CAD program. An expert system incorporating cost-estimating rules of thumb can be employed. In a more advanced design stage, the cost analysis must incorporate more detailed algorithms and rules.

Heating load. Parameters to determine the heating load of a building are based on climate, geometry, materials, and user type. The simulation tools range from microcomputer rule-based estimation programs [Schmitt 1985b] to the mainframe program DOE-2.1.C.

Cooling load. Small rule-based programs are employed to determine the equipment schedule. The simulation tools are the same as for the computation of the heating load.

Electric load. Watts-per-square-foot assumptions combined with an appropriate schedule, will yield a valid estimate for the cost sensitive peak electrical load. The simulation tools are the same as for the simulation of the heating and cooling load.

Structural feasibility. Structural reasoning systems are only in the beginning stage of development. Therefore, the evaluation of the structural feasibility of different design concepts will include a human judgement factor. Evaluation programs include SDU, a structural analysis and database program developed at Carnegie-Mellon University and the expert system HI-RISE [Maher 1985].

Circulation efficiency. The computer is used to calculate the areas and ratios and for visualization. Rules of thumb must be used to judge the overall circulation efficiency for the designed building.

Visual comfort. Visual comfort is a fundamental factor in user satisfaction and thus a measurement for the ultimate success or failure of a building. Functional considerations related to visual comfort such as specific daylighting requirements for studios, can be judged by the evaluator [Rush 1986]. The computer is used to calculate glare values and daylighting levels [MacGowan 1983] and can be employed to judge the result of the calculation.

Contextual responsiveness. The computer allows visual evaluation of the design alternatives in a given architectural context. Land use ratios and the impact of the design's shade on adjacent buildings and sites are computed and judged.

For all the above criteria, the computer is used as a tool to support evaluation and human judgement. The list of criteria must be expanded for a realistic problem and will change depending on the problem at hand and the tools available. A meta level expert system can add or subtract criteria to select and apply the appropriate programs at each level. The representation of all application results at the same absolute scale is not possible, because too many different units of measurement are involved. One solution to this problem, and also to the problem of visually recording the evaluation results together with the associated concept, is the *circle sector visualization*. The circle is divided into a number of equal sectors that correspond to the evaluation criteria. The circle radius represents a threshold of acceptability. For first cost, heating, cooling, and electricity, it represents the preset budget. For the structural, circulation, visual, and contextual criteria, it represents a minimum standard of acceptability. The radius of a sector is larger than the circle sector if the particular type performs better than the minimum standard (i.e., if its energy consumption is lower than the established energy budget), and it is smaller than the circle sector if the design alternative is below the minimum acceptable standard (for example, the circulation area is excessive). In the cases of non-existing quantitative evaluations, rule-based systems are used to determine the circle radius (see Figure 11.7a). The *weighted circle sector visualization* is similar to the circle sector visualization but is compounded by the fact that each sector in the circle is assigned a weighting factor that represents the relative importance of the criteria (see Figure 11.7b).

Sample Problem

Figures 11.7 – 11.10 show the application of the methodology developed above to a sample design problem, in this case a school of architecture

[Flemming 1986b]. A customized version of a drafting package, containing the building program, the building site (see Figures 11.7c and 11.7d), and massing manipulation procedures implemented in AutoLISP support the designer in the original layout of the building. Four alternatives on two different building sites are shown in Figure 11.8 for the sample problem. Each individual concept is selected and evaluated separately. The results are then displayed adjacent to the design concepts.

Type One is U-shaped and located on the east side of the existing Fine Arts building on site A, and is three stories high. The large studio and support spaces are on the north and the south side; other functions are concentrated in the eastern part of the building. Good visual qualities but poor circulation characterize this concept. The results of the evaluation are shown in Figure 11.9a.

Type Two is located on the north-east corner of site A and has four stories. It uses the existing Fine Arts building as a backdrop, not as an integral part. Entrance and main vertical circulation are at the north-east corner. Office, classroom, and support spaces form the east and north wings of the building, while the studios are located in the south-west corner. This solution offers very efficient circulation, but high cooling loads. Figure 11.9b shows the building and the trade-offs.

Type Three follows a well established scheme on the existing campus. It is located on a steep slope on site B. Three wings project out of the main building with the circulation running in an east-west direction. Offices and small scale spaces are on the south side, the large spaces occupy the wings. Good visual quality, but high heating costs are significant trade-offs in this scheme. Figure 11.10a shows the results of the simulations and judgements.

Type Four has a linear organization and is situated in the same location as Type Three. It is bermed into the ground, and only the second and the third floor are visible from the main entrance opposite to the existing Fine Arts buiding. The offices for faculty, staff, and graduate students are on the terraced south edge. All teaching facilities and studios face north. Except for foundation problems, this solution has no particular shortcomings according to the selected criteria. Figure 11.10b shows the results of the evaluation.

The final assessment of the evaluated concepts must be performed by the designer because too many incompatible facts and utterances of the design solutions must be considered. However, the use of expert systems to evaluate the design according to a set of criteria, gives this judgement a better foundation. A typical human final judgement on the four schemes could be as follows: As expected, the comparison of the evaluation results yields no one best solution, but gives indications of the strengths and weaknesses of a particular type in the given context. For example, the linear Type Four clearly demonstrates the capability of this type to accommodate contrasting orientations (used to advantage by allocating studios to the north and offices to the south) which, in turn, gives the opportunity to express fundamental functional distinctions on the outside. The type does

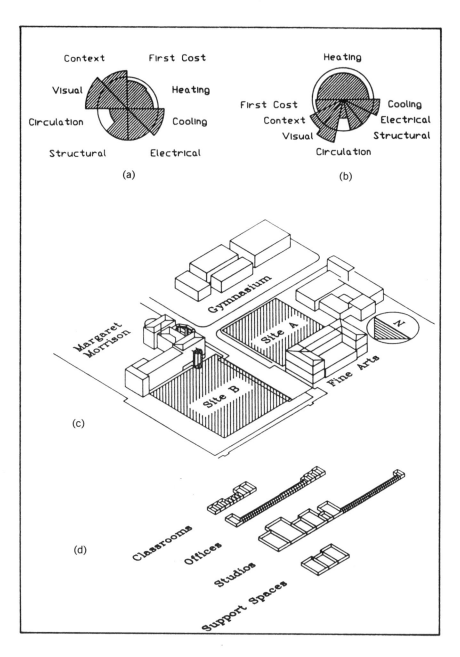

Figure 11.7. Building criteria visualization, building site, and building program.

238

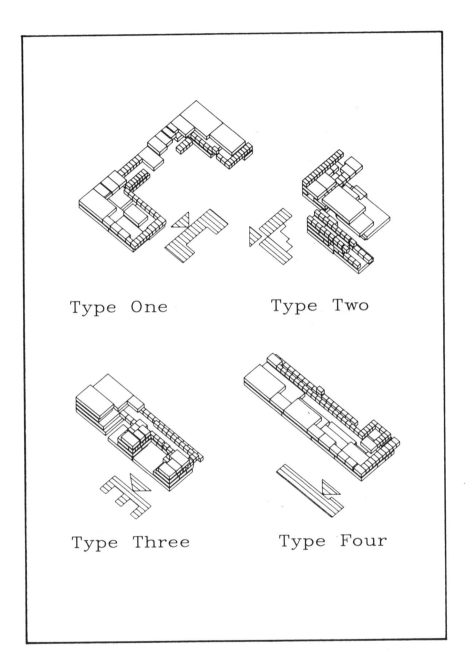

Figure 11.8. Computer aided concept development: Four possible results.

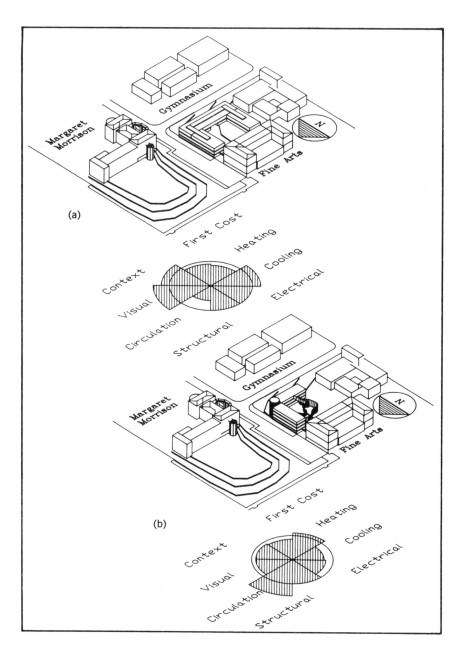

Figure 11.9. Top: Type One on site A and performance prediction. Bottom: Type Two on site A and performance prediction.

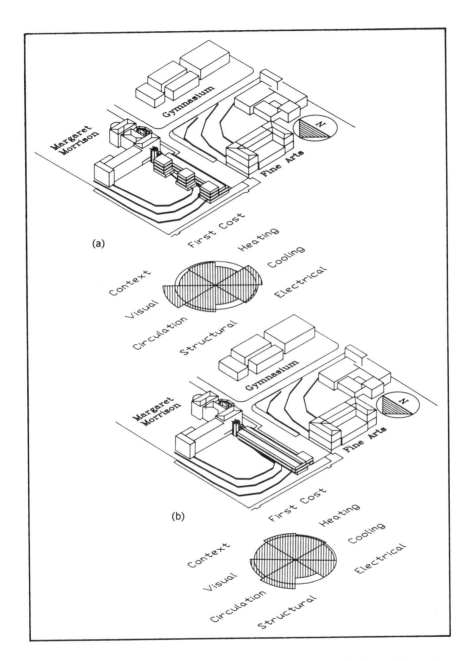

Figure 11.10. Top: Type Three on site B and performance prediction. Bottom: Type Four on site B and performance prediction.

not create outdoor areas of its own, but is able to complete such spaces in particular circumstances (in the present case, by defining the missing edge of a potentially very attractive space to the south). Type one, in contrast, forms together with the existing Fine Arts building a courtyard scheme with the almost opposite characteristics. It accommodates varying orientations with less ease and is harder to read from the outside. But the court offers the unique opportunity to create a protected interior open space that may be used in various ways. Furthermore, each major area is visible from other areas across that space; people can see each other at work, creating a sense of community not attainable with the same ease through other schemes.

☐ CONCLUSION

The present use of expert systems in architectural design evaluation is in its infancy. However, rule-based or frame-based programs are the available means to provide a framework for the integration of quantitative and qualitative criteria in design. The implementation of design evaluation expert systems is an expression for the paradigm shift from problem solving towards knowledge driven approaches in design evaluation. While the traditional algorithmic programs perform best when the *problem* is limited, evolving expert systems are most reliable for limited *problem domains*. The results produced by expert system evaluation as a combination of analysis and applied judgement, can be stored as rules to evaluate similar design solutions and to aid in the generation of design. This allows an effective feedback capability and eventually the programming of intelligent design systems relying on the knowledge base not of one person, but of a large array of relevant evaluations. This, in turn, will fundamentally change the design process and the process of evaluation.

☐ REFERENCES

Aikins, J.S. "A representation scheme using both frames and rules" in *Rule Based Expert Systems,* G.G. Buchanan and E.H. Shortcliffe, Eds. Addison-Wesley, Reading, Mass., 1984, pp 424-440.

Akin, O., *The Psychology of Architectural Design.* London, Pion, 1986.

Bonta, J. P., "Notes for a semiotic Theory of Graphic Languages" Paper presented to the International Conference on Semiotics, Ulm, West Germany, 1972.

Brooke, C., *The Monastic World.* Random House, New York, 1974.

Chase, W. G. and Simon, H. A. "The mind's eye in chess," in *Visual Information Processing,* ed. by W.G. Chase, New York: Academic Press, 1973.

Coyne, R.D., and Gero, J.S. "Semantics and the Organization of Knowledge in Design" in *Design Computing,* John Wiley & Sons, Spring 1986.

Fikes, R., and Kehler, T., "The Role of Frame-Based Representation in Reasoning," *Communications of the ACM,* September 1985, pp 904-920.

Flemming, U., Rychener, M., Coyne, R.F. and Glavin, T.J., "A Generative Expert System for the Design of Building Layouts," Department of Architecture, Design Research Center, Center for Art and Technology, Carnegie Mellon University, Pittsburgh, PA., 1986a.

Flemming, U., and Schmitt, G., "The Computer in the Design Studio—Ideas and Exercises that Go Beyond Automated Drafting," in Proceedings of ACADIA '86, J. Turner, ed. 1986b.

Frenkel, K.A., "Toward Automating the Software-Development Cycle," in *Communications of the ACM,* June 1985, pp 578-589.

Gero, J.S., and Coyne, R.D., "Knowledge-Based Planning as a Design Paradigm," in *Preprints of Design Theory in CAD,* (H. Yoshikawa ed.), Tokyo University, Tokyo, 1985, pp. 261-295.

Goel, V., "Assigning Locative Prepositions to the Spatial Relations Implicit in 3-D Geometrical Models of Objects and Schemes," Master Thesis, Faculty of Environmental Studies, York University, Ontario, Canada, 1986.

Hartkopf, V. "Warner Hall Energy Retrofit," Carnegie Mellon University, Institute of Building Sciences in cooperation with Dubin-Bloome Associates, Pittsburgh, PA., 1981.

Hayes-Roth, F., "Rule-Based Systems," *Communications of the ACM,* September 1985, pp 921-932.

Hayes-Roth, F., Waterman, D.A., and Lenat, D.B. *Building Expert Systems,* Addison-Wesley, Reading, Mass., 1983.

Hendrix, G.G. "Encoding knowledge in partitioned networks," in *Associative Networks: Representation and Use of Knowledge by Computers,* (N.V. Finder, ed.) Academic Press, New York, 1979, pp 51-92.

Herot, C.F., "Context in Sketch Recognition", Master's Thesis, Massachusetts Institute of Technology, Cambridge, Mass., 1974.

Hunt, E.B. *Artificial Intelligence,* Academic Press, New York, 1975.

Kalay, Y., Harfmann, A., and Swerdloff, L. "ALEX: a knowledge-based architectural design system," in Proceedings of ACADIA '85, P. McIntosh, ed., 1985.

Laseau, P., *Graphic Thinking For Architects And Designers,* Van Nostrand Reinhold Company, New York, NY., 1980.

MacGowan, D., and Schmitt, G., "A Study of the Influence of Visually Satisfactory Windows and Luminance Contrasts on Energy Conservation Strategies in Architectural Design and Retrofitting and in the Energy Management of Large Internal Thermal Load Dependent Buildings". Faculty of Architecture Research Laboratory, University of Manitoba, August 1983.

Maher, M.L., and Fenves, S.J. "HI-RISE: A Knowledge-Based Expert System For The Preliminary Structural Design Of High Rise Buildings," Report No. R-85-146, Department of Civil Engineering, Carnegie Mellon University, Pittsburgh, PA 15213, January 1985.

Newell, A. and Simon, H.A. "An example of chess play in the light of chess playing programs," in *Progress in Biocybernetics,* (N. Wiener and P. Schade ed.), Elsevier, Amsterdam 1965.

Pye, D., *The Nature of Design.* New York: Reinhold Publishing Corporation, 1964, pp 65-66.

Rush, D., *The Building Systems Integration Handbook,* John Wiley & Sons, 1986.

Schmitt, G., "Computers in the architectural practice". A two year survey of all Pittsburgh architects, Department of Architecture, Carnegie Mellon University, Pittsburgh, PA, November 1985.

Schmitt, G., "Microcomputer Based Integrated Energy Design Expert Systems: A Powerful New Tool," in Proceedings of the First National Conference on Microcomputer Applications for Conservation and Renewable Energy. Tucson, Arizona. February 1985.

Simon, H.A., *Sciences of the Artificial.* Cambridge: MIT Press, 1969.

Stiny, G., "A New Line of Drafting Systems," in *Design Computing,* John Wiley & Sons, Spring 1986.

Taggart, J. "HUNCH: An Experiment In Sketch Recognition," in *Computer Graphics,* W.Gilbi ed., Berlin, 1971.

Woodbury, R.F. "Representation and manipulation of geometric information in an knowledge based expert system," forthcoming PhD Dissertation, Department of Architecture, Carnegie Mellon University, Pittsburgh, PA, 1986.

12

THE ROLE OF SHAPE GRAMMARS IN THE ANALYSIS AND CREATION OF DESIGNS

Ulrich Flemming

Department of Architecture
Carnegie-Mellon University
Pittsburgh, Pennsylvania

The paper has three major parts. (1) It introduces *shape grammars*, which contain at their core a set of rules that can be used to generate designs based on various conventions and principles. Shape grammars can be used to explain and describe given corpora of designs with common features, or to develop new designs and to test the rules on which they are based. (2) Both types of applications are demonstrated by a realistic *case study*. The goal of the study was to analyze the historical housing stock in Pittsburgh's Shadyside district and, based on the results obtained, to develop new housing patterns compatible with historic precedents. Shape grammars proved useful in this context because they lead to more comprehensive results, which are stated with precision and rigor, and to a deeper understanding of the issues involved. The study also shows that our familiarity with this formalism has now progressed to a level where issues of architectural substance can be addressed. (3) A simple *shape grammar interpreter* is described, a computer program that accepts shape grammars and generates designs by applying its rules. Such programs are extremely helpful when a grammar is developed and tested. The present approach does not resolve the more intricate problems posed by these interpreters, but makes non-trivial applications like the case study possible.

Figure 12.1. An architect's sketch explaining the derivation of a design. Copyright Noel McKinnell. Reproduced by permission.

☐ SHAPE GRAMMARS–AN INTRODUCTION

Architects frequently use sketches like the one shown in Figure 12.1 to explain their designs. The sketch is to be read from bottom to top. It shows first a shape that looks more or less like an amorphous hill. This form is "geometrized" and turned into a regular four-sided pyramid in the next stage. In a third stage, pieces are cut out from the bottom of the pyramid, and finally, the top of the pyramid is divided into steps. The final shape describes the overall form of a particular building.*

The sketch itself demonstrates how a building mass can be derived in stages, where each stage transforms a previously created shape and elaborates it. The principles underlying each transformation are not restricted to the particular building under consideration and can be applied in various contexts. A convenient way to express these principles in a form that emphasizes their general applicability is to formulate them as *rules*. For example, from the sketch shown one can derive:

>*Rule 1*
>
>>IF you have a pyramid,
>>THEN you can cut pieces out of its bottom edge.

>or
>*Rule 2*
>
>>IF you have a pyramid,
>>THEN you can divide its top into steps.

I am using the term "rule" here not to refer to some sort of restriction (as in "rules and regulations") but in the sense in which it is used in Artificial Intelligence and "rule-based programming": a rule specifies some *condition* or *context* in which something can be done (the part that starts with an IF), and then indicates an *action* that can be executed under this condition (the part that starts with THEN). A rule thus describes an action that can be performed if certain conditions are met. It opens up the possibility for action rather than restricting it, and sketches of the type shown in Figure 12.1 suggest precisely rules of this kind.

In an architectural context, the notion of rules also arises from another direction. Buildings designed in a particular style or by a particular architect are often instantly recognizable because of shared features that distinguish them from other buildings. Architectural history and criticism pur-

---

*The American Academy of Arts and Sciences in Cambridge, Mass., designed by Kallmann, McKinnell and Wood; see *Architectural Record*, November 1981.

sue, among others, the task to identify and explain these features. This is often done by specifying *rules of composition* which underlie the buildings under consideration.

The more reflective and articulate among architects, from Vitruvius and the treatise writers of the Renaissance to present day practitioners, have often been able to state these rules explicitly. For example, a central theme for F. L. Wright and for architects of the Modern Movement inspired by him was the "destruction of the box," the definition of spaces that were not rigidly confined within four walls and more directly related to the outside, leading to an "open" or "free" plan. To achieve this effect, Wright recommends, for example, to avoid solid corners and to support roofs by freestanding walls or screens [Wright 1960, pp. 284-289], recommendations that again can be expressed as rules:

IF you are interested in an open plan,
THEN avoid solid corners.

or

IF you are interested in an open plan,
THEN support roofs by free-standing walls or screens.

Rules, then, appear as a rather general and unifying device to deal explicitly with various aspects of architectural design, a contention that finds support from observations made during current work with "expert systems", where it was found that rules provide a natural and effective format to capture and make operational the "effective special-case reasoning characteristic of highly experienced professionals" [Hayes 1985, p. 922], which is the task of these systems.

However, the rules that have been specified so far are expressed verbally, a formulation that has distinct disadvantages when one has to deal with shapes and their geometric qualities. For example, rules 1 and 2 are not very precise as to how the bottom of a pyramid is to be handled, or how its top can be divided into steps. They are certainly not operational in the sense that they specify a well-defined action. It is simply very difficult to precisely describe in words geometric properties or shapes. *Shape grammars* are particularly interesting here because they provide a means to formulate, in a precise and convenient manner, rules that deal with geometric objects and properties. (They are, in fact, very general computing mechanisms. The present introduction, however, is written for readers with an architectural background and tailored to their particular experience. A more detailed introduction is given in [March 1985], which also gives an extensive bibliography and traces the history of many of the ideas that influenced the development of the formalism.)

Figure 12.2, for example, restates rule 1 as a *shape rule*. It shows the

Rule 1

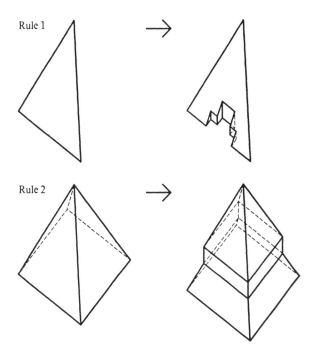

Rule 2

Figure 12.2. Specification of rules 1 and 2 as shape rules.

side of a pyramid to the left of an arrow, and the same side with its bottom cut out on the right of the arrow. The drawing on the left is called the *left-hand side* of the rule, and the drawing on the right is called its *right-hand side*. The left-hand side corresponds to the IF part in the verbal specification, and the right-hand side to the THEN part. The interpretation is the same: if a pyramid is given, its bottom can be cut out. But this time, the specification is more precise: the right-hand side shows the cut-outs in more detail and with greater clarity. It delineates precisely the boundary of the shape to be generated, except for parametric variations in the coordinates of the endpoints of the edges that define the boundary.

Figure 12.2 shows in a similar way a graphic specification rule 2. Observe that an application of this rule to a pyramid generates exactly one step. But the new shape ends again in a pyramid, and the same rule can be applied to this (smaller) pyramid to create a second step (see Figure 12.3). That is, rules can be applied *recursively* to shapes.

F. L. Wright's recommendations could be expressed in similar ways by rules that would indicate immediately how the desired effects could be achieved.

Shape grammars contain, at their core, a set of rules that can be used to generate shapes from other shapes. Each rule consists of a left-hand side,

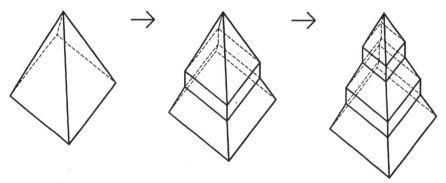

Figure 12.3. Shapes generated by recursive application of rule 2.

which is a shape, and a right-hand side, which is also a shape. The term *shape* denotes a configuration of edges or surfaces that describe a two- or three-dimensional form. By definition, a rule can be *applied to a shape* if the left-hand side of the rule is part of the shape (that is, the shape satisfies the condition specified by the left-hand side); the application consists in replacing the left-hand side by the right-hand side (that is, it carries out a specific action that transforms the old shape into a new shape). In order to start the process of generation, the grammar must contain, in addition to a collection of rules, an *initial shape*, because otherwise no match could be found for any left-hand side, and no action could ever be executed. For example, in order to start the process of design for either of the two rules that we have, a pyramid must be given at the outset (or it must have been generated by other rules that start from a different initial shape; in the simplest case, the initial shape represents not much more than an empty page).

Sometimes, actions have to be restricted to certain parts of a shape characterized by properties that are hard to discover by an inspection of its geometry alone. In this case, *labels* can be attached to certain points in a shape and can be referred to by the left- and right-hand sides of rules. For example, if we want to restrict applications of rule 1 to the bottom edge of a pyramid, we can label the center point of the edge with label *B*, say, and refer to this label in the left-hand side of rule 1 (see Figure 12.4 (top)). But if we do this, we must also redefine our initial shape and label the center points of its bottom edges appropriately.

Observe that an application of this new rule 1 removes label *B*; that is, the rule cannot be applied twice to the same edge. If we want to allow for this possibility, we would have to redefine the right-hand side of the rule. If, on the other hand, we want to express the fact that a bottom edge does not have to be cut out, we can introduce a rule like the one shown in Figure 12.4 (bottom) which simply removes a label *B* without changing the edge to which it was attached.

But rules 1 and 2 only apply to complete (sides of) pyramids (as indi-

Rule 1 (revised)

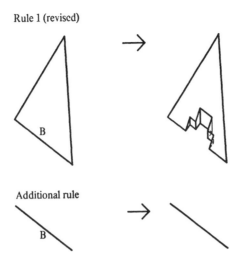

Additional rule

Figure 12.4. New rules.

cated by their left-hand sides). As a result, we cannot apply them both to the same evolving shape: rule 1 destroys the bottom edge of a pyramid and thus makes a subsequent application of rule 2 impossible; and rule 2 changes the sides of a pyramid and thus makes an application of rule 1 impossible. At least one of the rules would again have to be re-formulated if they are to be used on the same shape.

These examples intend to give readers a sense of the explicitness, precision, and rigor that can be achieved when developing a shape grammar. But they also suggest that this process takes time. An initial specification of rules might not work in the intended way and might have to be re-designed. The design of a suitable shape grammar is greatly helped by the fact that its rules are *constructive*. They can be used to actually *create* shapes that can then be inspected in order to pass judgment on the effectiveness of the underlying grammar (a process that is greatly facilitated if it is supported by a computer program able to interpret and apply shape rules; see Section 3). It is likely that during this process, the grammar under development will undergo numerous revisions, and it is exactly these revisions that, I believe, lead to a deeper understanding of the issues at hand than is possible with traditional, more intuitive approaches. A major goal of the present paper is to demonstrate this effect by means of a case study (see Section 2).

In general, such work can address two types of problems: (a) to explore the possibilities inherent in a given set of rules or conventions; or (b) to discover the rules underlying a given corpus of seemingly related designs [March 1985]. The first problem stresses the generation of new designs within a given set of conventions and tries to systematically explore the possibilities inherent in these conventions and their appropriateness for solving the problem at hand. The rules expressing these conventions (and as a result, the conventions themselves) might undergo changes in the process. The second problem deals with the analysis of given designs. But even in that case, grammars will be used in a constructive manner; the rules extracted from the given corpus will be used to generate designs, and these designs will be inspected in order to evaluate these rules. The grammar is again likely to undergo revisions.

In my experience, the constructive nature of the process and the surprises it holds in store almost inevitably create a spirit of exploration and discovery which I consider one of the true advantages of the approach, next to the precision and rigor it imposes on the work.

☐ CASE STUDY

The material presented in this section has been taken from a larger study that concentrated on the housing stock in Pittsburgh's historic Shadyside district. The study posed the following question: how can new construction be fitted into the fabric of the district so that its visual coherence and identity are not destroyed, but strengthened and, possibly, re-established (a full account can be found in [Flemming 1985]). An explicit goal of the study was to test the applicability of the shape grammar formalism to this type of problem. The study naturally fell into two parts: (1) an analysis of the existing housing stock (which was done by developing shape grammars that captured the underlying conventions and were able to reproduce this stock); and (2) the design of new patterns able to achieve the stated objectives (this was done by modifying the grammar developed in part (1) to take changed demands into account). The study thus addressed both types of problems introduced in the previous section.

Part 1

The housing stock that gives Shadyside its character was built between 1860 and 1910. It contains examples of all the major styles dominating residential construction during that period in the United States; among these, Queen Anne and Colonial Revival houses are particularly well represented. In analyzing these houses, we found that aspects of spatial organization could be separated from those of exterior articulation, and we consequently derived separate grammars to express the conventions underlying each of these aspects.*

A small sample of house plans is shown in Figure 12.5. All of them

---

*I am using the first person plural in the following when describing work done by the entire project team.

adhere to a form of space planning that Scully has called "peripherally additive" [Scully 1971, p. 14]. The main organizer of the plan is the hall which gives access to all other public spaces and thus forms the hub of the plan. Public spaces can surround this hall in various permutations as long as a parlor or reception room remains available at the front. The spaces surrounding the hall form a relatively compact core; that is, they fill more or less tightly a rectangular area whose regular boundary can only be broken by a few protruding rooms (an effect that is highly dependent on style and that will be addressed later). The depth of this core is restricted by the fact that at most two spaces are accessible from any side of the hall.

We tried to capture these principles through the rules of a shape grammar able to generate plans that obey those and only those principles. The

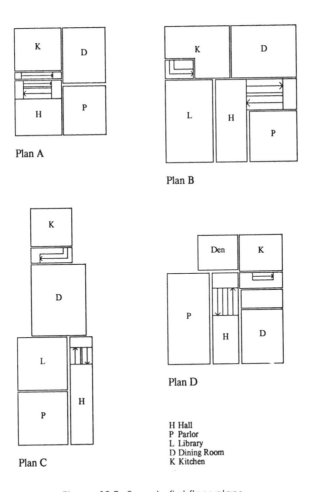

Plan A

Plan B

Plan C

Plan D

H Hall
P Parlor
L Library
D Dining Room
K Kitchen

Figure 12.5. Sample first floor plans.

initial shape consists of an entrance hall, given by a rectangle whose center point is labelled *H*, and of labels *F* and *B* that mark the front and back of the plan (independent of compass orientation; see Figure 12.6).

Rule 1 creates a compact core with the hall as its hub by adding a room from the side or back. This rule applies only to shapes in which the hall reaches the back or side (otherwise the newly added space could not be adjacent to the hall), and the back or side cannot be more than two rooms wide (otherwise, the newly allocated space would become too large). The

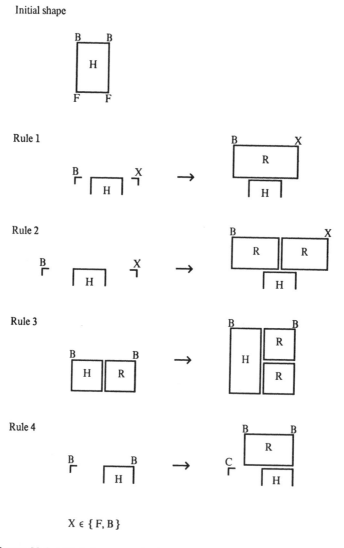

$$X \in \{F, B\}$$

Figure 12.6. Initial shape and selected rules from layout grammar.

hall and all other spaces that have been allocated previously remain unchanged. This rule can be applied to the initial shape to place a first room against the back or side of the hall, and it can be used again to add further rooms. The derivation of cores that are possible using this rule alone is shown in Figure 12.7. (Readers not familiar with shape grammars are strongly encouraged to follow this derivation step-by-step). It is important to note that rules can be used in reflected or rotated versions, which increases their power. In the present example, rule 1 could be used to generate mirror images of the plans shown in Figure 12.7 or, if the initial shape were rotated, rotations of these plans.

But rule 1 generates only small cores and is not sufficient to create the larger cores in our sample. We added rule 2 which allocates two rooms simultaneously from the side or back, provided the respective dimension is wide enough. Like rule 1, it leaves the depth of the hall unchanged. But for larger plans, this depth must increase, and rule 3 can be used to this

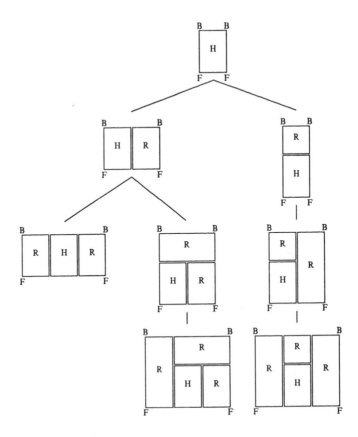

Figure 12.7. Derivation of layouts by application of rule 1.

end. It adds a room to a layout containing a room at the side of a hall and makes this hall deep enough to accommodate two rooms at its side. Taken together, these three rules are sufficient to generate all of the compact cores that we have come across.

But the requirement for compactness can be loosened at the back, where spaces can be added as separate volumes that are not integrated into the main mass of the house. In response to this, we added, for example, rule 4 which places a space against a back corner (provided the hall reaches this corner). In combination with rules 1 and 3, this rule creates layout 1 in Figure 12.8, which represents the core of plan C. But rule 3 can then again be applied to that layout, generating layout 2 for which we had no instance in our initial sample. It was only after we found plan D that we accepted this result.

The criterion that governs explorations of this kind is *correctness*: a grammar used for purposes of analysis should generate those and only those (partial) configurations of shapes that are legitimate; that is, they are either contained in the given corpus or follow principles generalized from that corpus.

A second criterion which I consider as important in this context is *expressiveness*: the grammar should describe as clearly and directly as possible the principles and conventions found. The next stage in the development of the present grammar, where we added a kitchen on the first floor, might serve to illustrate this point.

Plan C contains a kitchen that clearly does not follow the principles of peripherally additive planning; it has no connection with the hall and remains separated from the core of the house at the back. Examples such as this one led us initially to treat kitchens independent of the core. We specified, among others, rule 5 which adds a kitchen from the back (independent of the location of the hall) and designates an adjacent room as dining room (which is always part of the core); see Figure 12.9. But we also

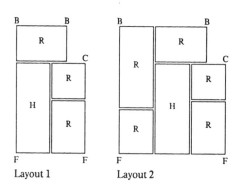

Figure 12.8. Two layouts generated by application of rule 3.

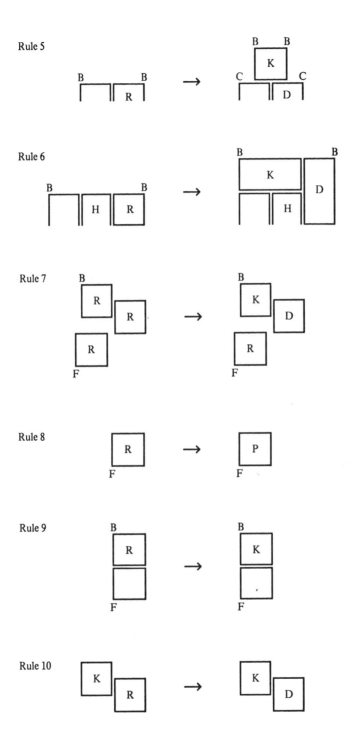

Figure 12.9. Evolution of kitchen rules.

have instances of kitchens that *are* integrated in the core (see plans A or B); it thus became necessary to define, for example, rule 6 which extends a given core to incorporate a kitchen and again selects an adjacent room as dining room.

The resulting grammar is certainly correct. But it is unsatisfactory because it obscures the fact that the kitchen does not always represent an exception from peripherally additive planning. It can be incorporated into the core like a public space and, in these cases, *should be allocated by the same rules*. I consequently decided to keep rule 5 and similar rules that produce the exceptions, but to replace the remaining rules by new rules that do not add a kitchen to the core, but select a suitable space from those that have been allocated by rules 1 to 3, which were designed for this purpose (this is the basic motivation behind the revisions of our initial grammar introduced in [Flemming 1987]).

Rule 7 represents my first attempt with this approach. It selects a room at the back and designates it as kitchen; it also selects an adjacent space as dining room; in addition, it assures that the kitchen does not reach the front and that a front room remains which could serve as parlor. But it proved difficult to express all of these concerns in a single, compact rule. It was easier and more elegant to incorporate these conventions in different rules that must be executed in sequence to generate the desired effects.

Rules 8 to 10 represent the most current version of this portion of the grammar. The allocation of a kitchen starts with rule 8, which selects a parlor at the front (this is the most direct way to assure that such a space actually exists). Rule 9 then selects an appropriate space at the back and designates it as kitchen, and rule 10 selects an adjacent room as dining room. (The sequencing of applications of these rules is accomplished by labels attached to the origin, a detail omitted here; see [Flemming 1987]). As a result of this revision, rule 5 and similar rules could also be simplified so that in the end, each rule expressed a single convention or a very small number of principles (or, in AI parlance, a "nugget" or "chunk" of information).

The criteria of correctness and expressiveness also governed further work on these grammars, which I can only summarize here. We needed a few additional rules to allocate a main staircase to a plan and to prepare it for articulation in three dimensions according to the conventions of a particular style.

The first rule used for this purpose was rule 11 (see Figure 12.10), which takes a room, extrudes it vertically and adds a second room with the same horizontal dimensions on top of it. If applied sequentially to all rectangles in a plan, this rule generates a configuration of spaces on two floors, where the layout of the second floor mirrors that of the first floor, an important characteristic of the houses under consideration (see the example shown in Figure 12.12).

Such configurations are ready to be developed and articulated according

Rule 11

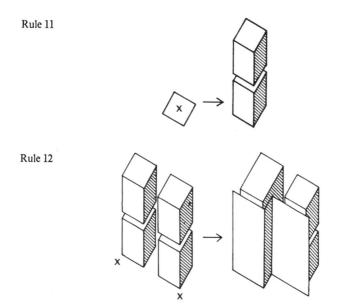

Rule 12

Figure 12.10. Selected rules for the articulation of a plan in 3 dimensions.*

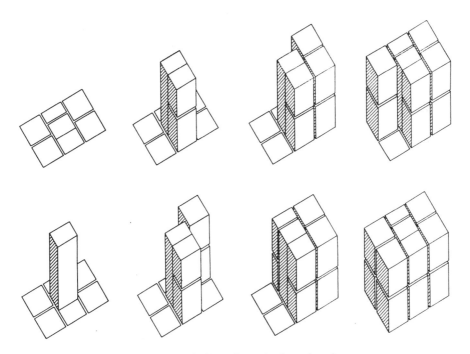

Figure 12.11. Stepwise extrusion of a plan.

*Figures 12.10 – 12.18 copyright Ulrich Flemming. Reproduced with permission.

to particular styles. We concentrated on Queen Anne houses, which dominated construction in Shadyside during the 1880's and early 1890's, because
they are geometrically the most complex. A basic rule used in the derivation of a Queen Anne house is rule 12, which selects a corner room at the
front or back and pulls it out, thus creating a break in the facade. This
rule, in combination with rules that generate similar effects at the sides, creates the irregular contours and "picturesque" silhouettes characteristic for
the style (see the examples shown in Figure 12.12).

We added rules to generate complicated roof geometries on top of the
second floor (see Figure 12.13) and to introduce various volumetric additions and refinements, notably wrap-around porches in various forms (Figure 12.14). Further rules could be added to elaborate individual elements
and to apply decorative details to an arbitrary level of resolution; Figure
12.15 shows, as an example, various bases of chimney breasts produced by
the appropriate rules.

Part 2

In part 1 of the study, the spatial organization of a house was separated
from its exterior articulation and dealt with first, an approach that is also
appropriate for the development of new patterns and types that are able to
respond to changed demands and that satisfy, at the same time, these

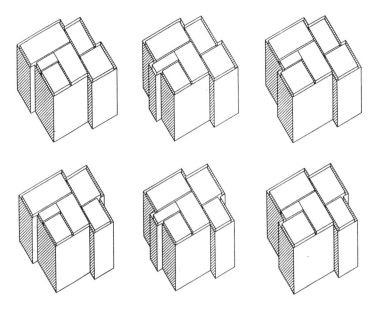

Figure 12.12. Examples of exterior walls.

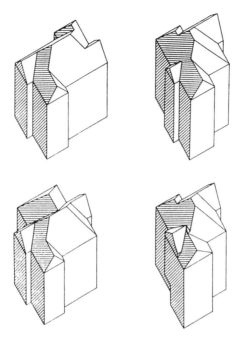

Figure 12.13. Examples of roofs.

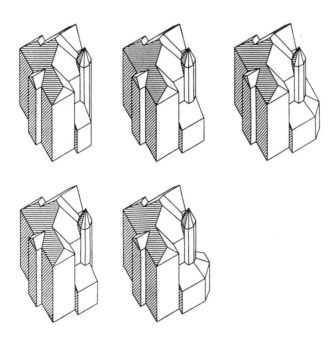

Figure 12.14. Porch alternatives.

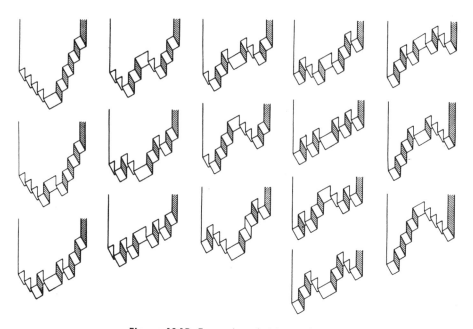

Figure 12.15. Examples of chimney bases.

demands through architectural forms derived from and compatible with the historic precedents in the district.

Our work in the second part had again to be limited to a representative case, which we selected from the "Village of Shadyside," a project that is currently under construction and that provided the initial motivation for our study (UDA Architects of Pittsburgh are the planners and designers; Montgomery & Rust of Allison Park, Pennsylvania, are the developers). The project consists of 68 townhouses and mid-rise condominiums with about 140 units. We concentrated on the townhouses in our study.

The basic organization selected for these houses by the developer is tailored for lots 40 feet deep and 22 feet wide. Each house contains its own garage in the basement, which is raised almost a full floor above grade. The garage is fully exposed at the front and aligned with the space above, forming a wider bay next to a smaller one that contains the entrance at street level.

Such houses can be placed next to each other in three distinct ways: (1) narrow and wide bays alternate in a regular sequence; (2) except for end situations, two narrow and two wide bays from two different houses are always adjacent to each other (that is, the two houses are mirror images); and (3) narrow and wide bays alternate in a more irregular manner. Examples of the three arrangements are shown in Figure 12.16.

In part 1, a basic house was generated from a configuration of stacked

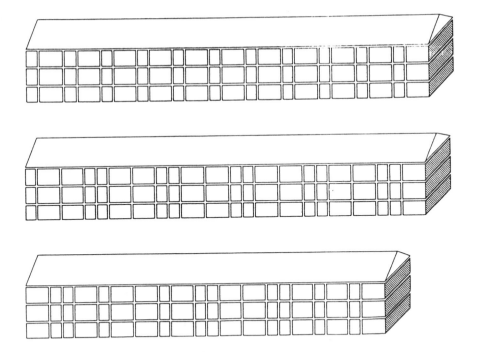

Figure 12.16. Possibile rows of townhouses.

spaces by rule 12 and similar rules which pull certain spaces out to form an irregular plan and silhouette. These rules can be adapted to produce similar results for a row of townhouses (see Figure 12.17). In rows where wide and narrow bays alternate, application of these rules creates a regular rhythm of protrusions (see Figure 12.17, top row). If two wide bays are adjacent to each other, they can be pulled out by the same distance (which aligns their fronts), or one can be extended farther than the other. In the first case, protrusions that are two spaces wide are created, and in the second case, a more irregular massing is the result. Both of these possibilities are shown in the center and bottom rows of Figure 12.17. The same figure shows how rules used to cover the irregular mass of a historic house can be adapted to cover rows of townhouses.

However, an obvious deviation from established patterns resulted from the very fact that we were dealing with townhouses; the gaps that separate detached houses from each other could simply not be duplicated in this situation. But this effect did not seem to be fatal. In the denser sections of the district, narrow houses are spaced very close to each other (sometimes less than one foot apart), which creates vistas down the street that are, in terms of scale and massing, indistinguishable from the ones created by rows of townhouses of the type shown in Figure 12.17.

These examples show how a grammar developed from an interpretation

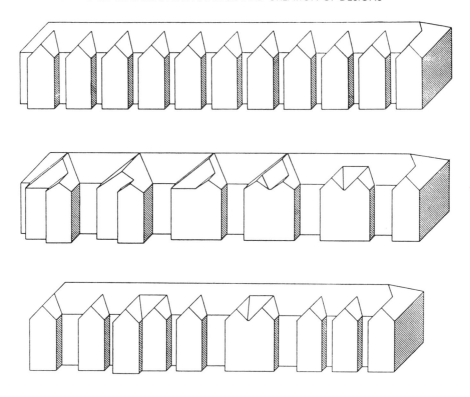

Figure 12.17. Massing possibilities for rows of townhouses.

of historic houses can be used to generate new forms that are compatible with traditional ones. In the present case, the scale, volumes, and massing that are created correspond closely to the historic houses in the district. In addition, the grammar creates regular or irregular sequences of gables facing the street, a motive that gives the streets of the district a characteristic boundary. The approach can be extended to the articulation of the gables themselves and other elements. Figure 12.18 shows, as an example, gable patterns derived from rules used in part 1 to reproduce historic precedents.

What evolves from these explorations is a collection of conventions or principles that produce desired effects or satisfy given goals. Expressiveness remains an important criterion for evaluating grammars that capture these conventions: each rule should express a single convention which, in turn, should be clearly related to the goals to be achieved. Correctness, on the other hand, is no longer a criterion (since there is no corpus to be reproduced) and is replaced by *appropriateness*, a criterion that is again evaluated in a constructive manner, namely by the systematic exploration of the possibilities inherent in a given set of conventions.

Figure 12.18. Gable patterns.

□ OUR PROLOG IMPLEMENTATION OF PARAMETERIZED SHAPE GRAMMARS

During the explorations illustrated in the previous section, shape grammars are developed and tested, sometimes through a number of versions. This process is tedious and error-prone if done manually and could clearly gain from automation. What is needed for this purpose is a *shape grammar interpreter*, a computer program that allows users to specify and apply the rules of a grammar.

So far, such interpreters have been developed only for non-parameterized grammars, in which the coordinates of the endpoints of edges in shape rules are constants, not variables [Krishnamurti 1980; Krishnamurti 1981]. (The concept of a parameterized grammar was first introduced in [Stiny 1977]; the standard technical reference is [Stiny 1981].) The representation and interpretation of parameterized shape rules pose intricate problems that, as far as I know, have not yet been resolved. But we found that, for example, the applications described in Section 2 allowed for simplifications which enabled us to develop an interpreter that is perfectly acceptable even if it does not resolve the general theoretical problems involved. The present section shows how this can be done with particular ease if Prolog is used as programming language. In fact, our experience with this approach has been so successful that we hardly missed having a general shape grammar interpreter available. (The section presumes that readers have some familiarity with Prolog; a good introduction can be found in [Cohen 1985]; the standard manual is [Clocksin 1981]).

All of the grammars used in our study work on domains bounded by polygons which, in turn, are made up of edges. For the sake of computational efficiency and ease of use, we treated these polygons as the primitives out of which shapes are composed, rather than the edges contained in them (for three-dimensional shapes, this also solves the problem that a set of edges not always uniquely determines the solid bounded by them). The layout grammar presented in Section 2, in fact, deals only with rectangles, each of which is labelled to indicate its function. We represented such a rectangle by the triple [L,[X1,Y1],[X2,Y2]], where L is a list of characters that make up the label of the rectangle and [X1,Y1] and [X2,Y2], respectively, are the coordinates of its lower left and upper right corner. A labelled shape is then given by the ordered pair [Q,P], where Q is a list of labelled rectangles and P a list of labelled points. The latter are still needed because not all labels in a labelled shape are associated with a rectangle; a labelled point in P is represented by the pair [M,[X,Y]], where M is the list of characters that make up the label and [X,Y] are the coordinates of the point.

Figure 12.19 shows the graphical specification of a rule from that grammar and our Prolog formulation of the same rule. When an attempt is

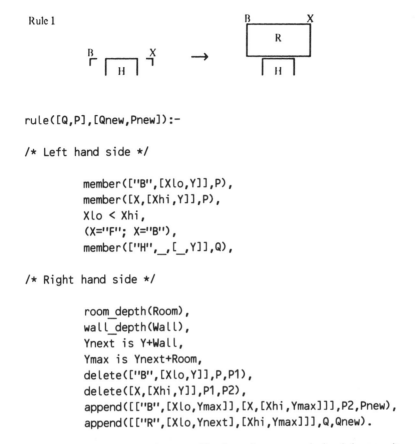

```
rule([Q,P],[Qnew,Pnew]):-

/* Left hand side */

        member(["B",[Xlo,Y]],P),
        member([X,[Xhi,Y]],P),
        Xlo < Xhi,
        (X="F"; X="B"),
        member(["H",_,[_,Y]],Q),

/* Right hand side */

        room_depth(Room),
        wall_depth(Wall),
        Ynext is Y+Wall,
        Ymax is Ynext+Room,
        delete(["B",[Xlo,Y]],P,P1),
        delete([X,[Xhi,Y]],P1,P2),
        append([["B",[Xlo,Ymax]],[X,[Xhi,Ymax]]],P2,Pnew),
        append([["R",[Xlo,Ynext],[Xhi,Ymax]]],Q,Qnew).
```

Figure 12.19. Graphical and Prolog specification of a parameterized shape rule.

made to satisfy this rule, the variable [Q,P] must be instantiated to a shape; it will be called the *current shape* in the following. When the rule is applicable to the current shape, it will instantiate [Qnew,Pnew] to the shape resulting from the application. The first five clauses in the body of the rule specify the predicates of the left-hand side. The first two establish that P contains two points labelled "B" and X, where the latter is a variable. If these points are found, their coordinates are instantiated, using the predicate member that can be found in introductory texts, for example [Clocksin 1981]. The next predicate succeeds when the first of these points is to the left of the second point, and the following predicate succeeds if the second point is labelled "F" or "B". The next predicate succeeds if Q contains a rectangle labelled "H" *so that the upper side of the rectangle is aligned with these points.* If all of these predicates succeed, the rule can be applied to the current shape; that is, the left hand-side is a subshape of the current shape. Along the way, a permissible assignment has been found for the parameters in the left-hand side, which are simply the variable terms in the predicates.

The formulation of the predicates could be kept short because under the selected representation, properties such as the fact that certain edges form a rectangle, are already implied and do not have to be laboriously established whenever a rectangle is called for. Readers should note, however, that the principles used in the formulation of the rule could also support more general formulations.

The remainder of the body specifies the right-hand side. But in contrast to the left-hand side, this part of the rule reads very much like traditional procedural code under sequential control. Its purpose is to construct the new shape. It first of all instantiates the variables Room and Wall, the standard room depth and wall thickness that are used throughout layout generation, by matching them against facts that must be asserted at a suitable place in the data base. For the generation of layouts, we used the following facts:

```
room_depth(100).
wall_depth(6).
```

The lower and upper Y-coordinates of the space that is to be added to the current shape are then computed. Finally, Q and P are modified to produce the new shape by means of the predicate append, which is used frequently in the literature to illustrate features of Prolog, and the predicate delete(E,Oldlist,Newlist) which produces the list Newlist from the list Oldlist by deleting the element E in Oldlist (this predicate can be written in a straight-forward manner).

This style of writing rules, in which the left- and right-hand sides show a distinct flavor, is very easy to learn, and that is its main advantage. In a more general and elegant formulation, the left- and right-hand sides would be *syntactically distinct* and contain a mechanism to pass parameters between the two sides. It could be used, for example, to "run a grammar backwards" to parse a given shape and to determine if it can be produced by a given grammar. But these issues again introduce complications that might as well be avoided for applications like the present one.

One problem has to be addressed, however, if a grammar is to be tested with some ease. Parameterized shape rules can be applied under transformations (rotations or reflections), and these transformations should be automatically generated. In the present case, only eight transformations are of interest: rotations by 0, 90, 180 and 270 degrees and the same rotations combined with a reflection in the y-axis, say. Rather than transforming a *rule* (manually or automatically), we decided to transform the *current shape*, which can be done automatically with great ease by transforming each pair of coordinates in Q and P, [X,Y], into the pair [A*X+B*Y,C*X+D*Y], where A, B, C and D are suitably selected coefficients. The following clauses assert the eight sets of coefficients needed for the present purpose.

```
trans_coeff(1,0,0,1).
trans_coeff(1,0,0,-1).
trans_coeff(-1,0,0,1).
trans_coeff(-1,0,0,-1).
trans_coeff(0,1,1,0).
trans_coeff(0,1,-1,0).
trans_coeff(0,-1,1,0).
trans_coeff(0,-1,-1,0).
```

The following clause asserts the initial shape:

```
shape([["H",[0,0],[100,150]]],
      [["F",[0,0]],["F",[100,0], ["B",[0,150],["B",[100,150]]]]).
```

Rule application is started by typing start. at the terminal, which initializes an attempt to satisfy the predicate

```
start:-
           shape(Shape),
           apply(Shape).
```

start instantiates shape to the initial shape (or any other shape asserted in the data base) and attempts to satisfy the predicate apply with Shape as argument:

```
apply(Shape):-
           trans_coeff(A,B,C,D),
           trans_shape(Shape,A,B,C,D,Transhape),
           rule(Transhape,Newshape),
           inv_coeff(A,B,C,D,Ain,Bin,Cin,Din),
           trans_shape(Newshape,Ain,Bin,Cin,Din,Finshape),
           disp_shape(Finshape),
           apply(Finshape).
```

apply is the work horse of the program. It is invoked with Shape instantiated to a shape. It first instantiates the transformation coefficients A, B, C, and D. It then transforms Shape to the transformed shape Transhape using predicate trans_shape, and attempts to satisfy a rule with the transformed shape as the current shape. If the rule can be applied, the new shape, Newshape, is subjected to the inverse transformation. The coefficients for this transformation are instantiated through a match with the following facts in the data base:

```
inv_coeff(0,-1,1,0,0,1,-1,0).
inv_coeff(0,1,-1,0,0,-1,1,0).
inv_coeff(A,B,B,D,A,B,B,D).
```

The resulting shape, `Finshape`, is then displayed, through the predicate `disp_shape`, and becomes the argument for a recursive attempt to satisfy `apply`. The predicates `trans_shape` and `disp_shape` are easy to write and not given here (for the latter, some graphics package must be used for the actual display). `apply` will fail eventually and backtrack, causing all rules to be applied to all transformations of shapes that were generated in the process.

Within this framework, various refinements can be introduced. An extension to three dimensions is trivial and was used throughout our work. To improve computational efficiency, it proved very useful to restrict application of certain rules to only a subset of the possible transformations; the rule shown in Figure 12.19, for example, should not be applied under reflections if X="B", as this would generate duplicates. In order to allow for this kind of control, the transformation coefficients used to produce the current shape can become additional arguments of the rule, which then checks if they are of the appropriate kind. In addition, the depth-first generation executed by `apply` can be interrupted by queries after each display, asking the user if the search should continue or backtrack to a previously generated shape.

I have outlined this approach for readers interested in gaining some experience with shape grammars with a minimum of effort. But the simplifications under which this is done should be kept in mind. In addition to those that have been discussed, I would like to mention an aspect that is often overlooked, but important for a proper understanding of the shape grammar formalism. Stiny has pointed out repeatedly that a shape should not be viewed as a *set* of edges or line segments: the sub*shapes* on which the left-hand side of a rule can match are not exhausted by the sub*sets* of edges contained in the shape. For example, the shape shown in Figure 12.20 contains two overlapping squares and would be specified in our representation by these squares. But a shape rule that works on squares might be intended to work on *every* square in a shape, including the smaller square formed by the overlap of the two larger squares in the present example. The simple matches performed by our program would not find this square, nor would it be found if we had used the standard representation of a shape as a set of "maximal lines," that is, a set of edges that cannot be combined with other edges to form a continuous line segment (these points are discussed in greater detail in [Stiny 1986]). Much of the simplicity of our approach is based on the fact that we match indeed only on sub*sets* of

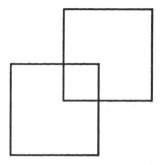

Figure 12.20. Shape consisting of two overlapping squares.

edges. To do otherwise would require a solution of the subshape recognition problem for parameterized shapes, which is not available at the present time.

☐ CONCLUSIONS

While developing our grammars in both parts of the study, we were forced to look at examples with a degree of closeness that is hardly needed if the analysis proceeds in the traditional, intuitive way. In order to be able to generate realistic layouts and to develop a house in three dimensions, we had to study our precedents in all aspects. We were forced, in particular, to deal with aspects of plan organization, massing, and articulation that are usually neglected in style descriptions, or are treated in less precise terms. As a result, we were able to demonstrate how the various parts and features of a house relate to each other and to explain its overall geometry. At the same time, we developed a solid basis for the derivation of new types that satisfied our goals. The main emphasis of part 1 carried over into part 2, where we again concentrated on issues of scale, massing, and overall geometry and were thus able to avoid a mere copying of isolated decorative features, which is characteristic of many developments with similar goals.

Work with shape grammars can thus lead to more comprehensive results which, in addition, will be stated with precision and rigor. Grammars that are correct, appropriate, and expressive normally go through several versions, a process likely to lead to a deeper understanding of the issues involved.

A case study was used to demonstrate these points and to convey the flavor of work with shape grammars. The constructive nature of this work should be appealing to architects or designers who conceive of their designs in a constructive mode, as indicated by the opening sketch. But the study was also intended to demonstrate that our familiarity with this formalism has now progressed to a level where we no longer have to demonstrate its feasibility, but can start to address issues of substance.

☐ REFERENCES

Clocksin W.F., C.S. Mellish *Programming in Prolog*, Springer, New York, 1981.

Cohen J. "Describing Prolog by its interpretation and compilation," *Communications of the ACM*, 28:1311-1324 ,1985.

Flemming U., (with R. Gindroz, R. Coyne and S. Pithavadian) *A Pattern Book for Shadyside*, Technical Report, Department of Architecture, Carnegie-Mellon University, Pittsburgh, PA, 1985.

Flemming U. "More than the sum of parts: the grammar of Queen Anne houses," *Planning and Design*, 14, 1987, in press.

Hayes-Roth F. "Rule-based systems," *Communications of the ACM*, 28:921-932, 1985.

Krishnamurti R. "The arithmetic of shapes," *Environment and Planning B*, 7:463-484, 1980.

Krishnamurti R. "The construction of shapes," *Environment and Planning B*, 8:5-40, 1981.

March L. and G. Stiny "Spatial systems in architecture and design: some history and logic," *Planning and Design*, 12:31-53, 1985.

Stiny G. "Ice-ray: a note on the generation of Chinese lattice designs," *Environment and Planning B*, 4:89-98, 1977.

Stiny G. "Introduction to shape and shape grammars," *Environment and Planning B*, 8:343-351, 1981.

Stiny G. "A New Line on Drafting Systems," *Design Computing*, 1:5-19, 1986.

Scully V.J. *The Shingle Style and the Stick Style*, Yale University Press, New Haven, CT, 1971, (revised edition).

Wright F.L. *Writings and Buildings* (selected by Edgar Kaufmann and Ben Raeburn), Horizon Press, 1960.

13

DESIGN BY ZONING CODE: THE NEW JERSEY OFFICE BUILDING

Matthew J. Wolchko

The Aybar Partnership,
Architects and Planners
Garfield, New Jersey

A generative system is described for a building type common to the highly urbanized region of northern New Jersey. The severity of zoning and planning ordinances common to many municipalities often imposes obvious restrictions on the building form. This necessitates the use of almost all available ground level space as parking and automobile circulation, with only a token lobby/vertical circulation core provided to reach the office building above. The spatial and quantitative relationships between various design components can be described in terms of grammar rules and procedural analysis routines. These rules and procedures must be used in concert to attain optimal solutions. By studying architectural design in such a constrained format, we may gain insight towards applications for a wide variety of architectural design problems.

☐ INTRODUCTION

Recent exploration of computer aided design tools often involves the use of a shape grammar to generate a desired building corpus [Downing, Koning, Stiny 78a, Stiny 80b]. A particular building, or group of similar buildings, is analyzed to discern an underlying schema that can be expressed in terms of grammar rules. These rules can then be applied to re-create one of the original building forms, or generate new variations on the theme. The building corpus selected is usually of a single architect, and seldom part of current practice.

It is suggested that shape grammars's can be effective in more generic situations for a wide variety of building types, if the purely spatial information contained within a shape grammar generative system is combined with the wealth of quantitative data necessary for executing a building design. A shape grammar rule is a dimensionless representation and must at some point be molded by context to become a valid part of an architectural design. For example, a grammar rule used to layout a grid of structural columns is ineffective if the span lengths it generates are too long to be safely or economically bridged. That information can be easily determined through simple structural calculations. Grammar rules with such procedural capabilities would effectively link spatial and non-spatial aspects of architectural design.

As a point of departure, a study of a distinct building type common to Northern New Jersey is undertaken. This building corpus is usually particularly effective for speculative office buildings, where maximizing usable (i.e. rentable) space is the primary criteria. What makes the corpus worthy of study is the obvious fashion in which spatial design problems are resolved through quantitative analysis.

In the following, several examples will be cited, designed, and executed by a variety of architects over a fairly wide area. All examples cited are influenced by the stringent zoning codes of their respective municipality. Requirements for parking and circulation, and restrictions on height and bulk, are the two major code issues. How these design criteria are resolved—and the expression of possible design solutions through the application of shape grammars and parameterized geometries—is discussed. The results should help illuminate how computer design aides can encompass both spatial and quantitative attributes of architectural design.

□ A CANONIC DESIGN SYSTEM

The use of shape grammars as a design generating system requires that the problem at hand be well defined. The algebra of elements and operations demands that the shapes involved are already understood, and that their use in a particular situation can be predicted. In the case of architectural design, a well-defined set of example buildings is examined, and the seminal spatial and conceptual ideas are identified and extracted. The plans, forms, and underlying scheme of the building corpus are then expressed in terms of shape grammar rules, a graphic algebra of building component parts that can be combined in the composition of architectural form. Often, the works used in such a study are from the hand of a single designer, or are firmly established in historical precedent.

The buildings examined in this study belong to a populous commercial typology. Although the locations and designers vary, there is a discernible common logic to all speculative office buildings. The basic design corpus consists of one or more stories of open office space, linked to a vertical circulation and service core. A fire stair, if required by building size and occupancy load, is connected to the primary core by a corridor that can either subdivide the office space or run along a perimeter wall.

The entire arrangement is elevated to a height that allows a required amount of parking to occupy the space below the first floor. In this scheme, the vertical circulation core is the only element to extend to grade; once the parking/circulation scheme is initially resolved, obligatory extensions of the design grammar are vertical. Figure 13.1 provides a basic synopsis of the building type. Subsequently, Figures 13.2–13.9 illustrate examples of the completed building. The diagrammatic site plans shown depict areas devoted to parking, vehicle circulation, column grid layout, and vertical circulation cores. Also, the outline of office space above is superimposed on the plan. Where applicable, greenspace (landscaping) is also shown.

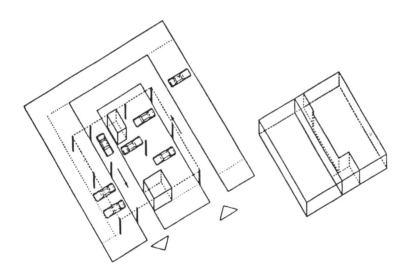

ground floor/site plan   typical upper floor

Figure 13.1. Typical example of building corpus. Office space is in elevated shell above parking area. Core areas at front and rear are the only non-structural elements that are on grade. Column grid spacing is a function of site context and circulation/parking requirements.

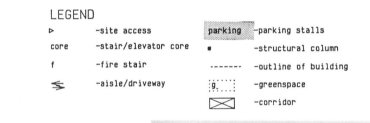

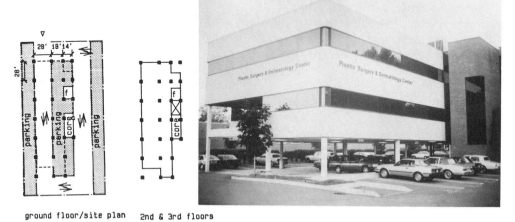

ground floor/site plan   2nd & 3rd floors

Figure 13.2. Two office stories with double loaded and perimeter parking. Paramus, N.J.

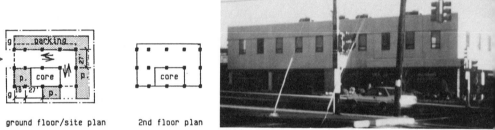

ground floor/site plan   2nd floor plan

Figure 13.3. Single office story with double loaded parking. Saddle Brook, N.J.

276

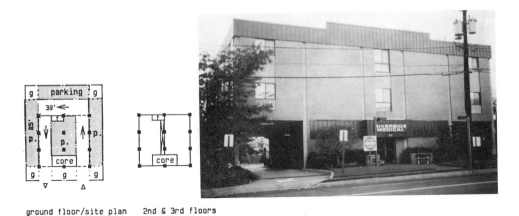

ground floor/site plan   2nd & 3rd floors

Figure 13.4. Two office stories with one way double loaded and perimeter parking in River Edge, N.J.

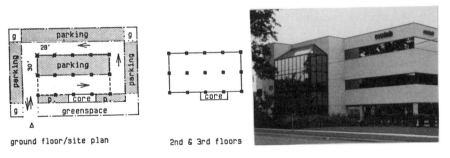

ground floor/site plan   2nd & 3rd floors

Figure 13.5. Two office stories with one way double loaded and perimeter parking in River Edge, N.J.

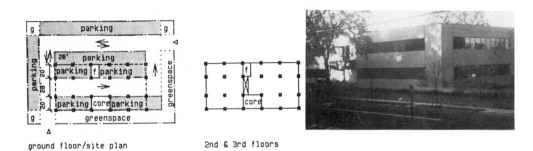

ground floor/site plan   2nd & 3rd floors

Figure 13.6. Two office stories with one way double loaded and perimeter parking in Englewood, N.J.

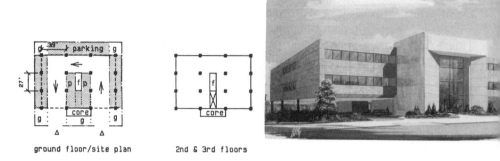

ground floor/site plan   2nd & 3rd floors

Figure 13.7. Two office stories with one way double loaded parking in Ridgefield, N.J.

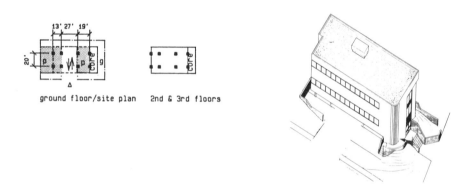

ground floor/site plan   2nd & 3rd floors

Figure 13.8. Two office stories with double loaded parking in Ridgefield, N.J.

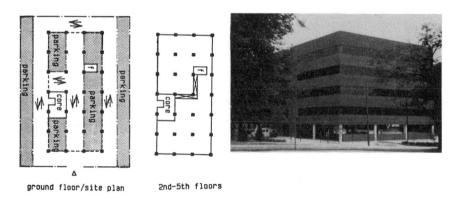

ground floor/site plan   2nd-5th floors

Figure 13.9. Four office stories with double loaded parking, underground parking level in Teaneck, N.J.

The examples depicted in Figures 13.2 – 13.9, ranging from tiny, almost residential scale projects to major low rise developments, all bear two points in common: a molding of the building exterior to conform with the zoning envelope, and a column grid with dimensions conforming to the requirements of automobile parking and circulation. Once these two major criteria are met, the building becomes a valid and buildable design. Most other aspects of design can be considered secondary, as their successful resolution is not critical to the ability to execute the building.

A shape grammar can be defined for this building corpus if certain parameters can be incorporated into the system. Parking and circulation, as stated earlier, comprise a major part of any feasible design in the corpus. Stall size and aisle width are fairly constant, while the required number of parking stalls is a function of building's square footage. The span for structural bays over the parking area is another criteria to be considered. A process for such a building design can be summized as follows:

GIVEN : a site

1. Define frontage.
2. Given a zoning code, define a building envelope that maximizes potential square footage.
3. Determine the number of possible stories through the analysis of height and bulk restrictions/limitations. Calculate total potential square footage.
4. Determine, through zoning/planning code, the required number of parking spaces.
5. Designate building frontage and vehicular access.
6. Apply grammar rules and parameterized geometries to select parking layout and vehicle circulation.
7. Locate primary vertical circulation core column grid layout. Also, if required, locate secondary circulation core.
8. Evaluate parking space/square footage ratio for conformance to code.
9. Revise building envelope as necessary to conform to code.

Not all of the tasks enumerated above are best solved, or can be solved, through parametric shape grammars. However, many of the criteria involved in the design process are straight forward numerical calculations, or require reference to a table of values and classifications listed in a zoning code. This implies the necessity for an integrated design system, wherein various stores of design knowledge can be rapidly and easily applied to assist in a design solution. The data flow diagram (Figure 13.10) depicts the process. As can be seen in the diagram, several data stores are called upon to provide design information, often at the impetus of some numerical value being determined. For example, parking lot layout schemes, a spatial/grammatical task, cannot be performed without first quantifying the desired number of parking stalls.

In a study of bungalow housing in Buffalo, New York, Downing and Flemming designated three classes of rule criteria: functional requirements, contextual requirements, and formal/aesthetic requirements. The restrictions imposed by zoning codes belong to the "context" category. Their application in the design process requires, however, the use of analytical procedures in addition to the shape grammar rules.

In the following sections, a series of shape grammar rules and procedures are described to solve the design tasks enumerated in Figure 13.10.

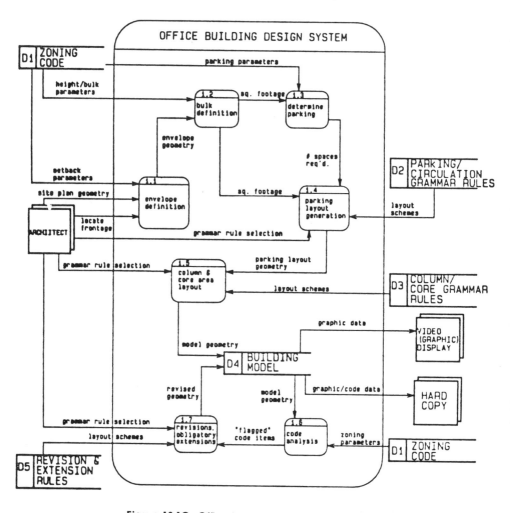

Figure 13.10. Office building design system.

☐ INITIALIZE THE PROCESS, CHECK THE CODE (PROCESS 1.1–ENVELOPE DEFINITION)

The first step in any design problem is to adequately describe the site. This will entail, most likely through a drafting system interface, the generation of a roughly rectilinear site plan. (Irregular sites, and triangular or trapezoidal sites with extremely acute corner angles, have been encountered. For brevity and simplicity, they are not discussed in this paper.) Bearings, dimensions, points of access, and designation of the applicable zoning/planning ordinance database are required.

The zoning code database is particularly essential to the scheme: it should certainly contain requirements for setbacks in all applicable zoning districts, height and bulk limits, a parking space to floor area ratio, parking stall dimensions, handicap access requirements, and any special requirements for corner lots, such as the location of curb cuts at specified distances from street intersections. While zoning ordinances vary from community to community, the topics they address are most always the same; as noted earlier, the most important issues are those relating to size/bulk and parking requirements.

Once the site has been described, a variety of markers should be located on the site to enable grammar rules to be applied. The first round of marker placements requires the designation of site and code frontage. This is usually, but not always, the same operation. As illustrated by the example in Figure 13.2, building frontage in a design sense may not always correspond to frontage in terms of zoning code. Grammar rules 1-4 are for the designation of site boundaries and the placement of access/context markers.

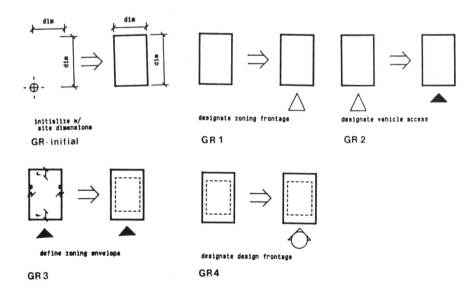

With the initialization phase completed, design aid subroutines can now be applied to further develop the building design. Referring back to the data flow diagram (Figure 13.10) specifying the system, the various component processes will be examined in greater detail, distinguishing what architectural knowledge base will be required, and offering some suggestions as to what form that data will take.

□ PROCESS 1.2/1.3–ENVELOPE DEFINITION/PARKING

Now that the site constraints have been firmly established, an overall building bulk/parking requirement ratio can be established. At this point, some heuristic would be necessary to get the process started. Expressed as an algorithm, consider the following:

```
ALG:  compute parking

CONST: town_code   (* access particular zoning ordinance *)

VAR:  site_area,   (* area of site *)
      req_stalls,  (* number of parking stalls required by code *)
      n_stalls,    (* number of parking stalls possible *)
      sz_stall,    (* size of parking stall in particular municipality *)
      aisle_%,     (* percentage of gross site area to be reserved
                      for circulation in this initial calculation *)
      g_park_area, (* gross site area available for parking *)
      flr_ht,      (* typical floor to ceiling height *)
      pkng_ht,     (* clear height of parking area above grade
                      [note : pkng_ht >= 8'-0''] *)
      code_ht,     (* maximum building height allowed by code *)
      n_stories,   (* maximum number as determined by calculation *)
      g_flr_area,  (* gross floor area *)
      z_envl_area, (* zoning envelope area *)
      p_ratio      (* ratio of cars/sq.ft gross building area, from
                      zoning code [example: 1 car per 250 sq.ft.] *)
(* START OF PROCESS 1.2 *)
(* calculate possible # of stories... *)
      n_stories := (code_ht - pkng_ht) / flr_ht;
      g_flr_area := n_stories * z_envl_area;

   (* PROCESS 1.3 *)
      req_stalls := g_flr_area * p_ratio;
      g_park_area := site_area * aisle_%;
      n_stalls := g_park_area / sz_stall;
```

```
if n_stalls >= req_stalls
   then GOTO (PROC. 1.4 - Parking layout generation);
else
   g_flr_area := n_stories * (z_envl_area * .9);
```

(* reduce floor area by 10% to correspondingly reduce
     the required number of parking stalls and repeat the
     process until the requirement is met ...*)

The execution of the above heuristic will only provide a "ball park figure" analysis of the crucial parking/building area ratio. Geometric and spatial evaluation is the obvious next step. This brings us to the next procedure in the system specification.

□ PROCESS 1.4-PARKING LAYOUT GENERATION

The effects of vehicular circulation and parking can now be brought into play to mold the building shape. The grammar rule shown below for parking lot circulation are dimensionless representations abstracted from the catalog of examples depicted earlier. Once a face (or faces) of the site has been selected for site ingress/egress, a pattern can be selected and dimensions added. Now some determination can be made as to how many cars can actually be parked on the site. Areas with potential use for parking stalls must of course be adjacent to a driveway aisle and must be of sufficient depth (a vector measured normal to the driveway aisle). Once the depth criteria is validated, the number of stalls can be fairly accurately calculated by simply dividing the length of the aisle/parking area boundary by

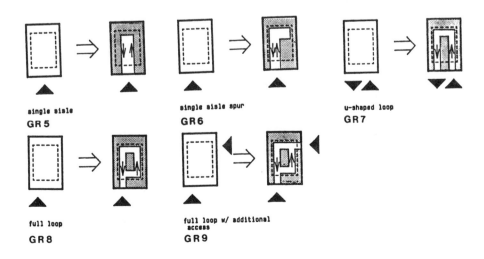

single aisle
GR 5

single aisle spur
GR 6

u-shaped loop
GR 7

full loop
GR 8

full loop w/ additional access
GR 9

the minimum stall width. This process may require several iterations until a satisfactory solution is discovered. It may also be helpful to refer back to Process 1.3 to determine whether additional building square footage should be added or deleted.

☐ PROCESS 1.5–CORES, COLUMNS, STRUCTURAL ANALYSIS

After the parking lot stalls and aisles have been laid out, we will have generated a scheme of loosely-packed rectangular regions. The primary office area, elevated above the parking level, must of course be supported by a structural system. The column layout, and corresponding span of beams and joists, must be designed to permit the flow of traffic in the driveway aisle(s) below, and should permit as much of the remaining ground level space as possible to be used for parking stalls.

Grammar rules 10-19, are intended to begin the process of laying out the structural column grid. Taking cue from the markers for site access, the rules locate columns in the corners of the zoning envelope (where they will not interfere with aisles or parking) in such a way as to insure free vehicular ingress/egress. These columns are shown filled solid. Columns that must be located via the parameters of parking stall dimensions or driveway aisle width are shown as empty squares. The parameters include: aisle width (approximately 24' for two-way traffic), stall length (18'-20'), and stall width (7'-6"-10', depending on the requirements of the municipality). The

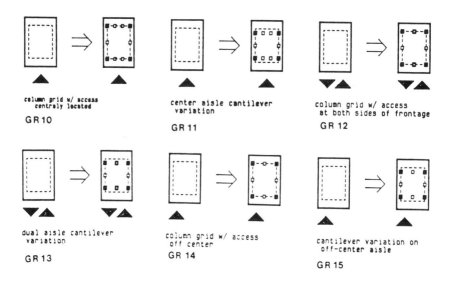

column grid w/ access
centrally located
GR 10

center aisle cantilever
variation
GR 11

column grid w/ access
at both sides of frontage
GR 12

dual aisle cantilever
variation
GR 13

column grid w/ access
off center
GR 14

cantilever variation on
off-center aisle
GR 15

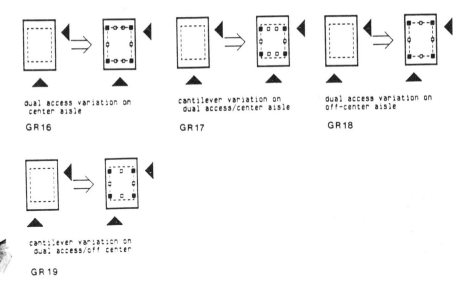

dual access variation on
center aisle

GR 16

cantilever variation on
dual access/center aisle

GR 17

dual access variation on
off-center aisle

GR 18

cantilever variation on
dual access/off center

GR 19

empty column symbol implies the replacement of that symbol with appropriately located perimeter columns, as shown below.

Interior columns, those not adjacent to any exterior wall, can now be placed by adding column lines, defining the grid, and locating columns at the intersections. Grammar rules for this operation are depicted in Grammar Rules 20-29. It must be noted that the grammar rules shown above depict the procedure schematically: in many cases columns will interfere with driveway aisles or parking stalls. Solutions to interference problems can be determined by calculation. Ideally, columns should be centered on the hairpin markings separating two parking stalls. A simple test procedure could determine if the centers of all the interior columns are coincident (collinear) with lines creating the parking stall layout (see Figure 13.11 below). The computation of such a test, the cross product of Pc (the column), P1, and P2 (the end points of the parking stall hairpin line) can be expressed as:

$$(Pc - P1) \times (P2 - P1) = (0,0,0)$$

Similar equations may be used to determine if columns lie within the bounds of a driveway aisle. Calculations are straightforward once the site plan has attained some degree of finished quality.

At the completion of the column layout phase, we will have amassed the majority of data required for basic structural calculations. Tributary areas can be derived from the graphic model, and with the addition of live and dead load suppositions, we can size structural members. Performing such calculations early in the design process can be beneficial: the problem of

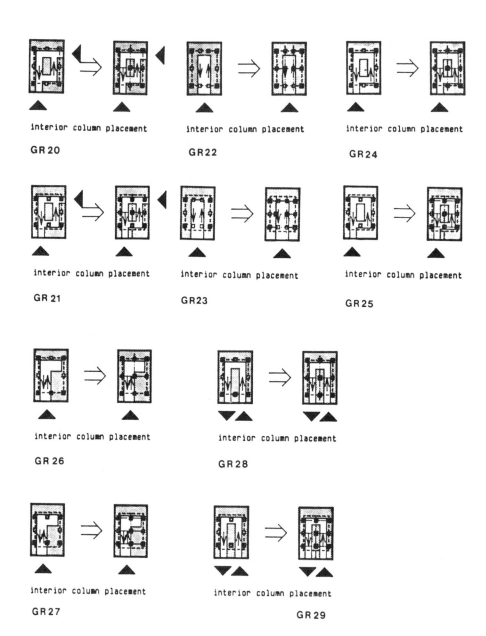

interior column placement

GR 20

interior column placement

GR22

interior column placement

GR24

interior column placement

GR 21

interior column placement

GR23

interior column placement

GR25

interior column placement

GR 26

interior column placement

GR 28

interior column placement

GR27

interior column placement

GR 29

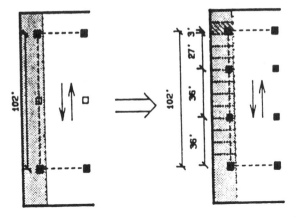

Figure 13.11. Interference testing for column grid layout.

maintaining sufficient floor-to-floor height (plenum space for services, long-span structural systems such as joist-girders, etc...) in relation to the over-all building height limit can be recognized and solved early on.

The design process can now proceed with the selection of the entrance and primary circulation core. A space adjacent to the front (site or design) face of the zoning envelope must be designated, usually in such a fashion as to enclose several columns. If the size (gross square footage) dictates, a second area for a fire stair and auxiliary exit must be carved from the parking area, usually adjacent to the rear face of the zoning envelope. Grammar rules 30-43 depict rules for core location.

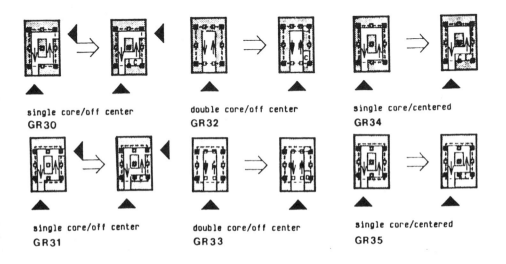

single core/off center
GR30

double core/off center
GR32

single core/centered
GR34

single core/off center
GR31

double core/off center
GR33

single core/centered
GR35

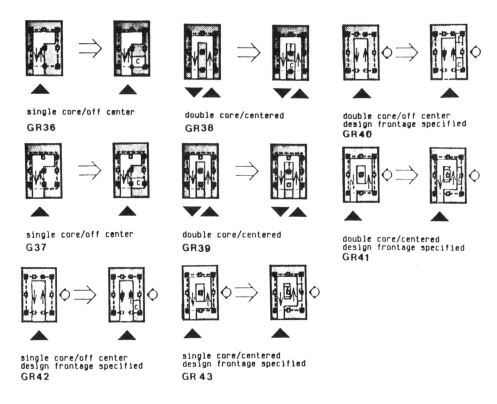

single core/off center
GR36

double core/centered
GR38

double core/off center
design frontage specified
GR40

single core/off center
G37

double core/centered
GR39

double core/centered
design frontage specified
GR41

single core/off center
design frontage specified
GR42

single core/centered
design frontage specified
GR 43

☐ PROCESS 1.7–OBLIGATORY EXTENSIONS/VOLUMETRIC ANALYSIS

By this stage of the process, the entire site plan should have some degree of "finished quality." Now it is appropriate to add the upper stories to the building as obligatory extensions to the ground floor model. This is simply a matter of extending the zoning envelope, defined in the early stages of the design process, vertically above the structural system and parking layout. This vertical stacking can continue for as many stories as was calculated in Process 1.2-BULK DEFINITION. Grammar rules for upper floor generation are depicted in grammar rules 44-48.

Large buildings may require two fire stairs, which must be connected by a corridor. Basic grammar rules for corridor definition are described in Grammar Rules 49-51. The appropriate use of these rules is again a procedural matter.

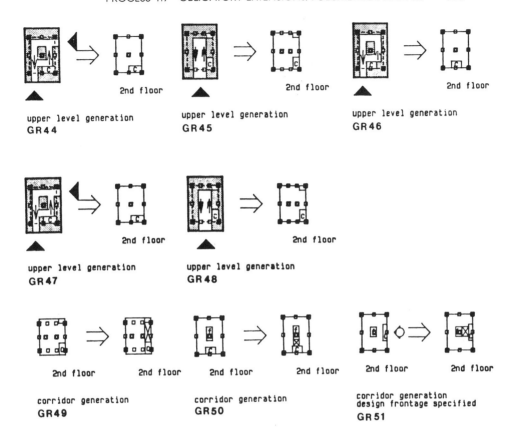

upper level generation
GR44

upper level generation
GR45

upper level generation
GR46

upper level generation
GR47

upper level generation
GR48

corridor generation
GR49

corridor generation
GR50

corridor generation
design frontage specified
GR51

Greenspace areas are designated by additional grammar rules during the final stages of design. Zoning ordinances often prohibit using the front setback area as parking. Also, site corners are unusable for parking, and are best used for plantings and storm water retention. Grammar Rules 52-53 depict rules to accomplish these design tasks.

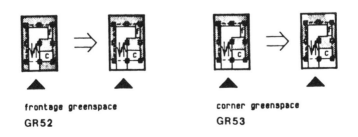

frontage greenspace
GR52

corner greenspace
GR53

☐ EXAMPLE : A "NEW" NEW JERSEY OFFICE BUILDING

The following building design was composed with the preceding grammar rules. Required procedural analysis is noted in the appropriate location, as it would occur in the execution of the design. The resultant shapes generated will be a site plan and a typical upper story, similar to those depicted in Figures 13.2 – 13.9.

It can be argued that the design process I have described is primarily a two dimensional exercise. This is the nature of the building corpus; the relationships between site plan/ground level and all subsequent upper floors is inherent to the design corpus. I have not touched upon any of a number of additional aspects of design: shade, shadow, texture, color, proportion, etc. In fact, no mention of facade, roof line, or articulation has been made. These elements are much more personal and peculiar to individual practitioners. Aspects of design that are not subject to great personal preference (or have been removed from the designers choice entirely) can be automated. This relieves the designer of the obligation to spend time and effort resolving these matters and allows greater attention to be spent working on those aspects of design that are really the architect's forte. Any computational design aid that takes some burden of time, effort, or tedium off the architects shoulders has merit if the designs it produces are acceptable in aesthetic and practical terms, are valid, and are similar to those that might be produced by a designer working without such aides.

☐ CONCLUSION

A comprehensive system for the computer aided design of a particular building type, an office building type common to northern New Jersey, has been specified. The system contains not only spatial generative tools (shape grammars), but also a variety of procedural analysis modules that have been employed to perform tasks that are not suitable for shape grammars. The methods and techniques required to generate solutions for a limited and highly restricted building type (such as the one discussed here) may prove useful in the configuration of new design systems for other building types.

☐ ACKNOWLEDGMENT

Thanks to the Aybar Partnership, Ridgefield, N.J., for the use of their computer facilities.

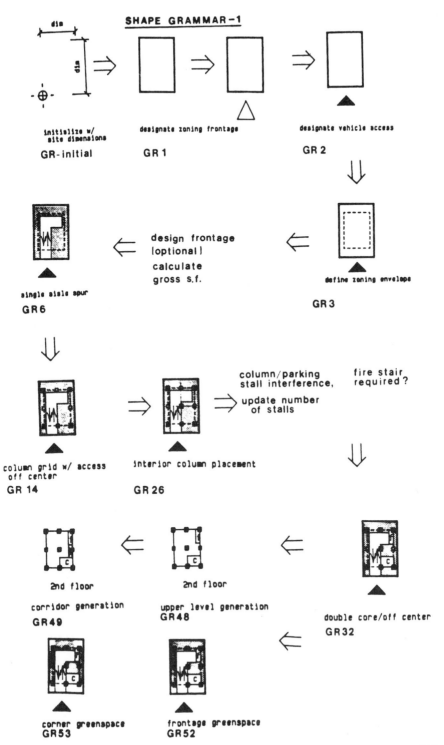

SHAPE GRAMMAR-1

initialize w/
site dimensions
GR-initial

designate zoning frontage
GR 1

designate vehicle access
GR 2

design frontage
(optional)
calculate
gross s.f.

define zoning envelope
GR 3

single aisle spur
GR 6

column grid w/ access
off center
GR 14

interior column placement
GR 26

column/parking
stall interference,
update number
of stalls

fire stair
required?

2nd floor
corridor generation
GR 49

2nd floor
upper level generation
GR 48

double core/off center
GR 32

corner greenspace
GR 53

frontage greenspace
GR 52

291

☐ REFERENCES

Borkin H. *Spatial and nonspatial consistency in design systems*, Environment and Planning B, 13:207-222, 1986.

Downing F. and U. Flemming "The Bungalows of Buffalo," *Environment and Planning B*, 8:269-293, 1981.

Fikes, Richard, and Keller, Tom "The Role of Frame-Based Representation in Reasoning," *Communications of the ACM*, 28(9):904-920, September 1985.

Flemming U. "On the representation and generation of loosely packed arrangements of rectangles," *Environment and Planning B*, 13:189-205, 1986.

Gero J.S., A.D. Radford, R. Coyne and V.T. Akiner "Knowledge based Computer Aided Architectural Design," I.F.I.P. Working Group, Working Conference on Knowledge Engineering in Computer Aided Design, Budapest, Sept. '84

Hayes-Roth F. "Rule-Based Systems" *Communications of the ACM*, 28(9):921-932, September, 1985.

Koning K. and J. Eisenberg "The language of the Prairie: Frank Lloyd Wright's Prairie Houses," *Environment and Planning B*, 8:295-323, 1981.

McIntosh, P.G. *The Geometric Set Operations in Computer Aided Architectural Design*, University Microfilms, Ann Arbor, MI, 1982.

Mitchell, W.J. *Computer-aided architectural design*, Van Nostrand Reinhold, 1977, New York.

Mitchell, W.J. "Formal representations: a foundation for computer-aided architectural design," *Environment and Planning B*, 13:133-162,1986.

Radford A.D. and J.S. Gero "Towards Automated Architectural Detailing," Working Paper, Computer Applications Research Unit, Department of Architectural Science, University of Sidney, 1984.

Spillers W.R. "Design theory versus architectural design," *Environment and Planning B*, 13:243-248, 1986.

Stiny G. *Pictorial and Formal Aspects of Shape and Shape Grammars*, Birkhauser Verlag, Basel and Stuttgart, 1975.

Stiny G. "Introduction to shape and shape grammars," *Environment and Planning B*,1980a, 7:343-351, 1980a.

Stiny G. and Mitchell W. "The Palladian Grammar," *Environment and Planning B*, 5:5-18, 1978a.

Stiny G. and Gipps J. "An Evaluation of Palladian plans," *Environment and Planning B*, 5:199-206, 1978b.

Stiny G. and Mitchell W.J. "Counting Palladian Plans," *Environment and Planning B*, 5:189-198, 1978c.

Stiny G. and Mitchell W.J. "The grammar of paradise: on the generation of Mughul gardens," *Environment and Planning B*, 7:209-226, 1980b.

Stiny G. "A Note on the Description of Designs," *Environment and Planning B* 8:257-267, 1981.

Stiny G. Editorial, *Environment and Planning B*, 13:127-132, 1986.

Zeaman J. "Beyond bland: good design can triumph over zoning," *The Bergen Record*, January 12, pps. F1-F6, 1986.

PART 4

DESIGN ASSISTANCE

Earlier parts of the book discussed the essence of design in general, and the knowledge that underlies its computability. The computational approaches to support or completely automate the design process that have been discussed demonstrate the difficulties of design computation. Yet, the two fundamental questions that are at the heart of computer-aided design research still remain unanswered: How can designers cope with the inexplicable difficulties of synthesizing seemingly unrelated ideas into a single whole, in imaginative new ways? And how can they exercise preference of certain qualities on account of others? Not only are *creativity* and *judgment* fundamental to design theory, but methods to aid them have tended to divide computational design models into ones that automate design as a whole, and ones that facilitate design through representation and evaluation of the emerging artifact.

The practical corollary to these questions forms the questions concerning the computability of design this book set out to explore:

1. What parts of the design process *could* be computed?
2. What parts of the design process *should* be computed?

Designers are able to cope with and manage complex design processes and achieve outstanding results. Perhaps it is not necessary to fully automate the process of design? Perhaps it may be more prudent to apply computers only in assisting designers in specific aspects of design?

The four chapters in this part of the book suggest precisely that: let computers do what they do best (analyze, visualize, etc.), and let designers do what they do best (synthesize, judge, etc.). The chapters propose that not all design tasks need to be computed in order to significantly improve design productivity and quality, and that a practical and feasible symbiosis between the capabilities of designers and machines could be constructed.

Which tasks are computable? Which tasks are not? Which tasks could but should not be computed? How can computational and manual design practices be combined without loosing design continuity? These are some of the questions discussed in this part.

The difficult question of computing intuition, or computationally assisting it, is discussed by Richard Norman in INTUITIVE DESIGN AND COMPUTATION. He describes the creative phase of design as embodied in the intuitive leap, which is sometimes manifested in a single sketch that comes after the gathering of information is complete and an idea is formed. He proposes that computers could assist intuition by generating alternative solutions that nurture the intuitive leap, and by providing an extensive knowledge base at the point of conception. By adding color, texture, and three dimensional display to the sketch, computers could also aid design comprehension and visualization, both at initial design phases and in design development.

Michael Cohen expands on the realistic visualization capabilities that computers can provide the designer. In RADIOSITY BASED LIGHTING DESIGN he presents a method for obtaining realistic visual images through lighting design and analysis, based on the radiosity method of computing radiative transfer within an environment. This approach leaves both the generation of the environment and the interpretation of the images to the designer, but provides him with rich and readily comprehensible information.

In A PARTNERSHIP APPROACH TO COMPUTER-AIDED DESIGN, Swerdloff and Kalay present a computable model of design in which the role of the computer can be shifted dynamically between passive representation/evaluation and active generation of design solutions. In this model the designer, rather than the system's programmer, decides what role the computer should assume at every stage of the process, allowing the designer and the system to respond to changing requirements, unforeseen problems, and emerging opportunities as they arise during the design process. The designer has the option to rely on the system to generate certain design solutions, if the system has sufficient data and knowledge to generate them. On the other hand, solutions could be generated entirely by the designer, who may rely on the system only for analysis, solution representation, and the provision of pertinent design information.

In Chapter 17, Franz Veit sums up the utilities of computational design methods that were employed in actual architectural design. In DESIGN AUGMENTATION IN THE ARCHITECTURAL PRACTICE, he shows how computer systems have been employed to aid, in various degrees, creativity, experience, and technical knowledge (facts) in the design of hospitals in the last 20 years.

14

INTUITIVE DESIGN AND COMPUTATION

Richard B. Norman

College of Architecture
Clemson University
Clemson, South Carolina

The creative phase of design is embodied in the intuitive leap that comes after the gathering of information is complete, and an idea forms itself to be manifested in one beautiful sketch.

The argument for computation in support of the intuitive process is well founded. The computer provides an extensive knowledge base at the point of conception and can function as a tool for the comprehensive visualization of an emerging design.

Computers could also aid design development, which comes after the intuitive leap has occurred, through displaying visually the implications of design decisions.

Computers, therefore, can aid in the design process by generating alternative solutions that nurture the intuitive leap, and can help design development. However, they do not partake in performing the intuitive leap itself, only facilitate it.

This paper builds an argument for using computers in the pre-design fact gathering and in the developmental phases of the design process, by demonstrating that they are as effective as or better than traditional design tools. It does so by exploring the use of computers to investigate the manipulation of line, form, pattern, and color as basic design elements, which provide a better understanding of design choices.

□ THE INTUITIVE PROCESS

The American Heritage Dictionary defines *intuition* as "the act or facility of knowing without the use of rational processes." It is a cognitive process, based on prior knowledge and insight. Thus, by definition, no mathematical, logical, or rational process can elicit intuition, which therefore defies computation.

The creative phase of the design process is intuitive. Design begins with a gathering of facts, sometimes simplistically, as in the Beaux-Arts tradition, and sometimes with elaborated structuring, as in Christopher Alexander's pattern language [Alexander 1977]. But there comes a point after all the gathering of information that an intuitive leap must be made. Given that intuition is not computable, how can computers facilitate it?

The process of design can be approached as a search for alternatives. By examining the choices available within any given architectural problem, it is possible to generate multiple solutions on which the intuitive leap is based.

Computers can perform this task well. The computer can be programmed to generate an inventory of *patterns* that are potential solutions to the design problem [March & Steadman 1974]. These patterns are mathematical, logical, and systematic repetitions of design elements. Appropriately generated, they can represent the range of formal solutions to the architectural design problem at different levels of abstraction and scale.

An extensive body of alternative solutions can be generated by structuring and limiting the formation of patterns on the computer. These combinations of form may uncover more ideas than can be achieved manually. Furthermore, this enumeration is thorough and can be analyzed. It provides invaluable information to a designer, and can free him from the tedious search for alternatives.

In other words, the search for alternatives is not in itself an intuitive process. Rather, it is a presentation of useful ideas, choices from which a design decision can be made. Perhaps it is a presentation of multiple intuitive leaps, but I would be more inclined to define the generated forms as choices from which to make the intuitive leap, since this process is more analytical than inventive.

□ TRADITIONAL REPRESENTATION OF INTUITION

Computer generated formative patterns are only one source of information that fuels the creative design process. It is doubtful, for example, that the shape of the Chapel at Ronchamp would be generated from a programmed inventory of form choices. Rather, Le Corbusier is said to have drawn his inspirations from such diverse situations as Greek fishing villages or from the habits of nuns. Often in his sketchbooks the substance of a design is found in one intuitive drawing (see, for example, Figure 14.1). Such sketches are not restricted to Le Corbusier. Among Frank Lloyd Wright's developmental sketches for the Johnson Wax Building was the first drawing that can be said to have captured the essence of the design concept. Such sketches are an instantaneous assimilation of gathered facts that simultaneously give form to the design, no matter how complex the designed building will be.

The Beaux-Arts Institute's approach to design illustrates this point. It idealized the moment of conception by forcing the student to an intuitive design [Drexler 1977]. At the Beaux-Arts, a design was initiated with a sketch exercise ("esquisse"). One page of carefully worded material was distributed to provide a program, conveying both the particulars of the building function and the hierarchy of spaces. The preparation of this design statement was in the best traditions of research. At the Beaux-Arts each student was literally locked in a closet, there to intuit his design concept as a sketch. In this initial sketch was to be embodied the essence of the emerging design. Each student had only the written program statement as a source for his design. Solutions represented concepts that were the sole creation of the student, his claim to originality. The essence of the design, the concept, had passed from the mind to the hand to the paper in that closet.

The ubiquitous "napkin sketch" is another example to a means of capturing the intuitive leap. It is credited with being the Modern Movement's last remnant of the Beaux-Arts tradition described above:

> A sad vestige of the traditional analytic or process drawing is the 'napkin sketch', stereotypically representing the flash of intuitive insight that structures the solution to an architectural project. Interestingly enough, it is the napkin sketch that within modern architecture seems to animate the otherwise lifeless program upon which so much depends. The napkin sketch, of course, was not new to modern architecture. It is only its intentional spontaneity and independence from traditional architectural form that was new. Its premodern counterpart is found in the Ecole des Beaux-Arts' esquisse. [Crow & Hurtt 1986].

Les premiers croquis

La chapelle de Ronchamp

Figure 14.1. The representation of intuition.

The napkin sketch is a procedure familiar to anyone involved in design process today. As an intuitive solution to the design problem it is common practice. Can the intuitive idea for a design travel from the mind to the hand to the keyboard or joystick in the computer room of the future? Is it in fact possible to replace the napkin sketch with a computed concept?

□ COMPUTATIONAL REPRESENTATION OF INTUITION

Architectural intuition is traditionally expressed as an arrangement of spaces and formal relationships. The pursuit of a particular organization, a "parti" as the Beaux-Arts called it, consists of manipulating the fundamental geometry of architecture. This endless variation of line and repetition of form is computable.

Computational techniques expand considerably the resources available to the designer. We have discussed their utility in generating and representing available choices (though not in the intuitive essence of a design). Computers also expand the techniques and methods available to the designer for capturing and representing the intuitive leap.

Traditionally we design by creating "lines" with a pencil. The pencil is a good media for design. It is a simple thing, much easier to understand and to use than a computer. But should it be a 4H pencil, or a 2B? Should it have a chisel point, a rounded point, or no point at all? One can draw beautiful lines and with a good pencil technique achieve a formidable composition. But the pencil, in fact any medium, introduces the issues of its own techniques. These are important issues, but they are not central to the issue of intuitive design.

The manipulation of line is the beginning of the design process. We pick up a pencil and draw. Through experience we are aware of the line drawings of da Vinci or of Le Corbusier, and our own work seems at first inferior. If we draw lines using our friendly computer we are really alienated, for these lines possess none of the warmth, none of the stylistic elegance of the master's sketches.

Yet at least part of what we admire are the drawings themselves, not just the objects they represent. The design process is full of such obstacles to inhibit comprehension of design. We must distinguish between "line" as object and "line" as an element of the more complex meaning of design.

The use of a computer at the point of conceptual design could be seen as an intrusion into our focus on the geometry of architecture. But the computer can also help, for it creates a "style-less" line. This is not bad. In fact it enables us to explore the uses of line as a design tool, void of any imposed questions of style. Media technique ceases to be an issue. The computer is a great equalizer. On its screen the lines which draw the master's designs are the same as the lines which you draw, only the designs which they represent are different. If we could see lines as design elements that are void of all stylistic consideration we might better understand how by their length, grouping and direction they form a design and express a design idea.

The old metaphor of line as a design abstraction may no longer be enough, though. The Television Generation expects a message with clear visual demonstration. The mental pictures formed during the golden era of radio have given way to the sharp visualizations of modern media entertainment. Today's designer could benefit by having a clear visual demonstration by computer of the forms he is inventing. His intuition would be reinforced with this improved visualization.

The techniques of three-dimensional modeling on the computer, if made simple enough to maneuver with dexterity, could contribute substantially to intuitive design judgement. So used, the computer would enrich the designer's vocabulary by illustrating form choices previously eliminated as too difficult to draw.

☐ COMPUTERS IN DESIGN DEVELOPMENT

The role of the computer in support of the intuitive design process has been discussed so far. It assists in gathering the facts, listing available components and developing patterns in support of the typology. Computers can also be used in the design development process which comes after conception. Between these two areas lies an intuitive design decision that has been made outside of the computational process. The utility of computers in design development lies in their ability to visually display the implications of design decisions in three-dimensional form, and with color and texture.

Suppose that our computer contained a city as part of its database. The image of a twenty story mass can then be seen on the corner of First Avenue and Park Place; it can rapidly be changed to a forty story mass. It can meet the street line or set back 50 feet to generate a plaza.

The urban pattern is probably the most complex pattern generated by man. The systems, rhythms and textures of the city are endlessly questioned and re-formulated by designers. The recognition of patterns and their determinants are basic to understanding the nature of design. Repetition of pattern and formation of texture are logical computer tasks. Through the study of pattern, many urban design issues can logically be approached by computer.

The perception of a building is dependent on the choice of color, both the color of the building and the color of its surroundings. Color can be used to shift the emphasis of an object or a building from horizontal to vertical. It can be used to alter the way in which we perceive form, manipulating the perception of a building to make it assume either a foreground or a background position.

Yet, in many ways color is the poor orphan on a list of design elements.

It has always been included among the list of these elements, the subject of a chapter in most design texts and the substance of a few notable design efforts. Yet a vast majority of architects have not involved themselves with color as a design element capable of their manipulation.

Computing may change this, for computer images are literally made of colors. They can be manipulated with an ease never possible by traditional methods. It is easier to fill an area with color by computer than it is with any other medium. Changing colors on the computer is as easy as processing words; the computer is the first instrument ever devised that permits free and uninhibited color analysis.

On the computer the effects of color changes on the mass and scale of a building can be seen and quickly modified. Computer color becomes an element of design that like line, form and texture can be used as the substance of design intuition. In comparison, the design dreams of yesteryear were in black and white.

□ THE FUTURE OF COMPUTATIONAL DESIGN

The computer has been established as an excellent design tool for both fact gathering and for the development of ideas. The facts about a proposed building which can be gathered with computers are exhaustive. They expand exponentially the methods of analysis and assimilation which traditionally begin the design process. This bank of information is capable of recording precedent, typology, and programmatic needs at a depth never before achievable. It is an overwhelming design resource, and therefore a catalyst to the intuitive leap.

After the conception of a design, the drawings that CAD systems can produce as the design process unfolds are a revolution in the communication of architectural information. The comprehension of design intent, which these systems foster throughout the building industry, cannot help but improve our environment. With a consistency of method which only the computer can foster, each aspect of a design is conveyed to all concerned. The information is received, recorded, and distributed by computation.

If those responsible for the design of our environment can exploit computation as both a source of design information and a repository of design ideas, then substantial progress will be made toward the computability of the design effort.

But between the analysis of a design and its development to a finished product lies the seat of intuition, the heart of the creative process. This intuitive leap, the first expression of the conceptual design, is not yet computed.

What must be asked is whether the methodologies of computation, in addition to their excellent supportive role, could actually achieve this intuition. In our excitement with computation, the argument is sometimes presumed. I believe, however, that the intuitive leap should remain the sole passion and turf of the human mind.

☐ REFERENCES

Alexander C. *A Pattern Language: Towns, Buildings, Construction*, Oxford University Press, New York, NY, 1977.

Crowe N. and S. Hurtt "Visual Notes and the Acquisition of Architectural Knowledge," *Journal of Architectural Education*, p. 11, Spring 1986.

Drexler A. *The Architecture of the Ecole des Beaux-Arts*, The Museum of Modern Art, 1977.

March L. and P. Steadman *The Geometry of Environment*, MIT Press, Cambridge MA, 1974.

15

RADIOSITY BASED LIGHTING DESIGN

Michael F. Cohen

Department of Architecture
Program of Computer Graphics
Cornell University
Ithaca, New York

A lighting design and analysis method is outlined and demonstrated which is based on the radiosity method for computing radiative (light) transfer within an environment. The input consists of the geometry of an environment, the reflective properties of the surfaces as well as light emission from light sources. The radiosity method, based on principles of conservation of energy, computes a balance of the light energy through a simultaneous solution for the complex inter-reflection and absorption of the light energy. Following an initial pre-process, various lighting conditions can be quickly analysed. Reflective properties can be varied effecting the secondary illumination within the environment. Primary and secondary illumination can be studied separately or in combination. The results can be displayed graphically from any angle providing the means for both quantitative and qualitative evaluation of a proposed environment. Sequences of images can provide further feedback though dynamic walk-throughs.

□ INTRODUCTION

The question of how computer technology should be applied to the problems of design is no longer a new one, however, a sufficient answer is still lacking. Perhaps the continuing explosion in computational power and

303

graphics abilities is changing the question even as we try to answer it. This paper will not attempt to present a complete answer to the original question. It will instead present an application which will, I hope, add evidence that computers, particularly when coupled with advanced display devices, can be a powerful aid in the design of physical environments. The function of the application is to model the illumination of proposed environments for purposes of lighting design and visualization. The mathematical technique is called the radiosity method.

The result of the radiosity analysis can produce a strikingly realistic image of the simulated environment. It is often argued that a realistic image obscures the real issues in architectural design. Abstractions, on the other hand, allow the designer to concentrate on a facet of the whole. There must be a process of breaking down a problem into its component parts and building it back up. The author has no differences with this point of view.

When the question relates to what kind of visual output is desired from computer simulations used as a design tool, a similar argument follows that there is no real need for realism (except for promotion, of course). Line plots or at most simple volumetric shapes provide sufficient information to analyze a proposed design. Why go to the trouble of creating realistic images?

The simplest answer is "Why not?". Technologies that are becoming available today will soon make realistic image synthesis affordable to most architectural firms in the near future.

A more meaningful answer is that all abstractions must have their roots in some reality. A realistic or complete database which contains enough information to render a realistic image, also contains information from which to extract and abstract. The ability to run computer analyses for lighting design, or HVAC considerations from the same database that can produce plans and elevations is a powerful tool. Inconsistencies within databases show up immediately to our eyes when presented with a realistic image. This generally is not the case with other forms of output.

The simulation of the interreflection of light in order to create a realistic image provides valuable information to the architect, designer or lighting engineer. Both the numerical output and the visual information can be used by the lighting engineer to evaluate the result of a proposed lighting scheme. In some cases the simulated environment can replace the need to build a physical model to study the visual impact of a design.

□ RADIOSITY

The radiosity method was originally developed to study radiative heat exchange within environments [Siegel & Howell 1978]. It was introduced to the computer graphics community in 1984 by [Goral et al 1984]. An algorithm introduced by this author in 1985 [Cohen & Greenberg 1985] provided the means to analyze the direct illumination and light reflection in complex environments by solving the problems involved with occlusion of one surface from another. The validity of the algorithm's results have been verified through physical tests which have been reported by [Meyer et al 1986]. Improvements in terms of power and efficiency have been subsequently published [Cohen et al 1986]. In recent years other work has been done, most notably by [DiLaura 1981; DiLaura 1982], to use radiosity type methods for lighting design and analysis.

In order to determine the need and value of graphic simulation, it is important to evaluate the ability of the resulting images to accurately represent the environment being simulated both quantitatively and qualitatively. An evaluation of the accuracy of the impression produced by viewing a computer graphic image on a CRT as opposed to a physical model has been made by [Davis & Bernecker 1984] and [Meyer et al 1986]. In each experiment, subjects were asked to evaluate the match between computer images and real world environments. Both experiments confirmed the ability of computer simulations to produce visual impressions similar to the real environment being simulated. The latter experiment which utilized the software described in this paper also found quantitative agreement by comparing radiometric measurements of the real world with the quantitative results of the computer simulation.

Through the ability to create realistic images from the radiosity data, the radiosity method becomes a tool both for lighting design/analysis, through quantitative results as well as for simulation of the visual impact of a design.

A short description of the theory and implementation of the radiosity method follows. This is followed by an example environment in which the outlined methods are illustrated.

□ THE RADIOSITY METHOD

The radiosity method makes one basic assumption, that all surfaces act as Lambertian diffuse reflectors, and involves four steps:

1. Providing a geometric description of an environment and specifying a subdivision of the surfaces into small discrete areas or "patches". The level of subdivision of the surfaces into patches effects the accuracy and the cost of the computation. As an initial design tool, a fine subdivision may not be necessary or desirable. As more accurate and realistic images are desired the same data base can be expanded through further subdivision. The surfaces must also be defined by their reflective (color) and emissive properties. Although all reflection is modeled as diffuse, the emission of the light sources

can be specified by its directional characteristics as well as its intensity. In this way, luminaires ranging from spotlights to diffuse ceiling panels can be simulated.

2. Computing the geometric relationships between each set of patches. These are termed the "form-factors" and define the fraction of light which leaves one patch that arrives at another. Through these terms the complex interreflection of light from one surface to another is accounted for. The form-factor computation is the most expensive part of the analysis. However, since it is dependent only on geometry, it needs to be performed only once for a given static environment.

3. Solving a set of simultaneous equations defined by the form-factors along with the reflectivity and emission properties of the surfaces. The solution provides the radiosity, or illumination of each surface in the environment. This matrix needs to be solved once for a monochromatic analysis, however, for full color, the equations must be formed and solved at three or four wavelength intervals.

    The designer or lighting engineer may not require or even desire the level of accuracy available from a full radiosity solution for realistic image generation. The complexity of the output can also be tailored to the type of graphics device available. Although full color 24 bit displays are required for realistic image synthesis, they may be an unnecessary luxury for the lighting designer.

4. The final step in the process is to display the results of the radiosity analysis from a given vantage point. This involves determining the visible surfaces from a given viewpoint and shading those surfaces based on the radiosity results. Sophisticated graphics devices perform these operation very quickly in hardware making it possible to "walk around" the simulated environment. Software implementations for this step can be created for any raster device, however, the characteristics of the display device will define the properties of the final image.

Different light sources can be turned on or off or modulated by repeating steps (3) and (4). Surface reflectivity values can also be changed in the same two steps. The bulk of the computation residing in the form-factor computation needs to be repeated only with changes in geometry.

The results of the radiosity analysis provide total illumination levels on each surface. The totals can be separated into direct and secondary illumination to study the effects of shadowing and interreflection. The secondary illumination due to interreflection plays a significant role in overall environment illumination levels. This process has previously been difficult to model accurately. An example environment follows, which is used to illustrate the power of the technique for architectural lighting design and visualization.

□ AN EXAMPLE ENVIRONMENT

The environment which is illustrated in the following images was modeled and rendered with interactive software developed at Cornell University's Program of Computer Graphics. Primitive objects such as room shapes, partitions, tables and light fixtures are modelled individually and stored as data files. These can then be read into an environment modeler and quickly assembled into a complete environment. Material properties, such as colors, reflectivities and emission values can be specified for each surface or object in the environment.

The surfaces of the environment are subdivided into patches through both automatic and interactive means, completing the required input for the radiosity analysis. Later refinements to the geometry and lighting and reflective properties can be made rapidly. Although the means for defining the environment are not discussed here, this aspect of the overall software system clearly plays a major role in the usefulness of the analytical methods contained in this paper. It is important that CAD systems maintain coherent three dimensional databases so that sophisticated analysis methods such as that outlined here can be applied.

All of the following images were created from a single set of form-factor calculations since the geometry remained constant. The form-factor calculations took approximately one hour on a VAX-780.

Three different types of light sources were modeled. Two windows on one wall are modelled as diffuse emitters. There are eight rectangular sources on the ceiling and five lamps (one above each table) which shine downwards. Three different lighting schemes were analyzed, each of which took an additional five minutes on the VAX mini-computer for the matrix solution. In the first set of images (15.1a and 15.1b) the windows provide the bulk of the illumination. There is also one desk light turned on.

Figure 15.2 illustrates the ability to separate the primary radiosity due to direct illumination from the sources (15.2a), from the secondary radiosity due to the interreflection of light from surface to surface within the environment (15.2b). The sum of figures (15.2a and 15.2b) is identical to figure (15.1a).

Figure 15.3 shows the same environment illuminated from the over head sources and figure 15.4 shows the environment illuminated from the desk lamps only.

Each image took approximately 15 minutes to render in software, however, hardware devices can now use the radiosity results to produce an image from any given viewpoint in about one second to allow a designer to "walk around" the environment.

These images were displayed on a 1280 X 1024 X 24 bit Raster-Technology frame buffer.

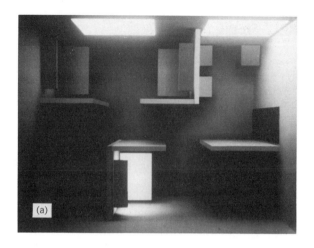

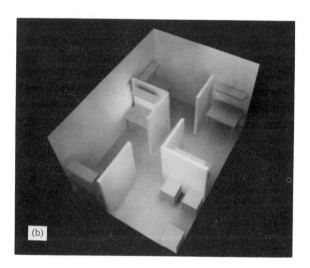

Figure 15.1. Environment Illuminated by Windows and One Desk Light.

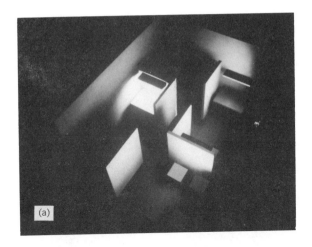

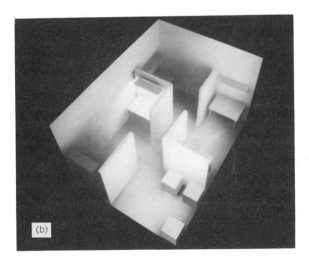

Figure 15.2. Separation of Primary and Secondary Illumination.

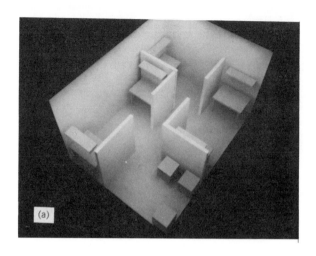

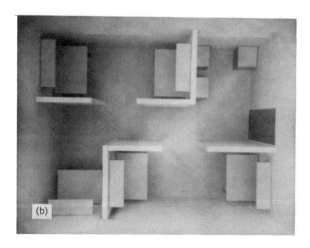

Figure 15.3. Environment Illuminated by Overhead Ceiling Lights.

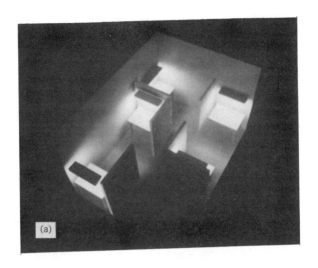

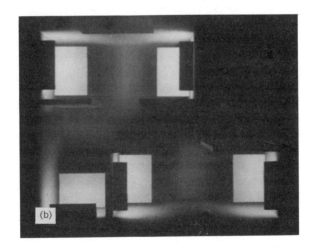

Figure 15.4. Environment Illuminated by Desk Lights.

☐ CONCLUSION

A system for simulating the interreflection of light within an environment, known as the radiosity method has been demonstrated for use in a lighting design system. The method allows the user to define different lighting schemes for an environment and to study the effects of the direct and secondary illumination.

Although the example environment was not presented in a quantitative fashion, the numerical results pertaining to illumination and radiosity values are available. An obvious question arises regarding the ability of the computer to redesign the proposed environment in order to achieve some defined goals. The original equations contain all the interrelationship between surfaces. Routines could be implemented to automatically adjust illumination levels until certain criteria are reached. The light reaching a particular surface could be modified both by increasing the output of the sources as well as by increasing the reflectivity of intermediate surfaces. An iterative process of redesign and evaluation could be performed automatically or through user control.

Perhaps of more importance is the ability of the radiosity method coupled with sophisticated display hardware to provide realistic qualitative simulation. This allows the architect, lighting designer and the client the ability to study the visual and aesthetic impact of a proposed design. New advances in display technology now allow the ability to "walk around" in the simulated environments.

The cost of the technology to produce images like those shown in this paper is rapidly becoming within the reach of most architectural offices. Given the software tools to define the 3D geometry and material properties of proposed designs, the radiosity method can provide a powerful tool for architectural design.

Clearly, realism is not the tool to address all architectural issues. It may obscure more fundamental issues in the early phases of the design process. The ability to study one aspect of a problem through the process of abstraction is an important design tool. Once a computer begins to simulate reality, however, various abstractions can be extracted from the full description. An example of this in the above paper is the ability to separate primary and secondary illuminations. The need for sophisticated databases which allow pieces to be selected from a coherent whole can not be overestimated.

No single tool will be able to address all the problems of design. It is important to continue to address the questions of how this technology can best be applied to the design of our physical environment.

☐ REFERENCES

Siegel R. and J.R. Howell *Thermal Radiation Heat Transfer,* Hemisphere Publishing Corp., 1978.

Goral C.M., K.E. Torrance D.P. Greenberg and B. Battaile, "Modeling the Interaction of Light Between Diffuse Surfaces," *ACM Computer Graphics,* SIGGRAPH, Volume 17, Number 3, 1984.

Cohen M.F. and D.P. Greenberg, "The Hemi-Cube: A Radiosity Solution for Complex Environments," *ACM Computer Graphics,* SIGGRAPH, Volume 19, Number 3, 1985.

Meyer G.W., H.E. Rishmeier M.F. Cohen D.P. Greenberg and K.E. Torrance, "An Experimental Assessment of Computer Graphics Images," *ACM Transactions on Graphics,* Vol. 5, No. 1, January 1986.

Cohen M.F, D.S. Immel P.J. Brock and D.P. Greenberg, "An Efficient Radiosity Method for Realistic Image Synthesis," *IEEE Computer Graphics and Applications,* Volume 6, Number 3, March 1986.

DiLaura D.L., "On Radiative Transfer Calculations in Unempty Rooms," *Journal of the Illuminating Engineering Society,* January 1981.

DiLaura D.L., "On the Simplification of Radiative Transfer Calculations," *Journal of the Illuminating Engineering Society,* October 1982.

Davis, R.G. and C.A. Bernecker, "An Evaluation of Computer Graphic Images of the Lighted Environment" *Journal of the Illuminating Engineering Society,* October 1984.

16

A PARTNERSHIP APPROACH TO COMPUTER-AIDED DESIGN

Lucien M. Swerdloff
Yehuda E. Kalay

School of Architecture and Environmental Design
State University of New York at Buffalo
Buffalo, New York

The use of computers for automating the processes by which artifacts are designed is limited by the difficulty in computationally modeling *discovery* and *judgement*—two of the most important characteristics of design. It has yet to be established whether the cognitive processes of discovery and judgement can be computed, and whether doing so will be in the best interest of design.

This paper proposes that discovery and judgement could be incorporated into computer-aided design *without their computation*, by integrating computational and manual design methods within a generalized design framework. It suggests that such integration will increase the utility of computer-aided design systems by allowing them to more fully support the creative facets of design. Such integration could be achieved by a *partnership* approach to computer-aided design, where design decisions are undertaken alternatively by the designer and by the computer. The implementation of the partnership approach is predicated on the ability to factor design into discrete tasks, each of which could be represented computationally, and the development of a control structure that can monitor the design process and manage the allocation of responsibility for achieving each design task between the designer and the system.

To support this argument, design is modeled as a search process that seeks one or more solutions that satisfy certain design objectives. Design is shown to be a special case of general problem-solving, comprised of two major components: design states and transitions between them. Using techniques developed by computer-aided design and artificial intelligence researchers, it is shown that both design states and transitions can be represented computationally, forming the basis on which the design process control mechanism could be founded. A conceptual framework for design process control, which is based on the partnership approach, is presented, and its potential for increasing the utility of computers in design is discussed.

□ INTRODUCTION

The growing complexity of modern artifacts and environments, and the socio-economic pressures to maintain an efficient design/build cycle, are forcing designers to seek new tools and methodologies that can help them cope with and manage the processes by which new artifacts and environments are conceived and created. This trend has been accelerated in the past few decades by developments in cognitive and computer sciences that have provided insight into some human thought processes, and have produced tools to assist them.

The application of computers to design has generally been associated with the notion of increasing the productivity of design professionals. The advent, and subsequent disillusionment, of computer-aided drafting has, more recently, focused the attention of researchers on developing fundamental computer-aided design measures capable of *qualitative* rather than more *quantitative* improvements, through the effective use of designers' creative resources in their pursuit of better solutions to design problems.

Computationally facilitating the creative aspects of design processes in disciplines such as architecture is difficult for several reasons. First, the process of design is ill-understood, and therefore defies the precise modeling prerequisite to its computation. Second, the prospect of incorporating computational means to assist design creativity has met with serious criticism from designers, who object to automation of the inherently human process of design. (It is interesting to compare their objections with criticisms of artificial intelligence.)

The difficulties in computer-aiding many design tasks, and the criticism against attempting to do so in the first place, suggests that not all high level design tasks could or should be computer-aided, and that it may be more prudent to integrate conventional and computational approaches within the overall design process. However, attempts to integrate computational and conventional design practices have tended to follow a rigid task allocation that is not suitable for supporting the exploratory nature of design, where insight and understanding of the problem often arise from the solution process itself, requiring modification of both objectives and means.

We propose that a flexible integration of computational and other design methods in a generalized design framework can be achieved through a *partnership* approach to computer-aiding the design process. This approach views design as a process of *search* for a satisfactory design solution. The search can be modeled by means of a state-transition graph, representing multiple alternative sequences of design goals. The responsibility for generating solutions that achieve each goal can be dynamically allocated between the designer and the supporting computer system, depending on the nature of each goal, the circumstances of the particular design problem, and the designer's own judgement.

The partnership approach to computer-aided design is predicated on the ability to factor the design process into discrete tasks, and to assign the responsibility for resolving each task either to the designer or to the computer. In discussing the partnership approach it is necessary, therefore, to establish the factorability of design into discrete tasks, and to develop computational means for their representation. It is also necessary to develop the means for allocating the responsibility for design task resolution between the designer and the computer, without loss of process continuity, and with guaranteed convergence on an acceptable design solution.

The paper is organized into three parts. First, the factorability of design is discussed, using a state-transition graph as a means to model the goal directed design process. Second, computational techniques for the representation of design states and the simulation of the transitions between design states are discussed, illustrated by examples drawn from computer-aided design and artificial intelligence. Third, a dynamic design task allocation control structure is outlined, along with a conceptual framework for its implementation.

☐ MODELING DESIGN AS A SEARCH PROCESS

To understand the process of design and its potential computation an abstract model may be used. Many models of design exist, in some cases differing widely from each other. Opinions differ more with regard to the methods designers use in executing the process, than with regard to the nature of the process itself. Most researchers agree that design is a complex, purposeful behavior which is directed at devising artifacts or environments that attain certain goals while abiding by certain constraints. Since no formulae exist which can translate design objectives and constraints into a self-consistent physical entity, design is necessarily described as process of search in which alternative solutions are constructed and tested for satisfying the objectives and abiding by the constraints. Design, therefore, shares many characteristics of general problem-solving processes as defined by Newell and Simon [Newell & Simon 1972; Simon 1969].

According to general problem solving theory, for every problem we may define a *solution space*—a domain that includes all possible solutions to the problem. Problem-solving can then be characterized as a process of *searching* through alternative solutions in this space, in order to discover one (or several) that meet certain objectives and therefore are considered "solution states." The word "search" is used here metaphorically to describe a process of *seeking* and *evaluating* alternative solutions, either to the problem as a whole or to its subproblems (Figure 16.1). The states need not exist prior to the initiation of the search process, but can be (and usually are) developed as it unfolds.

A "state" is meant to describe a specific recognizable phase of the design process (a "snapshot"), It can be comprised of a candidate solution to the design problem (a physical description), or of a set of objectives and constraints that a candidate solution must achieve (a functional description). The design process can be viewed as the application of operators that modify candidate solutions so they become less abstract or they attain particular design objectives. The transition process must be guided by heuristic knowledge so as to guarantee its convergence on a recognizable solution in "reasonable" time (if such a solution exists), and thereby bring the design process to a successful conclusion.

The transition from one state to another—a process that eventually brings the search closer to the desired solution state—is more difficult to computationally represent than the design states themselves. Simon and Newell propose the use of "means-ends" analysis to minimize the differences between the current state and the goal state, but caution that such analysis is effective only in "well behaved" solution spaces, where transitions cause no side effects that may steer the solution away from the goal

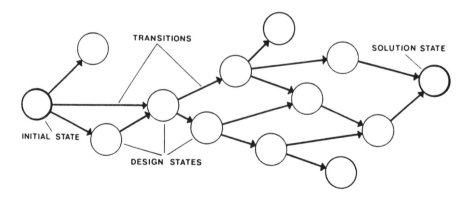

Figure 16.1. Design as a goal-directed search process.

rather than closer to it [Newell & Simon 1972]. Design is characteristically not such a well-behaved process, hence means-ends analysis must be augmented with inference based on knowledge, experience, judgement, and intuition.

☐ COMPUTATIONAL MODELS OF DESIGN STATES AND TRANSITIONS

Computer-aided design, as we view it, is founded on the premise that design states can be represented by symbolic mathematical structures that can be operated on to simulate the transitions from one design state to the next. By representing states and simulating transitions computers could generate, evaluate, and reason about designed artifacts and environments. The representation of states and the simulation of transitions, therefore, comprises the core of computer-aided design research.

Much progress has been made by researchers in the past two decades in computationally modeling (physical and functional) design solutions. It will suffice to mention here advances in geometric modeling [Baer et al 1979; Eastman & Preiss 1984; Kalay 1983b; Requicha 1980], design database development [Kalay 1983a; Lafue 1979; Rasdorf & Kutay 1982], shape grammars [Flemming 1981; Stiny 1980], and the more task-specific representation of buildings [Akin 1982; Eastman 1980; Eastman & Yasky 1984; Negroponte 1970], machines [Shu 1976], and integrated circuits (IC) [Mayo 1983].

Advances have also been made in simulating transitions as processes that generate and evaluate design solutions. These advances have been, for the most part, task-specific, such as space allocation [Buffa et al 1969; Shaviv & Gali 1979; Whitehead & Eldars 1963], and IC design automation [Mayo 1983; Mead & Conway 1980].

Such advances have not only provided some useful tools for computer-aiding design, but have also accentuated its complexities. It has become quite obvious that most of the above mentioned computational design aids are inadequate for supporting the *creative* facets of design processes. To accomplish that, the computational representation of design states and the simulation of the transitions between them must be extended beyond mere syntax to include semantic information as well. This will enable the computer to extract relevant information from the model, infer information which is not explicitly modeled, and select actions that will modify candidate solutions or design objectives in the desired manner, without having explicitly been directed to do so by the designer.

Augmenting the symbolic representation of states and the simulation of transitions by incorporating semantic information has been one of the major areas of investigation by the artificial intelligence (AI) research community [Bobrow & Winograd 1977; Winston 1984]. Of particular relevance to computer-aided design are techniques for symbolically representing "meaning," and heuristic search strategies.

The Representation of Meaning

The state of a physical artifact is naturally represented by the objects it consists of: their form and attributes, the relationships between them, and the rules for their manipulation. This is particularly true when dealing with artifacts such as buildings, machines, and integrated circuits. It differs from other domains of knowledge representation such as natural language or image understanding where most of the knowledge is derived from inferences made about the state of many independent units of data, each of which carries a relatively small amount of information by itself.

The representation of individual objects alone is, however, adequate for representing only the static state of artifacts. When viewed as an integral part of the dynamic design process, the representation of the dependencies between objects is as important as the representation of the objects themselves. Inter-object relationships, represented as links, provide the means to combine objects dynamically into meaningful assemblies and cause changes that are applied to one component to have an effect on other components as well [Kalay 1985].

Such dynamic representation relies on the ability to describe not only the object itself, but also the conditions it must meet, and those that have led to its current composition. It has, in fact, been argued that the representation of functional composition and dependencies are more important than physical form, since the latter can be derived from the former, that is, "form follows function" (see "Reasoning About Form and Function," by W.J. Mitchell, in this book).

Whether or not one accepts this argument, the importance of functional description is indisputable. Techniques that were developed for the purpose of representing semantic knowledge include frames, rules, and scripts [Buchanan & Shortliffe 1984; Ingalls 1978]. These and other techniques have been used in shape grammars and expert systems for computer-aiding design [Flemming 1981; Gero 1985; Kalay et al 1985; Landsdown 1982; Rehak et al 1984; Stiny 1980] (see also "Artificial Intelligence and Automated Design," by Shapiro and Geller, in this book).

Heuristic Search

Viewed as a collection of action rules, computer programs can easily execute lists of predefined tasks. If the application of the rules is well-defined, the program is said to be algorithmic: actions follow some predefined "recipe" which, given the same conditions, always yields the same result. Many problems, however, cannot be solved algorithmically, either because their solution procedure is ill-defined or because not all the information they require is available or accurate. Such problems make it necessary to use less specific and more adaptive solution processes (known as "weak methods"), which typically rely on trial-and-error techniques before they arrive at any solution. Such techniques are, by definition, comprised of search and evaluation, which have been described as essential components of design.

Systematic trial-and-error (the examination of all possible solutions to a problem to find one that meets the goal criteria) is applicable only to very small problems, because of the exponential number of alternative solutions. For any realistic problem the search process must somehow be directed so that the exploration of unproductive steps is minimized.

In some cases, it is possible to eliminate exploration of unproductive alternatives by using local information which is inherent to the particular states. More often, however, it is necessary to use information drawn from a broader perspective, perhaps even from outside the particular problem domain itself. Such information, which is used to guide the problem solving search process, has been termed "heuristic knowledge". It is often experiential, drawn from knowledge possessed by experts and accumulated over long periods of time while solving similar problems.

The particular importance of heuristic search strategies to computer aiding design is their usefulness in *controlling* the design process, in terms of both selecting the path of design development, and the means of implementing that selection [Coyne & Gero 1985]. This is the essence of Simon and Newell's "means-ends" analysis, which can be implemented by action-coupled difference tables [Simon 1969; Newell & Simon 1972]. As it will be discussed in the next section, these means may be computational or manual, depending on the particular characteristics of the emerging design solution.

☐ THE PARTNERSHIP APPROACH TO COMPUTER-AIDED DESIGN

We have seen how design can be modeled as a process of search and can be represented by the state-transition graph. We have also seen that states can be represented functionally by means of techniques developed in AI, and that the process of selecting tasks for achievement can be simulated computationally as a heuristic search strategy.

These computational methods are, nevertheless, insufficient to fully automate the design process. Difficulties arise when attempting to compute *discovery* and *judgement*, two major characteristics that distinguish design from other problem solving processes, and establish it as the epitome of intelligent behavior.

Discovery and Judgement

Discovery is the act of acquiring understanding about the design problem through its solution process. Archea has described this phenomena as "puzzle making," the process whereby the designer discovers how a given set of components and rules can be composed into meaningful structures that achieve specific objectives (see "Puzzle Making: What Architects Do When No One is Looking," by J. Archea, in this book). The implication of discovery is that both design objectives and means may have to be modified as the process unfolds. The inference of such implications in realistic design problems are, however, currently beyond the power of computational methods, although systems that "discover" in certain precise domains such as mathematics have been developed [Lenat 1982].

Judgement is the cognitive property that must be employed when the designer is faced with the need to choose between alternative or conflicting qualities, without a common or objective basis for their comparison. An example is the well-known trade-off between quality and cost often faced by designers. Judgement relies on subjective preferences, experience, and normative rules, all of which are unattainable through current computational methods.

Advances in cognitive sciences and artificial intelligence may provide the computational methods needed to simulate discovery and apply judgement. It appears that computer-aided design could substantially benefit from the inclusion of discovery and judgement. For lack of appropriate computational means, these tasks must, for the time being, be undertaken by the designer. A partnership approach to computer-aided design could facilitate the integration of non-computable discovery and judgement into computational design processes.

The partnership approach is based on the integration of computational and manual design methods in a generalized design framework where the responsibility for resolving design tasks is allocated dynamically between the designer and the supporting computer system. This allocation depends on the nature of each task, the circumstances of the particular design problem, and the designer's own judgement.

Control of Computer-Aided Design Processes

The partnership approach differs from other approaches to computer-aided design in the sharing of control between the designer and the computer. For our purposes, *control* is defined as choosing design tasks to be accomplished, initiating solution generating procedures, and requesting evaluations.

By and large, existing computational design aids fall into two main categories with respect to the control process:

1. Approaches where control over the design process is vested exclusively in the designer.
2. Approaches where control over the process is vested exclusively in the system.

All drafting and modeling approaches to computer-aided design, where the computer is used solely as a means for representing the emerging artifact, belong to the first category. The generation of design solutions and their evaluation, although relying on such representations, are initiated by the designer with little or no active support of the computer. Analysis systems also belong to this category. They provide the designer with means to measure specific performances of the designed artifact, but do not suggest how this information is to be incorporated in the process, if at all, leaving to the designer the responsibility for judging the relative importance of each measure of performance compared to others.

Approaches where total control over the design process is vested in the system, rather than the designer, include space allocation, shape grammars, and even expert systems. These approaches are based on computationally representing all the knowledge pertaining to the design of specific artifacts, to the point where the systems are capable of designing such artifacts given certain initial information (or acquiring it during the process). It is the system's responsibility to initiate the request for information and to decide how that information is to be incorporated in the design process. Given that the source of the information is the designer, he may influence the process, but only within the bounds set by the system.

The Partnership Approach

The approach proposed here will let control over the process of design be assumed alternatively by the designer or by the system. The assignment of responsibility is not fixed, but dynamically shifts between the partners. The decision concerning who shall assume control over a specific design task is based on the circumstances of the particular task, and the relative strengths and limitations of each partner. The process as a whole can, therefore, better respond to the problems and opportunities that arise during the process of design. This model is, in principle, closer to the way design is performed in practice, where several designers participate in the decision making process. Similarly, it is proposed that one of the partners—the designer in this case—will be considered more "senior" than the other, and will have priority in deciding which tasks will be controlled by whom. For example, the designer may choose to assume responsibility for the overall layout of the floorplan of a house, and let the system design the details of the kitchen and the bathrooms. If, however, the designer is undecided as to which task should be pursued next, the system may make that decision. The designer will also have the power to resolve "arguments," and to override decisions made by the system. The designer will be responsible for extending and modifying the knowledge base of the system (with the aid of the system's record of the decision making process). Each partner will monitor and critique the decisions of the other. This mutual evaluation will prevent human mistakes from going undetected, and will guarantee that system-generated solutions will be consistent with the designer's wishes. It may be possible to carry this analogy even further, whereby design opportunities missed by either partner will be detected and pointed out by the other.

The proposed partnership approach has been implemented to a limited extent, in the ALEX system for computer-aided participatory design of single family houses [Kalay et al 1985]. The goal of that project was to develop a system capable of helping clients design their own single family house, much as an architect would. Although control over the design process was retained by the system at all times, some issues of joint decision making were encountered, since the client's responses to system prompts were in the form of design decisions. The sequence of activities was controlled by the system, but the client could backtrack and modify decisions made earlier (either by the system or the client), to which the system would then respond with other necessary changes.

A Framework for Implementing the Partnership Approach

Implementation of the partnership approach in a computer-aided design environment is comprised of developing task-based design knowledge representations and a suitable design process control framework that will support task allocation. This framework consists of Design Goal Representation (DGR) and a Design Process Executive (DPE). Both components are augmented by task-specific knowledge bases and are complemented by an appropriate user interface (Figure 16.2).

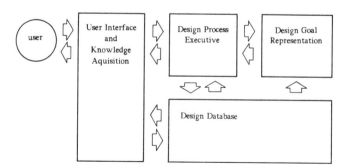

Figure 16.2. Conceptual framework of a CAD system based on the partnership approach.

This framework does not replace the design database of the system, where the designed artifact is stored. Rather, it relies on it for making decisions. The design database itself is generated and modified through design solutions that constitute the designer's or the system's attempts to achieve design tasks. However, the selection of design goals and the allocation of tasks for achieving them do not, in themselves, generate solutions. They only identify what objectives should be addressed by the solution generator and who should generate them.

Design Goal Representation (DGR)

To construct a working model of a computer-aided design system capable of supporting the partnership approach, *states* are defined as *design goals* rather than *design solutions*. Each goal is comprised of a set of context-dependent constraints that define the conditions a candidate solution must meet in order to achieve the goal. The major advantage and reason for this definition is abstraction: a goal is defined functionally, therefore it can be achieved by a large variety of design solutions whose particular composition is not explicitly defined. In addition, the goal definition itself can be modified by the designer if new knowledge is discovered through the design process. This definition of states also facilitates decomposition of the problem into tasks and subtasks, each represented as a goal. The hierarchical structuring of subgoals reduces the differences that must be bridged between successive design solutions. By reducing these differences the overall design problem may be reduced to a series of manageable tasks that can be solved by processes guided by information which is specific to the problem (e.g. square footage for a given room), and by project independent information which is part of the system's general knowledge base (e.g. typical layout of given rooms).

Subgoals are not necessarily sequential, and not all subgoals must be achieved in order to satisfy a given goal. Since their purpose is to facilitate the completion of design tasks rather than prescribe the flow of the design process, different combinations of subgoals that have been achieved may be considered sufficient to satisfy the goal itself. The achievement of particular subgoals depends, therefore, on the characteristics of the emerging design solutions. Since subgoals may require further decomposition to bring their complexity down to a manageable level, their structure resembles a tree hierarchy of nested subgoals. (An example and Prolog implementation of goals and subgoals is given in Appendix A).

Since states are defined functionally, evaluators must be employed to establish whether a proposed solution achieves each goal. (These evaluators do not replace, and should not be confused with, the means-ends analysis used by the DPE for goal selection.) Accomplishment of goal objectives and constraints need not be evaluated in cases where the solution generator is algorithmic or is otherwise based on inferential reasoning that guarantees generation of feasible alternatives. The constraints themselves may be shared by multiple goals, but their relative weights are goal-specific.

Design Process Executive (DPE)

The DPE monitors the progression of the design process and assists the designer in choosing the next goal to be achieved and in assigning the responsibility for generating a solution that achieves it to the designer or to the computer.

The particular sequence of goals that is chosen for achievement represents a *design plan*, or strategy. This sequence of goals ensures that adequate information exists at each phase of design, by virtue of achieving (completing) preceding phases, and ultimately reaching the solution state of design as a whole. In some cases, this sequence may be predetermined [Coyne & Gero 1985]. In other cases, the particular circumstances of the problem will require choosing goals based on the solutions that were devised for previous goals, thus transforming the process into a process that resembles opportunistic planning [Hayes-Roth & Hayes-Roth 1978].

In both cases, the DPE relies upon heuristic knowledge about the design process to perform the necessary means-ends analysis and guide the process towards conclusion. This knowledge is stored in a knowledge base that includes information about precedent design plans, and difference rules that support the means-ends analysis and are used to select goals when no precedent plan is found to fit the emerging design path.

The process of choosing goals for achievement and assignment of the responsibility for generating solutions that achieve them, are depicted schematically in Figure 16.3. (Its Prolog implementation is given in Appendix B.)

The generation of design solutions that accomplish specific goals represent the *transitions* in the state-transition graph. Solutions can be generated by the designer, or by the system if a solution procedure for the particular goal exists in its knowledge base, and if sufficient information exists to execute it.

User interface (UI)

An effective and friendly user interface between the computer and the designer is an essential component of a computer-aided design system based on the partnership approach. The UI allows the designer to graphically and analytically monitor the progression of the emerging design, apply judgemental decisions, and affect both the process and the design solution to reflect his preferences.

The UI also provides the conduit through which the various knowledge bases of the system can be augmented, modified and updated. The ability

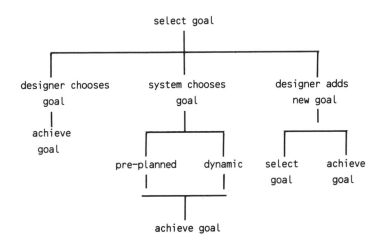

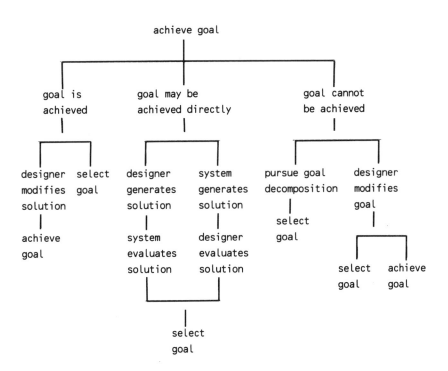

Figure 16.3. The Design Process Executive (DPE) schema.

to acquire new knowledge and update existing knowledge is a necessary feature to prevent early obsolescence of the system, and to improve its utility. In addition to fulfilling the important role of keeping the system current, knowledge acquisition also reflects the nature of design as an evolving process which constantly requires modification of knowledge and revision of methods.

□ SUMMARY

We have examined the design process from a problem-solving point of view and modeled it as a search process that seeks one or more solutions that satisfy certain design objectives. We have also seen how this search process can be described by a state-transition graph, and discussed some of the computational means that can be used to represent states and simulate transitions.

This exposition revealed that although computational techniques may be capable of representing both syntactic and semantic design information, and can simulate certain generative and evaluative processes, they are inadequate to support discovery and apply judgement. These tasks are better left to the designer, who must, therefore, be included in the computer-aided design process. This inclusion must be accomplished in a flexible and dynamic way, much like the partnership relation that support design in current practice.

A conceptual control framework, capable of supporting the proposed partnership approach, was presented. It is composed of Design Goal Representation (DGR), Design Process Executive (DPE), and User Interface (UI).

It is suggested here that computer-aided design systems that include control structures modeled after the partnership approach could improve the utility of time spent by designers, without sacrificing their ability to apply judgement, and the joy of discovery that are inherent to design processes.

□ ACKNOWLEDGMENTS

The authors thank Anton Harfmann and Bruce Majkowski for their helpful discussions during the writing of this paper.

□ REFERENCES

Akin O. "Representation and Architecture," in Akin and Weinel, eds., *Representation and Architecture*, Information Dynamics, Siver Spring MD, 1982.

Baer A., C.M. Eastman and M. Henrion "Geometric Modeling: A Survey," *Computer-Aided Design* 11(5):253-272, September 1979.

Bobrow D.G. and T. Winograd "An Overview of KRL, a Knowledge representation Language," *Cognition Science* 1(1):3-46, 1977.

Buchanan B.G. and E.H. Shortliffe *Rule-Based Expert Systems: The MYCIN Experiments of the Stanford Heuristic Programming Project*, Addison-Wesley, Reading MA, 1984.

Buffa E.S., G.C. Armour and T.E. Vollman "Allocating Facilities with CRAFT," *Harvard Business Review*, 42, November 1969.

Coyne R.D. and J.S. Gero "Design Knowledge and Sequential Plans," *Environment and Planning B*, 12:401-418, 1985.

Eastman C.M. "The design of Assemblies," Technical Report 11, Institute of Building Sciences, Carnegie-Mellon University, October 1980.

Eastman C.M. and K. Preiss "A Review of Solid Shape Modeling Based on Integrity Verification," *Computer-Aided Design* 16(2):66-80, March 1984.

Eastman C.M. and Y. Yasky "The Integrated Building Model and Database Scheme for the 2nd Phase of Integrated CAEADS," Technical Report, Institute of Building Sciences, Carnegie-Mellon University, February 1982.

Flemming U. "Structure in Bungalow Plans," *Environment and Planning B*, pp. 393-404, August 1981.

Gero J.S. "Expert Systems in Design and Analysis," Technical Report, Dept of Arch. Science, University of Sydney, Australia, 1985.

Hayes-Roth B. and F. Hayes-Roth "Cognitive Processes in Planning," Technical Report R-2366-ONR, Rand Corp. Santa Monica CA, 1978.

Ingalls O.H.H. "The SmallTalk-67 Programming Language: Design and Implementation," in Proc. 5th Annual ACM Symposium on Principles of Programming Languages, pp. 9-16, Tuscon AZ, January 1978.

Kalay Y.E. "A Relational Database for Non-Manipulative Representation of Solid Objects," *Computer-Aided Design* 15(5):271-276, September 1983a.

Kalay Y.E. "Modeling Polyhedral Solids Bounded by Multi-Curved Parametric Surfaces," *Computer-Aided Design* 15(3):141-146, June 1983b.

Kalay Y.E. "Redefining the Role of Computers in Architecture: From Drafting/Modeling to Knowledge-Based Assistants," *Computer-Aided Design* 17(7):319-328, September 1985.

Kalay Y.E., A. Harfmann, and L. Swerdloff "ALEX: A Knowledge-Based Architectural Design System," in Proc. of ACADIA 85, P. MaIntosh ed., 1985.

Lafue G.M.E. "Integrating Language and Database for CAD Applications," *Computer-Aided Design* 11(3):127-130, May 1979.

Landsdown J. "Expert Systems: Their Impact on the Construction Industry," RIBA, London UK, 1982.

Lenat D.B. "AM: Discovery in Mathematics as Heuristic Search," in *Knowledge-Based Systems in Artificial Intelligence*, Randall Davis and Douglas B. Lenat (eds.), pp. 1-25, McGraw-Hill, New York NY, 1982.

Mayo J.S. "Design Automation: Key to Future Technology," *High Technology*, pp. 17-30, November 1983.

Mead C. and L. Conway *Introduction to VLSI Systems*, Addison-Wesley, Reading MA, 1980.

Negroponte N. *The Architecture Machine*, MIT Press, Cambridge MA, 1970.

Newell A. and H.A. *Simon Human Problem Solving*, Prentice-Hall, Engelwood Cliffs NJ, 1972.

Rasdorf W.J. and Kutay A.R. "Maintenance of Integrity During Concurrent Access in a Building Design Database," *Computer-Aided Design* 16(4):201-207, July 1982.

Rehak D.R., H.C. Howard, and D. Shriram "An Integrated Knowledge-Based Structural Engineering Environment," in Proc. IFIPS WG5.2 Working Conference on Knowledge Engineering in CAD, 1984.

Requicha A.A.G. "Representations for Rigid Solids: Theory, Methods, and Systems," *Comput. Surveys* 12(4):437-464, December 1980.

Shaviv E. and D. Gali "A Model of Space Allocation in Complex Buildings," *Build International*, June 1979.

Shu H. "Geometric Modeling for Mechanical Parts," in Proc. of 4th NSF Conf. on Production Research and Technology, pp.10-15, Chicago IL, November 1976.

Simon H.A. *The Sciences of the Artificial*, MIT Press, Cambridge MA, 1969.

Stiny G. "Introduction to Shape Grammars," *Environment and Planning B*, pp. 343-351, July 1980.

Sutherland I.E. *SKETCHPAD: A Man-Machine Graphical Communication System*, PhD dissertation, MIT, Cambridge MA, 1963.

Whitehead B. and M.Z. Eldars "An Approach to the Optimum Layout of Single-Storey Buildings," *Architects Journal*, 1963.

Winston P.H. *Artificial Intelligence*, Addison-Wesley, Reading MA, (second edition) 1984.

☐ APPENDIX A: REPRESENTING DESIGN KNOWLEDGE IN PROLOG

A flexible model of design based on transitions through a set of design goals has been described as a framework for a computer-aided design partner. Based on this approach a prototype system written in Prolog has been under development. This appendix briefly describes the Prolog representation of the major forms of design knowledge that were discussed in the paper.

Design knowledge consists of plans, goals, constraints, evaluators, and generators. To support the use, modification and expansion of the knowledge base, major units of knowledge are represented declaratively as Prolog relations.

Plans

Simply put, a plan is just an ordered or partially ordered sequence of goals. That is, a plan can contain goals related by two types of operators:

1. `Gr --> Gs`
2. `Gr <-> Gs`

The first specifies a strict ordering (i.e. goal `Gr` must be achieved before goal `Gs`), and the second specifies that the order is irrelevant. For example, a plan to design and construct a bridge might consist of the three ordered goals of preliminary design, main design, and construction, represented as:

`(pre_design --> main_design --> construction)`

Each of the goals in a plan can, in turn, be associated with their own plans. For example, a plan for `pre_design` includes examining alternative bridge types, estimating their costs, and determining the overall appearance of the bridge:

`(bridge_types --> cost_est --> appearance)`

A plan for the `main_design` goal can include a detailed structural design and the production of drawings and specifications:

`(structural_design --> drawings <-> specs)`

The structural design goal can be further divided into substructure and superstructure design which may be achieved in any order:

`(substructure_design <-> superstructure_design)`

The purpose of plans, then, is to map out linear or hierarchical goal sequences, which if achieved will accomplish a particular design task.

More often than not, there are many ways of accomplishing a given task, that is there can be multiple plans. For example an alternative plan for `pre_design` might simply be:

`(calculations --> appearance)`

In order to aid in selecting the most promising plan in a given situation, plans must also include knowledge concerning their applicability to specific circumstances. Each plan has a set of preconditions that can be compared to the current design data base to assertion its relevance under given conditions. For instance the second pre_design plan may be sufficient for small bridges (spans less than 150 feet), but the first is more appropriate for larger bridges. Prolog representations of the two complete pre_design plans would be:

```
plan(p_031,
     pre_design,
     [small_bridge],
     (calculations --> appearance)
     ).

plan(p_032,
     pre_design,
     [large_bridge],
     (structural_design --> drawings <-> specs)
     ).
```

So in selecting a plan for pre_design, the possible alternatives could be examined and the one with the most appropriate preconditions chosen (i.e. plan p_031 would be used in the case of a small bridge, plan p_032 for a large bridge).

In general, a plan is represented as a Prolog relation of the form:

```
plan(PLAN_ID,
     GOAL,
     PRE_CONDITIONS,
     GOAL_SEQUENCE
     ).
```

where PLAN_ID is the identifying number of the plan, GOAL is the name of the goal that the plan is for, PRE_CONDITIONS is a list of conditions that relate the plan to the design, and GOAL_SEQUENCE is the set of goals which comprise the plan.

Goals and Their Constraints

A design plan is described in terms of the sequence of transitions between a set of goals. Each goal represents a set of design criteria and associated context-dependent constraints on the design solution. Criteria are, in a sense, the atomic units of design knowledge. They can be combined and recombined to define and modify the characteristics of the particular design solution. Each goal is treated as a separate packet of knowledge. For instance, the criteria for the pre_design and the specs goals are represented as the following Prolog relations:

```
goal_crit(g_020,
          pre_design,
          [span, depth, aesthetics, cost,
           redundancy, maintenance,
           constructability]
         ).

goal_crit(g_021,
          specs,
          [materials, tests, quantities,
           construction_techniques]
         ).
```

Since the criteria of each goal represent many aspects of design knowledge, a candidate design solution that satisfies some criteria is likely to violate others. Therefore, in addition to specifying the criteria which comprise
a goal, there must be a means to relatively weight them. To accomplish this
goals include knowledge about the criteria themselves, in the form of
context-dependent weight factors (constraints). A goal is associated with
one or more sets of constraints (criteria-weight pairs), each of which
specifies one possible combination of criteria which will satisfy that goal.
For example, two sets of constraints for the pre_design goal are represented
as:

```
goal_cons(g_020,
          pre_design,
          [(span,80),(depth,80),(aesthetics,50),
           (cost,95),(redundancy,85),(maintenance,60),
           (constructability,90)]
         ).
goal_cons(g_020,
          pre_design,
          [(span,80),(depth,80),(aesthetics,50),
           (cost,80),(redundancy,85),(maintenance,90),
           (constructability,90)]
         ).
```

Note that in the second alternative the cost criteria is less satisfied (i.e.
the initial cost is higher), but the maintenance criteria is better satisfied (i.e.
life-cycle costs are lower). So alternative constraints allow for alternative
design solutions and account for the trade-offs specified by each.

Criteria

Criteria can be thought of as context-less units of knowledge which are organized into context by the constraints (criteria-weight pairs) of the goals. Each criteria is associated with a database evaluator that determines satisfaction of the criteria by an analysis of the database. For example, the cost criteria could be represented by the following fact:

```
criteria(c_041,
         cost,
         STATUS,
         PROCEDURE_ID
         ).
```

where `PROCEDURE_ID` stands for an evaluation procedure that calculates the cost of the current design solution and compares it with the budget.

Generators and Evaluators

Candidate design solutions are evaluated against criteria to establish the accomplishment of the goals. Evaluative and generative operations respond to the context and organization of criteria. Evaluators are procedures that perform a specific analysis of the design database, such as cost estimation, structural analysis, etc. Each evaluator is capable of several levels of evaluation, depending on the particular phase of the design. This is accomplished by incorporating several sets of default values. For example, during preliminary design the cost estimation would be a rough approximation based on general considerations, while during the main design phase it would be much more complete, taking into account specific materials and joint details. Evaluators can be written in Prolog or another language (e.g. Pascal or C) which is most suited to its function.

Generators operate on the design to affect a change in the design state. The major part of a generator is its action, which is simply a procedure that operates on the database. Each generator also has a pre-condition (which specifies database conditions that must be true in order to invoke the action), and a post-condition (the expected results of the action). Generators can be thought of as very specific plans. They are represented by the form:

```
generator(GEN_ID,
          PRE_CONDITION,
          ACTION_ID,
          POST_CONDITION
          ).
```

☐ APPENDIX B: REPRESENTING DESIGN CONTROL IN PROLOG

The design process as discussed requires two kinds of decision making processes:

1. Deciding on the sequence of goals to be pursued by selecting several goals in advance (skeletal planning), or by selecting one goal at a time (dynamic planning).
2. Deciding on means to achieve individual goals by selecting appropriate design solution generators and evaluators.

Of course, in actual practice the design process is not so clear cut. For example a sequence of goals thought to be appropriate when selected may need to be modified due to unforeseen circumstances arising during the process of design. In addition, some information discovered during the process of achieving a particular goal may demonstrate the inadequacy of the original goal, leading to the redefinition of the goal itself. Each of these potential problems make it necessary to include an additional component in each of the decision making strategies above: a means to modify plans and a means to modify goals, respectively. An overall control structure, which enables the design process, while supporting a high degree of designer-computer interaction has been implemented in Prolog.

The two main predicates which perform the two above tasks are the goal_selecter and the goal_achiever. The goal_selecter allows three tasks: the designer can choose the next goal to achieve, the system can choose the next goal to achieve, or the designer can add a new goal. The system can select a goal either from a pre-planned sequence of goals (a design plan), or dynamically by employing means-end analysis.

```
/* User choose next goal to achieve. */
goal_selecter(GOAL) :-
        user_get_goal(GOAL1),
        goal_achiever(GOAL1).


/* Choose next goal to achieve from plan. */
goal_selecter(GOAL) :-
        get_plan(GOAL,PLAN),
        choose_goal(PLAN,GOAL1),
        goal_achiever(GOAL1).
```

```
/*  Choose next goal to achieve dynamically.  */
goal_selecter(GOAL) :-
        get_goal(GOAL1),
        goal_achiever(GOAL1).

/*  User add new goal.  */
goal_selecter(GOAL) :-
        add_new_goal(GOAL1),
        goal_selecter(GOAL1).
```

The goal_achiever enables the flow of control to satisfy the goal: either directly, by exploring sub-goals, or by modifying the goal itself.

```
/*  Evaluate criteria. If goal is achieved then  */
/*  user option or continue execution of plan. */
goal_achiever(CONDITION, GOAL) :-
        evaluate_criteria_set(GOAL),
        goal_satisfied(GOAL),
        user_option(CONDITION,GOAL),
        goal_selecter(GOAL).

/*  Try to satisfy GOAL directly. */
goal_achiever(GOAL) :-
        direct_goal_satisfy(GOAL),
        goal_selecter(GOAL).

/*  Try to satisfy GOAL by sub-goal exploration. */
goal_achiever(GOAL) :-  goal_selecter(GOAL),

/*  Modify GOAL.  */
goal_achiever(GOAL) :-
        modify_goal(GOAL,GOAL1),
        goal_achiever(GOAL1).
```

17

DESIGN AUGMENTATION IN THE ARCHITECTURAL PRACTICE

Franz S. Veit

Cannon Design Inc.
Grand Island, New York

Architectural design as a discipline combines artistic, pragmatic, and scientific aspects. The architect addresses these three areas with his creativity and experience as well as through the application of facts. Each area lends itself, to a varying degree, to the application of computers.

Creativity, while the most challenging topic, today ranks lowest in terms of computability. The area of experience has been captured successfully in several systems as of this date. The rate of success will increase as we become more familiar with expert systems and knowledge engineering. Facts, the primary objective of the computer from the very beginning, lend themselves most readily to computer applications. The processing of facts will be greatly enhanced by increasing compatibility of graphic and computing systems. Graphic systems must allow easy extraction and manipulation of the facts inherent in building design. The sample applications discussed here were developed and used successfully during a 17-year effort of integrating the computer into the design process within an architectural practice.

□ INTRODUCTION

Design as the central concern of the architectural profession traditionally implied artistic skills supported by a knowledge of materials and technology. With the increase in complexity of our civilization, societal, economic, and other concerns gained importance and are often more prominent than design issues. This emphasis is reflected in the areas of computer applications in the architectural practice. The majority of these applications serve to make the process more efficient but not necessarily more creative.

Aside from external influences this situation is also based on the nature of the design process, which evades the rigorous structuring necessary for computing. If we assume that design prerequisites are creativity, experience, and facts, then we can say that these three elements lend themselves, to a varying degree, to the application of computers. In the following material, computability for these three prerequisites is discussed and some sample applications, which have been developed and used successfully within the setting of an architectural practice, are reviewed.

□ CREATIVITY

During the creative phase of the project, the architect must incorporate varying qualities into the building design. Most of these qualities cannot be measured in objective terms and therefore evade accurate optimization procedures. In an interplay between intuitive search for a solution and an analytical study of the design parameters, the architect develops the form and content of the project. While doing that, he/she must envision the end result of the design effort before knowing its details, a condition which is opposed to the data processing approach where the total is the result of many details. At the current state of the art, computer applications in design, although less apt to aid in comprehensive solutions, are helpful in solving detail aspects.

Early examples of computer applications in design are space allocation procedures. Desired spatial adjacencies had to be expressed in quantitative terms and the programs would develop diagrammatic plan patterns either in a free form or within given building constraints. Using the computer for these purposes still proves to be successful where new spatial relationships have to be dealt with and the traditional manual approach would take many time-consuming iterations until the designer would become fully familiar with the required topologies of the project. The computer makes it possible to explore alternatives in a much shorter time. Furthermore, the following example illustrates how clients can become directly involved in the design process by filling out adjacency matrices.

TAG [Veit 1973], a computer-aided space allocation procedure, was applied to the design of a cancer research facility in Buffalo, NY. The mandated spatial relationships were rather unfamiliar to the architectural designers. In a joint effort between users and designers, relationship matrices were prepared, the program processed, and the results reviewed. The computer program produced bubble diagrams and indicated major traffic routes. These diagrams were then developed manually into floor plans.

While space allocation procedures are most useful in familiarizing the designer with new relationship patterns, they can also be helpful in reanalyzing typical patterns that have been used traditionally for certain design applications.

As design alternatives are developed, it becomes necessary to select one of them on the basis of comprehensive evaluation criteria. For the most part, this is a judgemental process. However, it is desirable to introduce quantitative data for comparison wherever possible. Gathering such data can become a very time-consuming process and is, therefore, often omitted. An example is the evaluation process for floor plans in hospitals relative to interdepartmental traffic. Obtainable quantitative data are usually not developed because of the laborious effort involved in getting a meaningful sample. In the case of a medium-sized hospital, one may have to consider several thousand daily trips, a magnitude that exceeds feasible proportions for a manual procedure.

The "Plan Analysis" computer program was written to aid in this situation. It simulates traffic activities and measures time and distances for movement of patients, staff, visitors, food, supplies, pharmacy items, and linen. Within given floor plans that indicate access points to the department/services considered, center lines of corridors, and elevator locations, the program traces the shortest route for particular traffic activities.

Comparing the results for various design alternatives allows one to determine which one performs best in terms of interdepartmental traffic. The program was applied to a number of hospital designs which led to the development of optimally achievable performance targets for various size institutions. Individual projects are then tested against these idealized profiles. Overall, the program provided a quantitative backup for design aspects that until then were dealt with mostly intuitively (see Figures 17.1 and 17.2).

Parallel with the development of the floor plan arrangements, the formulation of the building geometry takes place. A good designer visualizes the three-dimensional implications of the two-dimensional studies he/she is undertaking. In many cases the spatial/sculptural design goals influence the floor plan arrangement. This being the most elusive of all design aspects in terms of definition and structure, ranks lowest in terms of computability. The closest that some efforts may have come are those in the area of pattern recognition where, on an experimental basis, three-dimensional patterns where recorded by a computer and subsequent new patterns were generated [Negroponte 1970].

Not being able to understand clearly the forces we use when we give form to buildings and space, does not prohibit us from drawing some clues from its results in order to arrive at partial answers.

A consistent trend, particularly in more recent years, is an awareness and fondness of traditional visual forms. Modernism and high-tech architecture

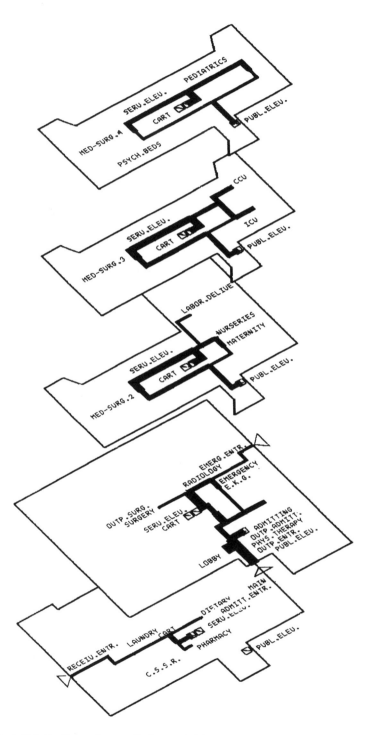

Figure 17.1. Traffic patterns with line weight expressing volume of traffic.

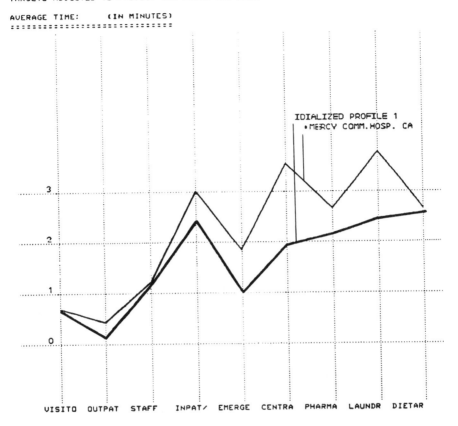

Figure 17.2. Average times for various traffic categories.

have not been able to provide the built environment with the richness that we seem to need and to which we have become accustomed in the traditional forms. One must disagree with Adolf Loos, an influential Austrian architect in the early part of this century and a pioneer for modernism, who has said: "The ornament is dead." The question is whether we have in our current culture and technology the source for a formal language that is unique to our time and that satisfies our esthetic needs.

In this respect, developments in the rapidly growing area of computer art are of interest. The algorithms used are as varied as numerical analysis based on the 12th century mathematician, Fibbonacci [Koch 1985], cell breeding algorithms by Fredkin [Scientific American 1986], and the theory of fractals by B. Mandelbrot [Mandelbrot 1982].

While these theories apply generally to two-dimensional geometries, work is currently done in various disciplines, i.e., molecular topology, that addresses multidimensional space and may impact the world of architecture.

As early space allocation procedures benefitted from quadratic assignment problems aimed at electronic circuit design, the next level of computability in architecture may be linked to progress in apparently unrelated areas of chemistry or physics.

Observing some of these developments leads one to speculate that eventually the currently purely intuitive order of a building geometry can be expressed in terms that are computable. Short of such far-reaching goals, experimental work is done by the author to utilize two-dimensional fractal designs for building graphics and floor patterns (Figure 17.3). Extending two-dimensional patterns into the third dimension generates architecture-like forms as seen in Figures 17.4 and 17.5.

Figure 17.3. Patterns created with fractal julia curves.

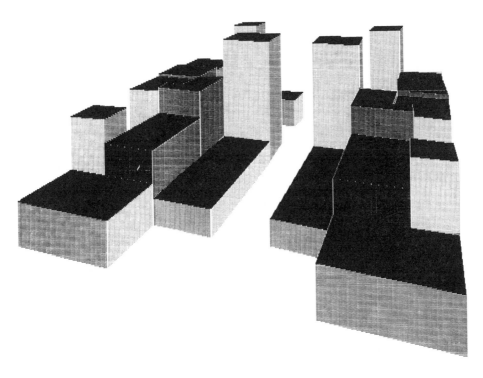

Figure 17.4. Three dimensional interpretation of Fractal julia curve.

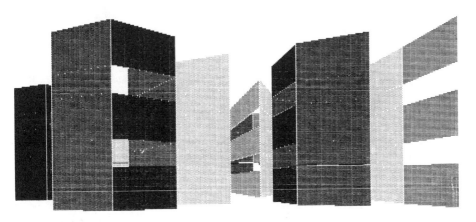

Figure 17.5. Three dimensional interpretation of Self-Avoiding Koch curve.

□ EXPERIENCE

Having ended the discussion on the computer's potential in augmenting creativity on a speculative note, the computability in the area of experience is on much more solid ground.

We consider an architect experienced when he/she can draw inferences from differing and often novel scenarios that allow him to apply a set of rules that he/she has acquired over a period of time primarily through exposure to a variety of related problems. In other words, gaining experience means building the heuristics for the decision-making process. It is assumed that this learning process may take some years in order to become effective.

In the area of computers, inference and rules are the key words for artificial intelligence. Current efforts in the area of knowledge engineering/artificial intelligence weaken the argument that experience cannot be formally taught. Particularly in areas with well-established rules, new software techniques (Lisp, Prolog) can simulate the reasoning that an experienced person would apply in certain situations. Expert systems have been successfully applied to the field of medical diagnosis, trouble-shooting for mechanical systems and character recognition, to name a few [Harmon 1985]. Each application has a clearly defined domain, an acknowledged set of rules and an inference mechanism that allows forward or backward chaining through a decision tree. Each application is absorbing the heuristics of the particular field.

In the architectural practice, a task that follows similar patterns is the task of space programming. In this task the architect applies a set of rules that translate information on activities, occupancy and space/furniture requirements into programmable floor area. These rules are applied first to primary spaces which then trigger secondary or support spaces. For example, in the case of a hospital, a building type with a particularly large number of planning rules, the number of surgical procedures determines the number of operating rooms, which in turn establishes the number and size of recovery spaces, etc.

The computer has been augmenting space programming for hospitals for several years. Early programs have not yet had the advantage of current artificial intelligence technology, but the basic objectives are the same. The programs referred to are HPS1 and VSPPR. Using an array of various rules, the logic of the programs guides the user in an interactive process through the steps in the development of the space program.

A feedback mechanism allows one to generate new rules or to modify existing ones based on the experience made with specific projects. HPS1 is geared toward the early stages of a project when volumes of various services and capacities are known and the overall scope of the project has to be established. The program applies the parameters to suggest ranges for departmental gross square footages. On a statewide basis, the New York

State Health Department is gathering data in a similar manner for the purposes of establishing planning guidelines.

VSPPR aids in the development of a room-by-room space list. In an interactive mode, the program asks for service volumes of departments, capacities, operating hours, and policies regarding organizational structures (see Figure 17.6.)

Both HPS1 and VSPPR provide the opportunity to test alternative assumptions within a much shorter time than can be done manually. Consequently, more alternatives will be considered in the planning process which lead to a better end product.

ST.ANN.V   181 BEDS

	PROC VISIT OTHER	DEP NET SQFT	NET PER BED	PERC OF TOT.	PROC PER NET	DEP GROSS SQFT	GROSS PER BED	PERC OF TOT.	PROC PER GROSS
MED/SURG NURS.UNIT	0.	22760.	126.	20.2	0.0	29588.	163.	20.3	0.0
I C U / C C U UNIT	0.	3870.	21.	3.4	0.0	5805.	32.	4.0	0.0
OB/GYN UNIT	0.	8890.	49.	7.9	0.0	11557.	64.	7.9	0.0
NURSERIES	0.	4980.	28.	4.4	0.0	7470.	41.	5.1	0.0
*** NURSING ********	0.	40500.	224.	36.0	0.0	54420.	301.	37.3	0.0
EMERGENCY DEP.	24000.	3722.	21.	3.3	6.4	5583.	31.	3.8	4.3
SURGERY/OUTP.SURG.	3270.	4870.	27.	4.3	0.7	7305.	40.	5.0	0.4
LABOR & DELIVERY	3035.	4730.	26.	4.2	0.6	8041.	44.	5.5	0.4
DIAGN.RADIOLOGY	27645.	4589.	25.	4.1	6.0	6884.	38.	4.7	4.0
NUCLEAR MEDICINE	4800.	940.	5.	0.8	5.1	1410.	8.	1.0	3.4
LABORATORY	112950.	4071.	22.	3.6	27.7	6107.	34.	4.2	18.5
CARDIO.PULM.CENT.	6280.	2000.	11.	1.8	3.1	3000.	17.	2.1	2.1
E.E.G. DEPARTM.	1000.	730.	4.	0.6	1.4	949.	5.	0.7	1.1
PHYSICAL MEDICINE	10250.	1750.	10.	1.6	5.9	2275.	13.	1.6	4.5
*** DIAGN/TREATM ***	0.	27402.	151.	24.3	0.0	41554.	230.	28.5	0.0
MAT.MANAGM.ADMIN	0.	1220.	7.	1.1	0.0	1586.	9.	1.1	0.0
SUPPLY PROCESSING	0.	3783.	21.	3.4	0.0	4161.	23.	2.9	0.0
PURCHASING DEP.	0.	660.	4.	0.6	0.0	858.	5.	0.6	0.0
STORES & RECEIVING	0.	4667.	26.	4.1	0.0	4900.	27.	3.4	0.0
LINEN SERVICE	0.	1540.	9.	1.4	0.0	1694.	9.	1.2	0.0
ENVIRONMENTAL SERV.	0.	1340.	7.	1.2	0.0	1474.	8.	1.0	0.0
MAINTENANCE DEPARTM.	0.	1580.	9.	1.4	0.0	1738.	10.	1.2	0.0
PHARMACY	0.	2760.	15.	2.5	0.0	3036.	17.	2.1	0.0
DIETARY DEPARTMENT	0.	9640.	53.	8.6	0.0	10603.	59.	7.3	0.0
*** SUPPLY ********	0.	27190.	150.	24.1	0.0	30050.	166.	20.6	0.0
EXECUTIVE MANAGEMENT	0.	1590.	9.	1.4	0.0	2385.	13.	1.6	0.0
FINANC.MANAGM	0.	3028.	17.	2.7	0.0	3331.	18.	2.3	0.0
NURSING ADMIN	0.	1200.	7.	1.1	0.0	1320.	7.	0.9	0.0
ADMITTING/DISCHARGE	0.	1640.	9.	1.5	0.0	1804.	10.	1.2	0.0
SOCIAL SERVICE	0.	350.	2.	0.3	0.0	385.	2.	0.3	0.0
MEDICAL RECORDS	0.	2130.	12.	1.9	0.0	2343.	13.	1.6	0.0
MEDICAL LIBRARY	0.	1420.	8.	1.3	0.0	1562.	9.	1.1	0.0
MEDICAL STAFF FAC.	0.	730.	4.	0.6	0.0	803.	4.	0.6	0.0
LOBBY & PUBL.SERV.	0.	3300.	18.	2.9	0.0	3630.	20.	2.5	0.0
AUXILLIARY	0.	500.	3.	0.4	0.0	550.	3.	0.4	0.0
*** ADMINISTR. *****	0.	15888.	88.	14.1	0.0	18113.	100.	12.4	0.0
PHYSICAL PLANT	0.	1650.	9.	1.5	0.0	1815.	10.	1.2	0.0
*** PHYS.PLANT *****	0.	1650.	9.	1.5	0.0	1815.	10.	1.2	0.0

Figure 17.6. Space summary generated with VSPPR. Utilization factors are indicated.

□ FACTS

The processing of factual data for the purposes of engineering design and cost estimating has been addressed with reasonable success over the past years. The effectiveness of these procedures is, however, limited by the extensive effort necessary to generate the data base required for computing. A project has to be fairly well defined in quantitative terms, which usually does not occur until the later stages of the design process, before these procedures can be applied. That means that the feedback is available when the conceptual thinking has been completed, and major modifications at that stage of the project often lead to a degradation of the original design intent. The goal is to turn what is now a sequential into a simultaneous process to the largest extent possible.

Developing a building's geometry with the computer addresses this issue since it offers the opportunity to generate a data base at the same time. Property extraction features of CADD systems are intended for this purpose. However, these features have not yet been developed to the same level of sophistication as the capabilities for the manipulation of geometries. Data extraction is still a somewhat cumbersome process.

Also, contrary to graphic data where generic formats like IGES and ISF aid in the communication between various systems, standardization is lacking for quantitative data. Translation software is needed to make the data extracted from drawings useful as input to engineering, cost estimating, or other procedures aimed at quantitative building aspects. As an example, in a facilities management assignment for the State of New York, drawings were generated with a minicomputer-based CADD system, and data was extracted with internally developed software and then post-processed with data management software (INFO by Henco Software) resident on a general purpose computer. Although CADD systems offer report generating features, they are usually less flexible than general purpose data management packages. Furthermore, processing of reports, engineering calculations, and cost estimating procedures are usually more cost-effective on general purpose computers than on graphic workstations.

It should be the aim of CADD vendors to make the data base generated with their systems easily accessible and compatible with other computer-based procedures.

□ CONCLUSION

The applications discussed in the preceding pages do not imply routine procedures in an architectural practice. They address special efforts in situations where it was felt that the traditional methods were insufficient for a given task. The desire to produce a better result warranted the effort to learn and apply a new process. This establishes the desire for depth and quality as the basis for computer applications that go beyond improved productivity.

As a professional deeply involved in a variety of traditional architectural tasks, the author benefitted from the insight that computer applications can provide into old, familiar problems. One learns to understand the architectural process better by analyzing its nature for the purposes of computability. On the other hand, studying successful computer applications in other disciplines points out methodologies that are of benefit to the architect.

Looking back at the developments over the last 20 years, we must admit that some of our earlier expectations are still unfulfilled. Nevertheless, the computer has had a great impact on the architectural profession and its supporting role will eventually turn into a decision-making role. Research in sciences will teach us a more rigorous approach to what is currently still a mostly intuitive process. We have to aim at breaking down that process into logical steps within a comprehensive system that addresses the varying aspects of design. Our understanding of building geometry will be enhanced by development in the field of topology. We will then be able to go beyond bubble diagrams in space allocation procedures to tentative building configurations and other architectural ingredients. While applications to the creative phase of the design process will remain the most challenging and exciting task in the field, we will gain more immediate benefit from expert systems that will gradually adopt the heuristics of the architectural process.

Increasing the compatibility of CADD data extraction procedures will help us in developing a unified data base that will save the significant effort that is still necessary to interconnect the various computer-based design systems.

Progress will be greatly enhanced by the proliferation of computer equipment within the profession. Increasing computer literacy and programming capabilities will enable the architects to understand better the available systems, how to combine them, and, in a few cases, how to develop customized procedures for purposes that are not yet fully addressed by the vendors. It is important to keep alive the dialogue between the academic world and the practicing architects as a balance to the flood of information driven by commercial interests to which architects are exposed. Given the rapid growth and the attention of a powerful industry, it is important to maintain a thoughtful analysis and discussion of the state of the art.

☐ REFERENCES

Harmon P. and D. King *A Expert systems,* John Wiley & Sons, Inc., 1985.

Koch K.H. *Kunst! Computer?*, Te-Wi Verlag, Muenchen, 1985.

Mandelbrot B.B. *The fractal geometry of nature*, W.H. Freeman and Company, 1982.

Negroponte N. *Architecture machine*, MIT Press, 1970.

Veit F. TAG: traffic study in building layouts, Tenth Annual Design Automation Workshop, Institute of Electrical and Electronics Engineers, Portland, OR, June 1973.

Wall paper for the mind: Computer images that are almost, but not quite, repetitive, Predicting chemistry from topology. *Scientific American,* September 1986.

18

COMPUTABILITY OF DESIGN

Bruce R. Majkowski
Yehuda E. Kalay

School of Architecture and Environmental Design
State University of New York at Buffalo
Buffalo, New York

The complexity of the physical environment has grown steadily over the years. Increased awareness and consideration for human factors and environmental impacts has been paralleled by pressures to maintain an efficient design/build cycle in their production. These forces encouraged designers to seek new tools and methodologies to help manage the proliferation of information. Recent developments in cognitive and computer sciences have provided insight to some human thought processes, and have accelerated the search for new design tools that embody them. In some disciplines, such as electrical and mechanical engineering, the introduction and use of computers have significantly accelerated complex design processes. Yet, in other design disciplines, such as architectural design, computational design aids have at best attained a marginal role. They fostered no major qualitative or even quantitative improvements, although attempts to develop appropriate design aids have been pursued as vigorously as in other disciplines.

In order to understand why computational design aids have succeeded in some disciplines but not in others, and what research directions should be followed to develop better computational design aids (or prove their development impractical) we must examine the nature of "soft" design processes, analyze their inherent difficulties, and establish the utility of computational methods that attempt to aid them.

The problem is epitomized by the apparent paradox posed by the title of this book. *Design* is an ill-defined process that relies on ill-understood practices such as learning, creativity, and intuition, as well as the judicious application of scientific principles, technical information, and experience. *Computable processes*, on the other hand, are by definition well-understood and subject to precise analysis and mathematical modeling, which qualify them for simulation by artificial computing devices.

The first problem we must address in our quest for computational design aids is the development of a precise, mathematically treatable *model* of the design process. This design model must resolve several seemingly insurmountable obstructions: the non-existence of a universally acceptable definition or description of the design process, and the lack of understanding of creativity and judicious decision making. Although achievements in the study of human problem solving and other cognitive processes have provided insight into some of these areas, the inability to clearly and precisely describe the design process casts serious doubt on the feasibility of defining a mathematical model of design. The very prospect of using computers to model and provide assistance in design decision-making has also met with serious criticism by designers themselves on the grounds that the inherently human process of design, like intelligence, cannot (or should not) be rendered to a computer.

The mere development of a computable model of design is, however, insufficient for developing computational design aids. The *knowledge* that is employed by designers must also be defined and computationally represented. Computational techniques that can acquire and use this knowledge in ways defined by the design model must then be developed. It is unclear, therefore, whether computational design aids can ever be more than *design partners* that work in concert with human designers.

☐ DESIGN PROCESS

Attempts to explain how people design, or even define what they do when they are said to be "designing," have been at the core of Design Methods research for many years. A definition shared by several researchers considers design to be a process of *mapping* from one symbol system to another; a process that transforms previous experiences and precedents into new spatio-temporal situations. The purpose of this mapping is to develop a strategy which, when implemented, will lead to the construction of an artifact or environment that will perform within tolerable margins of some prescribed behavior. Many researchers also agree that the mapping process resembles *search*, since no formula exists that will translate the performance requirements of the sought environment or artifact into a self-consistent physical (or organizational) assembly of parts. Opinions differ, however, with regard to the method(s) that are used to carry out this search.

One view regards the search as a process of *problem solving*, where alternative solutions are generated and tested until a "satisfying" solution is found. This approach to modeling design is predicated on the assumption that the characteristics of the desired solution, in terms of its objectives and constraints, can be formulated independently and prior to engaging in the process of seeking a solution that meets them. Accordingly, the search for a satisfying solution is goal-directed, and can employ means-ends analysis to guide it as it evolves toward the desired solution.

The assumption that the characteristics of the desired solution can be formulated prior to and independently of the search for the solution that meets them is, nevertheless, not universally accepted. In fact, some researchers argue that such knowledge cannot exist prior to the search itself, since the sought solution is unique, or the stated specifications may not represent the true intentions of the designer. Rather, the specifications develop simultaneously with the design itself, uncovering the hidden design intents as well as the constraints and opportunities of the evolving design. These specifications then form the criteria by which the solution is ultimately judged.

According to this view, the process of search resembles *puzzle making*—a search for the most appropriate effects that can be attained in unique spatio-temporal contexts through the manipulation of parts, following a set of combinatoric rules derived from precedents, symbols, and metaphors. This approach suggests that design solutions are seldom generated from scratch but rely, instead, on precedents that provide the initial "kit" of parts and rules.

Critics of the puzzle-making approach argue that although the search process generates insight that will be used to guide the generation and evaluation of the solution, some goals, objectives, and constraints must and do exist prior to the initiation of the search, in the form of design specifications. These specifications may be incomplete, and perhaps even contradictory and misleading, but they form an initial set of conditions that define the particular problem to be solved. As the design process unfolds, more specific constraints are added that redefine and narrow the problem statement thereby reducing the space of possible solutions. Solutions are generated by "fixing" values of design parameters, and are tested for compliance with the constraints. The selection of specific values may introduce new constraints or affect other parameters through constraint relationships.

This *constraint model* of design allows for goal-directed search (and thus supports the process of producing new solutions through means-ends analysis), and allows for adding new constraints as insight is developed during the search process. The fact that constraints are both a consequence of the search and its driving force raises several important questions: how are new constraints generated and evaluated? how are conflicts between incompatible constraints resolved? how can the model be applied to "soft" design specifications?

□ DESIGN KNOWLEDGE

The importance of knowledge for carrying out both complex and common tasks has been established and demonstrated by developments in artificial intelligence. In particular, Simon and Newell demonstrated the importance of using knowledge in solving "soft" problems for which strong solution procedures do not apply. Design is one of the most difficult problems, and accordingly it requires the application of considerable knowledge.

To be able to computationally aid design, some of this knowledge must be formalized and made accessible to the computer. Three related questions underlie the computability of design knowledge:

1. What is the nature of design knowledge?
2. How can it be computationally represented?
3. How can it be computationally used?

Design knowledge is both elusive and inconclusive. Given that the design solution we seek is unique (because it must fit unique spatio-temporal conditions), how can we apply previously acquired knowledge to its formulation? And even if such general knowledge could be of use, what is it comprised of, and how can it be stored?

Many researchers find a striking similarity between design knowledge and natural languages. In particular, both use symbolic structures to support ideation and communication. *Ideation* is the formulation of new concepts*; and *communication* is the conveyance of these concepts to other people. Design knowledge, like languages, is comprised of syntax and semantics. The syntax describes physical attributes, while semantics describe function.

Designers have developed a remarkable symbolic language both to help them form their ideas and to communicate them. This language is commonly represented by drawings and sketches. Unfortunately, neither the semantic nor the syntactic information contained in drawings is computationally accessible (since much of the semantically rich information remains in the mind of the designer). It relies, instead, on considerable amount of inference for its interpretation.

The search for computational means of representing both syntax and semantics of form practically describes the history of computer-aided design: first, two-dimensional drafting, then three-dimensional solids model-

---

*In *The Origins of Knowledge and Imagination* Jacob Bronowski points out how human speech differs from animal communication in that its purpose is not merely to inform others, but also influence them and the speaker himself (Yale University Press, New Haven, CT, 1978).

ing were computerized. Yet, neither method is able to computationally represent the semantics of form. Perhaps the major difficulties associated with computational representation and use of design information are due to abstraction and fuzziness, the hallmarks of design decision making.

Abstraction helps designers focus their attention on selected parts of the designed artifact, without being overwhelmed by details. It is context-dependent; therefore good algorithms have not yet been developed that can automate it. The difficulty of generating architectural drawings from three-dimensional solid models is an example: such drawings are not simple sectional projections, but rather context-dependent symbolic interpretations of selected parts of the building, drawn to different scales with different amounts of detailing.

Fuzziness allows sharing the responsibility for decision making between different participants of the design/build continuum by permitting certain facets of the design to go undefined until later stages of the process. Architects, for instance, seldom articulate the ductwork in HVAC systems beyond centerline routing and desired capacities. They rely, instead, on mechanical engineers and subcontractors to later fill in the details. Of course, this practice is itself difficult to compute, and thoroughly upsets the sequential nature of computation. Fuzziness is not always a positive attribute. It may lead to design/construction errors due to misinterpretation of the architect's intent, or due to incompetence.

The reliance of both abstraction and fuzziness on considerable contextual knowledge for their appropriate presentation and use is another hinderance to the computation of design knowledge. Moreover, *context* itself is often an interpretation of subtle clues derived from a variety of empirically acquired and validated knowledge of rich and sophisticated precedents. The very richness of these experiences and precedents may hinder the formation of new design concepts, which must, by definition, fit unique environments. The term "door," for instance, is commonly used to convey the essence of controllable access, but is also laden with (potentially misleading) semantic information that invokes visions of conventional form, materials, and modes of operation. If future systems are to reason about functional capacities (rather than merely parametric and combinatorial assembly of shapes) then there must exist knowledge relating the functional qualities and semantic information with various precedents.

Solutions to the problem of design knowledge representation are already emerging. Void modeling, an alternative approach to solids modeling, embeds the semantic information needed to distinguish containment conditions. However, semantic information concerning non-geometrical and functional properties is not represented. General solutions to the problem of design knowledge computational representation may come from AI research in *semantic networks*, which enable the representation of semantics and their use for reasoning about objects and their properties.

□ DESIGN COMPUTATION

The difficulties in modeling design and computing the knowledge it relies on have become apparent only through early attempts to automate the design process as a whole. "Design machines" preceded computational design aids, which gradually gave way to computer-aided drafting when the magnitude of the problems were realized. Yet, recent advances in artificial intelligence, coupled with the experience gained in two decades of research in computational and other design methods, raise the possibility of design automation once again. This has already been achieved in some engineering disciplines, such as the design of integrated circuits.

Attempts to automate "soft" design processes, such as architectural design, have been based on developing methods that automate the *synthesis* and *evaluation* of design alternatives (*analysis*, which precedes both synthesis and evaluation, is yet to be computed). Computational approaches to solving layout design problems in architectural floorplans led the way: although very limited in their abilities, spatial allocation algorithms, coupled with quantitative and qualitative evaluation procedures, represented the generate-test cycle. Their integration into one whole is difficult, however, since spatial allocation is typically done in the early phases of the design process, when the available information is scarce and abstract, while evaluation typically relies on elaborate information available only in the later phases of the process.

More recently, expert systems have been developed that expand the knowledge used by design generators beyond mathematical programming (i.e. the optimization of an objective function and the satisfaction of constraints). Expert systems assist in the generation, abstraction and evaluation of alternative design solutions while providing a framework for the integration of quantitative and qualitative criteria in design. However, their general implementation in design may be limited due to the magnitude and the availability of sufficient knowledge in the problem domain. Shape grammars offer another approach based on the concept of a graphical language employing production rules. The formalism can be used to analyze a given corpus of similar designs or to generate new designs based on rules extracted from a desired building corpus. The approach provides a means to integrate computational design methods commonly used by architects, such as historical building analyses and building code enforcement. These techniques, which make use of non-procedural languages like Prolog, Lisp and OPS5, promise to become one of the most significant developments for automating design solution synthesis and evaluation.

□ DESIGN ASSISTANCE

The difficulty of automating design stems not only from the lack of an accepted model of the design process and the knowledge it relies upon, but also a lack of understanding of the *learning*, the *creative*, and the *judgmental* processes that comprise design processes. Attempts to bypass the difficulties in automating knowledge acquisition, creative thinking, and judgmental decision making promoted computational approaches that *facilitate* design through the representation and evaluation of the emerging artifact, but not the processes that generate them.

These approaches are predicated on the observation that designers are able to cope with and manage complex design processes, and have for centuries achieved outstanding results without the aid of computers. Thus, perhaps it is not necessary to fully automate the process of design in order to significantly improve design productivity and quality. Rather, computers may assist designers by construing a practical symbiosis between the capabilities of designers and machines.

In order to develop and employ such design assistants, it is necessary to identify the tasks that are computable, and tasks that are not. Furthermore, it is necessary to decide which tasks could but should not be computed, and how computational and manual design practices can be combined without losing design continuity.

Attempts to achieve such symbiosis range from assisting designers in the creative phase of design, which is commonly believed to be embodied in the intuitive leap, to the appreciation of the emerging product through visually realistic images and detailed analytical tools. Computers could assist the associative process of intuition by generating alternative solutions that nurture the intuitive leap, and by providing an extensive knowledge base at the point of conception, on which the judgmental decisions could be based.

Realistic visual representation of the designed artifact is an aid similar to the use of telescopes to see distant objects that are not visible to the naked eye. It lets the designer infer semantic information directly, as he would from a physical scale model or real artifact.

Design assistance can also be interpreted as a *partnership* between the designer and the computer, in which the role of the computer can be shifted dynamically between passive representation/evaluation and active generation of design solutions. Such dynamics would allow the designer and the system to respond to changing requirements, unforeseen problems, and emerging opportunities as they arise during the design process.

In architectural practice, computers can assist in the creative, experiential, and information processing activities of design. Generative systems can assist in creative endeavors for developing specific components of design, while analytic applications may evaluate compliance with building codes and other design criteria. Information processing systems, such as cost estimators and specification writers allow the architect to manage the proliferation of paperwork and legal documents necessary for contract documents. Computers can also assist the designer in ascertaining the true intentions behind design specifications, leading toward building designs more responsive to the needs and desires of the client.

□ CONCLUSION

The issues raised in discussing models of design, representation and use of design knowledge, the use of computational design methods, and the integration of computer assists with manual methods, bring us back to the questions put forth at the beginning of this book: Can the process of design be described precisely enough to allow its computation? What factors make certain design methods and design disciplines more amenable to computer assistance? Is the pursuit of computational aids in "soft" design disciplines (such as architectural design) valid? Should the inherently human processes of creativity and intelligence be rendered to the computer, or should they be left to human pursuits? What directions should research follow to attain these and other progressive goals? Have the appropriate questions concerning the computability of design been addressed, or have some main issues been overlooked?

The ability to address and discuss the many issues raised in considering the complex, fragmented, and contradictory process of design and come to some conclusions seems to indicate that many of the questions were indeed valid. Extracting answers from this myriad of information presents a most formidable task. The central theme, however, is woven around three main ideas: the *desirability*, the *feasibility*, and the *utility* of computing design processes.

If we begin with the desirability of computing the design process, we must first address whether we should even attempt the endeavor and if we do, to what degree. Many researchers agree that the complexity of our designed artifacts and environments, combined with a multitude of socio-economic pressures, demand the use of new tools to help designers manage the process. This pursuit demands a clear definition of the problem domain and of its vital components. The ability to describe the design process in a sufficiently precise, consistent and accepted model is difficult due to the nature of design and the variety of definitions designers have applied to it. The various theories presented in this book view the process from several well defined but narrow vantage points. A more general model may include all these views complementing and augmenting each other.

The amount of knowledge required to perform the process of design is enormous. A method must be found to represent and organize this information in a self-consistent, manageable whole, capable of sustaining complex relationships, while advancing beyond simple combinatorial assemblage and groupings. Representing levels of abstraction, fuzziness and semantic information will provide design knowledge with higher levels of compatibility with the thought processes designers use during the activity of design. Artificial intelligence, psychology and cognitive science may provide additional insight into the mental processes and structures used to acquire and represent design knowledge. As research and externalization of design processes continues, a greater understanding of the process itself and its interaction with design knowledge will follow and provide better solutions.

As the process of design is rationalized, the feasibility of performing computational design tasks will become more explicit. We are presented with two options: computation of the entire design process; or computation of those parts of the process that are deemed computable. Proponents of the first approach contend that design may be viewed as science, and therefore, the entire process, in time, can be computed. If a mathematical model of design cannot be found, then symbolic representations such as shape grammars, expert systems and semantically charged abstractions may provide an answer to computing the design process. It is this approach that raises the most controversy for it attacks the very core of the design profession and raises the conflict of human/machine cohabitibility.

Proponents of the second approach contend that design is a form of art which is and should remain the sole domain of humans. Creativity, judgement and intuition are hallmarks of human activity that defy the rationalization required to compute them. Therefore, the computer is delegated to an assistant position, capable of performing the tedious and mundane details of the design activity, while allowing the designer to pursue those areas for which he is well endowed. The computer may also be used as a medium to support and enhance the human capacities for creativity and judgement through semantically rich images, evaluative processes and generative catalysts.

The utility of these endeavors becomes clear when compared to the benefits that other design disciplines have attained. The promise to provide designs and environments more responsive to human needs and requirements is plausible. The ability of the design professionals to partake more in the aspects of the design process that are enjoyable while delegating the tedious and mundane chores to the computer is also meritorious. However, the dependency on "the machine" and the humanistic issues raised will continue to surface as man pursues his exploration of the design process.

Asserting the feasibility, utility, and desirability of computing design processes or their components relies upon developing computational design models and knowledge bases that may be employed in the development of new sophisticated tools. This book did not not attempt to answer the question of design computability, but rather to raise and explore some of the issues it involves. It presents some general models of the design process, discusses computational representations of design knowledge, presents several approaches to the computation of design as a whole or its components that are most amenable to computation, and their possible integration within a single, unified design process. The four parts of the book present the major concerns that face the computation of design, and some of the different views and approaches proposed to solve them. It is hoped that the book may serve as a catalyst upon which the research of the future may rest and ultimately answer the question of design computability.

INDEX

Abstraction, 3, 28–29, 121, 214, 353
  analytical aspects, 215
  design, 137
    expert systems for, 213. *See also* Expert
     systems
  generative aspects, 215
  geometric, 129
  graphic language for, 215
  levels of, 119
  mapping of, 122
Applied science, 34, 45, 50
Archimodos, 171. *See also* Void, modeling of
Architectural drawings, 138
Architectural modeling, 142
Architectural practice, 337
Architectural reasoning, 224
Aristotle, 91
Art, 45, 48, 341
Artificial intelligence, 173, 344
Augmented transition network, 184. *See also*
  Semantic network
Axial skeletons, 146

Beaux Arts, 296–297
Black Box process, 1
Block structuring, 66, 71

Choisy, August, 92
Classical architecture, 92
Classification hierarchy, 77
Color, 299–300
Computability of design, 141, 354
  desirability of, 356
  feasibility of, 356
Computational tools:

generative, 191, 334. *See also* Spatial
  allocation problem
  heuristic techniques, 193
  for quasi-optimal building layouts, 192
  random techniques, 193
  valuative, 191, 334
Computer-aided design, 6
  assistance of, 354
  comprehensive, 121
  control of, 322
  generalized framework of, 322
  partnership approach to, 315, 321
  schematic, 124
  theoretic bases, 130
Configurational descriptive system, 112
Consistency, management of, 59
Constraints:
  algebraic, 64
  assertion of, 74
  definition, 77
  definitional, 77
  domains of, 73. *See also* Constraints, space
    of
  examples, 57
  functional, 77
  inequality of, 65
  invertible, 62
  particular, 57
  preferential, 77
  proliferation of, 76
  relational, 74
  as relations between variables, 57
  representation of, 332
  sources of, 56
  space of, 69. *See also* Problem space

Constraints (*Continued*)
  spatial, 119
  transformational, 74
  universal, 57
Control, 322, 335
Creativity, 80. *See also* Design, creativity

Data extraction, 346
Decision making, 118, 138. *See also* Design, as
    decision making
Definitions of design, 349
  conventional, 78
  defunct, 78
  standard, 78
Deontic:
  description, 100
  statement, corroboration of, 105
Design:
  abstractions, *see* Abstraction
  automation of, 354
  conceptualization of, 142
  constraints of, 56
  as craft, 2
  creativity, 80
  as decision making, 118, 138
  execution of, 142
  factorability of, 317
  goals, 317
  innovations, 96
  intent, 100, 104
    inference of, 105–106
  intuitive, 295
  media:
    computer-aided, 11–12
  partnership approach, 317
  as problem solving, 13, 118
    cognitive structures, 120
    "wicked" problem, 120
  program, 42, 44, 50
  solution of, 62
  specification of, 100, 104
    necessary impropriety of, 101
    paradox of, 103
  state of, 59
    hierarchies of, 124
    representing the, 122, 124
  synthesis of, 97
  theory of, 54
    functionalist, 96
Design knowledge, 179, 352
  attributes of, 180

class hierarchy, 181. *See also* Representation
    of design
communication of, 352
contextual, 353
externalization of, 1, 3–4
form of, 179
fuzziness of, 353
modality of, 180
part hierarchy, 181. *See also* Representation
    of design
positions, 179
syntax and semantics of, 352
Design language:
  of action, 122
  of form, 122
  grammar of, 226
  machine understandable, 111–112
  of plans, 122
  symbols of, 226
Design machine, 110, 354
Design methods, 4, 46
  formalization of, 6
  interactive, 11–12, 34
  iterative, 4
Design process, 104, 316, 350. *See also* Search
  control of, 322
  fundamentals of, 120
  integration of, 316
Discovery, 322. *See also* Intuition
Drafting system, 175
Dynamic task allocation, 322. *See also*
    Partnership approach

Empiricism, 44–45
Environmental qualities:
  description of, 63
  prediction of, 64
Evaluated model, *see* Void, modeling of
Evaluation:
  of activities layout, 202
  of building layouts, 202
  expert systems for, 231
  of life cycle flexibility, 208
  of room dimensions, 205
  traditional models, 216
Expert:
  domain of, 174
    epistemology, 174
    ontology, 174
Expert systems, 89, 97, 174, 213, 248, 354
  architectural, 221. *See also* Abstraction

in conceptual design, 233
in design abstraction, 222
in design evaluation, 231
External memory, 14, 18, 23, 29–30

Form, 298–299
utility of, 89
Form and function:
reasoning about, 89, 97
relation between, 89, 92, 94–96
Freedom, degrees of, 56. *See also* Constraints
Functional adequacy, conditions of, 91–92, 96
Functional equivalence classes, role of, 94–95
Fuzziness, 353

Galen, 90
Gaudi, Antonio, 135
Geometric model, 128, 299
problem of transition of, 129. *See also*
   Abstraction
Goals:
defining by AI system, 110
design as directed by, 317. *See also*
   Representation of design
representation of, 334
subgoals, 325
Growth of knowledge, 47–48, 50–51

Idea generation, logic of, 111
Ideation, 352
Information processing system, 14–15, 18–19,
   24, 32–33
Inheritance, 68. *See also* Representation of design
Instrumentalism, 44–45
Intelligent interface, 173
Intelligent machine drafting, 184. *See also*
   Drafting system
Interdepartmental traffic, 339
Interval values, 65
Intuition:
computational representation of, 298
leap, 295, 355
process, 296. *See also* Design, intuitive

Judgment, 97, 323

Kits of parts, 41, 44, 46–47, 49, 96
Knowledge:
base, 97
based system, 110, 174
engineering, 174, 344

representation of, 128, 173
in PROLOG, 330

Land form models, 165. *See also* Void,
   modeling of
Language of architectural form, 96–97
Learning, 355
Lighting design, 303
Logical inference, 93

Machine intelligence, 109–110
for teleological explanation, 109
MACSYMA, 65
Maintenance expert system, 173
Mapping, 350
Meaning, 43–44
Metaphors, 42–44, 46, 51
MMB Gehause part, 13, 21
Modern architecture, 96
Modern movement, 49, 248
Multi-story building models, 169. *See also*
   Void, modeling of

Natural languages, 352
Nonlogical reasoning, 67
Notes, design as, 31–32

Objects, classification of, 68
Optimization, 55

Paradigms for computer-aided design, 118
constraint model, 54, 351
Coyne-Gero model, 122, 126, 128
Eastman model, 121, 124, 127
Kalay model, 122, 125, 127
Mitchell model, 121, 123, 127
Parametric design elements, 96
Part hierarchy, 78
Partnership approach, 315, 321
Patterns, 296, 299
Planning, 122, 326, 331
Plausible reasoning, 68
Precedents, 42–44, 46, 51
Problem solving, 3, 13–14, 19, 24, 33–35,
   47–51, 350. *See also* Search, methods of
general problem solver, 120
Problem space, 14, 17–22, 27. *See also* Search,
   methods of
partitioning of, 71
representation of, 28–29. *See also*
   Abstraction

Problem space (*Continued*)
   scrutiny of, 69
PROLOG, 266, 330
Protected core, 47–48, 50–51. *See also*
      Protective shell
Protective shell, 48, 50–51
Psychotherapy, 46
Puzzle making, 40–41, 43–45, 47–48, 51, 350

Radiosity, 303, 305
   method of, 305
Rationalism, 44
Realistic imaging, 304
Reflection in action, 4
Relationships:
   causal, 107
   group, 125
   master-instance, 125
   part-whole, 125
   representation of:
      explicit/implicit, 124
      hierarchical, 124
   teleological, 107
Renderability, 80
Representation of design, 222
   dynamic, 320
   methods of:
      chunks, 223
      productions, 223
      state-transition graph, 317, 319
Requirements, 50
Rules, 247, 279. *See also* Shape grammars
   applied to shapes, 250
   systems of, 41–44, 49

Scully, V., 253
Search, 14, 17–18, 23–26, 225, 350. *See also*
      Problem solving
   goal directed, 317
   methods of, 27
      generate and test, 225
      heuristic, 225, 320
      hill climbing, 225
Semantic network, 177, 353. *See also* SNePS
Semantics, 119
   representation of, 128
Shape grammars, 245, 248–249, 273–274, 354
   advantages, 252
   applicability, 252
   criteria of evaluation, 256, 258, 264
   initial shape, 250, 254
   PROLOG interpreter of, 266

rules of composition, 247–248, 254
Shop drawings, 138
Site planning, 77
SNePS, 175
Solid modeling, 133, 143. *See also* Geometric
      model
   functional requirements of, 139
Solution space, 55. *See also* Problem space
Solving:
   constraints, 63
   in design, 62
   invertible contraints, 62
   logical, 67
   multiple solutions, 62
   nonlogical constraints, 67
Spatial:
   incremental definition, 128
   manipulation of design, 117
   relationships, 126. *See also* Relationships
Spatial allocation problem, 191, 338
Stiny, G., 270
Structuralism, 44–45
Styles, 252. *See also* Shape grammars
Subdesigns, ordered set of, 69–70
   heuristics for maintaining, 70
   pruning, 71
Summerson, Sir John, 96
Symbols, 42–44, 46, 51
   symbolic description, 123
Systems of computer-aided design, 117,
      179
   Calma DDM, 136
   Computervision CADDS-4X, 136
   McAuto BDS, 136

Task environment, 14, 19, 24
   constraints of, 18
Teleological structure:
   explanation of, 105–106
   inference of, 105–106, 111

Unique contexts, 41, 44–47
Universe of discourse, definition of, 95–96

Valuative criteria:
   evaluation of, 102
Value system, mapping of, 111
Variables:
   control of, 58
   introduction of, 59
Versatile Maintenance Expert System (VMES),
      173

Void:
  attribute assignment, 147
  compositional operations, 147
  container/contained, 144
  editing, 147
  exterior/interior curves, 154
  hierarchical structure of, 152
  interior spaces, 154
  modeling of, 143. *See also* Solid modeling
    levels of abstraction, 158–159
  operations of, 165
    arrangement, 166

    difference, 166
    intersection, 166
    scaling, 165
    union, 166
  regular/irregular, 148
  room tracing, 148
  three-dimensional model:
    horizontal faces, 155
    vertical faces, 157
  wall tracing, 148

Wright, F.L., 248–249